Pacific Battle Line

THE MACMILLAN COMPANY
NEW YORK · BOSTON · CHICAGO · DALLAS
ATLANTA · SAN FRANCISCO

MACMILLAN AND CO., Limited
LONDON · BOMBAY · CALCUTTA · MADRAS
MELBOURNE

THE MACMILLAN COMPANY
OF CANADA, Limited
TORONTO

By
FOSTER
HAILEY

Pacific Battle Line

NEW YORK

The Macmillan Company

1944

Foreword

THE UNITED STATES has been waging in the Pacific the most difficult war in history. And the least understood. The battleground is the world's greatest ocean, with its tens of thousands of islands. The battle line is a great arc extending 7,000 miles from the tropical regions of northern Australia to the bleak, fog-covered Aleutian Islands on the rim of the Bering Sea.

It is a warfare that is principally amphibious, a type of conflict our armed forces never had fought before and in which they had little training.

It is war on an animal level, a war of no mercy, a war with a foe whose ideals are as foreign to most of us as the names of the islands on and around which it has been fought, and as repugnant. It began with treachery and has been waged with a foulness which most Americans find difficulty in understanding.

For various reasons the full story of the war against Japan, or, rather, Japan's war on the United States, could be told only in part at the time. Even now it can be only a half-told tale. But time has made much information valueless to the enemy.

This book is an attempt to correlate the first two years of the Pacific war, to put events in their proper proportion in the world picture, to explain what has been done and why more could not have been done.

It is too early to make any broad evaluation of our strategy, even if anyone were capable at this time of doing that. Events are too near, we do not know the full effect on the enemy of certain actions, too many personalities are involved, to make that feasible at present.

The effort has been made to present the picture as it was, not as we might have wished that it was or as the American public generally may have evaled it on the basis of news stories that were allowed to pass the strict censorship.

Much of the material contained was gathered first-hand, as a correspondent for the *New York Times*, at sea and ashore with the navy, the marines, and the army, from Christmas Day, 1941, to the conclusion of the Aleutian campaign in August, 1943. All areas except the Philippines, the East Indies, and New Guinea were visited during those twenty months.

Where events portrayed were not actually participated in, the information has been gleaned from official records or from conversations with the men who took part in them.

No effort has been made to present this war as anything but what it is, the ultimate insanity of civilization. All of war is hard work, much of it is boring, a fact to which any man will attest who has taken part in one. But the exigencies of war also bring out in many men traits you would not know they had—patience under pressure, cheerfulness under great difficulty, stoicism under pain, raw courage in the face of terrible danger. An effort has been made to tell that too.

Here then is the record as one reporter saw it, a record written in blood and sweat, of the first two years of the war in the Pacific.

There are many reasons, of course, for writing a book. The principal reason for writing this one is this: that the men with whom I shared some of the hardships and some of the dangers deserve to have their story told, and told as objectively and factually as I can tell it. If they believe that I have made an honest effort to do that and have achieved some success, that will be satisfaction enough for "the correspondent from the *Times*."

F. B. H.

Little Neck, New York
December 15, 1943

Table of Contents

Illustrations

PART I

OUR WAR IN THE PACIFIC:
THE FIRST TWO YEARS

CHAPTER I

The Japanese Strike

COMMANDER "BEAUTY" MARTIN, commandant of the United States Naval Air Station at Kaneohe on the northeastern side of the Hawaiian island of Oahu, was in the bathroom of his quarters shaving at 7:30 A.M. the morning of December 7, 1941. Watching him was his small son.

It was a typical winter morning in the islands. The sun was shining through high, broken clouds. A warm wind stirred the curtains of the commandant's quarters.

From his bathroom window the commander could look out over the brilliant green lawns, past the wood-and-stucco administration building and the living quarters of the station personnel, over the top of the steel-framed hangar and workshops to the bay where the big seaplane patrol bombers, the PBY's, rocked gently at anchor on the morning tide.

As he remembered it later, he had just finished shaving one side of his face and was starting on the other when dimly on his consciousness was impressed the faint throb of the motors of an approaching flight of planes. He could tell from the sound they were not PBY's, his own ships. If he thought of it at all he probably surmised it was some of the army crowd out for an early morning patrol or training exercise.

The small son, as small boys will, had gone to the window when he heard the motors. His practiced eye saw something strange in the contour of the silver planes against the blue sky. (We could do a lot worse than to mobilize America's youngsters as plane spotters.)

"Daddy, those aren't our planes," he said, as he returned to the bathroom.

Seconds later the Japanese fighters roared over the station

[3

strafing the rocking PBY's, the hangar, the control tower, and the white-clad sailors and khaki-clad officers who at the first ominous crackle of the machine guns had raced from their quarters toward their battle stations.

So sure were the Japanese of the surprise, they executed no evasive maneuvers whatever but came in straight and low. The two planes assigned to knock out the control tower—a small, roofed structure atop a 300-foot hill in the center of the station grounds—were flying so low they fired up at the tower as they swept over the living quarters and up toward it.

Those were the first shots in our war with Japan. Minutes later other Japanese planes were over the navy field on Ford Island in Pearl Harbor, over Wheeler Field—the army fighter base near Schofield Barracks in the center of the island—and over Hickam Field, adjoining Pearl Harbor. Their task was to knock out the air strength on the island. Following them came the bombers and torpedo planes to attack the battleships, cruisers, and destroyers at anchor or tied up to the piers.

By 10:30 that morning, when two Japanese photographic planes circled over our mid-Pacific base to take the pictures later shown in Tokyo and Berlin, the destruction or immobilization of 95 per cent of our sea-and-air strength in the Hawaiian Islands was complete.

Five of our eight battleships in the Pacific were sunk, or sinking; the three others were damaged. Sunk also were the target ship Utah (armed with the latest antiaircraft guns and carrying hundreds of thousands of rounds of ammunition), the tender Oglala, and two destroyers. Another destroyer, the Shaw, was burning fiercely in dry dock and later exploded. Other ships, including three cruisers, had been hit. One hundred and seventy-seven of our planes, ranging from the latest-type fighters and bombers to an old amphibian rescue plane at Kaneohe, were torn and blasted by machine gun fire and bombs. Three thousand, three hundred and three men were dead or dying; twelve hundred and seventy-two more were wounded.

Only that Providence which seems to watch over fools and sailors had saved our navy from an even worse disaster. One of our two aircraft carriers in the Central Pacific, which had escorted reinforcements to Wake, was to have been in Pearl Harbor that Sunday morning, but an engine casualty to one of her escorting cruisers had delayed her arrival. She was still some miles at sea when the Japanese planes struck.

There is no reason to believe that had the two carriers been at their regular berths they would have escaped the fate of the battleships. None of our ships was protected by the antitorpedo nets that would have saved them from the worst damage. Had the carriers been sunk that day the early months of the war would have been even more desperate for this country than they were.

Fortunately, the Japanese too make mistakes. They concentrated on the battleships—which would have been of little use anyway in the early days of the war—and the airfields, and made no attempt to fire the oil tanks or demolish the shore establishments of Pearl Harbor. Had the United States lost that day its oil stores, dry docks, and workshops and the usefulness of Pearl Harbor as a fleet base, the situation would have been catastrophic.

As the sun progressed westward other Japanese air groups struck at the Philippines and our two isolated military posts of Wake and Guam. The latter, which Congress repeatedly had refused to fortify, fell with little or no struggle. Wake held out until December 23, Honolulu time, or perhaps a day later. Radio communication was lost on that day.

No nation ever went to war, or rather was pitchforked into war, as poorly prepared as was the United States in the Pacific. Nor has any great nation ever fought a major antagonist with less adequate equipment than was ours in the first two years. The United States has the Japanese to thank, not Washington, that Pearl Harbor and the Aleutians were not lost and our West Coast was not attacked. It just didn't happen to be Japanese strategy.

At the beginning of the war our island bases were largely

[5

in process of construction. Our air force was well trained but small. Our land armies were inadequate and only partially equipped. Less than half of our navy was in the Pacific, and it was spread over half of that great ocean. Nowhere were we ready to strike a telling blow at Japan or halt by force of arms any aggressive move she might make in Asia or the western half of Oceania.

Japan had been "telling the world" for years that our military strength in the Pacific and our development of bases there were menacing the peace of the Far East. There is no question that our forces later became a menace to her, but let us look at the record as of December 7, 1941.

Our only real naval base in the Pacific on that fateful December morning was at Pearl Harbor, seven miles out of Honolulu, twenty-four hundred miles from our West Coast and almost four thousand miles from Tokyo. Our only other dry docks in the Pacific were at Cavite, near Manila. They were not large enough for battleships. Cavite's principal use was as a repair base for destroyers, gunboats, and submarines which were our main naval strength in Far Eastern waters. Two days after the start of the war Japanese bombers knocked it out in ten minutes. Dutch Harbor, five hundred miles west of the Alaskan mainland, a quarter of the way out the Aleutian chain, was then only in the process of construction, and even today is of little consequence in our military position in the Pacific.

We had airfields at Manila, at Wake, Guam, Midway, and Pearl Harbor and were constructing others on smaller Pacific islands, but by no stretch of the imagination were they any menace to Japan. We did not have a single bomber on December 7, 1941, that could carry a full load of bombs to Tokyo from any of our island bases, let alone carry them there and then come back home. The American public may have been misled by stories of bombers with ranges of thirty-five hundred to seven thousand miles, but the Japanese militarists had not.

Our military installations were purely defensive, and inadequate. Moreover, every one we had was well known to the Japanese. We do not know to this day just how well developed or how strong are some of the bases Japan built up illegally, through the years since the First World War, in the Central Pacific islands she held under mandate of the League of Nations.

We were especially weak in the Philippines. And that was the one sure place where the Japanese would strike. Our land forces there consisted of eleven thousand regular army troops, federalized National Guardsmen, and marines; twelve thousand Filipino Scouts, and a poorly equipped Philippine citizen army of one hundred thousand. The latter group did little effective fighting.

Our air force in the Philippines, which had just been strengthened, consisted of 35 Flying Fortresses, 107 P-40 fighters, 108 miscellaneous other craft such as outmoded bombers, fighters and transport planes, and eight thousand men, pilots, and ground crew men.

At sea in that area we were even weaker. Our total naval strength in the Far East on December 7, 1941, consisted of one heavy cruiser, the Houston; two light cruisers, the new Boise and the old Marblehead; thirteen destroyers; between twenty and thirty submarines, of which six were the old S-boats; a squadron of six motor torpedo boats, and a few river gunboats, tenders and supply ships. The naval air arm—the famous Patwing 10—consisted of thirty-odd patrol bombers, the long-range but slow and lightly armed PBY's.

In three months this naval surface-and-air force was driven entirely out of the Far East, along with the British and Dutch ships and planes. A large part of it was lost, including the heavy cruiser Houston, several of the destroyers, nearly all the smaller surface craft, and all but five of the PBY's. The submarines were chased to Australia. The last hope was gone of reinforcement of the remaining soldiers, sailors, and marines, fighting gloriously but inevitably toward defeat on Bataan and Corregidor.

The major portion of our fleet was concentrated in the Central

[7

Pacific. But it was not as large, nor as great a part of our total naval force, as might have been expected and the American public believed it to be.

Only two of our seven carriers were there. A third was on the West Coast. Eight of our seventeen battleships were in Pearl Harbor, but all of them were old and slow and inadequately equipped with antiaircraft weapons and detection devices. Less than half of our light and heavy cruisers and about the same percentage of destroyers were in the Pacific. Several of these were doing convoy work.

The rest of our navy was in the North and South Atlantic and the Caribbean. It will be remembered that the United States had started a "shooting war" against the Nazi submarine in the Atlantic at that time and that Hitler stood in western Europe and Africa looking speculatively at South America, where his Fifth Column was hard at work.

CHAPTER 2

The Japanese Strategy

IN WASHINGTON Ambassador Nomura and Special Envoy Kurusu, who has an American wife who calls him "Daddy," were talking peace.

In Tokyo the Japanese war lords, headed by General-Premier Tojo and the late Admiral Isoroku Yamamoto, were planning war.

Japan at that time held all the main Chinese coastal ports; Formosa was a major air-and-sea base from which to strike at the Philippines. The French colonial government in Indo-China, abandoned by Vichy and too helpless to resist with its own resources, had been pushed to one side and the country taken over by the buck-teethed dwarfs from the north. Thailand was ready to join up on what looked like the winning side. She had been promised part of Indo-China, perhaps all of it. Burma, one of the less happy of the British possessions in the Far East, was led by ambitious men who thought they had nothing to lose by playing ball with Japan.

Spurred by the mounting potentialities of the American industrial machine, which was to become the arsenal of the democracies but had not reached that estate in 1941, and cheered by the preoccupation of our Navy Department with the German submarine war in the North Atlantic and the possibility of an invasion of South America, the Japanese decided the moment to strike had come.

Except for the attack on our fleet, their military moves could have been forecast years before. Japan's militarists had made no secret of their intention to seize, or dominate, all of East Asia. They even had mapped the extent of their empire, including all the territory they later won.

In the territories they intended to seize there was no military power that could stop them. The one imponderable was the United States, with its Pacific fleet. What would the United States do when Japan moved on the Philippines? Would it declare war? If it did choose to fight would it be able to carry out the classic pattern of Pacific war, a holding action in the Philippines until the fleet could fight its way through with reinforcements on the Pearl Harbor-Wake-Guam line?

The Japanese answer to the question whether we would fight if the Philippines were attacked obviously was in the affirmative. Otherwise they would not have attempted to immobilize our fleet. There are many persons in and out of the United States, in and out of the fleet, who are not so sure.

The No Foreign War Committee, headed by the Cedar Rapids, Iowa, editor Verne Marshall, financed by William Rhodes Davis, the oil speculator, and several wealthy Republican Roosevelt haters, and backed (behind the scenes) by Charles A.

[9

Lindbergh, had been largely discredited by the fall of 1941. But the America First Committee, with the same Lindbergh and Senator Burton K. Wheeler, the would-be presidential candidate, as its ideological leaders, was still strong and growing stronger in the Middle West.

The Philippines had been promised their independence, and the day was not far distant. Our sovereignty over those Far Eastern islands never had been popular with the great mass of the American public. Even if some of our ships had been sunk in Far Eastern waters and some of our people killed in the Philippines it is doubtful whether President Roosevelt, or anyone else, would have been able to get from Congress a declaration of war against Japan.

If the Japanese are half as smart as many persons credit them with being it would seem their best policy would have been to take a chance on that point, carry out their Far Eastern campaign and leave the American decision to destiny.

It is fortunate for the world, horrible as this war has been, that they did not. Perhaps German pressure had something to do with their decision to attack us, but that is doubtful. They showed the same overboldness then as they have since at such heavy cost to themselves; the overboldness which, by the terms of the Cairo agreement, eventually will cost them all their empire. White arrogance and mismanagement in the Far East gave them some excuse for attempting to enlarge their influence there. They had no reason to attack the United States. The way they attacked welded this country for war as nothing else could have done.

Once Japan's decision to challenge the United States was made, the problem was to immobilize our fleet so as not to leave an exposed flank while the Japanese armies moved south under naval escort to conquer the Philippines, the East Indies, Malaya, New Guinea, and the other islands of Melanesia.

Our method of fleet operation, a method imposed by our lack of bases and by the strict economy necessary under restricted

10]

navy appropriations, made that a fairly simple problem to solve. We had only one base in the Pacific. When the fleet wasn't at sea it was in Pearl Harbor or on the West Coast. The reason it was in Pearl Harbor so much of the time was because it required more than a million gallons of fuel oil a week to keep it at sea.

In our fleet exercises, of which the Japanese were close students, we already had shown them how such a base could be successfully attacked. The teacher was no less a person than Admiral Ernest J. King, later Commander in Chief (COMINCH) of the navy. Several years ago, in a problem of attack on the Panama Canal, Admiral King used exactly the same tactics the Japanese used December 7. He formed a striking force of two carriers, with cruiser and destroyer escort, and sent them against the canal behind a storm front. They were in striking range without detection, theoretically destroyed the canal locks, and escaped unscathed.

The Japanese had studied our fleet operations for years. They knew the fleet customarily came in for week ends. Their intelligence out of the Hawaiian Islands was excellent and extensive. They knew the facts of our army and navy patrols (even if our respective commanding officers of the two arms did not) and of the fleet disposition. From their submarines and fishing fleets in the North Pacific they kept a close check on the weather, a much closer check than we did. The only problem was to pick a time when the fleet would be tied up in Pearl Harbor, with precautions taken only against submarines and sabotage, and when the weather was propitious for a carrier task force to sneak in behind a cold front.

The plans had been long in the making. Our preparations for the attack on Attu in May, 1943, were begun four months before. Every nation has on paper plans for any war it may have to fight. Nations of good will, however, make their plans largely for defense. Such were those of the United States and the other democracies.

The groundwork had been well laid by Japan. Late in November her fleets and transport trains started moving. And so did the task force whose job was to knock out our fleet.

It was a grandiose undertaking. Undoubtedly every plane and ship available to the Japanese was thrown into that first effort. Even so, those early successes, especially the attack on Pearl Harbor, must have exceeded even Yamamoto's fondest hopes.

The task force assigned to the Pearl Harbor mission was composed of carriers. With them, undoubtedly, were the usual guards of cruisers and destroyers.

Cruising east and north from Japan, this task force followed a cold front down toward the islands. At sunrise of December 7, or shortly before, they launched the attack from a point about one hundred and fifty miles due north of Oahu. The Japanese made two major mistakes in their attacks on the United States. They attacked the ships instead of the shore installations at Pearl Harbor. They failed to follow up their initial advantage. By the time they had realized their mistake and could gather the men and the ships for the job—which was not for six months—it was too late. They underestimated, too, the fighting qualities of the United States Navy and its air force.

Had the Japanese, on that bright December morning of 1941, had the same force within striking distance of Pearl Harbor that they threw against Midway and the Aleutians six months later, they probably would soon have been sitting in the Hawaiian Islands. Our road ahead to victory would have stretched out much farther and more bitterly.

Few persons familiar with the situation will deny that the Japanese could have done it. They could have thrown twelve or more carriers against our three; war-trained pilots in superior planes against our peace-trained airmen flying obsolete fighters that didn't belong in the same league with the Zero; and could have fought our cruisers with battleships. Malaya, Sumatra, Java, New Guinea, the Solomons, and all the rest would have fallen into their laps like ripe plums had they chosen to make their main strike at the Hawaiian Islands.

Had the Japanese seized Pearl Harbor and been able to operate from there our whole West Coast would have been harassed. A landing on the coast would have been inconceivable, even as poorly defended as it was then, but carriers operating from the Hawaiian Islands could have forced the transfer of our great aviation plants eastward beyond the Rockies and rendered hazardous the operation of our shipyards. Submarines operating from a base only two thousand miles from the West Coast could have cut our supply lines to New Zealand and Australia, or at least have made the movement of convoys through the Pacific a perilous undertaking, subject to enormous losses.

The sinking or disabling of our entire line of battleships had an effect on which the Japanese hardly could have counted. It changed our fleet speed from eighteen knots to more than thirty. For there is little doubt that if the battleships had remained in commission they would have put to sea with the carriers and cruisers. The greyhounds would have had to suit their pace to that of the waddling bulldogs.

It may well be, too, that in disabling the battleships the Japanese prevented our navy from carrying through the long-studied plan of attempting to fight its way through to the Philippines with reinforcements. That probably would have resulted in an even worse disaster than was Pearl Harbor. Such an attempt could only have slowed, not stopped, the Japanese advance to the south and would probably have left us with no Pacific fleet at all instead of the small, fast and very effective one that remained after the Pearl Harbor attack.

The main flaw in the strategy of the Japanese was that they overestimated their own strength and underestimated the productive ability of United States industry and the fighting ability of the "soft" American man. They probably counted too on a Hitler victory in Europe.

The only Japanese hope after the early successes was for a

stalemate and war weariness on the part of the United States, allowing Japan to hold some of her conquests. If the declaration of Cairo by President Roosevelt, Prime Minister Churchill, and Generalissimo Chiang Kai-shek were to be put in force at the peace conference, that hope would be gone.

By the end of 1943 the issue in the Pacific was no longer in doubt. The only question was the length of time needed to overwhelm the Japanese military machine. A boy had attempted to do a man's job, and had failed.

CHAPTER 3

United States Strategy

THAT THE United States would have to fight Japan some day had long been accepted by our navy. Japan had the only fleet that was in any way a menace to us. She had the only bases from which our islands and continental cities could be attacked. Our national idealism and democratic principles were the main impediment to Japan's domination by force of all of East Asia.

For years the Naval War College at Newport, Rhode Island, had concerned itself with problems that had the Japanese as the enemy. As best it could, lacking funds for espionage, our navy command had kept track of Japanese activities, especially movements of the Japanese fleet. When that fleet put to sea so did the United States fleet, or what there was of it in the Pacific.

Our grand strategy when war with Japan came was, as explained before, to hold the Philippines and have the fleet fight its way through with reinforcements. The disabling of our entire battleship line knocked that plan into a cocked hat.

The psychological impact of the Japanese attack on Pearl Harbor was even greater than the physical damage to the fleet.

14]

The very audacity of the Japanese in striking us at our strongest point was as paralyzing to the admirals' nerves as was Bob Fitzsimmon's solar-plexus blow on Gentleman Jim Corbett.

For the first two months the Pacific fleet's activities were purely defensive, the first of the three great phases into which the Pacific conflict falls.

It was a terrific problem that confronted the fleet and our air-and-ground forces in the Pacific. The great arc we had to defend at all costs stretched seven thousand miles from the western tip of the Aleutians, through the Hawaiian Islands, the Fijis, the New Hebrides, and New Caledonia to northern Australia.

From Kiska to Midway there are no island bases from which our search planes can operate. Fogs and storms cover much of that great sea area much of the time. It was through this gap in the line that the Japanese striking force had come to attack Pearl Harbor.

Southward from Honolulu to New Caledonia most of our island bases—Johnston, Palmyra, Canton, Howland, Baker, and the others—were within air range of the Japanese bases in the mandated Marshalls. What bases we had were only in the process of construction. As late as May, 1941, we had no fighter protection at Canton, then one of the main stops on the air route from Pearl Harbor to Brisbane. We had only one squadron of inferior navy fighter planes, at Palmyra.

There were many civilian work parties on most of these islands at the start of the war, but in the first frenzied hours after the attack on Pearl Harbor all civilian workmen were ordered to leave by whatever transportation was available. I was told that the story of the group that left Canton on a barge in tow of a tug is one that makes the Nordhoff-Hall saga of Captain Bligh and the voyage of his longboat sound like a pleasure cruise.

The departure of the civilians left the islands held only by small forces of the army or navy, virtually without protection and dependent on their own resources to provide the fields to which fighter protection could be flown. It has been revealed that a force of twenty-six army men held Canton and built the air base there.

Until these island bases could be built up to a strength where they could defend themselves and from which our search planes could operate in comparative safety, with sufficient supplies of gasoline and food available, it devolved on the fleet to hold the line if it could.

To do this we had just the three carriers—the Saratoga, Lexington, and Enterprise—and a few divisions of cruisers and destroyers. It was not until midsummer of 1942 that the Pacific Fleet was strengthened to any extent. Tokyo Radio was not out of order in asking, "Where is the United States fleet?" Strict censorship, which probably was necessary although there is considerable evidence that the Japanese knew the answer to the question, kept the American public from being told the score.

With this force, which was pitifully small for the task it had to do, the navy set out to patrol our seven-thousand-mile defense line. It was a heartbreaking task. Because of the great areas to be covered the carriers could not operate together. If the Japanese had chosen to press eastward instead of southward any interception would have been a suicide venture for the carrier that ran into the Japanese, and most of the men knew it. Our fliers would have gone into action exhausted from the ceaseless dawn-to-dusk patrol. Many of them, in those first weeks, averaged eleven hours a day in the air, seven days a week. And no time and a half for overtime.

The navy's job was twofold. First, it had to maintain a constant patrol over as much of the Pacific as it could reach with its planes, its surface ships, and its submarines to prevent the Japanese from again sneaking in undetected for an attack on Pearl Harbor or, what would have been far worse and more demoralizing at that time, a strike at our plane factories in and around Los Angeles and Seattle or the shipyards there and at San Francisco.

16]

Secondly, the navy had to protect the ships that were carrying fighter planes, troops, workmen, and supplies to Hawaii, New Zealand, Australia, and other bases in the Pacific. None of these bases were self-sufficient. The Hawaiian Islands did not even raise what food was needed.

Most of the ships available were slow and poorly suited for the jobs they were called on to do. Train ferries built for operation on inland waterways were used to haul fighter planes to Honolulu. Many of the convoys moved at a speed as slow as six knots. Here again the Japanese missed their opportunity. Had they thrown more of their submarines against these convoys they could have forced a diversion of combatant ships from the westernmost patrols to convoy work, thus stretching even thinner our line of defense west of Hawaii and along the Australian supply route.

CHAPTER 4

Psychological Warfare

KNUTE ROCKNE, great football coach, always operated on the principle that a good offense was the best defense. The opposition couldn't make much progress as long as you held the ball and called the plays.

Our admirals took a page from the Rockne book. If the Japanese were not going to attack in the Central Pacific we would.

On January 31, or February 1, whichever side of the International Date Line you prefer to take, Vice Admiral William F. Halsey struck the first blow, a combined plane-and-ship bombardment of seven Japanese bases, or outposts, in the Gilbert and Marshall islands.

Halsey's two carrier groups, one led by the Enterprise, the

other by the Yorktown, which had just come out from the Caribbean, had been covering a convoy taking marine garrisons to Samoa and adjacent island bases. He was ordered to throw a scare into the Japanese on the way back and perhaps divert more of their sea strength from the South Pacific, where they were then busy mopping up the Netherlands East Indies and preparing for the ill-fated move against New Caledonia and New Guinea that was met and turned back in the Battle of the Coral Sea.

It took courage of the highest order to risk this operation. The many Japanese island bases gave the enemy unsinkable carriers from which to support their surface forces with air force. The destruction or crippling of either of our two carriers would have been a serious blow.

The results of the raids were much greater than had been expected. Sixteen ships, one a seventeen-thousand-ton former passenger liner of the Yawata class converted into an aircraft carrier, and forty-one Japanese planes, many of them two-motored Mitsubishi '97 bombers, were destroyed in the raid. Our losses were eleven dive bombers, at least six of which were victims of bad weather, and minor damage to one of our cruisers.

The psychological effect on the Japanese and our own people was even greater. Our fliers learned that their planes, the new Grumman Wildcat fighters, and their tactics were much better than the planes and tactics of the Japanese. Our ship captains learned they had little to fear from horizontal bombing. After two months of reverses, the operation gave our navy something to cheer about. It lifted home morale, which has an effect through letters on the men of the fleet. It battle-tested twelve thousand men. Above all it was something to do, definite action to relieve the boredom of constant patrol.

The operation was so successful, even if it did not divert the Japanese from their main goal or, probably, scare them much, that other similar operations were planned.

On February 24 Halsey, this time operating with only one

carrier, struck at Wake, and eight days later he raided Marcus, right in the front yard of Tokyo and the Japanese home fleet.

Far to the south the Lexington task force, under Vice Admiral Wilson Brown, later to be President Roosevelt's naval aide, started for Rabaul. Detected and attacked by eighteen two-motored bombers from Bougainville, of which sixteen were shot down, Admiral Brown withdrew into the Coral Sea. It was during this operation that the late Eddie (Butch) O'Hare, then a lieutenant junior grade, shot down five Japanese bombers and damaged a sixth in what was the finest single aerial exploit of the Pacific war.

Foiled in his proposed attack on Rabaul, which was not then the major base it later became, Admiral Brown took his force, which had been strengthened by addition of the Yorktown and her escorts, to the westward. On March 10, air groups from the two carriers climbed over the Owen Stanley Range in New Guinea to attack Japanese shipping off Salamaua and Lae. The Japanese were taken completely by surprise. Our torpedo planes and bombers sank two enemy heavy cruisers, one destroyer, and five transports, and heavily damaged several other ships, including two more cruisers. Three Wildcats sank a destroyer in strafing attacks, their hot .50-caliber slugs apparently touching off a torpedo war head or depth charges.

Thus in a period of forty-five days the Pacific Fleet with only three carriers had struck four times at enemy bases thousands of miles apart. It had sunk or destroyed twenty-six enemy ships, shot down forty-eight Japanese planes, and heavily damaged shore installations at nine island bases. Japanese personnel losses were not known but probably were fairly large, perhaps in the thousands. All this at a cost to us of fourteen aircraft, some fifty men, and damage to a cruiser. There are few parallels in naval history of so few doing so much at so little cost.

In addition to the psychological effect on the Japanese—the raid on Marcus gave Tokyo a real case of war jitters and led to a change in command—the raids also brought the information that Japan's air force was spread out much thinner than had been thought. Only a few Japanese fighters, and none of them the Mitsubishi 'oo (the Zero) had been encountered in the Marshall-Gilbert raids. Only float fighters had been met at Wake and at Salamaua and Lae. If the raids did nothing else they undoubtedly forced the Japanese to strengthen air defenses at their island bases.

While these raids were being made by the Pacific Fleet the Asiatic Fleet under Rear Admiral Thomas C. Hart was fighting a series of desperate delaying actions as it retired to the East Indies and then to Australia. In the Macassar Straits, between Borneo and the Celebes, four old four-piper destroyers of First World War vintage daringly ran through the Japanese screen of cruisers and destroyers at night and sank or heavily damaged nine Japanese transports. A combined Dutch-United States task force delivered heavy blows to the enemy in the Battle of Lombok Straits, the Battle of Bali and the Battle of Java Sea.

Our losses, however, were grievous. The heavy cruiser Houston was sunk, along with the destroyers Pope, Pillsbury, Edsall, and Peary, the former aircraft carrier Langley—used as a tender and plane ferry—and the tanker Pecos. Several other ships were damaged, including the light cruiser Marblehead. Practically all of the Dutch fleet and several units of the Royal Australian Navy also were lost.

Because most of the actions were fought at night and others at long range, the exact losses of the Japanese are not known. That they were much heavier than those of the United Nations, however, is without question. Japan's victories were not being won at a light cost. The United States and Dutch submarines also were taking a heavy toll.

CHAPTER 5

The Last Japanese
Offensives

BY MAY 1, 1942, the Japanese juggernaut had rolled southward
to the very shores of Australia. The little bandy-legged men from
the small island empire thirty degrees north of the equator had
swept through the Philippines, the Malay States, all of the Dutch
East Indies, and part of New Guinea to latitude 10 degrees South.
The only allied forces remaining in a continental-ocean area of
ten million square miles were a few thousand sick, bomb-shocked
American and Filipino soldiers in Corregidor. They surrendered
six days later.

Except for the long defense in the Philippines everything had
gone according to plan for the little men who would be masters
of a quarter of the world. Admiral Yamamoto was quoted as
saying he would dictate terms to the United States from the
White House in Washington.

Those were great days in Tokyo. Japan's slogan of Asia for
the Asiatics now appeared to have concrete meaning. The
Greater East Asia Co-Prosperity Sphere had been established.
The Japanese might have been said to have won their war.

The Japanese had suffered heavy losses, but these probably
had been discounted. The Japanese do not put a very high
premium on human life. Tokyo had been bombed by Jimmy
Doolittle's raiders, but after the first hysteria the Japanese must
have realized it was a feat that could not be soon repeated. They
had taken steps to see that it did not happen again as they began
an offensive to clear the Chinese from the coastal area below
Shanghai to remove the threat of establishment of air bases there.
Some of their islands had been raided, but no attempt had been

[21

made at landings and what damage had been done, except for ships lost, probably had been repaired in days if not hours. They had not lost a single inch of ground they had conquered. We could not touch their inner lines of communication with any airplanes we had, even if we had had enough planes in the Pacific theater to attempt it. Except in Burma and China the United Nations had no land contact with them. Early in May they again were on the move. An occupation force had moved on the Lower Solomons and had taken Tulagi and Guadalcanal without a struggle. Then down from the north steamed a two-pronged invasion force. One group apparently was headed for New Caledonia, the big French island which an American division had occupied in March but had as yet only partly fortified. The other was headed for Port Moresby, the precarious finger-hold a combined American-Australian force still held on New Guinea. In both groups were carriers, battleships, cruisers, destroyers, and transports.

In the aptly named Coral Sea, an ocean area larger than the Gulf of Mexico, was our two-carrier task force of the Lexington and the Yorktown, commanded by Rear Admiral Frank Jack Fletcher, aboard the Yorktown, and Rear Admiral Aubrey W. Fitch on the Lexington. The Yorktown had been at sea for almost two months. The Lexington, after the Salamaua-Lae raid, had returned to Pearl Harbor to reprovision and to have some new antiaircraft weapons installed. Her 8-inch rifles had been replaced by 5-inch dual-purpose guns, which could be used either against surface targets or against aircraft.

We struck the first blow. Admiral Fletcher took the Yorktown in south of Guadalcanal and sent his air group against the sixteen to eighteen Japanese combatant ships and transports lying in Tulagi Harbor and the roads off Guadalcanal. Again the Japanese were caught by surprise. Every one of their ships either was sunk or was badly damaged, and some of them had to be beached.

On May 7 began the historic Battle of the Coral Sea, the first

22]

great carrier engagement of naval warfare. In ships sunk for sure—one carrier on each side, a tanker and a destroyer for us and a heavy cruiser for the Japanese—the battle was a standoff. But the Japanese transports and their guard had turned back. They never tried again to take Port Moresby from the sea or to attack New Caledonia. The Japanese push southward at long last had been stopped.

The carriers Enterprise and Hornet, with their destroyers and cruisers, were just out of range of the battle. They had covered a landing of marines at Efate in the New Hebrides and had arrived in the Coral Sea too late to catch the retiring Japanese fleet.

Reconnaissance reports meanwhile had come of the withdrawal of large Japanese fleet and transport concentrations from the Southwest Pacific toward Japan. Some major move in the Central or North Pacific obviously was on foot.

Ships began to turn back to Pearl Harbor. All of our remaining battleworthy carriers—the Yorktown was not badly hurt—were down to the south, as were most of our other ships.

In the Hawaiian Islands all hands were on the alert. All air patrols were strengthened and extended, and the marine and army air arms on Midway were increased. Even the battleship divisions, which then were based on the West Coast, were ordered to sea. However, they were kept discreetly outside the combat area.

The morning of June 3, seven hundred miles west of Midway, a lumbering PBY, the navy's aerial workhorse, sighted one of the Japanese forces, two long lines of transport and cargo vessels escorted by cruisers and destroyers, steaming eastward.

At almost the same time, two thousand miles to the north, a flight of fifteen Japanese carrier planes attacked Dutch Harbor in the Aleutians.

The problem confronting our navy command in Pearl Harbor and Washington was, which was the main objective and which the diversion? The main striking force of the enemy had not yet been located. Army pilots attacking the transport train west of Midway reported a carrier with that group (apparently an error since they were not attacked by carrier planes), but it was certain the Japanese would not send out an attack force of only one carrier. Weather off the Aleutians was foggy as usual, but the attack on Dutch Harbor had been light, so it could be assumed the force there was small.

Our three carriers, under command of Rear Admiral Frank Jack Fletcher, aboard the Yorktown, and Rear Admiral R. A. Spruance, aboard the Enterprise (the Hornet was the third carrier), were northeast of Midway, prepared to join the battle either for the Aleutians or for Midway.

In addition to the contact with the transport train, the logic of the situation pointed to Midway as the main target. Seizure of that strategic island would bring Pearl Harbor within range of the Japanese two-motored bombers (the only Japanese four-motored planes are the slow Kawanishi seaplane patrol bombers). Midway too was far more important to us than Dutch Harbor. The United States fleet was held within striking distance of Midway to await developments. They were not long in coming.

In their arrogance the Japanese had miscalculated both the excellence of fleet reconnaissance and our admirals' ability to out-think and outmaneuver them. They launched their attack on Midway without waiting for a report from their morning search, which they made with slow seaplanes comparable to our cruiser and battleship scouts. They left their flank wide open.

First the marine and army planes from Midway and then the navy fliers from the carriers were on them. By midafternoon three of their carriers were sinking. None survived the night.

The remaining Japanese carrier, the Hiryu, meanwhile had turned eastward when the full picture was drawn to bring her planes within striking range of our carriers. She just didn't have enough to do the job. Two groups from her deck, the first composed of dive bombers, the second of torpedo planes, found the carriers and crippled the Yorktown but did not even attack the Enterprise or the Hornet. Planes from the latter two carriers

24]

found the Hiryu just before dusk that night, and set her on fire. She escaped back into the fog area, but the Japanese were unable to save her and she sank the next day after being abandoned by her escort.

With the Yorktown gone and with his flag now on the cruiser Astoria, Frank Jack Fletcher was out of the fight, so he turned command of the two other carriers over to Admiral Spruance. Fearful that the Japanese surface ships, which were far superior in numbers and fire power to the American vessels, might make a night attack, Admiral Spruance retired to the southeastward during the night. That was all that saved the Japanese from an even worse disaster.

With all four of their carriers sunk and other ships damaged, the Japanese fleet split into small units and ran for home. Some of them were found the next day by army planes from Midway and were attacked. The carrier groups, handicapped by the mileage they had lost the night of June 4, did not catch up with them until the morning of June 6. Most of our torpedo planes had been lost in the first attacks, but the dive bombers worked on the ships they could find, sinking at least two more cruisers and heavily damaging several destroyers. Then, fuel running low, our forces broke off the pursuit and retired eastward to refuel and re-form their air groups with the new planes that had been brought out by the Saratoga.

In the Aleutians, the Japanese planes returned to the attack on Dutch Harbor the afternoon of June 4. But that was the last time. Little damage was done in either attack.

Whatever plans they may have had for assaulting that outpost on the right flank of the Pacific battle line, the disaster at Midway and the unexpected opposition they received from army planes, based on Umnak to the southwest of Dutch Harbor, dissuaded them. They retired to the westward and on June 7 occupied Kiska and Attu, from which they were not driven for a year. They never attempted, however, to build either island into a major base. They even abandoned Attu for a month and a half

[25

that fall, but when we failed to take advantage of this fact they moved back in and finally had to be rooted out by army troops. Their Aleutian show failed in its main purpose of drawing off our fleet from the defense of Midway, but their occupation of the outer islands was a strategic victory for them, as it tied up many thousands of men and hundreds of planes for many months in Alaska and along our West Coast.

The twin-pronged drive at Midway and the Aleutians was the last great Japanese sea offensive. They have since been on the defensive.

CHAPTER 6

We Take the Offensive

IN THE Coral Sea and off Midway the Japanese had suffered two great reverses. After several months of uninterrupted advance they had at last been stopped. A more difficult task remained.

On June 7, 1942, six months after Pearl Harbor, the Japanese had won their empire. The task of the United States forces in the Pacific was to keep them from exploiting it.

The Japanese probably were content to hold what they had, if they could. Inside the territory they had conquered were all the raw materials they needed for making war.

The United Nations still were woefully weak in the Pacific. New Zealand's and Australia's imperial divisions were fighting Rommel in Africa. Others had been captured in Singapore. The flow of planes and ships and supplies to the Pacific war theater was only a trickle compared to what was going the other way. General MacArthur had only a token force of American combat troops and an air force of only a few hundred planes in Australia. Plans for the North African invasion already were under way, and a large part of our navy was earmarked for that job. Our command in the Pacific was particularly weak in sea transport.

The objective, therefore, had to be a limited one which would not overstrain thin resources. It had to be a point where our forces had land bases from which to support an offensive. There was a pressing need, too, to shorten the sea lanes of communication wherever possible. The most important supply route then as now was to Australia.

These are some of the factors that influenced the choice of the Solomons as the theater where the first offensive would be launched.

The Japanese had moved down the Solomons early in May, occupying the strategic harbor of Tulagi and the northern coastal plain of the big island of Guadalcanal, twenty miles to the south. They were hurriedly building a naval base at Tulagi and a land air base on Guadalcanal.

In addition to answering the requirements for a limited offensive—location within bombing range of our land bases in the New Hebrides, isolation from Japanese bases, and a short sea haul for transport trains—it was necessary to prevent the Japanese from developing Tulagi and Guadalcanal as bases. In Japanese hands the Solomons could become a menace to the Australian supply line and a continual bombing threat to the New Hebrides, which we had begun to strengthen in April; to New Caledonia, which had been made South Pacific fleet headquarters, and to the Fijis, Britain's main island possession in the South Seas and seat of her colonial administration.

There are many strategists who believe it would have been better to have thrown the men and supplies that were used in the Solomons campaign into New Guinea in an attempt to clean out the Japanese there and strike directly at Rabaul by the shortest route. But forces that might have been used in this theater were sent elsewhere.

Whatever the reasons, the navy and the marines, our only military arm trained in amphibious warfare, went ahead with

[27

the plans to attack the Solomons. What Lieutenant General Alexander Archer Vandegrift, later commandant of the Marine Corps, was to term "this modest operation" touched off one of the fiercest sea, air, and land campaigns ever waged.

The original plan, as it was understood through the fleet, was for the marines to seize the positions on Guadalcanal and Tulagi, then for the army, a division of which was in training in New Caledonia, to move in and take over while the marines moved on up to another position. What happened to that plan only the high command knows.

For over a month the marines received only a trickle of supplies, largely run in by old, converted four-piper destroyers that were considered expendable. If it had not been for the large supplies of rice and canned fish captured from the Japanese the marines would have been on very short rations indeed. They had no air cover for twelve days until they had completed Henderson Field and a squadron of their own pilots, in Grumman Wildcats, had flown in from the flight deck of the escort carrier that had brought them to the area.

It is not a pleasant chapter in the history of the Pacific fleet, those first two and a half months of operations in the Solomons. The Enterprise-Saratoga task force, aided by Flying Fortresses from the New Hebrides which were operating under the navy's direction, fought a successful battle against three carriers August 24 in what has been called the Battle of the Eastern Solomons. The late Rear Admiral Norman Scott, with the San Francisco, Salt Lake City, Helene, and Boise, turned back on October 11 one Japanese attempt to reinforce Guadalcanal. There also was a relatively ineffective but daring raid by the Hornet air group on Japanese positions on Bougainville and on the Shortland Islands.

But for most of those first ninety days the navy stayed strictly on the defensive, patrolling at slow speed up and down to the eastward of the Solomons. The fleet was showing caution at a time when some of the daring shown later when Admiral Halsey relieved Vice Admiral Robert Lee Ghormley in command of the South Pacific would have paid big dividends.

The Japanese meanwhile were running in reinforcements nearly every night and attacking the marine positions by air in the daytime and with surface vessels at night. Older marine officers who had served in the First World War said the shelling by battleships and cruisers the nights of September 13—14 and October 12—13 was far worse than any of the artillery barrages they had lived through in France twenty-five years before.

Our naval cautiousness, which was as much deplored by many naval officers as it was by the marines on Guadalcanal who were suffering the consequences, paid off in disastrous dividends. Cruising up and down and 'round and 'round in waters known to be infested with Japanese submarines, the American task forces finally reaped the rewards of their folly. The carrier Wasp was torpedoed and lost.

At the same time the Wasp was hit the whole bow was blown off one of her protecting destroyers, the O'Brien.

To fill the navy's cup of woe to overflowing, the South Dakota, new thirty-five-thousand-ton battleship that had just come to the South Pacific, ran on an uncharted pinnacle shortly after her arrival and had to go back for repairs. Fortunately, the damage was easily repaired and she was back in time to fight in the Battle of Santa Cruz and the night battle of November 14—15 off Savo Islands.

With the return of "Bull" Halsey to the wars in mid-October after four months in the States taking treatment for a skin affliction, the navy began to redeem itself. The Enterprise, repaired after her bomb damage of August 24, and the Hornet fought the successful battle of Santa Cruz, turning back the second major Japanese drive to retake Guadalcanal, and then came the great night battles of November when outnumbered, outgunned American ships hurled themselves against the Japanese navy, sank their ships and broke their spirit, saved Guadalcanal.

[29

The really magnificent job in the early stages of the Solomons campaign, however, was done by the marine and navy fliers, and later by the army pilots when they got the planes with which to fight. Always outnumbered, they never declined the issue, fought against great odds and died as brave men. Their greatest single feat was the destruction on November 14 and 15 of a complete Japanese transport train of twelve vessels, half of them the finest transports the Japanese had, loaded with an estimated thirty thousand to forty thousand troops.

That we would hold our position in the Solomons was never in doubt after mid-November. Supplies by the ton and men by thousands were poured into Guadalcanal. In late January the Japanese gave up and started their evacuation. On February 10 Major General Alexander M. Patch, U.S.A., who had succeeded General Vandegrift in charge of operations in the Solomons, announced that all organized Japanese resistance had ended.

Even before Guadalcanal was secured the marine, navy and army fliers, and navy surface vessels, were preparing the way for the move on up the island chain. The fliers were bombing the new Japanese airfields at Munda on New Georgia Island and Vila on Kolombangara Island nearly every day, and between January 5 and March 6 navy surface forces of light cruisers and destroyers made three night bombardment raids on the two Japanese strongholds.

In mid-February the Russell Islands, from which the Japanese had withdrawn when they abandoned the fight on Guadalcanal, were occupied and an airstrip built there. Then in June came the attack and capture of Munda and Vila and, on November 1, the landing on Bougainville. The Solomons campaign was nearing its end.

The successful attack in November on the Gilberts, the British islands which the Japanese seized soon after the start of the war, put the United States some two hundred miles closer to Tokyo but still farther away than we already were on New Guinea and in the northern Solomons. It did give us air bases from which to harass the Marshall Islands and prevent their use as air or submarine bases to threaten supply lines.

Contact with the Japanese still remained largely by sea and by air, except in China and along the Burma-India border. Even in those places the forces engaged at any one time never have been large. Japan had an army of at least one million five hundred thousand men which never had been in a major engagement, and large fleet units, especially 16-inch-gun battleships, that had not been in action. That fleet had to be brought to battle and destroyed before we could be well on the road to victory.

Japan's losses at sea, particularly in the categories of cruisers, destroyers, and submarines, and merchant vessels, were heavy. Whether Japan's ability to wage war could by these means be crippled sufficiently to make it unnecessary to inflict a military defeat on her army remained to be seen. Bases much nearer to the Japanese home islands were necessary before an attempt to bomb Japan out of the war could be made. We were only on her outer defense line. At the end of two years of war the road to Tokyo, despite the proven superiority of our men, our planes, and our ships, still remained a long, hard one.

CHAPTER 7

The Japanese Submarine Puzzle

ONE OF THE great puzzles of the Pacific war has been the failure of the Japanese to use their submarines more effectively. After the preliminary flurry along our West Coast in the first few weeks of the war, when Japanese undersea boats sank several tankers and unescorted merchantmen and bombarded Santa

Barbara, the waters east of the Hawaiian Islands were almost free from submarine activity, a boon that has been a large factor in movement of men and supplies to our Pacific outposts, to Australia, and to India.

It is estimated that at the start of the war Japan had 118 submarines, of which fewer than one hundred were what might be called modern, long-range boats of more than seven hundred tons. On the same date the United States had 111 pigboats in commission. How many midget submarines Japan had is not known. That is not important, since the two-man submersibles have played little part in the war. Japan had many island bases from which to operate on comparatively short cruises against our various supply lines in the Pacific. Yet against our submarine score to December 7, 1943, of 366 Japanese vessels definitely sunk, fifty more probably sunk and at least 112 hit and damaged, the Japanese submarine squadrons could boast only a score of our merchant ships.

One reason for the Japanese failure to attack our merchant shipping and troop convoys apparently was the Japanese strategy of using submarines against our combatant vessels. They are officially credited with sinking two aircraft carriers, the Yorktown and the Wasp, one of which previously had been damaged by air attack. They also have hit but not sunk several other of our combatant vessels. In nearly all of these successful attacks and a number of unsuccessful ones the Japanese have paid a heavy price.

The Japanese make wide use of their submarines as fleet screens. The Japanese fleet never goes to sea without submarines out ahead. During the early stages of the Solomons campaign the waters around those islands were fairly alive with the undersea boats. As many as twenty or thirty were believed to have been operating in the South Pacific at one time, which would indicate at least twice that number assigned to that area, half of them being at sea and the other half en route to or from station or at home being provisioned and refueled.

Japanese submarine losses have been very heavy. We claimed only five sure sinkings, three of these of two-man subs, and three damaged. The total is several times that. I have personal knowledge of more than ten sure sinkings and at least as many probables. In a period of less than a month in the Aleutians, while the Japanese were evacuating their Kiska garrison, there were four certain sinkings of Japanese submarines. Certainly the Japanese losses have been many times our own, which totaled fourteen in two years.

One reason for believing the Japanese losses to have been extremely heavy is their preoccupation with our task forces, which are well protected and counterattack sure, fast, and deadly. Attacking a convoy in the North Atlantic protected only by a few destroyers or corvettes is child's play compared to the Japanese task of getting within firing range of an American task force, with perhaps six to a dozen destroyers, and driving home an attack. Even if our destroyers cannot blast the enemy undersea boat to the surface, careful patrol of the area where he dived will keep him down, exhaust his air and kill the crew as surely as rupturing the hull would do it.

Air patrol, too, has made the submarine's work doubly hazardous in this war. A submarine commander now surfaces day or night at his own peril. No device yet has been constructed which will tell him while he is submerged when planes are overhead.

In contrast to the Japanese strategy, our own submarine warfare has taken a terrific toll of Japanese shipping, of which they had none to spare. In the early months of the war, when information on enemy ship movements was more important than a few sinkings, our submarines gave the major portion of their time to scouting. They were allowed to attack enemy shipping only when relieved on station and en route home. As our air search was extended, however, and the danger of fleet attacks on Pearl Harbor and our West Coast receded, the submarine skippers were turned loose to send Japanese shipping to the bottom. With the increase in our squadrons and perfection of attack techniques the submarine squadrons should take an increasing toll of Japanese shipping. The undersea war probably has been more of a deterrent to the Japanese war effort than any other single military factor, as all their raw products must be carried to the Japanese home islands in ships or airplanes, and they surely do not have the gasoline for any widespread use of air transport.

PART II

THE DEFENSIVE PHASE

Pearl Harbor, Three
Weeks After

THE WORLD was much too beautiful for war the morning after Christmas, 1941.

From the open port of the big Pan American clipper taxiing to her landing float in Pearl City could be seen the multicolored hills that rise as a barrier between Honolulu and the damp northeasterly trades. White clouds drifted along the crest of the red-and-green ridges and down the valleys toward the sea.

The sun had just cleared Diamond Head but had not yet warmed to its work. After the chilly trip from San Francisco at high altitude its heat was pleasant on the back of the neck and the shoulder blades.

The only sign that all was not right with the world was the heavy film of oil over the water, still bubbling up from the ruptured fuel tanks of the sunken ships in the harbor. Even it had beauty. The prow of the clipper shouldered the oily film aside, sending it rippling away in a rainbow-hued wake whose colors were so brilliant they hurt the eyes.

The tingling feeling of danger that had attended the departure from the clipper's Treasure Island base in San Francisco Bay the afternoon before largely evaporated in the outwardly peaceful aspect of the islands.

The overnight trip in the clipper had impressed anew a truth learned twenty-four years before in the North Atlantic, that war is uncomfortable and much of it boring.

The big airplane had been stripped of most of its peacetime plush furnishings. The berths and most of the lounges and seats had been ripped out to save weight and to make room for mail-

[37

bags and critical materials urgently needed in Hawaii. There remained only three small, fixed tables with built-in seats around them and two long lounges and two small seats in another compartment. The metal deck, even with a cushion on it, did not make a very comfortable bed.

The chief discomfort of the trip, however, had been the inability to see out. The small ports all had been covered with black paper. When the entry port was slammed on us, and locked, we couldn't even see the sea, which is all most sailors see. The young steward added a nice touch when he came around at what must have been sunset and carefully pulled all the curtains.

Aboard were Jim Kilgallen of International News Service, an old friend of many previous hurry-up assignments; Keith Wheeler, of the *Chicago Times*; Samuel Wilder King, Hawaiian delegate to Congress who was returning home for a first-hand look-see at what had been done; several navy technicians and even two yeomen for the Naval Intelligence Office in Honolulu.

Jim and Keith and I had felt somewhat embarrassed about taking passage on the clipper, fearing we were displacing more important persons or mail or critical war materials. Lieutenant Adam, the navy transportation officer who had okayed our passage, said he was freshly caught up on mail and we weren't displacing anyone of importance.

While riding out to Treasure Island in a navy station wagon, we had been talking about the war and speculating as to just what damage had been done by the Japanese at Pearl Harbor and what, if anything, the fleet was doing about catching the enemy carriers from which the attack had been launched.

We all had a feeling that the full story hadn't been told. None of us realized then, however, how small a part had been divulged. President Roosevelt had said our fleet was at sea seeking the enemy, and we entertained the hope that action perhaps already had been joined and it just had not been announced. The pictures released by the censor had indicated the principal damage in the raid had been to Honolulu itself.

Lieutenant Adam said his small son was asking embarrassing questions. The submarines of the Netherlands navy, which had put to sea on November 30 on the basis of American newspaper reports that war with Japan appeared inevitable, were reporting successes against Japanese forces, and the navy officer said his son was concerned about the lack of offensive action by the United States.

"Dad, what's our navy doing?" Lieutenant Adam said his son had asked him that morning. "The Dutch are doing all right. Where's our fleet?"

Although it was months before a complete answer to that question could be arrived at, a partial answer was evident sixteen hours later as the big car that carried us to Honolulu from the Pan American landing base in Pearl City was passing Pearl Harbor, which lies seven miles west of the city.

Across the oil-covered water, as the car rolled past the Fish Pond where several cruisers and destroyers were moored behind the antitorpedo nets, could be seen the slanting, fire-blackened foretop of the Arizona, the rusting bottom of the capsized Oklahoma, lying on her side in the mud, and on the near side of Ford Island the upside-down Utah. That sight was expected. To what ships, though, belonged the three rusting fighting tops astern of the Oklahoma?

Bob Casey, the ubiquitous correspondent of the *Chicago Daily News*, whose caustic humor was to enliven many a dreary blackout night in Honolulu and equally boresome days at sea, gave the best answer to that question several months later as we witnessed the final stages of the raising of the West Virginia.

"I have an impulse that is difficult to resist," said Bob, "to send a cable to Frank [Secretary of the Navy Knox, his employer and personal friend] announcing that the last one of the battleships he didn't say had been sunk has at last been raised."

[39

That momentary glimpse of the five sunken battleships—Arizona, Oklahoma, West Virginia, California, and Nevada—and the training ship Utah was the only evidence of damage as the big car slid on toward town, down Dillingham Boulevard, past the pineapple canning factory, across the River Street bridge at Hotel and on to the heart of the city.

Many of Honolulu's store windows carried the crisscross pattern of anticoncussion paper strips that has become familiar to most Americans on our seacoasts, but outwardly the city showed few signs that it was in the middle of a war zone. All the months I spent around Honolulu it never did. Even today it is a city of paradoxes.

It was many days before I got around to seeing the few burned buildings in Honolulu, and the tropic vegetation had such a head start by that time there was little evidence that they had been destroyed by any other instrument than that of normal decay. What few buildings were set afire in town, and what few people were killed and injured, were victims of our own shells, not Japanese bombs. There was some strafing of houses near airfields and of cars on the roads near Pearl Harbor, Wheeler Field and the Kaneohe Naval Air Station; but the Japanese, with those exceptions, limited their work of destruction to military objectives.

The explanation of United States shells being fired into the town is simple enough, and understandable. An antiaircraft shell has a time fuse. It will explode the shell so many seconds after it has left the gun—two seconds, four seconds, six seconds, and so on. If the fuse is not set or if it fails to work, as sometimes happens, the shell will not explode until it hits something. If it doesn't hit the plane at which it is aimed, it falls to earth and explodes on impact.

In the excitement of that morning, many fuses were not set. Those were the shells that fell in many parts of the city, did what damage was done and killed the civilians who died that day. It was not by design, but most of the shells fell in Japanese sections of the city. One fell in a street in front of Governor Joseph B. Poindexter's official residence, and spattered an automobile showroom with fragments.

The unreality of life in Honolulu in those days was illustrated by the strings of colored lights hung between the lampposts on Bishop Street, in front of the Alexander Young Hotel (they never had been lighted) and the wilted Christmas tree in the lobby, sagging forlornly in the sticky, midmorning heat of the day after Christmas. The tree remained there until Twelfth Night.

There already was quite a corps of correspondents in town: Bob Casey, H. R. Knickerbocker, Ed Angley and Harry Lang, the latter three all of the *Chicago Sun* (that city certainly was well represented); Wendell Webb, Tom Yarbrough and Jack Rice of the Associated Press; Frank Smothers, also of the *Chicago Daily News;* Frank McCarthy of the United Press, and of course the regular Honolulu Press Association men, Frank Tremaine and Bill Tyree of the UP, Gene Burns of the AP and Dick Haller of INS, who also doubled in brass as press agent for half the town.

They all had been through the mill, fingerprinted and photographed for this and that pass and passport, and all were well past the preliminary skirmishing with the censors. They could sit back and enjoy the enthusiasm with which we three newcomers attacked the problems.

Any feeling that Honolulu was not in the war zone passed with the daylight.

The busses made their last run soon after sunset. Late cars scurried along the streets with dimmed-out lights. Straggling pedestrians hurried their steps toward home. From then until sunrise Honolulu seemed a city of the dead, no lights showing, only an occasional police car or official truck or station wagon with dim blue bulbs moving through the empty streets.

Those who had business abroad could expect to be stopped at almost any corner by a command to halt, generally accompanied by the ominous clicking of a rifle bolt as a cartridge was driven home.

There were many itchy trigger fingers among the green territorial guardsmen and the almost-as-green regular army troops. The nights were punctuated with the crack of rifles and hysterical commands of "Halt, who goes there?" In the stillness of the streets sounds were magnified many times.

During the moon phases travel at night, afoot or in a car, was an eerie enough experience but not greatly different, except for the lack of headlights, from a drive through any countryside in a car whose lights were not working well. In the dark of the moon, however, the darkness was Stygian. No place ever was as black as Honolulu on a moonless night.

Admiral William H. Standley, who had been in Moscow before coming to Honolulu as a member of the Roberts Commission to investigate the Pearl Harbor attack, said the only place comparable to Honolulu in any war zone he had visited was the Russian capital. And in Russia there was no curfew.

Exceptions to the blackout were the Honolulu docks, the Pearl Harbor area and emergency defense projects, the principal military objectives. They all were lighted up every night like Christmas trees, a circumstance that caused considerable grumbling among Honolulu residents sweltering through the hot nights in their curtained and almost airtight homes. The explanation given the public as to why there had to be a blackout in the city and lights could burn around military objectives was that there were master switches to control the lights on the docks and at Pearl Harbor that could be pulled if there was an alarm, while it would take a corps of electricians to throw the switches necessary to black out the rest of the town. Privately, military authorities admitted the stringent blackout was enforced more as an instrument for control of the Japanese on the island than as a guard against enemy plane attack. Since 10:30 A.M., December 7, 1941, only one enemy plane has been reported over Honolulu, and even that one is questionable.

Violators of the blackout were dealt with summarily and severely. I was touring in a police car one brightly moonlit night when a trace of light was detected in the transom of the doorway of an apartment-house dweller in the Waikiki section. Since the doorway was six feet back under a porch and the light was hardly strong enough to carry across the street, I couldn't see that it was any heinous offense. But he received a summons nevertheless and the next day, in Provost Court, had the choice of paying a fine or giving a pint of his blood to the Red Cross, a method for recruiting blood donors that found no favor either with the citizens or with the Red Cross.

The first two months after the start of the war saw probably the most frenzied defense activity by the army and navy in the history of warfare. There were few scars of war about the city. The attack of the builders, however, was something different. Roads were being built all over the island. Hundreds of buildings were under construction. New trenches and gun pits were being dug every day. Every convoy brought hundreds of defense workers, many of whom had no more knowledge of the trades they claimed than had the men who hired them.

Out through the red hills and along the beaches of Oahu there appeared to be a soldier behind every bush and every sand dune. In less than two months there was a ring of barbed wire around the whole island. The face of the countryside changed by the hour. Pineapples would be flourishing one day. The next, a dozen bulldozers would be pushing the pineapple plants to one side and leveling out a new emergency airfield.

In practically every ravine leading down to the beaches men were camping in conditions more primitive than most of those I saw later on Guadalcanal and other advanced bases in the Solomons and New Hebrides. Within a twenty-minute drive

[43

of Honolulu, playground of the Pacific, were foxholes as muddy and as cheerless, if not as dangerous, as those on Bataan. Many of the soldiers had not been out of them for a trip to town since December 7.

The army and navy commanders, in those first few weeks, expected the Japanese to be back any day. They knew there weren't enough ships or planes to stop them if they came in force and that the destiny of the islands would be settled on the beaches.

Honolulu wasn't geared for the life it had to lead. Long lines formed outside the restaurants at lunchtime and started forming for dinner at 4 o'clock in the afternoon. Few restaurants were blacked out those first few weeks, and the serving of dinner had to be completed before sundown. Many went to bed hungry because they could not get from their work to a restaurant and then home before curfew. When they did get home, there was nothing to do but sit in the darkness, or go to bed. Blackout materials were expensive and almost unobtainable after the first few days.

Every day saw a few more store counters cleared of goods, with no replacements coming in. Prices began to mount. Eggs were ninety cents a dozen. Butter was seventy-five cents a pound. A steak was as precious as if it had been set with diamonds. One restaurant received three hundred sirloins one night. The news was all over town before the first one cooked had stopped sizzling. There was a near riot at the place. Steaks were reserved for regular customers. Knowing a head waiter was as important in Honolulu as it is in a New York night club.

Long-time Honolulans at first were excited by the war, then irritated by its restraints. Finally they became reconciled to the fact that their island paradise probably never would be the same again.

The bombs that dropped on December 7 did more than sink battleships and start a war. They changed a way of life that was one of the most pleasant in the world. No longer will a few missionary families and their companies rule the islands. The "Big Five"—the benevolent economic monarchs of the Islands—are only the "Little Quintet" now. The army and the navy are the collective Mr. Big. They bid fair to remain the dominant influence on Oahu for many years to come.

CHAPTER 2

Base Building

DURING THE first few weeks after the start of the war the one sure way to throw a Honolulan into apoplexy was to mention the army engineers.

Instead of scaring their children into obedience with threats of hobgoblins, Honolulu mothers told them that if they weren't good little boys and girls the army engineers would get them. They were the all-time, all-American bogy men.

Some of the criticism was justified. A lot of it was not. No organization ever had a bigger task suddenly handed it than was dumped into the army engineers' laps with the dropping of the first bomb on Pearl Harbor.

That afternoon Colonel Ted Wyman moved in and took over Punahou School, one of the most famous private day schools in the world. His men ripped up seats to make room for desks, threw books out of the windows, moved a grand piano out into the yard where the rain ruined it and, sacrilege of sacrileges, cut down all the night-blooming cereus that crowned the stone walls around the main buildings.

"Perhaps cutting down that cereus was a mistake," Colonel Wyman said one night, shortly before he sailed for the coast to take up a new assignment. "But look at the situation the morning of December 7. We all thought the Japanese would be coming in for a landing. The Punahou School was the only building in town with a wall around it. It stands at the mouth of the Manoa Valley, a good defensive position. The cereus would be in the way of machine-gun fire from the buildings against any attackers. I wasn't thinking about the tourists or anything else that day except finding the best defensive position I could for my headquarters."

In Honolulu the engineers seized everything they could get their hands on. They took over the interisland steamers, cutting off Honolulu from its beef supply on Molokai and Hawaii. They scoured the town for binoculars, draftsmen's supplies, trucks, rollers, sand and gravel, in fact everything that was needed to build airfields, barracks, docks, and warehouses.

The people of Honolulu saw materials disappear, but didn't see and couldn't be told where they went.

The day Japan attacked Pearl Harbor most of our now efficient air bases were only in process of construction. Some of them were only gleams in the general's and admiral's eyes. Civilian workmen were ordered to get off the islands as fast as they could. The army engineers were told to get in and take over the jobs where the civilian contractors had dropped them.

Materials taken in Honolulu were loaded on any kind of an old scow that would float and started south for Canton, Christmas, Baker, Howland, Fanning, the Fijis, New Caledonia, and other islands whose names never had been printed in American papers.

It was a job done in the best American frontier tradition. As their ancestors had built the railroads, with a pick or shovel in one hand and a gun in the other, so the army engineers carved out air bases over a four-thousand-mile string of uninhabited or only lightly settled islands, from 25 degrees North latitude to 40 degrees South.

What they did on Oahu alone would have been a full year's job in peacetime. When war came there were only three army airfields on the island. In less than six months there were twice that many, any one of them bigger and better than the peace-time fields. Miles of military roads had been cut to new gun positions.

One of the strangest jobs was the installation, as coastal defense batteries, of the 8-inch-gun turrets taken off the Lexington and the Saratoga. Exact copies in steel and concrete of the barbettes aboard ship were made out in the hills, complete with underground magazines and ammunition hoists, on top of which the big blue-painted turrets were installed. The first time I saw one of them I thought I had taken one too many drinks of oke (the highly palatable native distillation).

Around Honolulu, the work and the living were in a fairly normal pattern compared to the conditions encountered on the coral islands to the south, where the engineers rowed ashore in rubber boats and started to work. On most of the Pacific islands even water had to be hauled by ship. The engineers built airfields before they even had a place to live.

It was work and living of the most arduous sort. Here was none of the glamour of war. From the sudden tropic dawn to the quick blackness that falls like a blanket as the sun goes down, the men and officers of the army engineers, and later the navy construction battalions, the "Seabees," labored in tropic heat and torrential rain at all manner of prodigious tasks. Theirs were no 8-hour days. For months they worked twelve hours on and twelve hours off. After rassling a bulldozer around for twelve hours a man was so tired he didn't mind the mosquitoes or the heat or the bad food or the hard cot in a steaming tent.

During the first ten months of the war I twice flew the Honolulu-Noumea air-ferry route. On the second trip the big B-24 landed on hard-surfaced runways at every stop. It spent the night in a camouflaged revetment, where expert mechanics refueled it and checked its motors. I slept each night in army-operated "hotels," where there were clean sheets on the beds, a shower under which to wash off the dirt of the day, a club where a man could get a drink and a mess hall where he could eat a satisfactory, if not sumptuous, meal. I saw a movie every night.

It is still a grueling life for the men who man these unpublicized outposts in the Pacific. There is a rule of thumb that no man shall be kept on one of them longer than a year and no officer longer than a year and a half. For the first two years of the war, however, it was a rule "more honored in the breach than the observance."

A psychiatrist is a necessary adjunct of every island command. "I don't worry about the men as long as they are just griping about the duty," one doctor explained to me. "But when I find them sitting staring at the ocean, I know it's time to get them out of here."

All manner of excuses are given by some in an effort to escape the boredom of life on these tropic paradises.

The favorite story of Lieutenant Commander "Red" Welch, who was executive officer for many months on Palmyra, was that of the seaman who discovered after several months there that he had a congenital deformity of the spine, and, at the same time, that he was a Christian Scientist.

"He came to me one day with the story that he had such a backache he couldn't work and that the only way it could be cured was for him to return to San Francisco to consult a Christian Science practitioner," Red related. "His record didn't show that he ever had claimed any allegiance to that church before.

"I consulted the doctor and found that he did have a deformed vertebra. He had had it all his life, though, and the doctor said he saw no reason why it should suddenly begin to bother him.

" 'I'm sure I could grow a new bone in there in a month back in San Francisco, Mr. Welch,' he told me.

"I told him I could grow one faster than that, but I'd deliberate and let him know my decision.

"The next day he was back again. This time he had a new suggestion. He said he didn't want to cause the navy any inconvenience, so if he couldn't go to San Francisco he thought he could get fixed up in Honolulu instead. He knew a girl there who was a Christian Scientist, and perhaps two weeks would be enough to cure him under her treatment.

"I felt sorry for the lad, but there just wasn't any chance of any of us getting off the island under the conditions. We didn't have enough men as it was."

"What did you do with him?" I asked.

"Well," said Red, grinning, "we fixed him up with a stool so his back wouldn't bother him and set him to work peeling spuds and washing dishes in the galley. His back got well very quickly."

The soldiers and sailors who built the bases don't have any medals to wear on their blouses on dress parade. Most of them haven't seen a Japanese ship, plane or souvenir, and probably will not. But they, as well as the fighting men, deserve well from their country.

CHAPTER 3

On Patrol Aboard
the Lexington

IT WAS January 5, 1942. In two days it would be just a month since the Japanese planes had come snarling in from the north to knock out Hawaii's air strength and the Pacific fleet's battle line. The Lexington was headed out for another of the defensive patrols she had been sailing since that fateful day. She had been in port just long enough to refuel and reprovision.

She belied her bulk as the biggest fighting craft afloat as she slipped her moorings at the number one carrier berth on the west side of Ford Island in Pearl Harbor and steamed down the channel toward the sea.

The Lexington task force was the first to carry newspaper-

[49

men to sea. Aboard the carrier with me were Norman Alley, cameraman of the *News of the Day*, and Bob Bryant, of International News Photos. Aboard one of our escorting cruisers were Tom Yarbrough of the Associated Press and Frank Tremaine of the United Press. Aboard the other cruiser were Jonathan Rice of Acme and Ralph Jordan, of International News Service.

I had drawn the long straw among the five specials who had applied for the one place left over after the press associations and newsphoto and newsreel people had been taken care of, a program that was fair enough, since the press associations served many papers, but that sometimes made it difficult for a person representing only one newspaper to get around. I was congratulating myself on my luck. Later I wished I had lost, as had Wheeler and Casey, and had waited to ride the next one out.

Norman and Bob and I had boarded the Lexington the previous afternoon, had been assigned to our rooms by Lieutenant Commander "Pop" Healy, the First Lieutenant (Pop was killed in the Coral Sea), to our places at table by Lieutenant "Red" Gill, the air plot officer who was acting that month as mess treasurer, and welcomed to the ship by Captain Ted Sherman, the skipper, and Captain "Gotch" Dillon, the executive officer.

We began to like the navy right away. We hadn't had any beef for two weeks ashore. The Lexington served mignons for dinner. Honolulu had movies only in the afternoon—if you could get in. After dinner that night we saw Gary Cooper in "Sergeant York" from comfortably upholstered armchairs on the hangar deck. The stars shone down on us through the open elevator hatch.

Now it was a bright morning and we were headed out to sea.

There was little feeling of movement on so vast a ship in the quiet oil-covered waters of the harbor as she slid down past Hickam Field and the Ewa Plantation, where the navy was starting a new scrap pile of twisted metal salvaged from the sunken battleships and destroyers. The old scrap pile had been purchased several months before by Japan. Some of it probably had been returned December 7 and served its part in creating the new heap of fire-blackened plates and fighting tops.

As we cleared the harbor for the run through "Torpedo Junction" the thirty-three-thousand tons of the old lady began to quiver from the accelerating thrash of her propellers, driven by the most powerful engines of any combatant ship afloat. They generated 180,000 horsepower.

The escort ships had preceded her outside and were maneuvering on either flank of the carrier's proposed track, sweeping for the hostile submarines that then infested Honolulu waters. Motor torpedo boats were churning along at high speed, setting up a water turbulence that would interfere with the sound-gear of any listening Japanese boat.

The Lexington's great flight deck, 880 feet from its down-curving fantail to its blunt only slightly narrowed bow and 105½ feet from scupper to scupper, was bare of planes. They had flown in to Ewa Field, the marine base, when the Lexington had entered port, so as to be available if they were needed to oppose another Japanese attack. They circled now high above their mother ship like silver birds against the blue sky. We could hear faintly the drone of their propellers biting into the cold, high atmosphere at which they flew.

We were headed southeast to make a defensive sweep between Pearl Harbor and the Marshalls. But first there was to be the usual target practice to accustom the crew again to the roar of the 8-inch guns with which the Lexington then was equipped, the wicked bark of the 5.38's, and the chatter of the automatic weapons. Off in the blue sky, out of sight of the ship, some of the Lexington's planes were flying the usual long-range patrols and the rest were engaged in their own drills, practicing dog-fighting and firing at sleeves towed by the scout bombers.

Just before luncheon the planes came winging home. The landing of a carrier group is a thrilling sight that does not become

[51

stale with repetition. The planes returned in formation, circling the ship until all were ready to land. Then, group by group, they peeled off to form, at intervals and low altitude, a great landing circle.

As soon as her planes were in the circle and the arresting gear that stops them when they hit the deck had been set in place, the carrier picked up speed, turned into the wind, and the signal officer began flagging them in.

The recovery is made into the wind, as is the launching, to take as much advantage of natural resources as possible. The stronger the wind, the less speed the carrier has to make to get the knots of breeze across the flight deck necessary for a safe landing by the planes.

The signal officer stood on a narrow platform on the port side near the stern, silhouetted against a large square of canvas that also served to break the wind for him. In either hand he carried a large paddle similar to a table-tennis bat but larger. It was covered with bright cloth.

As each plane swung in astern on the same course as the ship and only a few feet above deck level, the pilot glued his eyes on the signal officer and followed his directions. In effect the signal officer flew them in. If the left wing was down he dropped his left arm. If the right wing was low he dropped his right arm. If he thought the plane was coming in too slowly he motioned with both paddles for the pilot to lift her.

The pilot had to have complete confidence in the signal officer and follow his directions without question. At that altitude he could not judge to the nicety required, the exact trim of his plane, or its height above the water.

If the plane was coming in on an even keel, at the proper speed, and if it had its hook down to catch the arresting gear and its wheels down properly to take the shock of the landing, the lending officer gave the pilot the "cut" signal, a sharp over-and-down stroke of his right arm.

If, however, the plane was not in good trim, was coming in

with one wing high or the tail down, or too fast, the signal officer would wave off the plane by rapidly scissoring his two paddles above his head. Then the pilot would gun his engine and rejoin the landing circle for another try.

Few wave-offs were needed for the Lexington's fliers. Although there was a sprinkling of youngsters among her four squadrons of fighters, scouts, bombers, and torpedo planes, most of her pilots were veterans of carrier operation. A cake was presented to Lieutenant Commander Hamilton of Torpedo 2 during our cruise for making his 500th landing (or maybe it was his 5,000th) on the Lexington.

Her most interesting squadron was Fighting 2, led by Lieutenant Commander Paul Ramsey. The squadron had several commissioned pilots, including Lieutenant Buzz Borries, of Annapolis football fame, but when it was first organized, the second fighter squadron to be formed, it had consisted of only two commissioned officers, the squadron commander and the executive. All the rest were NAP's, enlisted pilots. Its ensigne still was the enlisted pilot's crow, the designation of rank worn on the sleeve similar to the chevrons of a non-commissioned officer of the army.

An aircraft carrier is the most intricate machine of war built. In addition to the arms and armament carried by other ships she also houses airplanes, and the repair shops to keep them operating. She must carry not only fuel for her boilers but also gasoline and lubricating oil and spare parts for her birds. All this means a bigger complement of officers and men than any other war vessel requires. The Lexington had a wartime crew of more than twenty-five hundred men.

The whole life of the carrier is geared to that of its planes and their crews and pilots. Meals are served to suit the convenience of the fliers. They have their own medical officers, flight surgeons who themselves are fliers and have an intimate appreciation of the mental and emotional strains that beset the man in a plane.

[53

An aircraft carrier is no place for a person seeking a rest cure. All ships are noisy. A carrier is bedlam.

Long before the routine pre-dawn general quarters was sounded on the Lexington the pilots, radiomen and mechanics were routed out of bed and were served an early breakfast.

Already wearing their yellow rubber life jackets, the Mae Wests that are worn deflated, and carrying their helmets, goggles and flight boards, the pilots stumbled through the dimly lighted passages to the wardroom.

After they had eaten they were briefed on the day's operations. Because of the small ready room on the Lexington, which was adequate only for peacetime operations, the briefing was done in the wardroom. On a big blackboard on the bulkhead was the vital information needed on wind and weather and the day's operational plan. Any known friendly ships in the day's search area were plotted. When not in a combat area where enemy planes or ships were likely to be encountered there generally was a training program, which was outlined on the board. Occasionally the squadron commander would address his pilots, amplifying the written orders.

The briefing completed, the pilots would settle back for a last cigarette and cup of coffee before the orders came over the loud-speaker system for them to get topside.

It was still dark outside as the pilots filed through the narrow passageways and climbed the ladders to the flight deck. The planes were lined up on the after part of the deck, mechanics and armorers swarming over them for a last-minute check.

On the bridge the air officer, Commander Herbert Duckworth, was at his station on the port wing, surveying the dark deck below. Finally, the report coming that everything was in readiness, the bull horn bellowed the order, "Pilots, man your planes."

The groups of yellow-jacketed men, only dimly seen clustered around the amidships island, threaded their way through the closely packed planes and climbed into their cockpits. Their

54]

parachutes already were in the seats, and they had only to slip into them and adjust the safety belt for the takeoff.

"Start your motors," was the next order, the bull horn amplifying the quiet voice of Commander Duckworth to a roar that was audible on escorting ships a mile and a half away.

The Lexington meanwhile turned into the wind and began picking up speed. With a strong wind blowing she would not need to turn as many knots as on a clear day. Say a wind velocity of thirty knots is necessary across the deck. If there is a ten-knot breeze blowing, then the ship need make only twenty knots.

The motors of the planes coughed a few times as the starter turned them over, then settled to a throaty roar. Blue flames spurted from the exhausts.

As the eastern sky brightened and the horizon became a distinct line the final order was given, "Prepare to launch aircraft." The first one taxied up to the starting line amidships, where the starting officer stood, flag in hand.

There an armorer made a final check of the bomb and the release apparatus, and gave a thumbs-up signal to the pilot.

The starting officer waved his flag in small circles, to order the pilot to rev up his motor. Taking a quick look forward to see that the ship was not dipping into a wave and that the way was clear, he swung his flag in a long sweeping arc in front of his body from left to right, ending with it pointing forward.

The pilot released his brakes, shoved his throttle ahead to full and started to roll. The plane seemed to move painfully slowly at first.

"He'll never make it," I thought, as the distance rapidly decreased between his plane and the bow, where he must be airborne or plunge into the water.

But the carrier planes are built for quick acceleration. The tail came up before it had moved more than a few yards and before the flight deck was exhausted it began to rise. Slowly at first, then rapidly.

As fast as the planes could be brought to the starting line they

[55

were sent charging down the deck and into the air. The dawn patrol was on the wing.

Almost before the last plane had cleared the ship, the carrier began her turn back to her planned course, a course to which she must hold, come hell or high water, until the air group she had just launched had returned to her deck. Only dead reckoning can be used by the pilots of the carrier planes. The ship must be where they expect her when they come winging back from their patrols of one hundred, two hundred, or three hundred miles. In bad weather an error of seconds at 200 knots would put them miles off their course. It was always a surprise to me that more of them were not lost.

As soon as the last plane was away and the ship had turned back on her course, the order was given to "Secure from flight quarters" and the mechanics, officers, and fliers who were not going up that day filed below for breakfast.

Every day of our ten-day cruise the same procedure was repeated. Planes were recovered for refueling while others were launched to take up the patrol. For miles ahead, on either flank and astern of the force, the planes kept an unbroken watch during all the daylight hours for hostile aircraft, surface ships, or submarines.

The fliers of the Lexington had been doing such patrols since December 7. For a few days after the attack every plane was in the air from dawn to dusk every day. Some of the pilots logged as high as 250 and 300 hours that month. They all were beginning to show the strain.

"This is man-killing," said Captain Sherman one day as we sat talking in his outer cabin, his black cocker spaniel frisking around our chairs. "I hope to get some replacements for my pilots soon and let the boys have a rest. Someday, it may be soon, they will have to fight and I don't want them going into action worn out. They'll be like a boxer who has overtrained. They'll have left their fight in the gym."

Part of the strain was pure boredom. On patrol above the sea there was nothing to see but the sea and the clouds. Before we returned to Pearl, Commander Duckworth allowed Norm and Bob and me to take a ride one day with three dive-bomber pilots.

Norm wanted to take some movies of carrier operations, and especially some simulating actual combat. Ensign E. D. Willems and Lieutenant (jg) Armand, who later was to win the Navy Cross for his part in the Coral Sea battle, were assigned to take us up.

The flight deck looked even shorter from the rear seat of the SBD than it had from the bridge above, but we were up safely just when it seemed we were going to go plop off the bow into the sea. Lieutenant Armand had preceded us, and as soon as we had cleared the ship the two planes joined up and climbed above the clouds, which were about 5,000 feet that day. Then we began the maneuvers that had been agreed on previously while we were sitting in the wardroom. This had been accompanied by much hand waving to simulate a plane in flight.

Willems first climbed above the other plane and then dived on it as though attacking. The first dive gave me a good example of centrifugal force. I was leaning over attempting to adjust the seat, when Willems peeled off and dived on the other plane. I attempted to raise up just as he swept past the tail of the other ship and then zoomed to gain altitude for another pass. I couldn't raise my head. It was as though a giant hand were placed firmly in the middle of my back holding my head between my legs.

After a few more maneuvers, we sailed over to a hole in the overcast for a simulated dive-bombing attack. Norman and Armand had gone down below to record it. We were at about 6,000 feet altitude, I noticed on the instrument panel in front of me.

"Hold your hat, here we go," Willems advised me through the interphone system, and then he dropped his wing and peeled off.

Straight down we plummeted. The wind screamed past the greenhouse like a banshee. We broke through the hole and out underneath. The sea was rushing up at us at 200 knots. Just as it seemed we must crash into the blue water, now so close the small froth on the wave tips was plainly visible, Willems dropped his flaps, at the same time pressing the button on his machine guns. The plane shook from the recoil, and acrid burnt-powder smoke swirled around the cockpit. Below us on the blue surface of the water the .50-caliber bullets stitched a pattern of small white geysers. Then Willems hauled back on the stick and we straightened out in a long glide.

"Some fun, eh?" the big, blond youngster said through his interphone as he turned in his seat to grin back at me through the network of radio sets and gear on the platform separating pilot and rear gunner.

Finally Norm had shot all his film and as the two planes maneuvered wing tip to wing tip, Lieutenant Armand kissed his hand to us, indicating the play was over, and we shoved off on the patrol to which we both had been assigned.

For two hours more we flew back and forth, back and forth, across the ever-changing, ever-the-same face of the sea. Then, our patrol ended, we turned back toward the carrier.

From 2,000 feet up and ten miles away the flight deck that had looked so big when standing on it appeared to be only the size of a postage stamp.

Willems fell into formation with the other planes of the returning patrol and we circled the ship in the landing circle.

It had seemed the planes I had watched from the deck had landed with a jolt that must have almost snapped the neckbones of the fliers, but the shock, as the arresting gear caught our hook, was surprisingly gentle.

As soon as the plane was seen to be securely held, the landing crew rushed out to release the hook, the barricade of steel wire that would have stopped us had anything happened to the arresting gear, was dropped, and we taxied up the deck to clear the after end for the planes behind us.

"Gets damn tiresome sitting on a 'chute pack for three hours, doesn't it?" said Willems, grinning as he saw me gingerly rubbing my posterior as we climbed down the ladders and threaded the

58]

passageways toward the wardroom. "You get callused after a while," he continued, philosophically.

While Norm and Bob and I were thanking our pilots for our ride, we were told that it had been a pleasure for them as well as for us. It had broken the monotony of a routine patrol.

Only one incident occurred during our patrol to ease the boredom for the pilots.

One morning two of the fighter pilots, patrolling together as the fighters always did, sighted an enemy submarine on the surface, limping along on a course for the Marshalls. Since the enemy commander was on the surface in broad daylight it appeared probable he already had been attacked and hurt. They dove at him but he must have seen them, for he crash-dived. They came back to the carrier and reported.

Lieutenant (jg) Rinehart and C. E. Brewer, an NAP, his wingman, went out for a check. To their surprise, there was the Japanese submarine back on the surface. Climbing into the sun, they waited for the two torpedo planes that also had been sent out. The TBD's were armed with depth charges. Soon they came over the horizon.

As the TBD's started their run out of the sun at the enemy submarine, the Japanese opened fire briefly with a deck gun, then slammed the lid and tried to dive again. The sub was half awash as the American torpedo planes crossed it and dropped their ash cans, and the fighters dived out of the sun, their machine guns blazing.

"We could see our tracers bouncing off his deck as he went down," Rinehart said that night, "so I know the bullets were going into him. And don't let anyone tell you those .50 calibers won't tear a hole in anything they hit.

"I should judge he was about ten feet under the surface when the depth charges let go. The first one lifted his bow over at least ten or fifteen degrees and the next one shoved it back. I'd have hated to be in that pigboat."

Rear Admiral Wilson Brown, who was in charge of the force,

sent two destroyers to the position where the attack had been made. They found the water covered with oil and some debris floating around, but were unable to get a sound contact.

As an indication of the extreme care the navy exercises in its claims, Captain Sherman, after talking with the fliers and getting a report from the destroyers, reported only that the submarine apparently had been badly damaged. Lack of any great water turbulence after the explosion of the depth charges inclined him to believe the sub might have gotten away.

Whether it did or not, the attack did much to lift the spirits of the fliers, and of the whole ship. They had been assiduously looking for the enemy for over a month, and this was their first contact with him. It was with new eagerness now that each patrol set out on its appointed rounds.

Rinehart's return to report the attack caused almost as much of a flurry as his original contact report. He had written out his report and wrapped it up in the small bag of beans that is used to drop messages on a ship's deck. He came barreling in at full speed to drop it, Brewer on his port wing. As he swooped across the flight deck, at bridge level, he had to turn his plane on its side to avoid nicking the stack with a wing tip. Just hanging on his prop, he slid past the bridge, where everyone was taking cover, thinking he was going to crash, and neatly deposited his beanbag at the feet of Admiral Brown.

Under other circumstances he might have been reprimanded, but he escaped with only an unofficial reprimand from Paul Ramsey. Fighting 2's skipper was having a cup of coffee when Rinehart came down to the wardroom.

"As I was saying," said Paul, raising his voice so Rinehart would hear him, "I shall make out the report this way; 'Paragraph one, commendation; Paragraph two, denunciation; Paragraph three, no further remarks.'"

Rinehart joined in the laughter. He was feeling pretty good. Captain Sherman had just commended him for using his head and waiting for the arrival of the TBD's before making his attack.

"I can beat you at a game of acey-ducey, Skipper," he told Ramsey. And he did.

Four months later at Noumea I was talking to Ensign N. A. Sterrie, of St. James, Minnesota, who had piloted one of the TBD's that attacked the submarine; an NAP named Talkington had piloted the other.

I was asking about various officers and men I had met on the January cruise, to find how they had fared in the Battle of the Coral Sea.

"How about Rinehart?" I asked.

"He didn't come back from the strike," Sterrie said.

The submarine attack was the only thing to disturb the monotony of the days and we all were glad, a few days later, when Diamond Head showed up out of the early morning mists as we headed for the harbor entrance.

Lieutenant Commander Terry and I were having a last cup of coffee before he had to go to the bridge when we felt an explosion and then, in quick succession, three more.

"Depth charges," said Terry as we left our coffee and hotfooted it for a forward gun sponson, from where we climbed to the deck.

Five or six miles away a seaplane was circling, dropping smokepots, and one of our escorting destroyers was just turning to make another run over the spot where, even at that distance, we could see a spreading film of oil, and occasionally a big bubble of water.

"There's your water turbulence, the lack of which the captain was worrying about on that one our gang hit," Mr. Terry said. "There doesn't seem to be any question about that one."

I don't know. I tried vainly for two days ashore to get more information about the attack.

"Submarine? What submarine?" I was asked, when I inquired.

Pearl Harbor was a funny place in those days.

[61

We returned to find the other correspondents out with another task force. Then on February 1 word came that Halsey had attacked the Marshalls. For two days I damned the "lucky straw" that had sent me out with the first group. I knew Wheeler, who had been considerably disappointed at not making the initial trip, and Casey, would be laughing heartily.

Anyway it had been a swell cruise and I had met a lot of grand people. Some of their affection for the old Lex they had communicated to me. I was as sad as they must have been when I heard she was resting on the bottom of the Coral Sea.

CHAPTER 4

The Japanese Problem

IN HONOLULU, the first few months after Pearl Harbor, the Japanese Problem (spelled with a capital P) almost dwarfed the war against Japan. Everyone talked about it. You met it walking down the street, clerking in the stores where most of the Hawaiian and haole (white) clerks had quit to take defense jobs from which the Japanese were barred. It even was parading in army uniforms, helmeted, armed, sullen.

Whenever two persons got together for more than a casual greeting the Japanese Problem was sure to be raised. Influential pineapple and sugar-cane people who needed the Japanese labor and were afraid all the alien Japanese might be interned gave elaborate dinners for newspaper correspondents from the States so they "wouldn't get the wrong idea" about it.

To show its popularity as a conversation piece and an ever present obsession, there even were jokes made about it. The favorite was about the army sergeant who, debarking from a transport and seeing two of the Japanese members of the Hawaiian Territorial Guard patrolling the pier, grabbed his rifle in alarm and shouted to his men, "My God, we're too late."

The census of 1940 put the total population of the Hawaiian Islands at 426,654 persons, of whom 156,849 were Japanese. Some 35,000 of these were aliens who had been brought to the islands as laborers on the sugar and pineapple plantations and were barred from citizenship. The remainder were the sons and daughters and grandsons and granddaughters of the original immigrants, neisi who had been educated in the public schools and at the University of Hawaii. Many of them had attended schools on the mainland. By right of birth all of them were citizens of the United States. If their parents had registered their birth at the Japanese consulate they also were citizens of Japan, holding the so-called dual citizenship—if such a status is possible—that was an issue in the islands every election.

Prior to the war there were no restrictions on the Japanese, except the social and economic barriers that were no less real because they were unwritten. Japanese, both Hawaiian-born and aliens, were employed at Pearl Harbor and at the various army fields and camps. The army G-2, navy intelligence and the Federal Bureau of Investigation each kept a separate and wary eye on them, especially during the last few critical months before the Japanese planes came in, but there apparently was little cooperation among the three. A Japanese alien suspected of espionage and whom the FBI had been seeking for months was discovered at Wheeler Field, army fighter base, on December 8. He had been working there as a laborer for some time.

The Japanese, with their own language schools, their own textbooks filled with pro-Japanese propaganda, their Buddhist temples, lived largely in one section of town. Most of the younger Japanese, American citizens, spoke poor English—despite their education in the public schools—and excellent Japanese. Few of them had intermarried with the Hawaiians, as had the Chinese and Filipinos. What few Japanese-Caucasian marriages had occurred were largely between Japanese girls and white soldiers

[63

of the regular army on duty in the islands. Weeks after Pearl Harbor, when a newspaper correspondent with a pocketful of credentials found difficulty getting into a navy yard or an army post, he could, when finally admitted, see the Japanese wives of army sergeants squatting around the doorsteps of the non-commissioned officers' homes adjoining Wheeler Field, presumably discussing the war their ancestors were waging against their husbands' country and their husbands.

How many of the Japanese were loyal no one can say. Some persons who should have been familiar with conditions before the war put the non-loyal Japanese, those who would have supported an enemy invasion of the islands, as high as 35 per cent of the total. W. A. Gabrielson, chief of police of Honolulu, placed the percentage much lower than that. He said Japanese on his force did more than the army, navy or FBI in rounding up suspects on December 7 and the following days, ferreting out many whom the other agencies could not find.

One of the most used arguments to prove the loyalty of the overwhelming percentage of Japanese on the islands was that there was practically no sabotage before, during, or after the Japanese attack. What few incidents there were obviously were on the initiative of the saboteurs and were amateurish.

That does not prove anything. Any organized sabotage would have been done under orders. It would have been carried out only when an invasion was planned and under way, when it would have the maximum effect. It was not Japanese strategy to land on Oahu on December 7. Ergo, no organized sabotage.

There is no question that there was a well organized espionage system, one that must have used hundreds, if not thousands, of agents. As late as two months after the attack on Pearl Harbor, information still was being sent out of the islands to the Japanese by short-wave radio, by direct physical contact with the Japanese submarines, and by visual signal to submarines off shore. Lights blinked in the hills around Honolulu every night during the blackout through December and January. It is quite probable that even today information as to United States ship and troop movements is being sent out of Honolulu by Japanese spies hidden among the preponderantly Japanese population.

The United States leaned over backward in its handling of the Japanese. During the prohibition days, from December 7, 1941, to March 5, 1942, white bootleggers were given much more severe sentences in Provost Court than were Japanese convicted of listening to short-wave radio, possession of weapons, and like offenses. One Japanese saboteur who was discovered to be suffering from both tuberculosis and syphilis was given the best medical care and fed on milk and eggs and steaks at a time when local residents found difficulty in purchasing those items.

The one issue on which nearly all Honolulans united was the Hawaiian Territorial Guard. It had been authorized by the October session of the territorial legislature to take the place of the National Guard Regiment that had been federalized the previous spring and which was doing guard duty on the island of Hawaii at the outbreak of the war. It was the Japanese units of this National Guard organization that were brought to the States, trained, and later saw action in Italy.

On December 7, when the Japanese struck, Colonel P. M. Smoot, adjutant general of the territory, hastily organized the Territorial Guard. Ninety per cent of the volunteers were Japanese youngsters who had received military training at McKinley High School or had belonged to the ROTC at the University of Hawaii. The remainder were largely older men who were former Hawaiian national guardsmen.

A distinctive uniform had been authorized for the guard but had not yet been manufactured, so they were outfitted by the army, armed with army rifles, machine guns and grenades. The only way they could be distinguished from regular army soldiers was by means of a brassard bearing the letters "HTG."

These territorial guardsmen, most of them young, were placed on guard duty at newspaper offices (the Honolulu *Advertiser* protested and had them withdrawn), cable stations, power sta-

[65

tions, bridges, and other strategic spots. For two and a half months, until the situation became so explosive that action had to be taken and the territorial guard was "inactivated," an army euphemism for disbandment, the safety of Honolulu's vital services was in their hands.

Long before they were inactivated, a high military officer who protested that his hands were tied (he didn't say by whom) pointed out to newspaper correspondents the danger of having men obviously of the Japanese race parading the streets in army uniform, armed with army weapons.

Perhaps all of them were loyal. Although they were the ones who did most of the promiscuous shooting at night in the early days of the war, they carried out their guard duties efficiently. There was not a case, so far as I know, of sabotage at any of the vital places guarded by them.

But, as the previously mentioned high army officer said, What if it had been the strategy of the Japanese to attempt a landing and as few as one or two of the uniformed, armed territorial guardsmen were disloyal, tore off their arm bands and started shooting—who could have identified friend or foe?

"No man in uniform will be able to trust any other," he said; "we will be shooting each other all over the island."

Admittedly the Japanese Problem was a difficult one to solve. Aside from the purely physical problem of interning all Japanese, or transporting them to the States, the island depended too much on their labor. They did most of the clerking in the stores, they made up the major portion of the personal servants of the residents and were the workers on the pineapple and sugar plantations and the small truck farms that provided vegetables for the islands.

The main complaint by the haoles against the handling of the problem was the tender manner toward convicted law violators and the lack of frankness by the army in explaining measures it was taking to control the Japanese.

The curfew and blackout, for instance, which were the most

severe in the world, were not so much a protection against attack as a method of keeping the Japanese at home. To avoid discrimination against any one race, the rules covered all persons. And it was of doubtful value even then. Japanese engaged in espionage must have found the blackout a perfect cover for their clandestine movements. Enough police cannot be placed throughout a blacked-out city to prevent the movement of any person who doesn't want to be seen and uses the alleys and backyards as his path.

There was much evidence that it didn't work. One policeman patrolling the Japanese section of the city saw several shoes parked on the porch of one small house; it is an old Japanese custom to remove the shoes when entering the home. The policeman investigated. Slipping close to the wall of the house, from which no light was showing, he heard a radio operating inside. Breaking down the door, he found ten Japanese squatting around a short-wave radio tuned to a program from Japan. Although it was a clear violation of several laws, the ten were let off with relatively minor sentences. There were many other similar incidents.

The Japanese did little themselves, as a whole, to inspire confidence in their loyalty. The police organized a small group that gave valuable help in collecting information on activities of suspected espionage agents. Several hundred gave their blood at the Red Cross bank, although their numbers fell off sharply when one hog farmer died a few hours after he was drained of a pint of blood. They participated in other loyal activities.

But many of the Japanese clerks in the stores were surly to white customers, pointedly ignoring them to wait on members of their own race or denying they had articles asked for when they were in plain view on the shelves. Another correspondent and I, dressed in army uniforms, practically had to trip up a Japanese waitress in a restaurant one day before we could get her to stop at our table and take our order.

There were exceptions to this attitude, of course. I have never been better served than by the Japanese waiters at the Halekulani Hotel, and there was the group that worked with the police, one of whose meetings I attended, about whose loyalty there could be no question.

"These boys are gambling on an American victory more than you or I," Chief Gabrielson said as we were leaving the meeting. "Can you imagine what the Japanese will do to them if they ever take this island?"

That was said at a time in the spring of 1942 when a lot of thoughtful persons, wondering why the Japanese had not attempted a landing on December 7, fully expected them to try it at some not too distant date.

Whatever the loyalty of the Japanese, it was a negative rather than a positive allegiance. There was no forewarning of the December 7 attack, and the closemouthed attitude taken by those against whom there was no suspicion hampered our various intelligence agencies in gathering evidence against the active espionage ring. This was shown by the relatively small number of those who were taken into custody, which was less than five hundred. Even the most liberal-minded Honolulans agreed the percentage of disloyal Japanese was greater than that. And most of them agreed, too, that the most active traitors probably were not among the older aliens, who had found in Honolulu a much more pleasant existence than they had enjoyed in Japan, but among their embittered descendants who were American citizens but had little reason to love the land of their birth.

There is considerable evidence that the Japanese in the Hawaiian Islands had a forewarning of the attempted invasion of Midway in June, 1942, which would have been followed by all-out bombing of Pearl Harbor and Honolulu. Several Japanese women quit their jobs as domestics in Honolulu during May and went back to their homes on other islands. This may not have been widespread, but three families I knew there lost their maids during this period. Asked for a reason for their departure, the girls said they had been ordered home by their parents.

The viewpoint that the Japanese-Americans, not the alien Japanese, were the most probable traitors was given point by the Niihau incident.

Niihau is a small island of the Hawaiian group lying to the westward of Kauai. It is owned by a missionary family, the Robinsons, who had maintained it as a private, feudal paradise. There the Hawaiians lived as they had before the coming of the white man. Before the war, no casual visitors to the island were allowed to spoil its primitive beauty by their presence, or to corrupt its inhabitants. Once a man quit his job with the Robinsons and left the island he could not return.

There were no white people on the island on December 7, only the Hawaiians and two Japanese, one an alien, the other his American son. A Japanese flier, whose plane had been damaged during the Pearl Harbor attack, made a crash landing there, and escaped uninjured.

The Hawaiians, who are the most friendly persons in the world, helped succor him. There was no radio or cable or telephone to bring them news of the undeclared war that had been started that morning by the Japanese.

The Japanese aviator immediately set up his little oligarchy. And who, would you guess, was his assistant gauleiter? Not the alien Japanese. He wanted no part of this queer business that he didn't understand. It was the son who eagerly joined forces with the enemy.

The Japanese flier, through the son, who acted as his interpreter, told the natives that the Japanese had seized the Hawaiian Islands and that he had been sent to take charge at Niihau. They would obey him, or else. To back up his claims he had his pistol and a machine gun he had taken from the wrecked plane.

The Hawaiians still made no resistance, even if they did accept his story with some dubiety, and thus things stood for two days.

Then, the arrogance of the little flier and his assistant becoming irksome, the Hawaiian manager decided he had better find

[69

out what was going on. He dispatched five of his workers to set a fire on a headland, a signal of distress to the Robinsons on Kauai, and, to supplement that, a party to paddle to Kauai in canoes.

The absence of the workers being noticed, the Japanese flier asked the manager where they had gone. Not being satisfied with the explanation, which was that they merely were somewhere on the island, he ordered him to call them back. An expedition consisting of the manager, his wife, the Japanese flier, the young Japanese-American, and one or two other natives set out, calling for the missing workmen as they went.

The Japanese flier, becoming more and more nervous as the minutes passed with no response from the missing men, finally told the manager, through the interpreter, that if he did not produce the men immediately he would be shot.

"I raise my hands to show I do not know where they are," the manager said, telling the story to friends, "and he fire shot at me. I think that may be mistake but when he fire second time, then third time, I get mad."

Rushing at the Japanese, the big Hawaiian picked him up and threw him head first against a stone wall. Then he started for the young Japanese-American. The latter, armed only with a shotgun, fired one barrel at his attacker and then turned the gun on himself and committed suicide. The manager's wife, meanwhile, had jumped on the Japanese flier, who had been stunned when his head struck the stone wall. Armed with a rock, she literally beat out his brains.

The Japanese Problem is one that will remain with the residents of the Hawaiian Islands even after the war is over. Not even those secretly disloyal to the United States will want to return to a Japan that will be as impoverished as will the Empire of the Rising Sun after this war has been lost. Those who are citizens cannot be deported. Non-assimilable, prolific, they must be a continuing and increasing problem. Cessation of the war will not bring peace to them.

CHAPTER 5

The Far Eastern Campaign

DISTURBING as was the situation in the Central Pacific, which was fraught more with terrifying potentialities than with actual attack, it could not compare with that of our forces and those of our allies in the Far East. There it was desperate and hopeless from the very beginning.

The Japanese struck simultaneously against the three major Far Eastern land bases of the United States and Great Britain, from Formosa and the China Coast against Hong Kong and the Philippines, and from Indo-China and Thailand against the Malay States. They used their fleet to cover the three operations.

The Hong Kong and Malayan campaigns did not last long. Hong Kong, cut off from support either by land or by sea, capitulated on Christmas Day after a valiant defense by the small British and Canadian garrison. Singapore was surrendered on February 15.

In the Philippines the combined United States-Filipino force fought on until April 9 on Bataan and held out until May 6 on Corregidor, the island fortress in Manila Bay. But it always was a hopeless fight. There never was a chance that reinforcements would get through.

Against the little more than token force we had in the Philippines the Japanese threw an armada of an estimated eighty vessels and two hundred thousand men. As many as two hundred planes in a single day supported the invasion. The wonder is not that we lost the land battles in the Far East but that our forces held out as long as they did.

Lacking men to hold all the beaches and, after the first few days, the airplanes to attack the Japanese war vessels and transports at sea where they were most vulnerable, General MacArthur fought only delaying actions through the hills while withdrawing his forces to Bataan and Corregidor. Manila was declared "an open city," although that did not save it from the Japanese, who there showed they had no intention of waging war under any of the accepted rules of international conflict.

Our naval facilities, at Cavite in Manila Bay and Olongapo in Subic Bay, were one of the first and primary targets of the Japanese. Olongapo was not very active as a base, and was abandoned. With no air protection, Cavite was knocked out in ten minutes. What small vessels and submarines remained after the withdrawal of the surface forces to the south operated from small docks on Corregidor and Bataan until they too had to leave, or stay and be destroyed.

As one grim day succeeded another, the tragic results of not getting our air force off the ground when word of the Pearl Harbor attack was received became more apparent. Even had all the planes been in the air December 8 (December 7 in Pearl Harbor), the Philippines could not have been held. But the Japanese would have had to pay a higher price than they did. The damage the few surviving planes did was an earnest of that.

Patched up B-17's continuously attacked the Japanese transports landing troops off Aparri in the Lingayen Gulf and south of Manila, and P-40's repeatedly attacked enemy forces in Subic Bay and off Bataan, but it would have taken "clouds of planes," such as Premier Paul Reynaud begged for when France was falling, to have stopped the invading forces.

It might be well here to bring into the open the question as to whether Captain Colin Kelly, our first national hero of the war, sank the old Japanese battleship Haruna, or merely hit it with a bomb.

There is no question that he hit and damaged the ship. One reconnaissance report was that she had to be beached. There is reason to believe, however, that she was not sunk but was salvaged by the Japanese and was back with the fleet within a few months.

Enough American ships have been bombed for navy men to know that one or two bombs, even thousand-pound bombs, may not even sink a destroyer, let alone a heavily armored battleship, unless by some freak it penetrates a magazine. The probability that the Haruna sank under attack by one B-17 does not appear reasonable.

The Kelly saga is like so many others. Once a communiqué is issued or a newspaper story relating some great deed is passed by the censor and published, neither our army nor our navy likes to admit that it may have been too hasty in its claim, and to set the record straight. Certainly the truth can detract little from Captain Kelly's bravery in attacking the Haruna and then, his plane afire, staying at the controls while his men bailed out, thus forfeiting his own life.

The real battle of the Philippines was fought on the Bataan Peninsula, a heavily wooded, hilly finger of land that forms the western enclosure of Manila Bay. Corregidor is off the peninsula's southern tip.

The Bataan forces consisted of thirty-five thousand men, of whom about ten thousand were white men—soldiers, sailors, and marines. They had twenty tanks and thirty-four 155-millimeter guns. They were under command of Lieutenant General Jonathan Wainwright, a tall, taciturn man who is one of the great military leaders of this war.

The command in the field had been turned over to General Wainwright by General MacArthur, who, after the evacuation of Manila, retired to Corregidor.

General Wainwright threw his defense line across the neck of the peninsula and dug in to fight the Japanese as long as it was humanly possible. At that time all the Flying Fortresses were gone. The air force consisted of four P-40 fighter planes.

Among General Wainwright's troops was a combined marine-navy battalion of a thousand men composed of marines who had been evacuated from China, the personnel of the Cavite navy base, and the crew of the submarine tender Canopus.

Under the urging of Lieutenant Commander Frank Bridgett and Lieutenant Malcolm M. Champlin, an aide on the staff of Rear Admiral Francis W. Rockwell who had won the Navy Cross for destroying oil stores in Manila Bay under the very noses of the approaching Japanese, General Wainwright allowed them to use the battalion as lookouts and guards along the peninsula's exposed beaches.

This beach guard of men, most of them untrained for that sort of warfare, did heroic work in defense of Bataan. On three different occasions they fought off Japanese landing attempts, killing an estimated one thousand of the enemy in the Tuol River pocket, a thousand more at Quinauan Point and several hundred more at the Pantingan River.

As lookouts they marked the position of Japanese ships in Subic Bay that were attacked by the P-40's and the motor torpedo boats of Lieutenant John Buckley's squadron.

All through January, February, and March the American-Filipino forces held the peninsula against continuous pressure from the Japanese, who were being constantly reinforced. Their ammunition was being brought to them by submarines.

This was a defense by men who knew they were not going to be relieved, whose only end could be death or surrender. Most of the time they were on short rations. They were under both day and night air attacks by low-flying planes that attacked anything they could see moving through the thick forests, now torn and shattered in many places by bombs and shells. All of them were weakened by malaria and dysentery.

On April 9, with the food and most of the ammunition gone, 90 per cent of his men ill, General Wainwright surrendered to the Japanese. Several hundred men refused to obey the last order of their general to lay down their arms, and escaped to Corregidor.

In the meantime General MacArthur had gone to Australia,

traveling part of the way by motor torpedo boat and the rest of the way by air, to assume command of the Southwest Pacific. Manuel Quezon, president of the Philippines, and his family also escaped by submarine, as had Admiral Rockwell and his staff and other key personnel.

Twenty-seven days after Bataan fell, Corregidor, now under shellfire from Bataan, surrendered. Except for guerrilla activities back in the hills of Luzon and Mindanao, the two largest islands of the group, the Philippine campaign was over.

Most of our Far Eastern fleet, such as it was, was at sea when the Japanese struck, including sixteen of the eighteen submarines based on Manila. One of those in port escaped. The other was destroyed as it lay in dry dock.

The two "capital" ships of the Asiatic squadron, the heavy cruiser Houston and the new light cruiser Boise, were south of the islands. They were ordered to join up and escort the plane ferry Langley, and the tankers Pecos and Trinity, aboard which was most of the navy's Far Eastern supply of torpedoes and depth charges, to Singapore and Surabaya, Java. They passed a Japanese force en route, but battle was not joined.

Meanwhile the two British capital ships in the Pacific, the Prince of Wales and the Repulse, a battleship and a battle cruiser, respectively, were caught by a Japanese plane force without an air cover and were sunk December 10 while trying to support the defense of Malaya.

The story of the naval campaign in Far Eastern waters is one of retreat from one port to another. Singapore was under air attack and soon to fall. Balippapan, on Borneo, soon was rendered untenable. Then it was Surabaya's turn.

The ships were dogged by submarines and planes, bombed out of one harbor after another and, finally, almost all destroyed. Only the Boise, Marblehead and a few destroyers escaped, the Boise to Bombay for repairs, the Marblehead to the States, and the destroyers to Australia.

It was a fighting retreat, though. On January 14 four old four-stacker destroyers, the John D. Ford, Pope, Parrott and Paul Jones, made a night attack on a Japanese force in the Macassar Straits, a thousand-mile-long passage between Borneo and Celebes, and sank at least nine Japanese transports.

The Boise started north with the destroyers on word of the approach of the Japanese force, reported as twelve cruisers and destroyers, and thirty transports. En route she hit an uncharted pinnacle, tearing loose several plates from her bottom and bending her keel, and she turned back.

Alone, the four little "cans," armed only with 4-inch guns, continued on their mission. Showing no lights, they steamed through the Japanese screen, a destroyer passing within a few hundred yards of them, and closed with the transports. Up the line they went, firing torpedoes from either side at the big, darkened Japanese transports. Then, their forty-eight torpedoes expended, they turned and ran back through the force, firing their 4-inch guns at the sinking vessels. They could see their wakes upsetting life rafts and boats in which the Japanese were abandoning ship. Several of the enemy ships blew up when they were hit.

The Japanese had been caught so completely by surprise that the small American force was able to make its escape without damage. Although the communiqué claimed only six enemy vessels definitely sunk, a Dutch submarine commander who was stalking the Japanese force and watched the battle from a few miles distant said he saw nine enemy ships go down.

The Battle of the Strait of Macassar was the first United States naval engagement in Far Eastern waters since Admiral Dewey sailed into Manila Bay in 1898 and destroyed the Spanish fleet.

Three weeks later the Ford and three American destroyers, the Stewart, Edwards, and Pillsbury, joined up with the Dutch cruisers Java and DeRuyter and the Dutch destroyers Tromp and Piet Hein and made another successful night attack on another Japanese landing force in the Badang Straits off Bali. In the confusion of this night action several Japanese ships were seen to be firing on each other. The exact results of the attack were not determined but aerial reconnaissance the next day and reports of survivors from the Piet Hein, which was sunk, said many Jap ships had been beached, others had capsized in shallow waters and more were heavily damaged and listing.

The Houston and Marblehead and two Dutch cruisers, meanwhile, had been attacked by Japanese planes on February 4 and the Marblehead heavily damaged. The Houston was hit but retained her integrity. The Marblehead started back for the States. The Houston, with American destroyers, then joined forces with the Dutch ships, under the Dutch commander, Rear Admiral Karel W. F. M. Doorman, and continued on the prowl for the Japanese forces.

By mid-February the allied American-Dutch forces were practically without a base from which to operate. Singapore had fallen. Priok and Surabaya were under increasingly heavy air attacks. Even Port Darwin, the only large port on the northern coast of Australia, was under heavy attack. The Japanese sent more than two hundred planes over Darwin on February 19 and 20. Among the ships sunk was the American destroyer Peary. The Japanese transport trains still were rolling inexorably southward, gobbling up island after island.

An allied command had been set up, headed by General Sir Archibald Wavell, with Admiral Hart in command of the sea forces, but it was only a paper organization that never really functioned. It was soon discontinued.

What little air force the Dutch had was largely reduced by losses, and the Australians were pulling back, for defense of their own country, what few forces they had left in the Dutch East Indies.

To the everlasting credit of the United States Navy, it stayed until it was released. Our admiralty had promised the Dutch the American ships would help them defend their islands as long as there was any hope. That pledge was honored, at the cost of many American lives.

[77

On February 27 was fought the last major naval engagement of the Far Eastern campaign. Against a Japanese force estimated to have included two battleships, seven heavy cruisers, two or three light cruisers, and thirteen destroyers, Admiral Doorman led his little Dutch-American-British force of the DeRuyter, Java, Houston, the British heavy cruiser Exeter, and the light cruiser Perth and ten destroyers.

In the steaming Java sea, the allied force fought the Japanese at long and close range intermittently for several hours, through the long afternoon and into the night. While the destroyers feinted and laid smoke screens and attacked, the allied cruisers drove on to engage the Java-bound transport train which the Japanese combatant vessels were protecting. The odds were too great.

A joint United States-British communiqué, which was in much greater detail than the customary United States Navy pronouncements, described the battle of the Java Sea and the subsequent loss of most of the United Nations vessels engaged, as follows:

"On the afternoon of Friday, February 27, an Allied Force consisting of H.M.A.S. Perth, H.M.S. Exeter, the U.S.S. Houston, and the Dutch cruisers DeRuyter and Java were at sea north of Surabaya. The Allied cruisers were accompanied by a group of British, Dutch and U.S. destroyers. The force was under the sea command of Rear Admiral Doorman of the Dutch Navy, whose flag was flying in the DeRuyter. The whole naval force in the area was under the strategic control of Vice Admiral Helfrich of the Royal Netherlands Navy.

"At 4:14 P.M. on February 27 this Allied Force made contact with a Japanese force about halfway between Bawean Island and Surabaya. The Japanese force consisted of at least nine cruisers, of which two were of the Nati class of ten thousand tons, armed with ten 8-inch guns. The Japanese cruisers had with them two flotillas of destroyers.

"Action was joined at extreme range. Almost at once one of

the Japanese destroyer flotillas launched an attack, but this attack was driven off by the fire of Allied cruisers and one of the enemy destroyers was seen to be hit by shells from H.M.A.S. Perth. Soon afterward the other Japanese destroyer flotilla delivered a torpedo attack. While action was being taken to avoid these torpedoes H.M.S. Exeter was hit by an 8-inch shell in a boiler room. This reduced her speed and forced her to drop out of line. Only one of the torpedoes launched in this attack took effect. This hit the Netherlands destroyer Kortenaer, and she sank.

"Three destroyers were ordered to counterattack the Japanese destroyers, who were retiring under cover of a smoke screen. Very little information is available about the result of this counterattack. H.M.S. Jupiter reported seeing only two enemy destroyers, both of which she engaged with gunfire. H.M.S. Electra was not seen after she had disappeared into the smoke screen, and it is presumed that she was sunk. As soon as Allied cruisers, including the Houston but without the Exeter, which was unable to keep up, drew clear of smoke they again engaged the enemy, this time at shorter range. Less than half an hour later the enemy cruisers turned away under cover of a smoke screen. It was seen that one of the enemy's heavy 8-inch-gun cruisers had been hit aft and was burning fiercely.

"Admiral Doorman led his force about and chased the enemy to northeastward, but he failed to regain touch with the enemy in the fading light. After nightfall the Allied cruisers sighted four enemy ships to westward and engaged them, but without definite knowledge of the results.

"Admiral Doorman attempted to work around these enemy ships in order to locate the convoy which was expected to the northward. This was found to be impossible owing to the high speed of the enemy, and Admiral Doorman then turned his force to southward to approach the coast of Java, intending to sweep to westward along the coast in an attempt to intercept the Japanese invasion convoys.

"Half an hour after this Allied Force had turned to westward

[79

along the Java coast H.M.S. Jupiter was disabled by an underwater explosion. She sank four hours later. H.M.S. Jupiter was not far from the mainland of Java, and a number of survivors have already reached Australia. A U.S. submarine assisted in the rescue of fifty-three survivors.

"At 11:30 P.M., when the remaining Allied cruisers were about twelve miles north of Rembang, two enemy cruisers were sighted between our ships and the coast. Our ships at once engaged, and a number of hits were secured on the enemy. The DeRuyter was hit by one shell. Afterward the DeRuyter made a large change of course, presumably in order to avoid torpedoes fired by the enemy. The other Allied cruisers were following the DeRuyter when underwater explosions occurred simultaneously in the cruisers DeRuyter and Java. Both these Dutch cruisers blew up and sank at once.

"It is impossible to estimate with accuracy the damage inflicted upon the enemy during these actions of February 27. Observers in the Perth consider that one Japanese 8-inch-gun cruiser was sunk, a second 8-inch-gun cruiser damaged and a destroyer sunk. It has also been reported that a cruiser of the Mogami class was set on fire and three destroyers seriously damaged and left on fire or sinking.

"H.M.A.S. Perth and U.S.S. Houston, which had received some damage in this action, reached Tanjong Priok at 7 o'clock the morning of Saturday, February 28. Five U.S. destroyers reached Surabaya after the action.

"With the enemy in command of sea and air north of Java in overwhelming force, the Allied command was faced with the problem of extricating the remaining Allied ships from a very dangerous situation. The way to Australia was barred by the six-hundred-mile long island of Java, with the straits at either end of it under enemy control.

"After dark on February 28, H.M.A.S. Perth and U.S.S. Houston left Tanjong Priok with the intention of passing through Sunda Strait during dark hours. During the night an enemy report from H.M.A.S. Perth was received which indicated that she and the U.S.S. Houston had come into contact with a force of Japanese ships off St. Nicholas Point at about 11:30 P.M. Nothing, however, has been heard from H.M.A.S. Perth or the U.S.S. Houston since that time. The next of kin of the U.S.S. Houston are being informed accordingly.

"The same night the Exeter, which was capable of only half speed, left Surabaya accompanied by H.M.S. Encounter and the U.S. destroyer Pope. On the forenoon of Sunday, March 1, the Exeter reported that she had sighted three enemy cruisers steering toward her. No further word has been received from the Exeter, Encounter, or the U.S.S. Pope. The next of kin of the Pope are being informed accordingly. The Dutch destroyer Evertsen encountered two Japanese cruisers in Sunda Strait. She was damaged and was beached.

"The destroyer H.M.S. Stronghold and the sloop H.M.A.S. Yarra are also missing and are presumably lost.

"It has not been possible to form any accurate estimate of damage inflicted on the enemy by these ships during these actions."

While the surface battle was raging in the Java Sea, the Langley and the Pecos, the former loaded with fighter planes, were headed for Java from Australia when they were attacked by a Japanese carrier air group. The Langley was so badly hurt she sank. Survivors were picked up by the Pecos, but, with daylight, the Japanese planes were back and sank the tanker.

Of the little American squadron that had fought so bravely for three months, only the Boise and the Marblehead and a handful of destroyers and submarines were left. They, and the ships that were gone, had written one of the bravest and finest chapters in American naval history.

PART III

THE OFFENSIVE-
DEFENSIVE PHASE

The First Raid

UNDER THE steady hand of Admiral Nimitz, some order had begun to emerge from the chaos by late January, 1942, and the decision was reached to begin the harassing raids on Japanese bases which, although they did no really crippling damage to the enemy, did serve to boost the morale of the American public, and especially that of the fleet.

The aircraft carrier Yorktown, whose air group was to play such a gallant part in the Coral Sea and Midway battles, had transited the canal and joined the Pacific fleet. Every day more destroyers, many of them still in their East Coast dazzle camouflage, were arriving at Pearl Harbor, and some of the ships that had been damaged in the December 7 attack were back, or preparing to join. Retirement or destruction of the Japanese submarines that had been operating off the mainland and on the sea lanes to Honolulu had released still more ships for offensive operations.

Although all the plane losses of December 7 had not been replaced, the army fighter strength in the islands had been increased even beyond what it had been before the start of the war, and new fields had been built or were being built on all the islands. The dispersal that was lacking on December 7 had been achieved. It would have taken a much bigger air force now than the Japanese had used on that fateful day, to knock out the islands' air protection.

Still it was a great risk that was taken. We still had no battleships in the Pacific that could be used offensively; our island bases along the supply route to Australia still were only thinly manned.

Much of the Japanese fleet was engaged in covering the advance to the south, but it was known that they still had more in reserve than we had in total in the Pacific, and there was no assurance, except intelligent guesswork, that a striking force would not be sent against Midway, or some of the islands on the sea road to Australia.

It took moral courage, and confidence of the highest order in the ability of our air groups, to send one-half of our Pacific carrier strength within range of land-based enemy planes. But that was what was done.

Admiral Halsey, then a vice admiral, with his flag on the carrier Enterprise, had safely escorted a convoy of marines to Samoa, providing air protection against enemy carrier attack or interception by submarines.

He was ordered to strike the Japanese bases in the northern Marshalls. Rear Admiral Frank Jack Fletcher, with the Yorktown task force, was to hit simultaneously at Makin, in the Gilberts, and Mile and Jaluit in the lower Marshalls.

At that time we knew little about the Japanese strength at any of the atolls singled out to feel the first offensive thrust of the fleet.

The Marshalls were one of the three groups of former German-owned islands in the Pacific that had been mandated to Japan by the League of Nations. There had been evidence for years that Japan was fortifying many of these islands, building airfields, dredging sheltered anchorages, building up stocks of fuel and ammunition. British and American diplomacy, however, had barred all efforts of our Navy Department to force an inspection either by ourselves or by a League commission. Now we had to do it the hard way.

Before the carrier raids, we had only the scanty intelligence our submarines had brought. Incidentally, their chief task in the early days of the war was reconnaissance. Then it was more important to know the disposition of the enemy fleet than it was to sink a few of his ships. From the submarine skippers we had learned something of the strength of the Japanese bases in the islands through study of ship movements to and from them.

PILOTS MAN YOUR PLANES

Two stub-winged Grumman fighters wait on the starting line for the signal to take off from their carrier while their big brothers, the Grumman torpedo bombers, line up waiting their turn. The TBFs have not yet extended their wings, which are folded to simplify handling and stowage aboard ship. The wake to the right indicates the carrier is turning into the wind to launch her brood.

CINPAC IN ACTION

Admiral Chester W. Nimitz, the "brains" behind the United States Navy's successful fight against Japan in the Pacific, at one of his rare meetings with the correspondents in his office at Pearl Harbor. Calm, patient and brilliant, Admiral Nimitz is equally at home in the conning tower of a submarine, on the flag bridge of a battleship or in his quiet, air-conditioned office from where he directs the far-flung movements of his rapidly growing Pacific Fleet. "Cinpac" is the Navy abbreviation for Commander-in-chief Pacific Fleet.

Some of this information was of little value in the raid. The navy had believed, for instance, that Jaluit was the main Japanese base in the Marshalls. Little was found there.

This then was the situation on January 31 as Admiral Halsey turned back from his convoy job and set his course for the Marshalls and Gilberts.

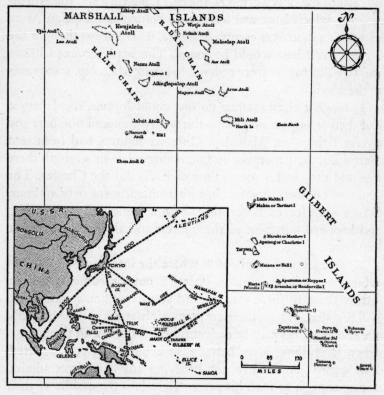

"The Marshall Islands are so numerous and the conditions under which the Japanese had operated (allowing no one to visit their mandated islands) made it difficult to know just where to strike," reported Captain Miles Browning, then a commander and Admiral Halsey's chief of staff. "But we had a certain amount of information as to where we might find worthwhile targets."

[87

The plan of operations for the Enterprise task force that Admiral Halsey commanded directly was for the carrier to go right in among the atolls, so as to be able to strike in any direction necessary, and at the shortest possible distance, and for her accompanying cruisers to bombard the two islands on the eastern edge of the chain.

Two of the heavy cruisers, the Salt Lake City and the Northampton, which later was lost in the Solomons campaign, were sent with a destroyer escort to Wotje, where it was thought the biggest naval base would be found. The heavy cruiser Chester and two destroyers were ordered to attack Maleolap, some miles to the south.

Through a circumstance no one could foresee, the Japanese had their strongest air group—thirty two-motored bombers and twelve fighters—at Maleolap. Only six fighters had been sent there from the Enterprise to immobilize what air strength there was and they had a rough time of it. So did the Chester. The Japanese bombers attacked her intermittently for over an hour, before a reinforced Enterprise air group caught them refueling and knocked out most of the fighters and all but seven of the bombers.

Maleolap was the only atoll where the information from our submarines was incomplete. That was not surprising. The main enemy strength there was air; and you never know where you will find that. Where there are many air bases, as in the Marshalls, the enemy planes may be concentrated at any one of them. Elsewhere everything went better than could have been expected. The enemy, apparently not believing any American admiral daring enough to stick his carrier right into the middle of their bases, looked everywhere for the Enterprise except the right place. They didn't find her until late afternoon when most of their planes had been destroyed and she, her mission completed, had recovered her planes and was on her way home.

How fortunate a circumstance this was can readily be seen when it is understood that once a carrier has launched her planes she must maintain the course and speed that will put her where the fliers have been promised she will be, and at the exact time planned. If the Enterprise had been found and attacked by the Japanese planes, the evasive maneuvers she would have had to carry out might have taken her over the horizon from the rendezvous point and left her striking air groups hunting for a landing deck that wasn't there.

As it was, Admiral Halsey was enabled to maneuver her as he had planned and use his limited planes to the greatest possible advantage. As each group of planes returned to the ship to report what it had found and attacked, and what enemy installations or ships remained to be destroyed, they were refueled and rearmed and sent back to the attack. Where the first strike had cleaned up the situation, the planes that had been on that operation were sent to a more troublesome spot. Where ships were found, as at Kwajalein, the admiral concentrated his torpedo planes and dive bombers. Where there were enemy planes remaining to be disposed of, as at Maleolap, he concentrated his fighter strength.

Carrier operation is the most intricate of all naval maneuvers since it must be geared to the three-hundred-mile-an-hour pace of the airplane and requires close timing, especially in uncertain weather conditions. Fortunately the weather in the Marshalls was excellent, simplifying for the planes the task of finding the carrier on their return from each strike.

"We threw our main air effort at Kwajalein because our information indicated that was the biggest base," Captain Browning explained.

The haul was even bigger than was hoped for. In the harbor was found a concentration of fifteen to twenty ships, including an aircraft carrier, one of the converted seventeen-thousand-ton Yawata class liners, a modern light cruiser, several submarines, three ten-thousand-ton fleet oilers and other smaller tenders and supply ships.

Ashore, on Roi, the largest island of the group, was found a

[89

modern air base with paved runways, hangars, and a modern village. It obviously had been under construction for many years, in contravention of the regulations for mandated territories, a fact the peacemakers might keep in mind when considering any promises made by the Japanese statesmen after the war is won and when conditions of control of Pacific islands in the future are being considered.

The fighters and dive bombers quickly immobilized the enemy planes and shore facilities, shooting down six Japanese fighters in the air and destroying others on the ground, and then turned their attention to the ships. Twenty-two hits with large caliber bombs—probably thousand-pounders—were made on various of these ships. Two hours later an attack by torpedo planes accounted for more destruction.

"Of the ships in the lagoon," the Captain said, "confirmed sinkings or total destruction included the carrier, the cruiser, the three oilers, at least two of the submarines, and one of the larger tenders or supply ships. Two to five others were heavily damaged."

After knocking the enemy fighters out of the air, our own fighter pilots had a field day strafing barracks and Japanese personnel.

Two of them saw one unlucky Japanese attempting to flee on a bicycle across a narrow causeway that connected two of the islands. They decided to give impetus to his flight with some .50-caliber slugs.

"He was pedaling like mad," one of them said later in describing the scene. "I missed him my first run, although I kicked up the dirt all around. I think my wing man hit him, for he tumbled off the bicycle. He got up again and was trying to mount when I swung around and pressed the button again. He didn't get up.

"You know," he continued, "I felt sort of sorry for the little so-and-so. He probably didn't know any more what the war was about than I do."

On Wotje an airfield was found, but no planes; and the cruisers and destroyers that did the bombarding there were enabled to carry out their assignment without aerial interference. The air strike from the Enterprise hit first, strafing hangars and gun emplacements and setting many fires. Then the ships moved in for their firing run and completed the destruction. All but two of the four or five supply ships, of four thousand to five thousand tons, and several small mine sweepers and patrol craft were sunk either by the planes or by ship's gunfire, all five shore defense batteries were silenced, and probably 90 per cent of all shore installations were either destroyed or heavily damaged. The two ships that were not claimed as positives, because they weren't seen to sink, were left in bad shape, one beached and the other down by the stern.

What later appealed to the crew of the Salt Lake City as an amusing incident occurred while she was on her firing run at Wotje. They were firing at one of the shore battery positions. Through an error in calculation one of the salvos was hurled between one hundred and two hundred yards to one side of the target. To the amazement of the gunnery officer and spotters, who were cursing their error and correcting it when they saw the shells landing wide, a towering sheet of flame followed the shell explosions. They apparently had put their salvo by error right into the middle of some camouflaged oil tanks.

"They must have thought our intelligence was perfect on that one," said Lieutenant George O'Connell, then the assistant gunnery officer. "We knock off firing at the battery just long enough to blow their oil tanks sky high and then sort of dusting our hands and saying 'Well, that's that!' we go to work on the battery again."

Lieutenant Commander Staff Crowley, then senior aviator on the Salt Lake City, said he saw one little Japanese gunner he'd like to commend for bravery. Staff was spotting for the guns, a few thousand feet over the island and had a ringside seat for the whole show.

"The fighters had strafed this gun position and had either

knocked out all the other gunners or scared them away, leaving just one little guy to do all the work," Staff said. "I watched him for several minutes. He'd run over to the ready box, get a shell and lug it over to the gun and ram it home. Then he'd point the gun and fire it, run back for another shell, load it, point the gun, and fire. No one could have blamed him if he'd taken to the tall timber, as we were throwing shells all around the position."

"Did they finally knock out his gun?" I asked.

"I don't know," Staff said. "I had to shove off about my business. He was still going strong the last time I took a look."

The Salt Lake City's navigator, Commander Church Chappell, also expressed admiration for the captain of the small Japanese patrol vessel that left the harbor and gave battle to one of our destroyers.

"You can think what you want to about these people," Church said, "but I'd be willing to chip in for a tribute to that skipper. He had only one three-inch gun to fire against the four 5.38's of our destroyer, but he never wavered. He fought his little ship as well and as bravely as any of our officers could have done."

This, remember, was before Midway, where the Japanese shot down our parachuting aviators, and before Guadalcanal where marine stretcher bearers were murdered by wounded Japanese they were attempting to aid. But it was after Pearl Harbor, the wreckage of which all of them had seen. It was an attitude of mind, a compassion for a helpless enemy, a willingness to recognize a brave act no matter by whom performed, that is more or less general throughout the fleet. I have talked to few men who had any feeling of personal hate for the individual men whom they were forced to fight, and kill.

While the Enterprise fliers and our three cruisers and several destroyers were striking at Kwajalein, Wotje and Maleolap, the fliers of Admiral Fletcher's task force were flying from the Yorktown to attack Jaluit, Mile, and Makin. Unlike the attack by Halsey's force, the cruisers with the Yorktown did not go in for shore bombardment, the whole job being done by the fliers. Bad weather hampered them.

Jaluit, which had been thought for years to be the main Japanese base in the Marshalls and the probable starting point of the carriers that attacked Pearl Harbor, received the brunt of the American attack. Unfortunately, it was not as big a base as our intelligence had indicated it would be. Only two ships of any size, auxiliaries of from seven thousand to ten thousand tons, were found. There was only a small airfield, with packed dirt runways, and no land planes, and shore installations were not extensive, consisting only of a few shops, barracks, and a radio station. Antiaircraft fire was light.

The Jaluit attack group flew into bad weather on the way in and had to split up into sections. Some of the planes climbed over the storm and made a conventional dive-bombing attack from twelve thousand feet. The others went in at low level. One of the enemy ships was hit by several bombs, and was afire and sinking when last seen. The other ship was not hit, and received damage only from near misses. Both were heavily strafed by the fighters.

Even less was found at Makin, the British port which the Japanese had seized several weeks before, soon after the outbreak of the war. The only ship found was an auxiliary of five thousand to eight thousand tons, probably a seaplane tender. It was hit by several heavy bombs and was afire and sinking when the fliers left. Two patrol seaplanes found on the water were strafed, set afire, and destroyed. The only antiaircraft fire came from the ship, the fliers reported.

One by-product of the Jaluit-Makin-Mile operation was the gaining of a certain degree of immortality by one of the Yorktown pilots, Lieutenant Elbert Scott (Go Get 'Em) McCuskey. He later was to prove at Tulagi and in the Coral Sea and Midway battle that his fame was well deserved.

Lieutenant McCuskey, a big, grinning, slow-talking pilot from Stuttgart, Okla., was on defensive patrol over the Yorktown as she was retiring that day. Then he spotted one of the big four-motored Kawanishi patrol bombers used for reconnaissance work by the Japanese. Somehow it had escaped the fate of its brethren at Makin. It was bent on tracking the force until an enemy striking group could come up.

McCuskey reported his find to the ship and the fighter-director told him, "Go get him, McCuskey," thereby hanging on the Oklahoman a nickname destined to stay with him the rest of his life. McCuskey and his wingman, Ensign Adams of Hiawatha, Kansas, went to get him. A Kawanishi, although slow and cumbersome, is no sitting duck. It bristles with machine guns and has a 20-millimeter cannon.

As Ensign Adams, who was ordered by McCuskey to stand by while he made his pass at the enemy, wrote in a letter that was made public by Admiral Nimitz, it was like watching a small terrier pursue a larger dog from a vantage point on the other side of a tall fence.

The Japanese pilot, wanting nothing to do with McCuskey, started dodging in and out of the clouds, with McCuskey after him. Finally they both disappeared into a large cloud. Then burning pieces of airplane began to come out of the bottom of the cloud. Adams, on the outside, didn't know whether it was the Japanese plane or McCuskey's fighter that had been blown to pieces inside that white opaqueness. He didn't have long to wait. Over the fighter circuit came McCuskey's excited voice.

"I got him, I got him, I got the sonofabitch," McCuskey yelled. "I just shot his ass off."

I have heard the story, although I haven't confirmed it, that when Captain Buckmaster of the Yorktown, anxiously waiting word from McCuskey, got the report from air plot, he turned to the boatswain's mate at his side and excitedly told him:

"McCuskey just shot his ass off. Pass the word."

Nothing was found at Mile except a narrow strip cut through the palm trees which might have been preliminary clearing for an air strip. No shore installations were seen and there was no opposition of any kind. The disappointed fliers had to go back home without finding anything to shoot at.

Our total losses for the seven attacks were eleven scout bombers, the famous SBD's that have played so heroic a part in the Pacific fighting. Six of these were apparently victims of weather on the Jaluit and Makin raids, as none were seen to have been shot down on those two missions. Four were lost to enemy fighters and AA at Kwajalein, and one at Maleolap. They just "failed to return," an epitaph for many a brave youngster.

The enemy's confirmed losses were sixteen ships sunk, many more damaged, forty-one planes shot down, and others probably destroyed in hangars and on the ground. Three important air and naval bases were severely messed up.

Although the physical damage to shore bases was not great, the loss of ships was a severe blow to the Japanese at that time, and the effect on morale must have been even greater. It undoubtedly forced them to hold more air and sea forces in the Marshalls than had been based there before. It showed them that the Pacific Fleet dared to, and could, attack their outlying island bases.

Captain Browning said that the ferocity with which the remaining Japanese bombers attacked the Enterprise "was such as to indicate desperation."

"The Japanese commander had been caught with his pants down," he said; "he knew that if he didn't do something to offset the results of our attack he was going to catch hell. He probably did."

One of the Japanese planes that had been set afire during the approach to the Enterprise, either by one of the attacking American fighters or by antiaircraft fire, attempted a crash landing on the carrier's deck and almost succeeded. He hit near the outboard waterway, shearing the tail off a parked dive bomber, but then plunged on over the side into the sea. It was the first evidence of suicidal tendency of some of the Japanese pilots, and gave rise to a host of stories picturing all the Japanese soldiers and fliers as willing to sacrifice their lives to score on our ships or planes, a theory that just isn't true, as our fighter pilots already had learned that day. They found the Japanese fliers didn't like to close with them. The Nips would fire a burst at extreme range, then turn away.

Even if the damage to the Japanese, except to their pride, was not great, the effects of the raid on American morale were of the utmost importance.

When the task force streamed into Pearl Harbor a few days later the shore was lined with cheering soldiers, sailors, and yard workmen. Officers and men from the ships found it difficult to get any work done, so overwhelmed were they with congratulations from the men who had survived Pearl Harbor and wanted to cheer those who had exacted the first small measure of vengeance.

CHAPTER 2

No Rest for the Weary

THERE WAS little time for congratulations for the men of the striking force. There was too much to be done. Other tasks already had been planned for the Yorktown-and-Enterprise task group, and the officers and crews of the various ships had to be about the preparations for them.

A return to Pearl Harbor and Honolulu in those days was no rest cure. A condition of alert had to be maintained on all the ships, with the antiaircraft batteries fully manned all day, and steam up to turn the engines on short notice, for the specter of Japanese invasion still hung heavily over the islands. No one could understand why they hadn't come on in December 7. The least that was expected was another carrier raid. Two carriers and their escorts were a more shining mark to shoot at than the battleships that had been sunk two months before.

Even without the in-port watches, there was more than enough to do in preparing the ship for another strike; replacing the ammunition that had been expended, loading provisions, making repairs and installing new equipment.

It is difficult to visualize the preparations that must be made in getting a combatant ship ready for sea. Food of all kinds must be taken aboard for from three hunderd to twenty-five hundred men (respective complements of a destroyer and an aircraft carrier or battleship) to last them for ninety days or more. And the navy eats well—fresh vegetables, fresh meat of all kinds, ice cream mix, flour for bread and biscuits, coffee, sugar, salt, pepper, and other condiments. An aircraft carrier would take aboard as much as four hundred tons of supplies for one trip.

There is hardly a trip that some part of the warship's intricate machinery does not break down or become so worn that replacements or repairs are necessary. In those early days of the war, too, new antiaircraft weapons, improved equipment and gadgets always were waiting on the dock for installation every time a ship came into port.

Almost before the lines were on the dock, or the chain made fast to a buoy, yard officers would be conferring with the gunnery officer, the chief engineer and the first lieutenant on what repairs would have to be made, or could be made, while the ship was in port.

All night long the ammunition and provisions would be going aboard. The riveting guns chattered from dawn to dawn. Living in a steel hull where every sound is carried through the bulkheads and echoed along the passageways was almost more of a strain than being at sea in danger of enemy submarine or plane attack.

What small percentages of the crews were allowed to go ashore found little to entertain them there. The liquor ban still was in effect, the few movies—operating only during the daylight hours—could take only a small part of those trying to get in. The few restaurants served much less satisfactory food than could be had aboard ship, and the men had to stand in line to get even that.

The Royal Hawaiian Hotel on Waikiki had been taken over as a rest center for submarine crews and the fliers, but the vastly larger group of destroyer, cruiser, and carrier sailors, who led almost as hard and dangerous a life as the men of the "pigboats" and the fliers, had no place set aside for them. They milled around the Honolulu streets, after a crowded and tiresome trip in by bus from Pearl Harbor, buying bootleg liquor at $25 to $35 a fifth or standing in line at the few sporting houses along Hotel and River Streets.

Many of the men, caring neither for liquor nor for bought women, stayed aboard ship for the full time in port. It was a relief for the majority when the word was passed to make preparations for getting under way. A semblance of civilization, a reminder of the homes they had left and the girls and the life they knew back in Missouri and Illinois and Texas and elsewhere in the States, was more disturbing than the complete lack of such reminders when the ship was at sea.

The officers fared little better than their men. Their small club at Pearl Harbor was operating, but it closed early, and there was no place else for them to go. The families of most of them had been evacuated to the mainland. Even if they had friends in the city who would have liked to entertain them, they were not allowed to accept. An officer had to have a "bona fide" family ashore to get overnight liberty.

CHAPTER 3

Rolling Down to Wake

THE MIDDLE of February the gig picked us off the dock at the submarine base at 11:30 and headed out across the oil-covered waters of Pearl Harbor, past the rusting flame-twisted foretops of the sunken battleships, to put us aboard the task force to which we had been assigned.

There were Keith Wheeler of the *Chicago Times*, James Joseph Custer of the United Press, Bill Hipple, who was to cover both for the *Honolulu Star-Advertiser* and the Associated Press, Bob Casey of the *Chicago Daily News*, and myself. While waiting on the dock for Joe to arrive (Joe was late for everything, except the piece of metal that lodged in his head off Savo six months later and cost him the sight of his left eye), we learned that Joe and Keith Wheeler were to ride the Enterprise, Bob and I were assigned to the Salt Lake City, and Bill was to be on the other cruiser, the Northampton.

The previous two hours had been busy ones for all of us. One of the disadvantages under which correspondents labored in attempting to cover the naval phases of the Pacific War was that of never knowing when they were going some place, or where they were going. Sometimes we were put on a ship two days ahead of time and lay off the Fish Pond in Pearl Harbor fighting mosquitoes and ennui. Other times we hardly had an opportunity to pack a toothbrush. The latter had been the case the morning of February 14.

One of my chores, between getting my laundry back and a suit that was at the cleaner's, was to register for the "metal draft." You know, the registration of 38-to-45-year-olds, who had silver in their hair, gold in their teeth and lead in their pants. Considering the circumstances under which I was living, my registration for army duty seemed somewhat incongruous. As the months passed it seemed even more so.

Anyway, there we were in the gig, heading out across the harbor.

The Enterprise was the first stop. They were preparing to take in her gangplank as we pulled in under her counter, and Joe and Keith scrambled aboard just in time.

As we backed away from the carrier berth on Ford Island and headed for the cruiser anchorage off the Fish Pond, we saw the Northampton already headed down the channel for the sea and the Salt Lake City backing out of her antisubmarine nets to follow.

"Can you take aboard two passengers?" our escort bellowed to Captain Elias Zacharias, who was standing on the wing of the "Swayback Maru" conning her out of the harbor.

"Surely, send them aboard," Captain Zach called back, and Commander Dolecek, the First Lieutenant, put over a cargo net amidships. It was up that net that Bob and I panted while a couple of sailors threw over lines to haul our baggage up after us.

Bill Hipple never did make his ship. He waited a few days, then left on the carrier Yorktown for a sixty-day cruise in which he saw little. He left her just a few days before the Coral Sea battle, thus missing one of the first big stories of the war.

It was like old home week for Bob on the Salt Lake City. He had ridden the cruiser on the Marshall-Gilbert raids, and both the officers and men considered it a good omen that he was going out with them again.

"This means we must be going places to do things," one of the sailors said as we were greeted and led into the wardroom for the inevitable cup of coffee, always making on the three electric burners just outside the officers' galley. "You people wouldn't be coming aboard unless something was planned."

"You know as much as we do," we told them. "Maybe they're just taking us out for gunnery practice."

As our cruiser followed the Northampton down the channel through the sparkling morning and headed out to sea, the carrier's air group was taking off from Ewa Field, where they based while their ship was in port. Our destroyer escort already was outside, forming an antisubmarine screen.

As we cleared the nets at the entrance to the harbor, the big cruiser began to shake under her increased speed, her clipper bow sending white water curling away on either side.

Japanese submarines were still active around the islands at that time, two and a half months after the Pearl Harbor attack, and the task forces came in and went out hell-bent for election. The sailors called the entrance through the mine field "Torpedo Junction."

Following in Bob's wake, since he was the old hand on the ship, I was introduced to Captain Zach, who, as Bob had promised, was affability itself; Commander George Carter, the new executive officer; Lieutenant Commander Tyree, the gun boss; and Lieutenant Commander Howett, the communications officer.

"You'd better get your lunch," the Captain warned. "We're going to have some gunnery practice this afternoon."

At luncheon I was introduced to the rest of the officers: Ted Kobey, the chief engineer; Staff Crowley, the senior aviator; Commander Hayes, the ship's surgeon; Lieutenant Commander Byrd, the supply officer; Lieutenant George O'Connell, one of the gunnery officers; Lieutenant Dave Hawkins, the assistant first lieutenant; Lieutenant Jim Brewer, the assistant gun boss. It developed in conversation that Jim and I had lived only a few blocks apart in Little Neck, Long Island, during the years he was out of the service and working for Macy's.

"We came a long way from Little Neck to get acquainted, didn't we?" said Jim. On a rough estimate we placed it at about six thousand miles.

Just as we were finishing lunch general quarters was called over the loud-speaker system.

"When it's just routine," Bob explained, as we climbed up after Mr. Tyree to the fire-control station at the top of the foremast, "they just sound the alarm and announce it. If you hear the bugle on this ship, though, hop to it. It will be the real thing."

Fire control was an armored pillbox at the very top of the foremast, which, on the Salt Lake City, was one of the tallest in the navy. A narrow platform ran completely around it.

"You feel like Shipwreck Kelly on top of a flagpole up here," Bob said as we puffed up the last long ladder, squeezed through the hatch and joined Mr. Tyree and Lieutenant John Boland, who was doing the spotting that day, on the outer walkway.

The equivalent of three stories below us stretched the ship, all guns manned, tearing along the deep blue sea in full battle condition. Off the horizon, almost lost in the haze, we could see an old four-stacker destroyer towing the target, a twenty-foot square of light wood and canvas that was only a dot on the ocean at eighteen thousand yards. It was difficult to see how any accurate sight could be taken on such a small object.

The other cruiser, steaming along a thousand yards ahead, first opened fire, the boom of the guns reaching us several seconds after flame and brown powder smoke had gushed from her rifle barrels and gone streaming down the wind.

While her salvo was still in the air our own main battery let go. John had warned Bob and me to hold on, telling us that the mast tip would whip around from the recoil of the guns. It was well he had. The shock was so great, if we had not had a firm hold on the screen, we would have been thrown off our feet.

No matter how you brace yourself for the shock of the guns, the first salvo is an ear- and nerve-shattering impact. One of the reasons for having gunnery practice the first few hours out of port is to accustom the crew again to the roar of the guns, the smell of cordite, to bring them again to the realization that war is thunder and lightning and killing.

It was my experience that practice firing is worse, so far as the nervous shock is concerned, than actual battle. Many others, both officers and men, have told me their reactions were similar.

Before the start of the war, a naval surgeon said (perhaps it was Dr. Hayes), there always were several cases of hysteria among the crew the first time a ship went out for gunnery drill after a long period in port or at sea without firing. After the start of the war, however, it was seldom they had even one. In twenty months on the Pacific I saw only one man become hysterical either during gunnery drill or in actual combat; and he did not break until after several hours of firing.

The Northampton's first salvo was over and wide, and ours was little better. Our second salvo was nearer and then the other eight were right on, as perfect a firing practice as ever I saw. None of the splashes were more than 3 mils off the target. Most of them threw up spray over the target itself.

"She's a left-handed ship in a lot of ways," Bob screamed against the wind whistling around our ears, "but she can certainly do the thing that counts, fire those guns."

Which was a good thing. For in the months ahead the old Swayback Maru was destined to do more fighting, and do it more effectively than any other heavy cruiser in the fleet.

After gunnery drill Bob and I were assigned our rooms and settled down for the many weeks ahead. Bob, as he had on the previous trip, moved in with Commander Church Chappell ("His mother must have had a sense of humor when she named him," Bob chuckled). Church was the navigator and, like the captain, slept in an emergency cabin on the bridge when the ship was at sea. I moved in with Ensigns Blum, Ware, and Kotencamp. It was a room designed only for two, and the spare bunks were so placed that a fat man would never have been able to negotiate the narrow passageway to the wash basin near the outer bulkhead. Fortunately, we were all slim. Being below decks, without portholes, it was always nighttime down there. We lived in a world of electric lights, white and blue.

Dick Blum and Chuck Ware were watch officers and had to stand one-in-four, that is, every fourth watch of four hours. "Cotton" Kotencamp and I were the "passengers." Cotton was a flier, but the weather was so rough most of the time on that trip that the cruiser's planes seldom were sent out. When they did fly, they were used for antisubmarine patrol and, in case of bombardment, such as at Wotje and Wake, as spotters for the guns.

The watch-standing ensigns were considerable of a trial to Cotton and me. One or the other always seemed to have the mid-watch, from midnight to 4 A.M., and the messengers who came down from the bridge to call them always had to arouse the three of us who didn't have the watch, before finding the right man. Then, after a night watch, one of them always was in his sack during the day when Cotton and I were wide-eyed and wakeful. Having no watches to stand, we always had all night in, every night.

Considering the cramped conditions under which the sailors live—officers and enlisted men alike—it is a continuous marvel how they manage to stand each other and get along so well together. Not that there were ever any hard feelings in Room 7. By some strange alchemy we all got along like fleas on a dog.

The most pleasant part of a day at sea is the dinner hour in the evening. The excellent food, excellently cooked on most ships, is part of it. But it is more than that. As in civilian life, it marked the end of another day's work. In the early days of the war, when old formalities still hung on, everyone changed from the working khaki of the day to more formal blues or whites. The white tablecloth, gleaming silver, gold braid of the uniforms and brilliantly colored campaign ribbons made each dinner hour a festive occasion.

The food at sea is something to make the mouth of a ration-harassed civilian drool. T-bone steaks that covered half the plate, filet mignons that fairly fell to pieces, all the butter you could eat, fresh salads the first few days out and on some ships every day, ice cream and cake for dessert. Have it served by an attentive colored boy with no barrier to seconds, and you have a simulation of a gastronomic paradise. And all that for an average through the fleet of a dollar-a-day mess bill for the officers. The men, eating only a trifle less sumptuously, pay nothing. The officers have to buy their own food. The low cost is explained by the fact that the officers' mess has no pay roll to meet, since the officers' cooks and the mess boys who prepare and serve the food are regularly enlisted men, and the mess buys from the ship's stores, which means at wholesale.

The second day at sea was Sunday. Except for church services in the morning, the day means little in ship's routine at sea. Certain activities, such as painting, scraping and various training classes, are suspended, but the same watches are kept, the usual cleaning is done, and gunnery practice goes on as usual.

Captain Zacharias went on the loud speaker after church to tell the crew our mission. He explained that it "probably will be the same as last time [the attack on Wotje], an attack on the Marshalls."

At the time I thought it unduly secretive on his part not to tell the exact objective, which I heard rumored ashore was to be Eniwetok, a Japanese base on the western fringe of the Marshalls, southwest of Wake.

His caution, however, was proved to be well-founded. A day or two later plans had to be changed and the force received its new orders, which were to attack Wake only.

I heard later that the original plan had been for the Enterprise group under Admiral Halsey to hit Eniwetok one morning and Wake the next, on the way back home, while the Yorktown task force, which had left Pearl Harbor a few days after we did, was to strike elsewhere in the Marshalls. Grounding of a transport on Canton Island while unloading troops and supplies there made it necessary to use the Yorktown force to screen her while salvaging attempts were made.

We had only three operating carriers in the Pacific at the time

—the Lexington was the other—and when some unexpected incident occurred, like the grounding of the transport, plans had to be quickly changed to meet the new emergency. Torpedoing of the oiler Neches in mid-January, after the Lexington had set out on a mission, caused the cancellation of those plans. It seemed as though not only time but the gods were on the side of the Japanese in those early, desperate days.

That Sunday, as the force forged on west, brought the news of the fall of Singapore. By that time, however, bad news of the war in the Pacific had become so common that one more disaster seemed no more than was to be expected. As I remember it, there was little discussion of the British surrender even in the wardroom, where the gloomy strategic picture was realized more vividly than in the crew's quarters.

There was too much to do aboard ship to worry long about disasters elsewhere.

In addition to keeping the ship going—an enormous housekeeping job whose problems are complicated by the corrosive salt air—preparing for action and then fighting it, each ship in the fleet also was a great training school. Classes were held every day in various subjects, from operation of a lathe to construction of a monkey's fist, the weighted knot at the end of the heaving lines and signal halyards.

Every day, too, there were various battle drills, and the planes from the carrier were off on some training operation every day the weather was favorable for flying. The third day out, February 16, our cruiser went off from the force and streamed a target three hundred yards astern, at which the dive bombers and fighters made several practice runs.

The fantail was crowded the first afternoon of such practice, everyone not on watch going out to watch the show. Everything except the bombs was on a strictly war basis. The squadrons would climb from the carrier to attack altitude, and then, taking advantage of every wisp of cloud, would come screaming down at the cloth target in a simulation that was so real it made the hair rise on the back of the neck. They dropped small practice bombs that burst with realistic flash as they hit the water. One day one of the planes put its bomb right on the small target, only 6 feet square, tearing it to bits.

Although sometimes the planes would tow a target at which our gunners would shoot in the nearest thing that could be devised to simulate actual conditions, most of our antiaircraft gunnery, especially that of the 5.20-caliber AA rifles with which many of the ships then were equipped, was practice firing at bursts fired from another ship.

Casey, who was something of an expert on the inadequacy of antiaircraft fire to stop a plane attack—he had lived through the great London blitz of September, 1940—nearly fell off the searchlight platform when the first shell from our cruiser exploded right on the edge of the target burst fired by the carrier. When several more exploded within lethal range, he was almost speechless.

"I only hope they do that well when the Japanese planes come along," he said fervently.

Two days later, on the 18th, occurred one of those accidents that can be more depressing than a major disaster.

The weather turned sour after the carrier had launched her afternoon search planes. When the hour came for recovery one was missing, a torpedo bomber with three men aboard. The carrier sent up a great cloud of smoke from her stack, hopeful that it might serve as a signal to guide the wandering pilot home. It was obvious, however, that the smoke would be of little value. A strong wind was blowing, that dissipated the smoke almost before it had cleared the stack, and the low overcast made it doubtful that what remained could be seen for any great distance.

Just before he went down into the sea the pilot opened up briefly on his radio to report his difficulty and allow the ship to get an approximate bearing on his position.

Whether through accident or design, one of the men in the missing plane forgot to throw the switch which would shift their circuit from the broadcast band to the interphone, and radiomen, straining their ears on all the ships in the fleet, heard them discussing what they would do.

"I've still got some gas left," we heard the pilot say. "A power landing will be safer than a dead stick. Do you think we should go down now or shall we keep on looking for the ship?"

"Let's keep on going as long as we can," we heard the answer.

But it wasn't long before the pilot came on the air again, checking on his two men to be sure they were ready to climb out, and telling them, "I'm going down now. Hold on to your hat."

After that silence.

It is a terrific responsibility that descends on the commander of a force at sea when an accident like that occurs. It is one he can delegate to no one else. A man must feel like God.

In the larger view of the war, one plane and three men were of little consequence. Yet it is one of the heartening things about our war effort, that everywhere we have operated on the principle that no man's life shall be sacrificed unnecessarily.

There were plenty of reasons for not turning back for an attempted rescue. The plane was down fifty miles astern of the force, which meant that nine ships, with six thousand men aboard, would have to go a hundred miles out of their way to attempt a problematical rescue. The sea was making up, and there was a very good chance none of the men in the plane had survived the landing on the rough water. Too, it might well have been that some Japanese radio operator had been listening in just at that time on that circuit, getting bearings as had our ships, and a submarine might have been close enough to keep a rendezvous.

Down off the Marshalls, twenty days before, three other men off the Enterprise had gone down under similar circumstances. A search had failed to find them, and the force had gone on.

We didn't know it then but these three, Dixon, Pastula, and Aldrich, were to live one of the great sagas of the sea, survive thirty-four days in their little rubber boat, and land safely at Danger Island.

All eyes on our bridge were on the Enterprise, waiting tensely for the decision. It was not long in coming. Up to her yardarm whipped the colored signal flags that ordered a change of course to take the force back through the approximate position of the lost plane. There was an almost audible sigh of relief.

Never was a maneuver more smartly executed. The nine ships, as though every man had been anxiously waiting for the order that was given, swung in great circles and headed back for the rescue attempt.

A thin, cold rain fell through the early evening, but at 11 o'clock, when we were at the estimated position of the little bobbing raft with the three men, the skies had cleared and the stars were out.

Halsey had ordered the force into a scouting line, so that the ships were spread over several miles of ocean. As we steamed slowly through the night every vessel turned on its battle and running lights.

Men who otherwise would have been below in their bunks, resting for their watches ahead, lined the rails, straining their eyes through the darkness for the possible pin point of a flashlight beam, or the cry down the wind that would mark the position of the little bobbing rubber boat.

For fifteen minutes we steamed slowly along. No flashing light was seen. There was no sound save the sigh of the wind. The ships' lights blinked out one by one, and over the force dropped the blackness of night.

This is a story with a happy ending. At dawn the next day Admiral Halsey launched a special search group to take one more look for the missing men. In mid-morning one of the planes came barreling back to drop a message on the carrier announcing he had found the men. A destroyer was sent at full speed to pick them up.

We learned later that the missing pilot was Ensign Tom

Eversole. When the search plane had found him it had swooped low to drop smoke bombs to mark his position for the other planes and the rescue vessel. Despite his relief at being rescued he was sore about the nearness to the rubber raft with which the smoke bombs had fallen.

"Sit out there all night in the cold and then you have to try to knock my head off," he told the culprit. "Fine thing."

Eversole had quite a time rounding up his shirts. The fliers, who never kid themselves about how long are their chances of life, had made a pact that the shirts of those who didn't come back were to be divided, khaki shirts being hard to get at that time in Pearl Harbor. They had marked Tom off the list and had divided his shirts.

The three men in the little raft never saw the fleet the night before, as it steamed past them lighted up like a Christmas tree.

February 22, our eighth day at sea, we rendezvoused with a fleet oiler and refilled our tanks.

Refueling at sea is a task the United States Navy has, through long practice, refined to a science. Other navies use similar procedures to ours but none of the rest, including the Japanese, ever have done it so many times as have our ships. The vast distances of the Pacific make it necessary.

With the tanker steering a steady course, the ships to be refueled—one on either side—come up astern, send over the lines, and then, on great booms, swing the big fuel hoses across. Tenuously joined by ten-inch manila lines, they steam abreast for an hour or more while the pumps send the heavy fuel oil surging from the oiler's great tanks into the smaller fuel storage spaces of the combatant ships.

While the oil is being pumped other lines are rigged, across which mail, provisions, and sometimes even spare machine parts are hauled in big canvas sacks. It is possible for a ship to keep fully fueled and provisioned for months at a time without ever going near a port. In the early days of the war, when secrecy as to our fleet position was of the utmost importance, task forces sometimes stayed at sea for weeks without ever even coming in sight of land.

When the sea is rough there is the danger of the two ships being thrown together, with serious consequences. I have seen dozens of such refuelings in fair weather and foul weather, by day and by night, and never yet have I seen two ships even touch their sides. It is a marvel of teamwork and hairline calculation.

An odd accident occurred during our first refueling. A ship's baker, wandering topside for a breath of air and to watch the refueling, came out of a hatch just as a line was being shot over from the tanker. The line is attached to a long brass rod, the diameter of a .45-caliber slug. The slug then is shot out of a gun, somewhat like a sawed-off shotgun, by a small powder charge. It trails the light line behind it. The slug travels with considerable velocity, since the carry is sometimes for a hundred feet or more, and there were strict rules that it always be fired into the air at an angle of forty-five degrees to avoid hitting anyone on another ship. In his haste in a rough sea to make a connection, the man firing the gun from the tanker aimed it to pass through a passageway just aft of the wardroom.

The baker and the bullet arrived in the passageway at the same time. The line-carrying slug struck him in the face just to the left of his nose. It passed on through his mouth and out the back of his neck, spearing him like a fish. A sailor had to cut the line on either side of the boy's head to free him from the slug and the long snake of line to which it was attached. Fully conscious, the boy walked down two decks to the sick bay (navy slang for the ship's hospital) for treatment.

For several days it was touch and go whether he would survive but when we pulled into Pearl Harbor two and a half weeks later, the youngster was topside asking if he could go ashore. Dr. Hayes was as proud as if he had given birth to the boy, and took him ashore to show the other doctors.

Dr. Hayes explained that the slug, being blunt-nosed, had

pushed its way through the network of veins and arteries in the back of the mouth and the neck without cutting many of them. The roof of the boy's mouth was fractured, several teeth and part of his upper jaw bone were knocked out, and he had a very sore neck, but there was nothing that could not be repaired; it probably has been long before this.

While all this was going on up north of Wake, three thousand miles to the south a young navy lieutenant, just a year out of flight school, was performing the greatest single aerial exploit of our war.

CHAPTER 4

The Remarkable
Mr. O'Hare

THE LEXINGTON, biggest and best of our aircraft carriers, was churning along through Coral Sea bound for Rabaul.

She was the flagship of Vice Admiral Wilson Brown. With her escort of heavy cruisers and destroyers, she was going in to give a pasting to the newly established Japanese base on New Britain.

It was February 20. The war was two and a half months old. The Lexington still was looking for her first action. During most of those two and a half months she had been at sea, doing a constant patrol up and down and around and around west and south and north of Pearl Harbor. Her fliers were so sick of flying they could spit a hole in the ocean.

There had been no announcement to the crew of the mission, but everyone knew they were getting into hot waters. The increased speed of the ship indicated they weren't too far away.

The course was northwest toward St. George Channel, separating New Britain from New Ireland.

Up in Flag Plot, Lieutenant "Red" Gill, one of the many football-playing Gills from the University of California, and his aides were busy plotting in various air search groups from the Lex who were out scanning sea and sky some two hundred miles ahead and on either side for enemy planes or ships.

Then came a report that nine enemy bombers were coming in from the direction of Bougainville. "Sound general quarters." Through the big carrier—thirty-five thousand tons of steel and aluminum, driving engines, big electric dynamos, cavernous airplane hangar, and officer and crew quarters—sounded the gong, supplemented by announcement over the loud speaker. On the flight deck the motors of the fighters sputtered and then roared into life. Bright-colored flags passed the word to the other ships. The Lex turned into the wind and started launching planes.

Except in cases of utmost emergency, when an attack group from an enemy carrier is coming in, or the ship is in extremis, some fighters are always held in reserve. This day on the reserve list happened to be a stocky, dark-haired young man from St. Louis, Lieutenant (jg) Eddie H. O'Hare and his wingman. His shipmates called him "Butch."

A graduate of Annapolis, class of '37, O'Hare had put in for flight training and had graduated from Pensacola in 1940. He had come out to the fleet as an ensign and in due time had won his half stripe.

There was little to distinguish Butch from any other young man in uniform. He was not antisocial, but neither was he the life of the party. I had spent ten days on the Lex in January on a security patrol covering a convoy moving south. Even after I saw Butch in Pearl Harbor, following the Lexington's return, I didn't remember him, and I have a good memory for faces. Butch just wasn't the type to stand out in a crowd.

Lieutenant Commander John Thach, one of our leading fighter pilots, led the Lex's fighters against that first group.

[113

Attacking in pairs, our pilots began to knock them down.

"They burn satisfactorily," observed Commander Duckworth, the Lexington's air officer, as he watched first one, then another of the two-motored Mitsubishi '97's fall flaming into the sea. Only three of the first flight reached bomb-dropping position, and Captain Frederick (Ted) Sherman avoided them all by swinging his ship.

It was the first fight the Lexington fliers had been in, and forgetting that other enemy bombers might be on the way, our fighter pilots took off in full cry after the three survivors that had dropped their bombs and now were headed for home. All three were shot down, one after a chase of one hundred miles.

Now it was O'Hare's turn to go up. The other fighters were running short of gasoline and ammunition. He climbed into his plane, waited for the thumbs up from his mechanic, and the signal from the launching officer; then pushed his throttle forward and flew off the deck to put on the greatest one-man aerial show of the war.

O'Hare and his wingman, who missed his share of immortality when his guns jammed and he had to drop out of the fight, had hardly reached altitude over the carrier when word came that another flight of nine enemy planes was approaching and to "go get them."

The Lexington's pilots were flying the new Grumman Wildcats, the stubby-winged little fellows that only then were beginning to come out to the fleet (only eight were built the month before we got into the war) and which it is no exaggeration to say did more than any other one single instrument of war to save the day for the United States in the Pacific.

Twelve miles from the carrier, at twelve thousand feet, O'Hare and his wingman found the Japanese. There were nine of them again, flying in a V of V's.

The Mitsubishi '97 is no bargain to fight. It has wing and tail guns and a 20-millimeter cannon in the turret. Nine of them

114]

firing at once can throw up a curtain of lead a fighter plane is lucky to live through.

As O'Hare and his wingman closed in from above they each pressed the red button on the stick to test the guns. Butch's barked satisfactorily, shaking his plane with their recoil, but Bennett's jammed. He dropped back and headed for the carrier at full speed.

"I realized it was up to me to repulse them," O'Hare said. "There wasn't much else to do but go in shooting."

So he did.

There are many methods of approach in a plane attack—from dead ahead, which the fliers call "scissoring," or from dead astern, which was the most simple and carried the least danger, until all countries started putting in tail guns. The tactics our navy fliers were using were to approach at an angle from above and astern. It is the most difficult of all approaches, as the fighter must fire a deflection shot, that is, not at the plane but ahead of it. It is very much like skeet shooting, where the gunner must lead the target.

Swooping in at better than three hundred miles an hour, O'Hare swept past the Japanese bombers, firing as he went. The last two on the left side dropped out smoking.

Not waiting to see the results of his first shots, he swung on across the formation, regained his altitude and swooped down on the Tail-End Charlie on the right.

Up again and again a swoop, this time on the next man on the right side of the V.

No man ever had a more appreciative audience. From O'Hare's first contact with the big dun-colored, two-motored enemy bombers twelve miles out, the whole action was in full view of the fleet, which was charging along at flank speed. It was action at better than three miles a minute, as the Japanese planes were making two hundred knots, which is roughly two hundred and twenty-five miles an hour.

Six times the lone American plane, only a speck against the

blue sky that arches over the Coral Sea, swooped on the melting enemy column. Five of the nine planes were down before they were within bombing distance. Observers on the ship said three of them were falling in flames at one time. The crew on the Lexington were shouting: "He's got one," then, "He's got another." Everyone was in a frenzy. Even after the ship's anti-aircraft had opened up on the enemy, the little snub-winged fighter with the begoggled, grim-faced youngster at the stick swooped in for one more pass. The sixth plane began to smoke but continued its run and dropped its bombs ineffectually. As it turned to limp away for home Johnny Thach, who had re-armed, refueled and again taken off from the carrier, caught it and shot it down.

The God of Battles was riding the Wildcat with Butch O'Hare that day. Someone may equal the feat before this war is over, but no one will surpass it, for this reason:

O'Hare's plane carried four .50-caliber machine guns, two in each wing. He had three hundred rounds of ammunition for each, about forty seconds of shooting.

Anyone who has pressed the trigger on a machine gun knows what an irresistible impulse there is to keep on the pressure until the feed line is exhausted. What greater impulse there must be when the target is a live enemy, not just a moving piece of canvas.

Yet here was one lone flier, in his first fight, with nine enemy planes boring in to attack his ship, the whole responsibility of aerial defense on his shoulders—and he conserved his ammunition so carefully that he was able to shoot down five of the nine planes and damage a sixth. He was making every bullet count.

O'Hare knew he couldn't afford to miss, so he was closing each time to about one hundred yards on what he called "my objective" before pressing the button. That way he was getting a maximum spread from his four guns, and doing a maximum amount of damage. None of the Japanese planes floated long enough for anyone to count the bullet holes, but it wouldn't have been surprising to find in each plane its exact share of the total. Never did heart and hand synchronize more perfectly.

O'Hare was telling his story in the lounge of the BOQ (Bachelor Officers' Quarters) in Pearl Harbor.

"What system of attack did you use?" he was asked.

"Fire till they catch fire," said "Butch."

And what did he think about when he found himself up there alone with the nine enemy bombers and his wingman dropping out with jammed guns?

"You really haven't any choice," said O'Hare. "You've got to go in."

Much has been written and said about the fanatical bravery of the Japanese. Eight hundred of them charged the army line on Attu and, the charge spent, committed suicide. Japanese officers on Guadalcanal ran at machine gun positions, screaming and waving their Samurai swords. That is fanatical insanity. Is it any wonder that the American fliers, people like Mr. O'Hare of St. Louis, with their calculated bravery, have proved themselves a match for the little buck-toothed men who think their emperor a god, and dying for him a privilege? Our fliers have no emperor to die for. They want to live to enjoy the country they are fighting to protect.

When the story of O'Hare's exploit was told he was detached from his ship and ordered to Washington. He probably was truthful when he told friends there he didn't know why he had been called home. He soon found out. In the President's office in the executive wing of the White House Mr. Roosevelt handed to O'Hare's pretty wife the highest-prized decoration for valor this country can bestow, the Congressional Medal of Honor, and asked her to put it around her husband's neck.

"For valor, above and beyond the call of duty," the President said.

Lieutenant (jg) O'Hare was advanced thirty numbers in permanent grade, received a temporary commission as a Lieutenant Commander, with a fighter squadron of his own, and was sent back to the Pacific.

Now Butch is gone.

A great flier and a very brave man died when Lieutenant Commander O'Hare fought his last battle off the Marshall Islands the night of November 26, 1943. He disappeared while protecting his ship from an enemy torpedo plane attack.

CHAPTER 5

Wake Island Dead Ahead

AFTER REFUELING, the Halsey task force pushed on west and north. The weather was cold and the sea rough. The name "Pacific" applies to the greatest of oceans only if you are speaking of that part of it which lies between latitudes 25 degrees North and 25 degrees South. Beyond those latitudes, in both directions, it is anything but pacific.

New orders had been received. The plan now was to attack Wake alone, with the two cruisers and two of the six destroyers going in to bombard. The carrier with its destroyer escort would lay off some seventy-five to one hundred miles and send in its planes.

After we had left Pearl Harbor an army bomber had flown over Wake and secured some excellent photographs. These were developed and flown out to the task force by a navy patrol bomber from Midway. Dropped on the carrier's deck, they were sorted and distributed to the bombarding ships by one of the destroyers.

In this maneuver the destroyer comes up astern of the ship to which it is to deliver the official mail, called "guard mail" by the navy, shoots a line across to the receiving ship's after deck,

118]

THE ODDS WERE NINE TO ONE

Lieut. Commander Eddie H. (Butch) O'Hare (left) and his squadron leader, Lieut. Comdr. Johnny Thach, discussing the action off Bougainville, the Solomons, February 20, 1942, when Butch took on singlehanded in his Grumman Wildcat nine two-motored Japanese bombers, shot down five of them and damaged a sixth. Twenty-one months later, then leading his own squadron and holder of the Congressional Medal of Honor, Lieut. Comdr. O'Hare went down in a night battle with Japanese planes off the Marshalls obeying his own simple creed when sighting the enemy to "go in shooting."

A LADY TO THE LAST

The aircraft carrier Lexington in her death throes May 8, 1942, after a dive-bombing and torpedo plane attack by the Japanese in the closing phase of the Battle of the Coral Sea. The Lex's skipper, Captain Ted Sherman (now a Rear Admiral), was still aboard her when this picture was taken. An American destroyer can be seen nosing in toward the doomed ship to pick up survivors.

THE CORAL SEA, MAY 7, 1942

An American plane-borne torpedo has just crashed into the side of a Japanese aircraft carrier of the Ryukaku class, helping complete destruction already done by dive bombers and other torpedo planes. She sank soon after this photograph was taken, literally torn apart by ten torpedo hits and twelve to fifty bombs on her flight deck.

and sends across the mail on a breeches buoy arrangement of lines. It takes only a few minutes, during which the two ships maneuver at the same speed.

The aerial photographs, showing enemy gun installations and fuel and ammunition dumps, were closely studied by the fliers and gunnery officers.

Wake atoll is composed of three islands, Wake, Peale, and Wilkes, which form a rough letter V with Wake as the base. The islands lie roughly at a southeast-northwest angle, with the base to the southeast. The open end, to the northwest, between the tips of Wilkes and Peale Islands, is crossed by a coral reef that is out of water at low tide.

The carrier planes were to attack the installations on Wake and Wilkes and any ships inside the lagoon, or off shore. The two cruisers and two destroyers assigned to do the bombarding were to give their attention to Peale, coming in from the west for their firing run up the island. On Peale was the seaplane ramp built several years before by Pan American Airways in inaugurating its trans-Pacific air route. Still standing, too, were the original Pan American buildings. The Japanese had installed a power plant and ammunition and fuel dumps on the island.

Studying the maps laid out on the green cloth of the wardroom table and noting the small size of the islands and lack of cover, it was hard to conceive how the small garrison of marines and navy men we had on the island at the start of the war could have held out as long as they did—fourteen days—against the Japanese.

Although by now it was well known by all hands that Wake was the objective, no formal announcement had been made. Captain Zacharias waited until the next day for that, by which time we were headed south for the objective. First meeting his officers in the wardroom, he explained in detail to them the plan of attack.

It might be explained here that the captain of a combatant

ship at sea has little contact with any of his officers and crew. His quarters are on the upper decks near those of the senior officers, the heads of departments such as the chief engineer, the executive officer, the gun boss, the surgeon, the supply officer, the communications officer, and the navigator. He eats alone, except when he invites one of the officers to his mess, and only rarely does he go to the wardroom, the officers' messing and living space.

The captain is always available to anyone who has business to take up with him, and of course, is in contact with the watch officers, the navigator and the communications officer on the bridge, which is his home at sea.

The presence of the captain in the wardroom, then, was a special event. It had been heralded over the loud speaker, which the sailors called "Donald Duck," in a characteristic announcement.

"Now here it is," the announcer said; "all officers not on watch will meet in the wardroom at ten hundred hours for a conference with the captain."

Promptly at 10 A.M. Captain Zach, ducking his head to clear the low door, strode into the wardroom, where everyone immediately jumped to attention.

"Carry on," he said, smiling, as he took a seat at the head of the table.

"Since I last spoke to you," he began with no further preliminaries, "there has been a further change of plans. As it now stands we are going to carry out the same operations against Wake as we did against Wotje. We will have more planes here than we did at Wotje [where the Enterprise split her air group to strike simultaneously at four Japanese bases]. Our own planes will be launched an hour before sunrise. Tonight, an hour before sunset, rig them out ready for launching.

"As you know, we are going south now and should get better weather all the time.

"I don't anticipate much opposition from the air, but we must be prepared for it. I hope we will be as successful as our ships were yesterday at Bali where, first reports indicate, we sank or badly damaged between seventeen and thirty-five enemy ships. [The official communiqué claimed only two Japanese destroyers sunk.]

"I'll make an announcement to the crew of our plans at 1330 [1:30 P.M.]."

There were a few questions about details of the bombardment, and then he rose to go. The whole conference had not lasted fifteen minutes.

He paused for one more word.

"This is a routine matter," he said. "Let's go about it without any excitement."

That morning, as we bored south at around twenty knots, with action distant only twice around the clock, the atmosphere of the ship had become tense. Captain Zach's matter-of-fact analysis of the situation, however, and the easy way in which he handled himself—he was one of the best down-to-earth psychologists I have ever met—the tension was gone.

Some of the officers returned to their study of the Wake maps, while others resumed interrupted chess or acey-ducey games.

Ted Kobey, the chief engineer, seized this opportunity to talk me into a tour of his domain below decks. All chief engineers are inordinately proud of their steam-heated, stinking engine rooms, or perhaps it's just that they are miserable and want company. Whatever the reason, they are never happier than when escorting some hapless visitor through their labyrinth of hot pipes, oily driving rods and slippery gratings.

Mr. Kobey's conducted tours always were well stage-managed. This day he had arranged a tryout of a new asbestos suit his engineers had made. It was built to resist live steam, to enable a rescuer to enter an engine room or fireroom where steam lines had been broken. It really worked, although the water tender who donned it and allowed live steam to be shot at him said the bald spot on his head "felt like it had been parboiled."

Ted and Staff Crowley also were working on a small evaporator for shipwrecked aviators, to weigh only four or five pounds. The evaporator was designed to provide potable water for a week for a man on a rubber raft, using a small can of canned heat as the energizing agent. It was based on the principle of expansion of gases. It didn't work on the first trial.

The steam-heated tour required most of the afternoon. The sun was setting as we climbed back to the chill air of the main deck.

As darkness fell, the cruisers parted company with the carrier and drove on through the night, grim, gray shapes on a grim, gray ocean, toward dawn and the attack.

CHAPTER 6

Hell on Wake

VENUS HUNG like a small moon in the eastern sky as the two carriers and two destroyers drove in on Wake.

The ships had run south most of the night, but now they were on the Wake latitude and heading almost due east. The speed had been increased. Occasionally the clipper bow of the Salt Lake City would cut the top off a wave and send white spray spattering against the Number One turret.

Going from the bright lights of the wardroom to the darkness of the upper decks, it was like playing blind man's bluff to find ladders that led to the bridge. After the eyes became accustomed to the darkness, however, it was surprisingly light.

Breakfast had been like that of any other morning, except earlier and a bit more hurried. Few lingered for a third cup of coffee. Everyone was anxious to get to his post. The mess boys,

122]

too, were in a hurry. They had to get breakfast served, the rugs rolled up, the tables pushed back and the wardroom readied as an emergency dressing station before they responded to general quarters and took their battle station in the magazines.

Everyone appeared to have slept well and to have a hearty appetite. I have heard and read a lot about prebattle strain, but I have seen few signs of it among the officers and crews of the ships I have ridden. An occasional strained face, outward evidence of taut nerves, has been the exception that proved the rule. Perhaps it is because navy men are so much under the threat of attack, from submarines or aircraft, whenever they leave port in a war area, that familiarity has bred contempt. The sea always is uneasy. The men who ride it are calm.

Despite the warm latitudes in which we now were running, only 18 degrees north of the equator, it was chilly on the small platform just above the bridge which Casey and I had selected as our battle station. We were making around twenty-five knots into a wind that was almost as strong. We pulled our kapok life jackets about our necks and stood behind the big ship's bell to let it break the wind for us.

All was ordered confusion on the decks below. Men were moving to battle stations. Captain Zacharias, his tall form muffled in a blue great coat, was pacing up and down the after end of the bridge.

Two of the ship's four scouting planes were on the catapults. As the light increased, their motors were started, spitting blue flame from the exhaust pipes.

The horizon became a distinct line marking where sea and sky met, and it became obvious it was to be a late sunrise. A bank of clouds spread all along the eastern horizon.

There was a flash of flame from the cruiser ahead. Above the roar of the plane motors and the sigh of the big blowers sucking air down to the firerooms, we heard a signalman yell, "Northampton launched her first plane, sir."

"Very well," said the captain, then to the yeoman following

him around the deck with the telephone line, "Stand by to launch two planes."

The motors of our two planes roared even louder against the wind. The plane crews were only black shadows against the lighter gray of the ship and the planes. They moved around, making last minute checks. Then the flash of the explosive charge and the starboard plane, with Staff Crowley at the controls, shot off the catapult and winged its way toward the lightening eastern sky. The starboard catapult was swung in, the port one swung out, and swish, away went Lieutenant Cheney. The Northampton, meanwhile, had launched all four of her planes and soon the six from the two ships joined up and started circling the formation, gaining altitude.

The sky turned from black to purple to blue to pink, and soon long, golden streamers shot up across the sky from behind the low cloud bank that still hung along the eastern horizon.

It was impossible to light a cigarette in the wind of the open platform. I was just preparing to duck under the bell, which was fine for that purpose but a confounded nuisance otherwise on the small platform, it was so large, when there were several flashes of fire from the destroyer and cruiser ahead of us and, a few seconds later, a series of black shell bursts high and to the north.

"What's that?" I yelled, inanely.

"Enemy planes," Bob yelled back, noting the time in his notebook—7:18.

We swept the area of the bursts with our glasses, but could see nothing, so I went ahead with the cigarette lighting. It had been an hour since the last one below decks. Besides, weren't the Enterprise planes supposed to be already pasting the atoll? Perhaps we had fired at some of them by mistake.

I was just drawing in the first few satisfying drags from the cigarette when I saw my first enemy plane. It was just a black dot against the golden eastern sky, coming down in a steep glide. Our own 5-inchers barked into action.

The Salt Lake City wasn't the Japanese target. For some reason, probably because it was difficult to estimate the size of the ships from eight thousand or nine thousand feet, the enemy flier picked out the leading destroyer. All the ships of the force were firing at him, but the bursts were all behind or to one side of the hurtling black dot that swept down to fifteen hundred feet, then leveled out and zoomed back up again. A geyser of water shot up near the bow of the can. It had been much too close for comfort.

The four ships of our force were maneuvering radically, swinging first right, then left, to discommode the diving planes as much as possible. At 7:30 one of the enemy fliers dived on the Northampton, but he missed her by a wider margin than his fellow pilot had missed the can. At 7:35 a third one dived, but he pulled out at two thousand feet or higher, and his bomb was far wide of the mark.

One of our signalmen thought the Northampton's guns had hit one of the Japanese planes and that it had exploded in the air. By that time, however, the sun had cleared the cloud bank and was shining directly in our eyes, so it was difficult to tell whether the black blob of smoke marked the death of an enemy plane or merely was where two antiaircraft shells had taken off simultaneously. The chief quartermaster, for whom the captain had secured a camera, snapped a picture which could be interpreted either way.

We had gotten a good look at the enemy planes as they dive-bombed the other ships, and it was agreed they were float-type fighters. They appeared to be carrying only hundred-pound bombs.

Our own planes, meanwhile, had disappeared to the east.

The force had gone up to flank speed when the enemy planes were sighted, and rapidly drew up to the firing course. At 7:45 the admiral, aboard the Northampton, gave the signal to open the shore bombardment. Wake was a dark pencil line along the horizon, seventeen thousand yards away.

[125

The first salvo of the 8-inch rifles almost shook Bob and me off our precarious perch. The guns were firing directly into the wind, which whipped the burning scraps of powder bags and the yellow smoke back into our faces.

The blazing early-morning sun so blinded the men in fire control that the gun boss waited until his first salvo had landed to check his range. It seemed like a long time, but it was only a few seconds, until there was a flash on shore—right on the target —and a great geyser of smoke and sand shot into the air. With this check against the range, the guns opened up in earnest.

Under the curtain of smoke now rising over Wake from the effects of our shells and the bombs of the Enterprise fliers, who had missed the atoll on the first sweep but now were over the islands, we could see the enemy shore batteries firing at the ships. At that distance the muzzle flashes looked like flashlights. The first enemy salvos were a thousand yards short of the two cruisers but were falling all around the two destroyers, which had closed the range to bring the island within easy reach of their 5-inch guns.

We continued to close, and soon our 5-inch dual-purpose batteries also opened up against the island. When all ten 8-inch rifles and the secondary batteries fired at the same time, their recoil seemed to push the big fourteen-thousand-ton cruiser sideways through the water, an impression that seemed to be borne out by another picture which the chief quartermaster took and which has been widely printed.

At 8:05 the cruisers as well as the destroyers were within range of the enemy shore batteries, three of which still were firing. Casey and I had counted eleven "flashlights" operating along the beach ten minutes before. Whether the others had been knocked out by the plane-and-ship bombardment or whether the gunners merely were blinded by the smoke rolling down over their positions we couldn't tell.

The three enemy batteries still operating were dropping shells all around the American ships, but without scoring any hits.

The shells were falling on either side of the Salt Lake City. Soon the admiral ordered a change of course that would put us outside their range.

Captain Cobb, in charge of the marine detachment aboard and an assistant aircraft defense officer, was searching the sky on the side away from the island, on the alert for enemy planes, when one enemy shell fell right through the field of vision of his glasses.

"The glasses brought it so close I thought it was coming down in my vest pocket," he said. It was a hundred yards over, as close as any of the enemy guns came to scoring a hit on our cruiser.

All hands were too busy watching the enemy-held positions to worry too much about the possibility of our ships being hit. All hell was raging on the atoll. A big explosion had followed the landing of one salvo, indicating a hit on an ammunition dump, we hoped, and then there was a string of explosions. These were great orange-colored blobs of flame, mushrooming two hundred feet or more in the air, and followed by clouds of black smoke. They seemed to be in a pattern, spaced some two hundred yards apart. The fliers later reported they came from gasoline tank cars, dispersed along a narrow-gauge railway paralleling the beach of Peale Island, against which the ship bombardment was directed.

At 8:20 the admiral turned his force away and headed northeast for the rendezvous with the carrier. The Salt Lake City had pumped twenty-five rounds, or two hundred and fifty shells, from her 8-inch rifles and as many more rounds from her secondary battery of 5-inch guns. It would seem to have been enough to have blasted everything above ground on the narrow sand-and-coral island.

As we retired, the three islands of the Wake atoll seemed to be on fire their entire length. There still must have been a lot of Japanese around, though, for we could see many enemy anti-aircraft bursts. It was an indication that the Enterprise fliers still were active.

The force received its last dive-bombing attack at 8:30, one of the float fighters diving to unload his light bomb at the trailing destroyer. It fell a hundred yards ahead of the can.

The guns had hardly ceased yammering at this invader when a lookout reported a large, unidentified plane paralleling our course. He had seen it pass between two large cloud formations. The antiaircraft batteries trained toward it, raising their short, ugly snouts in the air.

The clouds, which had formed since sunrise, hung only some three thousand feet above the ocean. Out of one of these, as we watched, came a flaming plane. Like a fiery comet it fell into the sea. Above it rose a column of oily black smoke, shot through with fire at its base. To one side an unburned section of wing fluttered down, twisting and turning like an autumn leaf in the wind.

A smaller plane shot out of the cloud after it, warily circled the pillar of smoke, then made off eastward.

"He was a Jap," a signalman chortled. "That last one was one of ours."

Two weeks later, in a hotel room in Honolulu, I heard the full story of the flaming plane. It was a big, four-motored Kawanishi, one of three that got off the water at Wake before the Enterprise fliers arrived to strafe and burn three of its fellows. Three of our fighters attacked. Lieutenant Commander Mc-Cuskey, skipper of Fighting Six, made the first run on the enemy bomber, setting one engine afire. Lieutenant Bayers made his pass and got a second motor. Then Lieutenant Roger Mehle went in. As he stopped firing and zoomed away for another run, the big enemy flying boat blew up. Chunks of metal as big as a man's fist were found imbedded in Mehle's Grumman Wildcat when he landed back on the carrier.

The pillar of smoke from the flaming Japanese plane was not yet out of sight when lookouts reported a small vessel broad on the starboard bow. A destroyer was sent over to take a look. Before she could get within identifying range, a group of our dive bombers sighted the four-hundred-ton Japanese patrol craft and started strafing it.

The destroyer went in cautiously, not certain how heavy armament the enemy ship carried. When it became evident that it would be a difficult job to sink the enemy vessel from a distance, since the sea was picking up and it made a bobbing, uncertain target, the destroyer closed and blasted it out of the water.

The brush with the enemy vessel had made the destroyer's gunners trigger-happy, and as the six seaplanes from the two cruisers came putt-putting out of a cloud directly ahead of the formation, she opened up on them. Identification was quick, happily, and she knocked off before any of them were hit, although several bursts were close enough to shake up the little two-seater biplanes.

Little time was wasted in picking up the planes, which landed on the water and taxied up alongside the ship, from where they were hoisted aboard by a crane. They had been in the air almost four hours and were running short of gasoline.

With our gooney birds aboard, everyone began to rest easier and Captain Zach ordered that hot coffee and sandwiches be sent to the gun crews. The ventilation system was reopened to pump some fresh air below decks, and sandwiches and coffee were set out in the wardroom for officers who could be spared.

It was only 9:30, but it seemed like twenty-four hours since breakfast, and food never was relished more than the somewhat slimy ham sandwiches.

Everyone was in high good humor. The job had been done, no one had been killed or even hurt. One of the youngsters on a 5-inch gun, sitting on the deck munching a sandwich and drinking hot, black coffee, grinned at Casey and me as we started below.

"Just like a picnic," he said. Which could have meant either the food or the firing. Perhaps both.

Staff Crowley, who had reported to the captain when he

came aboard from his plane, was in the wardroom almost as soon as we were. As usual Staff was bubbling over with information and good humor. He certainly took his war easy.

"Did you see those Japanese planes?" he asked. "Were they slick! One of them made a couple of passes at me. He was going so fast it seemed my old crate was standing still. I tried to flag him down so we could land and talk it over. I was willing to trade two SOC's for his ship." "SOC" is the official designation for the cruiser plane, Scout Observation Curtiss.

"My rear gunner scared the Japs after the second pass," Staff continued, "and may have hurt him some. The gunner said his bullets were going right in the guy's propeller. I was too busy getting out of his way to look."

Staff said the bombardment was accurate, he thought, and had knocked out most of the shore batteries. He and the other cruiser pilots all had carried bombs and had dropped them on the small dock in the lagoon, the place where the Pan American passengers formerly had landed. There were no ships inside.

"The carrier gang certainly was raising hell," Crowley reported, "strafing and bombing all three islands. There wasn't much antiaircraft, and I doubt if we lost any planes."

We learned later that only one failed to come back, a dive bomber piloted by a kid named Foreman. Other carrier pilots saw him going down, smoking. They thought he might have crash-landed in the sea or on the island and been captured.

The eating in the wardroom was to the point, but the talk was desultory. George O'Connell went to sleep in his chair, a half-filled coffee cup still in front of him. Staff Crowley and Dr. Hayes resumed their interminable game of acey-ducey, but the rest of us were gradually relapsing into somnolence when the loud speaker began to wheeze, and then came the captain's voice:

"We have sighted a vessel on the horizon. One of the destroyers has gone over to investigate."

Before you could say "Admiral Nimitz," the wardroom and

the crew's mess hall were deserted, as all hands scrambled back topside to see what was going on.

We had hardly hit the open deck before the destroyers opened fire, as though announcing "Investigation completed. He's a Jap."

So there would be no charge of favoritism, the admiral, this time, had sent another destroyer to investigate. She wasted little time, opening on the Japanese patrol boat—similar in size and armament to the one sunk two hours before—from about five-thousand yards and closing the range at high speed. One of the first shots hit the enemy vessel amidships. A quartermaster with a long glass said he could see men going over the fantail.

The little Japanese ship was wallowing, badly hurt, as the cruisers and the other destroyer swept on past. The original destroyer was circling carefully, like a terrier walking stiff-legged around a cat.

A signal hoist was two-blocked on the can and one of our signalmen read it off. Addressed to the admiral on the Northampton, it said: "Request permission to pick up survivors."

"Permission granted," came the answer.

From the Salt Lake City bridge we saw the destroyer cruise carefully through the spot where we last had seen the enemy patrol vessel and then come to almost a stop as she sighted five bobbing heads in the water.

It was only then I noticed the big plane, off in the clouds some fifteen-thousand yards away, cruising slowly up and down the course of the American force.

"It's a Kawanishi," Lieutenant John Boland volunteered. "He's been shadowing us for an hour. We can hear him sending the letter 'k' over and over. I suppose he's trying to guide a bomber strike from the Marshalls to our position."

The admiral had broken radio silence to tell the carrier about our unwelcome visitor and ask for some fighters to knock him down. There was nothing our force could do about it. Our planes had no business tangling with a well armed four-motored patrol bomber, and he stayed well out of range of our antiaircraft guns.

The destroyer, intent on rescuing the survivors of the Japanese patrol vessel, paid no heed to the Japanese bomber, which finally made a run on her and dropped a bomb from a high altitude, but without effect.

There was no criticism on the Salt Lake City of the act of the destroyer in risking herself to save five enemy sailors.

"Poor little bastards," said an officer compassionately as we watched through glasses. "They never had a chance. It was like a couple of Austins getting in the way of a fleet of 10-ton trucks. They must not have gotten the word from Wake that we were around, or else they didn't expect us to retire in this direction."

After the second patrol boat had been sunk, a modified Condition Three was set, with the main batteries secured but all antiaircraft guns manned. Luncheon was served as usual, and then those who were not on watch crawled into their bunks for a few hours' sleep.

The early morning clouds had cleared away and the day was sunny and warm. The decks were covered with sleeping men, to whom the sun was a welcome visitor, after ten days of storms and cold weather.

There was some concern on the bridge about the failure of the carrier planes to arrive and the continued presence of the snooper, who kept his vigil just outside the range of our guns, but elsewhere the ship quickly settled down to normal sea routine. It was as though the morning and the roar of the guns had never been.

As the hours passed with no enemy attack, even the captain began to doubt that one would be made.

"We apparently caught them completely by surprise," he said.

Full vigilance was maintained, as it always was, the captain dragging an armchair out of his emergency cabin and sitting there to keep a weather eye peeled at the western sky.

The sun was going down, a great golden ball, when the enemy planes, two of them, came.

They came from dead astern, right out of the sun, high and fast. They were almost at their bomb-dropping position when they were sighted. The captain and navigator saw them at almost the same time and Church, who had the deck, ordered full left rudder. Suddenly the 5-inch rifles began to crack and shellbursts blossomed behind the enemy planes.

Out of the bays of the two big bombers fourteen-thousand feet above us came four black specks that turned to silver as they dropped. Time seemed to stand still as they fell toward us. It was like a slow-motion picture.

Two marine gunners, leaning against their 1.1 quad-mount battery, unemotionally watched the bombs falling.

"Looks like they're going to hit," said one.

"Yeah, sure does," said the other.

The big ship was turning now, slowly. It soon became clear they were going to miss. They fell into the sea, to starboard and slightly astern.

"Damned good bombing," said Lieutenant Tate, one of the aviators. "He was right on. Lucky we were turning. Those eggs landed right where we would have been if the navigator hadn't ordered the rudder hard over. If you see them in time you always can evade the bombs of a high-flying plane. You see, the terminal velocity of these falling bombs is only five hundred feet a second. From fourteen thousand feet that makes it twenty-eight seconds for them to reach the target. If a ship is making thirty knots, which is better than a half-mile every minute, and if she turns just as the bombs are dropped [which is what he had done] she's a quarter of a mile away by the time the bombs hit. Dive bombing is the only answer against ships."

As the two enemy bombers, which apparently had gone unscathed through our antiaircraft fire, disappeared back the way they had come, the snooper also shoved off. Night came down quickly, as it always does in the lower latitudes, and all hands except the watch gave up the vigil on deck and went below for a late dinner.

There was a long discussion at dinner of bombing and anti-aircraft fire and detection devices.

Late that night, as I was taking a last walk around the bridge before turning in, I heard an amusing epilogue to the day's crowded events. It seems the chief petty officers had tuned their radio to a station that was rebroadcasting a speech by President Roosevelt.

"He had just come to the part where he said, 'We shall strike the enemy wherever and whenever we can find him,' " reported my informant, "when wham, wham, wham! those four Jap bombs lit right off our fantail. The damn radio nearly fell in my lap."

That speech probably was the most poorly timed of any the President ever made.

CHAPTER 7

Marcus Addenda

"Ever hear of an island called Marcus?" asked Ted Kobey two nights after the Wake attack as he, Commander Dolecek, Lieutenant Commander Byrd and I were playing bridge in the wardroom.

"No, why?" I answered.

"Just wondering," said Ted.

The game went on, with me wondering. (If I remember correctly, Ted and I were right in the middle of setting our opponents seven tricks at two clubs doubled. Mr. Byrd had opened his mouth at the wrong time.)

After the game, by means that must remain a military secret,

I ferreted out the meaning of Ted's cryptic question about Marcus.

Admiral Halsey had received a message telling him that if he considered it advisable he had Admiral Nimitz's permission to attack Marcus. There was nothing that Admiral Halsey liked better than an opportunity to attack a Japanese base. It was like asking a grizzled pit bulldog if he would like a nice pan of chopped meat.

We picked up the tanker the next day in what the men of the task forces had come to call "Halsey weather," that is, cold and stormy. Such weather is unpleasant but a good protection against detection. The sea was too high, however, to risk refueling unless it was necessary, so the admiral continued on a northeasterly course. Finally he found what he wanted, a fairly calm sea near a fog bank. If any "bandits," as enemy planes were called, came snooping around, he could run into the fog and lose them.

The force refueled without a hitch, and that night at sundown the Enterprise and two cruisers started southwest for the pinpoint Japanese island that isn't even charted in most popular atlases and which lies only nine hundred and ninety miles southeast of Tokyo.

"Sailing Directions for the Pacific," the official navy guide to such out-of-the-way places, revealed that Marcus was only of some seven hundred acres extent. What was there, no one had the faintest idea. The sailing directions indicated that the last American ship to visit Marcus was a survey vessel that had called back in the 1880's.

No one even pretended to like this job. There couldn't be much to destroy on Marcus; perhaps a radio direction-finding station, an emergency airfield, a few naval stores and buildings. We were going—a carrier and two cruisers—right into the backyard of the Japanese home fleet. There could be no preliminary air reconnaissance. It seemed like a lot of risk for a small objective.

Captain Zach was sure the strike at Marcus would be very upsetting to the Japanese.

"What if a Japanese task force came within a thousand miles of San Francisco?" he said.

He admitted that you couldn't win a war merely by scaring the enemy, but that conditions being what they were, it wouldn't do any harm to say "boo" once in a while. That was about all this raid would be.

The captain held his usual prebattle conference with his officers, explaining that this was to be solely an attack by planes, with the two cruisers remaining out with the carrier. That night he also told the crew of the plans, although not the objective, a reticence which I still don't understand, as nearly all of them already knew it.

"We have to accompany the carrier on a small job she has to do," was the way Captain Zach expressed it.

After leaving the tanker and the destroyer, which also left us with no guard against submarines, the three-ship force wasted little time, batting along toward Marcus at high speed. When you traveled with Halsey you moved fast. The cruisers acted as a plane guard when the carrier was recovering aircraft, the Northampton hauling one fighter pilot out of the water one morning without even slackening speed.

Early the morning of March 4 the force was within striking distance of Marcus. Squalls had been encountered during the night, but the sky was clearing as the Enterprise turned into the wind and sent her planes away. A great lunar rainbow arched across the storm clouds in the eastern sky as the first plane took off, a much revered symbol of good luck among the Polynesians. Such night phenomena are not uncommon in the Pacific, but there never was a more brilliant display than that morning.

The attack on Marcus was planned as a predawn strike, with the first planes dropping flares to illuminate the target for the dive bombers and torpedo planes, which were serving that day as horizontal bombers.

Over the attack circuit, the fliers could be heard gabbing away about the weather. There were some clouds, but the bright moonlight enabled them to keep formation easily. The air was clear over Marcus, and the raid went off like clockwork.

First evidence that our planes must be nearing the objective came from the Marcus radio station, which apparently began frantically calling any ships in the vicinity. Again Tojo had been caught with his kimono off.

A runway was found on the little island, and a hangar. If there were any enemy planes they must have been in the latter, which went up in a cloud of smoke and pyrotechnics. None got off the ground. The radio station, from which the Japanese probably had been taking bearings on any American radio sending in the North Pacific, went up in one burst as did storage tanks, ammunition dumps, troop barracks and antiaircraft positions. The airfield on the island indicated that Marcus may have been used as a ferry stop for planes en route from Tokyo to Wake or the Marshalls.

To make it more confusing for any Japanese ships or bases that might be listening in on the radio frequency they were using, the fliers blatted away as though the whole carrier strength of the navy was making the attack.

"Hornet group, attack," they ordered. And so on down the whole list—Saratoga, Lexington, Ranger, Yorktown and Wasp.

It must have caused momentary confusion, because Tokyo Rose announced the attack as having been made by a much larger group than actually participated, but not for long. Lieutenant Dale Hilton, and his radioman-rear gunner were forced down at sea only a few miles off Marcus after their plane was hit by AA fire. That night the Japanese knew the composition of the American force that had made the daring raid.

"I don't know how they got it out of them," one of Hilton's fellow fliers said. "We'd talked about what we would do if captured, and that information [names of the ships] would have been the last thing Hilton or Leaming, the gunner, would have told them."

The two American fliers had been seen to land their plane in the water and get out in their rubber boat. It was assumed the

Japanese had picked them up. Later, Lieutenant Hilton was quoted on the Tokyo radio, along with other war prisoners.

After the planes had been launched, there was nothing to do but listen on the attack circuit, keep a sharp lookout for any Japanese ships or planes, and wait.

At 7:45 A.M. the first planes began returning from the attack, and the Enterprise turned to pick them up. The wind had shifted meanwhile and was blowing directly out of the southwest, the direction of Marcus. There was nothing to do about that, so-o-o-o the force turned back and started running at high speed right for the enemy. That was a fine kettle of fish. Enemy traffic on the air indicated there were a lot of Japanese ships not too far away—and here we were, having to head right back for them instead of hightailing it the other way.

When a carrier group is returning from an air strike all hands start counting the returning planes. The first group back were fighters, and they seemed to be all right; then some torpedo planes, then eighteen dive bombers. There still were twelve dive bombers missing. Finally, at 8:20 they came over the horizon, flying high and fast. One, two, three, four, began the count. It went up to eleven, and then there were no more. One plane was missing; that was Hilton's, although we didn't know it then.

Never was a plane recovery watched more intently than was the Enterprise's that morning. A groan would go up whenever a flier made a bad approach and had to be waved off, to make another try.

"Come on, get those babies aboard," one of the signalmen said fervently, "and let's get the hell out of here."

Finally the Enterprise had all her eagles aboard and, with a fighter cover hovering over the force, Halsey turned east at flank speed.

Remembering the retirement from Wake eight days before, and the snooper we had with us who guided the bombers in for the sundown attack, it was comforting to see our own fighters buzzing around. Night never was more welcome, though, than the stormy one that settled over the three American ships at sundown.

Admiral Halsey, meanwhile, had advised the two cruisers, by visual signal, of the results of the attack and had given "well done" to all hands.

Ordinarily, it was considerably boresome to listen to the English-language broadcasts by Radio Tokyo, which were about all we had been able to tune in since leaving Honolulu, February 14. Tonight, though, it was fun. The dastardly enemy had made another of those cowardly attacks on the brave sons of Nippon, Tokyo screamed. They had paid dearly for it, however, an incredible number of planes being claimed. Tokyo residents were warned to obey the rigid blackout that had been decreed, as the enemy might be planning an attack on Honshu, which would be repelled as valorously as the raids on Wake and Marcus. (She didn't know it, but she was just thirty-four days early with that.)

Captain Zacharias was delighted.

"The Japanese lose their heads completely when the unexpected happens," he said. "They can make beautiful plans, but when something goes wrong, they can't improvise. If we can get away without interception, and it looks like we shall, this little trip will have been worth while."

Every ship and plane the Japanese had probably was thrown into the search, but Halsey had too big a start, quickly found bad weather, and came out without being sighted by enemy planes, ships, or submarines.

We picked up the tanker and the destroyers the second day, and then the force turned for home.

Several nights out of Pearl Harbor as we were pitching and rolling along north of the islands in a northeaster that whipped the Central Pacific for two weeks with rain and cold winds, came word of a "bombing attack" on Honolulu. We spread out to make a search.

It was a cold rainy night in Honolulu. Even had there been no blackout there would have been few persons on the street. Late in the evening a plane flew low over the city and dropped a bomb, or bombs, in Nuuanu Valley on the edge of the town. The army said examination of the bomb fragments showed them to have been of Japanese manufacture. The explanation was that it must have been a small plane, launched from a submarine.

Stanley Johnson, of the *Chicago Tribune*, who had just arrived in Honolulu and was reading in his blacked-out hotel room, said he heard the plane come low over his hotel and that it definitely was multimotored.

The most widely believed of the stories told about the bombing was that a few minutes after the bombs had exploded, the "enemy bomber" landed at Hickam Field. But the army denied categorically that it had any training flights in the air at the time. Besides, they said, any plane that had to jettison its bombs was under strict orders to do so over the sea, not over land. But then, the night was dark and stormy.

We listened assiduously for anything Tokyo Rose might say about that one, but all was silence.

After the first alarm no one else seemed much concerned about the attack, so Admiral Halsey resumed his course toward Pearl Harbor, and the longest liberty for his men since December 7.

CHAPTER 8

On the Beach

THE RETURN to Pearl Harbor March 10 was more exciting for the men of the fleet than either of the attacks that had been made; the red and green hills of Oahu a much more welcome sight than the white coral beaches of Wake. All hands were topside for the fast run in from "Torpedo Junction" to safe anchorage behind the torpedo nets off the Fish Pond.

There was no welcoming committee along the shore this time, though, as there had been for the return from the Marshall-Gilbert show. The force had maintained radio silence, and the only information either the American public or the admiralty had was what had been broadcast by Tokyo.

For the men of the fleet, the return was the most pleasant they had had to that time, or have had since. The Lexington and Yorktown task forces, the only other two carrier groups we had in the Pacific, were down to the south, and the town was not nearly as crowded as it had been a few weeks before. Too, the prohibition on sale of beer, wine, and liquor had been lifted, and instead of having to pay $25 to a bootlegger for a bottle of scotch or rye of dubious ancestry, the sailors could march into a bar and get a foot up on a rail. Sundown curfew and blackout still were in force, but transportation to town from the yard had been improved.

For me the return was something less than pleasant. There was always the struggle with the censors and the difficulty, ashore, of getting straight information on fleet activities. Then, too, returning correspondents at that time were held incommunicado until their stories were released, which might be for two or three weeks. In addition to these usual irritations I found myself in the doghouse, with my navy credentials suspended. Captain Zacharias informed me the night before of the message (that had been copied all through the fleet) announcing the suspension, but he had no information as to the reasons. He had received the message several days before but had seen no reason to worry me and had delayed telling me until the last minute, a courtesy that was much appreciated.

A check with army headquarters disclosed that my army credentials still were in order and that I would be welcome to write any stories I wished, and which would pass the censor, on its activities. Along with suspension of my navy credentials, however, also had gone suspension of my cable privileges, since the

[141

navy also controlled that, so I was reduced to sending my dispatches by mail.

The navy public relations officers, meanwhile, denied any knowledge of the reasons for the suspension, saying the message had come from Washington. It had ordered my credentials lifted "for violation of censorship." Of course I know what led to the navy action, but to this day I never have been given an official explanation. Decision to restore the credentials was made two weeks after the suspension, but because of the slowness of mail, even official mail, I did not get them back for over a month.

I go into the details of my personal troubles because it shows to what extent confusion reigned as to the policy of handling fleet correspondents.

These were but small matters, however. The Japanese still were pushing south, moving down through the Netherlands East Indies toward Australia and the British islands of the South Pacific. General MacArthur had left the Philippines by PT boat and plane, and was busy organizing Australian defenses around Port Darwin and Townsville. American troops had arrived safely to augment the Australian home defense forces. The forces available, however, were not large for the task ahead. The imperial troops of the Commonwealth were all abroad, either captives of the Japanese in Malaya or fighting in Africa against Marshal Rommel.

Admiral Brown, after being turned back from his proposed strike at Rabaul in February, had returned to Pearl Harbor and then gone back south with the Lexington and Yorktown. There was a concentration of enemy ships at Salamaua and Lae, two small ports almost due north on New Guinea from Port Moresby. The admiral took his carriers in south of the army base the following morning, and sent the navy planes across the Owen Stanley range to hit the Japanese force.

Dropping down out of the clouds that cloaked the mountaintops, the carrier striking groups fell on the Japanese vessels.

142]

There were two heavy cruisers, two light cruisers, five or six destroyers, and ten transports or cargo vessels.

The Japanese had not yet established a land air base and had only three float-plane fighters to contest the American attack. They were shot down quickly. Then the air group began to work on the ships, bombing, strafing, and launching torpedoes.

The two heavy cruisers were sunk, one of the lights was badly hit and when last seen appeared to be sinking, and the other was damaged. Three of the destroyers probably were sunk, one by machine-gun fire from fighter planes that apparently touched off a torpedo war head or ammunition magazine. Another destroyer was damaged. Five of the transports or cargo ships either were sunk or so badly hurt that they had to be beached. Four other transports were damaged. The tender for the float planes was heavily hit, as were two gunboats and a mine sweeper. Shore installations were bombed and machine gunned. Our loss was one plane.

The action was so swift and deadly that even the fliers did not know the full extent of the damage. The attack gave General MacArthur a breathing spell in which to reinforce his fingertip hold on New Guinea.

Combined with the heroic work the small force of the Netherlands and United States submarines were doing to harass the long Japanese supply lines, the carrier raids—the last two at spots three thousand miles apart—must have brought to the Japanese realization that they were in for a long, hard fight. Tokyo Rose did not have the same assurance these days when she posed the rhetorical question over Radio Tokyo, "Where is the United States fleet?"

Early in April, while my new credentials still were in transit from Washington, the other correspondents were ordered to report to Pearl Harbor for a new "fishing trip," which was the expression used to describe the departures with the fleet. There were rumors that something very mysterious was afoot, but the high command had taken few into its confidence.

Our newest carrier, the Hornet, had come from the Atlantic to join the Pacific fleet. On the Pacific coast she had picked up the sixteen twin-motored Billy Mitchell B-25 bombers which Jimmy Doolittle, then only a Lieutenant Colonel, was to lead against Tokyo in a daringly conceived and executed raid. The Enterprise, and her cruisers and destroyers, including those that had participated in the Marshall-Gilbert and Wake-Marcus raids, left Pearl Harbor to escort the Hornet on her perilous job. Again, Bull Halsey was given command of the force. He was suffering then from the skin affliction and gout that finally put him on the beach just before the Battle of Midway, but he refused to give up and return to the States for treatment.

Going far north into the bad-weather zone, as the Enterprise force had done for the Wake-Marcus raids, Admiral Halsey led his two-carrier group toward the Japanese home islands.

The raid was elaborately planned and, but for the breakdown of communications, might have been carried out with little or no loss. The plan was for the carriers to go, if possible, within four hundred or five hundred miles of Tokyo for a late afternoon launching. They were to hit Tokyo and its industrial suburbs just before dark, then fly on to hidden Chinese airfields, which were to be lighted on receipt of word that the American fliers were on the way.

The weather was all that could have been hoped for, squally and with low visibility that screened the approaching ships from the enemy air searches. Unfortunately, the force ran into two small Japanese patrol vessels the morning of April 18, while they still were some seven hundred miles from Tokyo. Escorting cruisers quickly polished them off, but it was feared they had given the alarm. Colonel Doolittle and Admiral Halsey decided to launch the B-25's immediately.

Half a gale was blowing as the Hornet turned into the wind. Colonel Doolittle himself took the first bomber off the flight deck, lifting the big ship into the air with many feet to spare. He was quickly followed by others, without a single mishap, and the American naval force turned for home.

As it turned out, the Japanese patrol vessels apparently had not given the alarm, because the fliers were over their targets without interception.

The early launching, however, caused a mixup in communications. The American fliers, many with damaged planes, arrived over the China coast. They cruised around until their gasoline was exhausted, then either crash-landed their planes in the surf, as did Captain Ted Lawson, or bailed out and let the planes go down. Some of them landed within the Japanese lines and were captured and, according to Radio Tokyo, executed.

Again, because of the necessity for radio silence and because no one in Washington knew for several days what had been the fate of the bulk of the planes and crews, the American public first got its information from enemy sources. President Roosevelt in a joking manner that found little echoing laughter in the fleet or the army air force, said the raid had been made from Shangri La.

What damage was done, no one on our side knows for certain. All sixteen planes were believed to have reached their objectives and dropped their bomb loads, which were of relatively small size because of the long flight, but included many incendiaries. Radio Tokyo was in a frenzy. Different announcers gave contradictory reports of the damage. Several high officers were reported to have taken their own lives.

Certainly, the raid jarred loose the last bit of complacency the enemy high command might have had. It proved that the long arm of America could reach across more than five thousand miles of ocean and strike at the very heart of Japan.

Although the raid was purely a stunt, it was a courageously executed one. In their hearts, the picked army crews who flew the B-25's must have felt they were going to their death when they pushed forward the throttles and roared off the Hornet's deck that gray morning six hundred and fifty miles from Tokyo. It was a miracle that so many of them survived.

As had the earlier raids by the carriers, the successful execution of the raid on Tokyo gave a big lift to the men of the fleet. Every precaution was taken to keep secret the exact method of the raid, but within a few hours of the task force's return to Honolulu it was known all over town just who had done the flying and from what ship they had flown. Even those who could only add to four were able to put two and two together. Except for the names of the ships involved, the manner of the raid could have been no secret to the Japanese. They also can add.

I had felt rather badly about missing the show, but when the other correspondents came ashore and told me they not only had been forbidden to write anything but had been asked to sign an affidavit that they wouldn't even tell their offices where they had been or what they had seen, my impatience at the slowness of the air mail subsided somewhat.

Except for the Tokyo raid, there was little Pacific war news during April about which to cheer. Our army and navy were feverishly building bases along the supply route to Australia, but these were all vulnerable to air-and-sea attack, being lightly held. The Japanese had moved steadily and inexorably through the East Indies, were firmly established on the northern coast of New Guinea, and, in a few days, were to start down through the Solomons. The Japanese tide of conquest was at the flood. Nowhere had they been stopped. Our submarines still were being used largely for reconnaissance, and were not yet in sufficient force to seriously imperil the Japanese.

Late in April came a call from Pearl Harbor that the exchange of documents with Washington had been completed and that my new credentials awaited me. Admiral Halsey, with the Enterprise and Hornet, had left a few days before to escort a convoy of marines to the south where preparations already were being made for the coming offensive against the Solomons. The lack

146]

of shipping space was so great that the combatant ships carried along deckloads of supplies.

I was told that if I wished I might follow them on a tanker that probably would refuel them somewhere down south. I accepted and went aboard an old fleet oiler, on May 1. To my surprise and satisfaction I found another passenger aboard, Captain Ernest G. Small. He was going out to relieve Captain Zacharias, who had his orders for the Office of Naval Intelligence in Washington, a place for which he was well fitted.

Before I left Honolulu, however, I had taken a ride on an army bomber to see the erupting Mauna Loa on the island of Hawaii. The big volcano, relatively inactive for several years, had started spouting lava, April 26. Scouting planes as far as two hundred miles from the scene had reported seeing the first great red glow against the sky the first night.

Volcanologists of the University of Hawaii had predicted the eruption almost to the hour, and any Japanese submarine in the area must have been able to see what was going on, but the army decided it would serve no purpose to give the enemy information it might not have, so the fireworks were kept a military secret, that is from all except several hundred thousand persons in the Hawaiian Islands.

The lava flow was not immediately endangering any military establishments, so it was not bombed for several days. Then a few bombs were dropped where the cooling crust had provided a tunnel through which hotter lava could flow. The idea was to break the crust and spread the lava so it would cool more quickly. The crater of the volcano itself, contrary to popular conception, is never bombed.

The lava flow, which was coming from a fissure in the side of the twelve-thousand-foot volcanic peak, looked exactly like all the pictures I had ever seen of such phenomena. Boiling at a temperature of several thousand degrees, the lava occasionally threw great bulbous masses of white-hot rock high into the air. All along its course flames rose and fell. Patches of white sulphur

[147

dotted the mountainside, and the red volcanic dust stirred up by the mountain's activity tinted the clouds with sunset hues in mid-morning.

Two thousand feet above the mountaintop and a mile to one side, the heat of the lava flow could be felt through the plastic nose of the big Flying Fortress where we passengers crouched in our oxygen masks watching the fiery spectacle. The war was turning out to be the best sightseeing trip I had ever hoped to take.

The lava dust still was in my hair when I put my sea bag and typewriter aboard the oiler and headed south on her with two other tankers and a destroyer escort.

The oiler was a survivor of the last war, 450 feet long, with both oil and gasoline tanks and storage spaces. Fully loaded, she displaced as much water as a heavy cruiser. Her listed speed is fourteen knots, but it would take a good following wind to push her that high now.

The fleet tankers do one of the most important, least appreciated, most dangerous, and most monotonous jobs in the fleet. Because there are never enough of them, they seldom stay long in port, going alongside a dock only long enough to fill their tanks. Heavily loaded as they are these days with aviation gasoline, they make a flaming torch when they are hit.

Because so much of their space is taken up with fuel tanks, the accommodations for a wartime crew are limited. There are some quarters forward. The majority live aft over the engines, which is pleasant in the higher latitudes but sheer misery along the equator, especially at night when the ship is blacked out and all hatches are battened down. Because of the inflammable cargo, smoking on deck is forbidden. In rough weather even the elevated catwalks are likely to be swept by seas at any minute.

Except for hot nights, the trip south was a pleasant interlude in my Pacific travels. The wardroom mess was small, which made for quick acquaintance and close companionship. Since we were dodging trouble, not looking for it, and there was nothing much to be done if we did run into a submarine or a Japanese task force, it was not difficult to relax, sun-bathe on the topside and admire the gorgeous tropical sunsets that followed us all the way.

The oiler, like most of the fleet oilers, was officered largely by reserves. She was under the command of Commander Coloney. He and the executive officer were the only Annapolis graduates aboard. Her navigator, chief engineer, first lieutenant, and gunnery officer all were old tanker men. The junior officers were young reserves from various college ROTC's. None of them knew a great deal about navy regulations or fleet maneuvers, but they did know their ship, they knew how to keep her clean, and they could rig for fueling quick as a cat could wink its eye.

We plowed along through the bluest of all seas for seventeen days, dropping off a Standard Oil tanker at one base. Another oiler left us the next day.

Because of the limited radio facilities, we weren't getting much news. We knew there had been a big battle in the Coral Sea, for the radio news report said so. But it gave no details. We were to the southwest and heading for the trouble area.

All now was confusion, so far as Captain Small and I were concerned. His ship, the Salt Lake City, was detached from Halsey's force and sent to reinforce the Australian squadron. The other ships of the force, including the cruiser Vincennes for which I had orders, were headed back north. We passed them one night, or perhaps it was the other way around.

Instead of refueling any of the naval forces churning around the Coral Sea, we went on into port, where the hundred thousand gallons of aviation gasoline we carried was eagerly received by Rear Admiral John S. McCain, later to head all naval air, but then ComAirSouPac, which translated, means Commander Air, South Pacific. On his flagship I met some of the survivors of the Lexington, whom I had met when I made the trip on her in January, and learned that the grand old ship had gone down.

I had been on the fringe of the first great carrier battle of naval history.

CHAPTER 9

The Battle of the
Coral Sea

IT WAS May 7 west of the International Date Line in the Coral Sea, a bright, fairly cool, sunny morning such as cannot be surpassed in the world.

Pushing their big hulls through the long swells of that bluest of seas were the aircraft carriers Lexington and Yorktown, and their escorting cruisers and destroyers.

The force was in charge of Rear Admiral Frank Jack Fletcher, called "Whiskey Jack" by the more irreverent of the sailors who had served with him, a salty, tattooed officer from Iowa (from which so many sailors and admirals come). He had his flag on the Yorktown, the 19,900-ton NRA carrier that had been built in 1933-34 with pump-priming moneys asked for by President Roosevelt. She was Admiral Fletcher's first carrier command. He preferred cruisers.

Second in command was Rear Admiral Aubrey W. Fitch, chunky, easygoing sailor and flier who later was to head all the air forces in the South Pacific during the Battle for the Solomons. He had his flag on the Lexington, the grand old lady that had been planned as a battle cruiser but converted to a carrier after the Washington disarmament conference of 1922. Almost nine hundred feet long, with a beam of one hundred and five feet, she and her sister ship the Saratoga were the biggest carriers afloat. The thirty-three-thousand-ton Lexington bore the designation CV-2, the lowest in the navy. The Langley, converted into a plane ferry and tender, had been CV-1. She now was at the bottom of the sea off Java. The Lex's size and slow turning abilities were to cost her her life.

REAR ADMIRAL FRANK J. LOWRY

Small but mighty skipper of a heavy cruiser in the Battles of the Coral Sea, Midway, Guadalcanal and the Eastern Solomons. He was awarded the Navy Cross for his courageous and seamanlike handling of his vessel, promoted to flag rank and sent to the Mediterranean where he directed the successful landing at Anzio, below Rome. When he turned over command of his vessel to another captain his crew collected fifteen hundred dollars which they presented in his name to Navy Relief, Inc., the Navy's welfare agency that helps the families of men in the service.

AN AMERICAN DISASTER

A torpedo, from a pack of enemy submarines that intercepted an American carrier force in the South Pacific September 15, 1942, during the Battle of the Solomons, had just thudded into the side of the American destroyer O'Brien. The O'Brien made port safely but was lost while enroute home for repair. In the background is the aircraft carrier Wasp, which had been hit by three torpedoes from the same enemy undersea force a few minutes before. The Wasp was abandoned and sunk later the same day.

The Coral Sea was familiar territory to the men of the two carriers. The Yorktown had been there continuously since late February. The Lexington had been in and out of the area twice. On March 10 the two ships had joined in the raid on Salamaua and Lae.

The morning of May 7 they were running westward at high speed in search of an enemy force of two carriers, cruisers, and destroyers that had been sighted by an army patrol plane the previous afternoon heading south past the Solomons at twenty knots. They expected to sight the enemy off the Louisiade Archipelago, the chain of islands that extends southwestward from the peninsula of New Guinea.

For a month the Japanese had been concentrating ships and men and planes in the East Indies and the Marshalls preparatory to extension of their conquests south and east. They had occupied the ports on the islands of Buka and Bougainville in the Northern Solomons and on May 1 had moved down to Tulagi and Guadalcanal.

Three days before this morning, on May 4, Admiral Fletcher had taken the Yorktown in south of Guadalcanal and sent in her air group to sink the occupation force of twelve to fifteen ships. Unfortunately much of their cargo already had been unloaded and work started on an airfield on Guadalcanal.

The Yorktown strike had been unusually successful. Every ship of the enemy force had been sunk. Our total loss had been three planes. The Lexington group was held in reserve that day to take care of any enemy reaction.

Now the Japanese were on the move again, apparently headed for Port Moresby and New Caledonia, the Free French island on the eastern rim of the Coral Sea that had been occupied by an American army division in March. Ahead of their transports and supply vessels the enemy had sent two carrier groups to clean out the American force he knew was there. Admiral Fletcher led his two carriers and their escort ships against the westernmost of the two main enemy forces.

An early morning search was launched. An hour and a half after dawn one of the scout planes, an SBD armed only with light bombs, sighted one of the Japanese carriers, about two hundred miles away, just where it had been expected the enemy would be found. The American air groups were ready and immediately took off for the attack—dive bombers, torpedo planes, and fighters.

Flying through brilliant sunlight, the American air groups of more than fifty planes each caught the Japanese unprepared and were on the carrier, identified as the Ryukaku, while she still had most of her planes on deck. She was turning, trying desperately to get into the wind to launch her birds when the first bomb struck.

The American attack was beautifully coordinated. The dive bombers screamed down from fifteen thousand feet, coming in from all points of the compass, and at the same time the torpedo planes were making their water-level attack.

"The Japanese are funny people," one of the torpedo plane pilots reported. "When we started in for them the enemy escort vessels all turned away from the carrier and left her all by her lonesome.

"When she saw she wasn't going to get her planes away, she started to circle. It was like shooting a duck in a barrel. I just slowed down until she reached that part of her circle where I had a broadside shot at her, then I went in and let her have it."

No less than fifteen heavy bombs and ten torpedoes hit the Japanese carrier in a space of less than five minutes. She went down like a rock, literally torn to pieces. It was considered doubtful that more than a handful of her crew of an estimated two thousand men escaped. Late-arriving American fliers, seeing the Ryukaku sinking, turned their attention to her escorts and polished off a heavy cruiser.

It was during this attack that Lieutenant Commander Bob Dixon, leader of one of the Lexington dive-bombing squadrons, sent his now famous triumphant message: "Scratch one flattop."

This slangy description popularized in the navy a phrase little used before for carriers.

The other enemy carrier, which must have been somewhere not too far away but which was not sighted by our fliers, meanwhile had sent up her air group to look for the American force. They didn't find the carriers immediately but instead flew across the path of the fleet tanker Neosho, which had refueled the force the day before and was on her way to Noumea for another load, and her escorting destroyer, the Sims.

Without any air protection, the two ships were doomed. One of the first dive bombers to scream down hit the Sims near the stern. She sank almost immediately. The Neosho, with her fuel tanks empty and thus serving as watertight compartments, was hit by eight or ten bombs but refused to sink. She took aboard the Sims's survivors and floated for several days, surviving another attack late the afternoon of May 7 by another formation of Japanese planes. She and the Sims claimed to have shot down several of the attackers. She still was floating when a destroyer found her. They removed her crew and the Sims's survivors, and sank her with torpedoes. The Neosho was one of our newer tankers, of 18,250 deadweight tons and with a speed of between eighteen and twenty knots.

It was not until late afternoon that the enemy planes found the American carriers. The weather had changed meanwhile, and the American force was now under a low overcast, with occasional rain squalls. Warned of the approach of enemy planes, the carriers had their fighters up to meet the enemy planes and shot down more than a score of them. Not an enemy reached torpedo-launching or bombing distance.

One of the strangest happenings in the Pacific war took place over the Lexington in the gathering gloom that evening. Several Japanese planes, seeking their own carrier, sighted the Lexington instead. Seeing the American planes circling for a landing—all navies use more or less the same procedure in recovering planes —they joined up, thinking they were over their own flattop. One of the destroyers first discovered they were enemy planes, turned a searchlight on them, and opened fire. It would have been interesting to have had one or two of them land on the American flight deck before discovering their mistake.

The Japanese fliers realized their error of identification when the tracer bullets and shells from the American ships began to whistle around their ears. They shoved off, making no attempt to attack the American ships. A few minutes later they were landing on their own carrier, only thirty miles away. In the bad weather the two opposing forces had steamed almost within gun range of each other. Neither, however, cared to risk the issue in a night engagement and both steamed opposite courses.

The night of May 7, the score stood high in favor of the American force. One Japanese carrier and one heavy cruiser had been sunk. At least twenty-five Japanese planes, probably more, had been shot down. We had lost only six planes, and the destroyer.

All through the night the American force ran east and south. Before dawn search planes were in the air again seeking contact with the enemy. They thought they had only the one remaining Japanese carrier to deal with.

At 8 A.M. they learned otherwise. Two scouts reported sighting a new Japanese task force of two carriers, two or three battleships, several cruisers, and destroyers. It was two hundred miles due north. It could not have been the force attacked the previous day. This new group apparently had come down from the Marshalls to the eastward of the Solomons. Again the Lexington and Yorktown air groups were ready and took off for the enemy's position.

Part way to their objective, the American attack force passed the Japanese air group headed for the American carriers. Apparently scouts from each force had sighted the other at about the same time. With only preliminary skirmishing between the opposing fighter groups, the two formations flew on past each other to carry out their original mission.

This time when the American air groups picked up the carriers they found the Japanese fighter planes waiting for them. Fighting their way through the Zeros they put at least three or four bombs and several torpedoes into one carrier, identified as the Shoho and an uncounted number of bombs and torpedoes into the other. Although the detailed navy communiqué on the action, which was issued a month later, claimed only damage to the Shoho, and did not mention the other carrier, the fliers who made the attack believe the Shoho sank and the other carrier, if she did not sink, was so badly damaged she had difficulty getting home and was out of action for months. They identified the second flattop as of the Zyukaku class.

Two hundred miles to the south, while our planes were attacking the Japanese carriers, the United States ships and planes were battling the Japanese striking force of dive bombers and torpedo planes. Every available American plane was in the air, including some dive bombers that took off without bombs to attack the enemy torpedo planes.

In the enemy attacking force were an estimated 105 planes, the striking groups from two carriers. They concentrated on the Lexington, because she was the biggest and obviously could not maneuver as radically as could the Yorktown, which was one of the best built and handiest carriers we had.

Screaming down out of the sun—it was another beautiful day, with only scattered clouds—the enemy fliers put five torpedoes and at least two heavy bombs on the Lexington and one thousand-pound bomb into the Yorktown. Here again, and this time on the debit side of the ledger, the official communiqué differed from the stories of eyewitnesses. Stanley Johnston of the *Chicago Tribune*, the only newspaper correspondent with the force, said in his graphic description of the battle that he felt five torpedoes strike the big Lex. The official version said she was hit by only two.

The Japanese paid heavily for their limited success. The American carrier cover of eight Grumman Wildcat fighters and eight Douglas Dauntless dive bombers knocked an estimated forty to forty-five enemy planes out of the sky, and guns of the two carriers and their escorts accounted for nineteen or twenty more. The toll might have been even higher had the four Lexington fighters had enough altitude to intercept the first wave of Japanese dive bombers. The enemy planes came in at fifteen thousand feet, three thousand feet above the American fighters, who could not get to them before they had started their dives.

The battle was over, at both ends of the two-hundred-mile-long fighting axis, in a matter of minutes. In aerial warfare or even surface sea battles the action is sudden, deadly, and of short duration. Both sides began retiring at full speed.

Aboard both American carriers, damage control parties were at work while the bombs were still dropping. Damage to the Yorktown was not serious. The bomb had penetrated several decks and killed two score men, but the fire it set had quickly been brought under control and she was steaming at full power.

Admiral Fletcher liked to tell a story about that hit. Just after the bomb struck, one of the talkers on a telephone circuit identified himself and asked permission of the officer in charge of the circuit to secure his phones; that is, to disconnect them.

"Why?" the officer asked.

"Because a bomb just passed through this compartment, sir," came the answer.

"Aren't they swell kids?" the admiral said. "I think I'd have chucked those earphones and been out of there so fast I'd have left a smoke trail. But not that youngster. It was his post, and he stuck to it until he was given permission to leave. The officer told me the youngster didn't seem to be excited at all."

Aboard the Lexington, a much more desperate fight was being waged. The old lady still was able to turn her engines, despite the extensive underwater damage, but fires were raging in half a dozen different places. Lieutenant Commander "Pop" Healy, her first lieutenant and damage control officer, who never liked to talk about the war but only about his family back on the Pacific Coast, was leading the battle to save her. Battered bulkheads were shored up. Compartments where fire and smoke made it impossible for damage control parties to work were closed in the hope the fire could be smothered.

Meanwhile the Lexington planes that had made the attack on the two Japanese carriers, along with the Yorktown's striking force, were coming back. The holes in her flight deck had been boarded over and she turned into the wind to recover her brood.

No one knew, then, how serious a trouncing in plane strength the Japanese had taken, and it seemed imperative that all planes be rearmed and refueled for any eventualities ahead. So the Lexington's gasoline system was opened and the highly volatile, high-octane gasoline started flowing through the pipes to the empty tanks in the planes on deck.

Steaming along at twenty knots, her fires apparently under control, the Lexington suddenly was rocked by a series of interior explosions and fire spread all through her lower decks. Although at the time it was thought a delayed-action bomb might have exploded, it later was decided that the explosions were of gasoline vapors. The gasoline pipes apparently had been twisted by the beating she had taken from bombs and torpedoes. When the gasoline started flowing the vapors leaked into compartments where fires still were burning, and were ignited.

The fires set by these gasoline explosions spread through the ship as if driven by a gale, and in a few minutes had burned out most of the telephone and electric lines. A human chain had to be formed to pass orders from the bridge to the engine rooms where the faithful engineers, firemen, and electricians were sticking to their posts.

Several destroyers were ordered alongside the stricken carrier to add their firefighting equipment to the emergency units still operating on the Lexington, but it was no use.

Admiral Fitch told Captain Sherman:

"Better get the men off, Ted."

Just before sundown the word was passed to abandon ship. Lines and nets were let over the side, life rafts were cut loose and the crew of more than two thousand men began sliding down them to the water, from where they were picked up by the small boats from the cruisers and destroyers.

Admiral Fitch and Captain Sherman, holding to a tradition as old as ships, were the last to leave. As Captain Sherman left her deck for the last time the magazine where were stored the war heads of her planes' airborne torpedoes exploded, literally tearing her apart amidships.

Still she refused to die. One of the destroyers, aboard which were many of her survivors, fired a spread of torpedoes into her side. Lower and lower she sank, and finally disappeared. A flier cruising above the place where she had been said he could see her white-hot hull fathoms down in the blue water. Men stood at the rails of the escort ships and cried unashamedly.

Only 8 per cent of the Lexington's crew were lost. Among them was "Pop" Healy, who was not seen again after the gasoline explosion. Despite the horrible burns many had suffered, only a few of the survivors died on the rescue ships.

The Battle of the Coral Sea was over. In three days of actual fighting spread over a period of five days, American fliers had destroyed two enemy aircraft carriers, one heavy cruiser, two destroyers, several transports, and some small vessels. Other ships, including another enemy carrier, had been badly damaged. More than one hundred enemy planes had been shot down. Enemy personnel losses were estimated at three thousand to four thousand.

Our own losses were the Lexington, Neosho, and Sims, and twenty-one aircraft. Our personnel losses were less than five hundred men.

The tide of Japanese conquest had at long last been turned back.

CHAPTER 10

Prepare for Action

EVEN BEFORE the Coral Sea other Japanese moves were in process of preparation.

Up through the Marshalls, Carolines, Marianas, and Bonins the Japanese were building up an imposing array of logistics that indicated a major effort eastward. All our sea strength was down south.

Admiral Halsey, with his flag on the Enterprise, had led a task force south in late April to reinforce marine garrisons in areas where bases were being built up for the start of the push toward Tokyo. With him were the Hornet and the usual cruisers and destroyers.

Halsey had been too far away when the Lexington and York-town tangled with the Japanese carrier groups in the Coral Sea, the Japanese having retired rapidly to the northward after the loss of their second carrier on May 6, but he had stayed in the area just to be sure they didn't come back. Once that was certain he turned north toward Pearl Harbor and the great day that was coming.

The Yorktown also was on her way back to Pearl Harbor to get her emergency repairs and go north to Midway to meet her destiny.

After the Lexington was lost, Admiral Fletcher had led his force southeastward, part of it going to one base and the rest to another base that rapidly was being converted into a major American sea-and-air base. The uninjured Lexington survivors, and as many of the wounded as could be moved safely, were put aboard transports and started back to the States.

I was hearing just enough disquieting reports about developments to the north to make me wonder whether my tentative

[159

plans to look over some of the new bases in the South Pacific might be a case of fiddling while Rome was burning. Captain Coloney, commanding an oiler, was good enough to send a dispatch to Pearl Harbor for me, asking for advice. He also took me aboard the tender that Admiral McCain was using as his flagship, to meet the admiral. I put the question squarely to him, whether I should go back or stay.

"Better get back north, son," he counseled.

I started looking for transportation. The ban on correspondents' flying, which was lifted a few months after it was imposed by Admiral Halsey, was not then in force, so when I saw a big Coronada, the navy's four-engined flying boat, coming in a few nights later I went over to see about getting a ride. A navy doctor had the same idea. He had two hundred and fifty pounds of luggage, and weighed two-ten himself, and was promptly turned down. The big flying boats had to count every pound.

I bearded Lieutenant Commander Bill Nation in the wardroom of the tender and asked him how about my going.

"How much do you weigh?" he asked.

"About 170 dripping wet," I told him. Then, before he could ask about the baggage, I said its weight only totaled about sixty pounds, with my typewriter, and I would leave it all behind if he didn't have room for it.

"No, I guess we can handle that much," he said. "I've still got a little leeway. Be over here at 7:30 in the morning with your gear and we'll shove off."

The trip up through the new island bases—Suva, Canton and Palmyra—was none too reassuring.

In the Fijis we had a good air base but only two squadrons of fighters, and at Canton none at all. There was a beautiful airfield at Canton, on which eight Flying Fortresses en route to Australia were sitting the night I was there, but not a fighter to protect them. And Canton was only a little over six hundred miles, easy bombing range, from Japanese air bases in the Gilberts. There wasn't even any barbed wire along the beaches. The few army

160]

troops on the island had been busy building up coral breastworks a few rods back from the beach, but there was no protection against air attack. The air warning system consisted of two lookouts on a fifty-foot tower, and a hand-wound siren.

It was a beautiful night as we stepped out of the lounge of the former Pan American Airlines hotel after watching a movie. A bomber's moon hung like a great crystal ball in the eastern sky.

"I don't understand why the Japanese don't hit this place," mused Bill Nation as we stood smoking before turning in. "I think that every time I come through. They'll never find an easier way to cause a lot of trouble and knock out a lot of bombers."

It was comforting to realize that the Japanese make just as many mistakes of strategy and tactics as anyone else.

Palmyra was better, but not a great deal. Captain Gordon Rowe, the navy commander there, had twelve Brewster Buffalo fighters, outmoded but better than nothing. But he had to rely for protection more on the weather than his own resourcefulness.

By working his entire force of marines and bluejackets from dawn to dusk, Captain Rowe had succeeded in completing the airfield that the civilian workers had left only half done when they all were ordered off the job on December 7. In addition, he had built a cross strip. The beaches were well guarded by barbed wire, and the defenses were deep dug and well camouflaged.

The main defense of Palmyra was, and is, that it rains there all the time. The annual fall is more than three hundred inches. Shades of the Dust Bowl!

The ferry pilots say that when you're flying south out of Honolulu all you have to do is go about eight hundred miles, then look for the biggest storm area. In the center will be Palmyra. Captain Rowe said finding Palmyra wasn't quite as simple as that. He kept an old amphibian plane wound up and ready to go day and night. When he got a message from some army planes, obviously wandering around with little idea where they were, he'd take off in his "duck" and lead them in. Despite his efforts, three Fortresses had been lost recently, and he felt badly about it.

"I wish they'd do a better job of teaching these boys navigation before they send them out here," he said. "They're good kids, but it's murder, the little some of them know."

The stay at Palmyra was all too short. We were away before it was light, on the last leg for Pearl Harbor.

I still wasn't quite convinced that Admiral McCain knew what he was talking about as the big flying boat eased down to a water landing off Pearl Harbor. I had a vision of a bath ashore, a couple of days swimming off Waikiki, and some mail.

As I climbed out of the plane a naval officer came to meet me. "Hailey?" he enquired.

I told him yes, wondering what I had done now to irritate the powers-that-be.

"I was told to bring you to CINPAC immediately," he said. "Let's get your luggage cleared by the customs" (life still went on as usual, it seemed, even in a war zone) "and I have a station wagon waiting for you."

CINPAC had more gold braid floating around through the passages than I ever had seen. Something big was coming up. I was told all the other correspondents already were at sea; my papers were made out, and I was to go aboard the Astoria immediately.

In an hour and a half after landing I was on my way to the biggest air-sea battle of history, where the Japanese tide of conquest finally came to its crest and broke against the thin blue line of navy men and ships who for so many weary months held the seven-thousand-mile Pacific battle line against overwhelming odds.

The Battle of Midway

THE EARLY morning of June 4, 1942, was cool and cloudy northeast of Midway where the three American carriers and their escorts were standing westward through the blue-gray swells of the Central Pacific.

There was a feeling all through the fleet that this was a day of decision. The enemy transport train that had been sighted the day before seven hundred miles west of Midway had continued eastward toward our westernmost island base after attacks by Flying Fortresses and torpedo-carrying navy Catalinas. The light attack on Dutch Harbor had convinced the admiralty that the show there was only a diversion for a greater effort.

The Japanese striking force must be near, though it had not yet been sighted. Planes from Midway and from the carrier force were ranging thousands of miles of ocean looking for it.

The three United States carriers, the Hornet, Enterprise and Yorktown, all we had in the Central Pacific at the time, were maneuvering in a broad scouting line, hull down from each other.

The American force was under command of Rear Admiral Fletcher, who had command in the Coral Sea battle. He had his flag on the Yorktown. Rear Admiral R. A. Spruance was aboard the Enterprise and Rear Admiral Marc A. Mitscher had command of the Hornet. In charge of the cruiser divisions acting as escorts were Rear Admiral T. C. Kinkaid, who later was to command both North Pacific and Southwest Pacific naval forces, and Rear Admiral W. W. (Poco) Smith, who had been chief of staff for Admiral Husband Kimmel.

First word of the enemy fleet came at 8:30 from Ensign Howard D. Ady of San Antonio, who was flying one of the big lumbering Catalinas on a search two hundred miles north of Midway.

Men of his crew sighted an enemy observation plane, then a cruiser. Neither, apparently, saw the American plane.

"We were flying through rain squalls," Mr. Ady said, "and as we came out of one we saw the main Japanese force coming out of another. There was a long front of ships, two big carriers, some other big ones that I believe were battleships, some cruisers, and a lot of destroyers.

"It was an hour after sunrise and from their position, running into the wind, I believe they either had launched their planes or were getting ready to."

At almost the same time, Lieutenant William A. Chase, of Altoona, Pa., flying a sector closer to the island, sighted the Japanese attack group heading in.

"It looked like the whole sky was full of planes," he said. Forgetting the rules about encoding reports, Lieutenant Chase immediately opened up on his radio in plain voice to warn of the approaching enemy force.

"Fortunately they didn't see me," he said, "and after reporting what I had seen I ducked into a handy cloud and stayed there."

The Japanese striking force of ships, it was learned when all reports were in, consisted of four carriers, two battleships, eight heavy cruisers, eighteen or twenty destroyers, and two or three small aircraft ships, from which float-type search planes were launched.

It was divided into two groups. The first, from which the attack on Midway was launched, was composed of three carriers, four heavy cruisers, and ten destroyers. The carriers were the Kaga, Akagi and the Soryu.

Fifty miles astern of the striking group was a support force of one carrier, the Hiryu; two battleships, four heavy cruisers, eight or ten destroyers, and the aircraft ships.

The enemy transport train, that had been sighted and twice attacked west of Midway, consisted of ten transports, carrying some thirty thousand to forty thousand men, four heavy cruisers, and eight destroyers. Midway between the striking force and the transport train, almost due northwest of Midway, were two Japanese fleet oilers, escorted by two destroyers. Southwest of Midway, coming in from the Marshalls without escort, were two heavily loaded supply vessels.

When the first report reached Midway all hands were ready. Immediately the planes started taking off. There were six new Grumman Avenger torpedo planes, twenty-seven Douglas Dauntless dive bombers, manned by navy and marine pilots; four B-26 army medium bombers, whose pilots had received a few days' instruction on torpedo attacks and were carrying "tin fish" that morning instead of bombs, and sixteen army Flying Fortresses.

Without fighter escort, because the twenty-five outmoded Brewster Buffalo fighters and the few Grumman Wildcats were needed to defend the island against the incoming Japanese attack planes, the American striking force set sail for the carriers' reported position.

They found the enemy ships where they had expected to find them, and attacked through a screen of Japanese Zeros. Just what damage they did is not known in full detail, for many of the planes did not return. All of the Flying Fortresses, attacking from a high altitude, returned safely. They believe they got three bomb hits on an enemy carrier. The two B-26's that came back reported a possible torpedo hit. Untrained at such work, they had gone in at such steep, fast glides that it was thought possible all their torpedoes had sounded, passing under the enemy ships.

One group of sixteen marine dive bombers (the marines fly the same planes as the navy) attacked the small Japanese carrier Soryu, which probably was carrying mostly fighters to provide the air cover for the striking force. The eight who came back said they had scored three hits. Another group of eleven dive bombers, of whom only five returned, reported two hits on one of the escorting battleships.

Meanwhile the American carrier force, hearing the reports from the Catalinas, had closed the distance between the two

[165

forces at better than thirty knots. Two hundred miles separated the two opposing carrier groups when the first contact reports came in. That was a bit too far for safe operation of the fighter escort, if they were going to have much flying time left for fighting once they reached the enemy position.

The Hornet and Enterprise launched their attack groups when about one hundred and seventy-five miles from the estimated enemy position. The Yorktown squadrons were held in reserve, and took off an hour later.

Whether because the ferocity of the first attack by the Midway-based planes dissuaded the Japanese admirals from pressing on, or whether it was the original plan to retire back into the fog area some hundred miles astern of them, the enemy striking force turned north soon after the first attack was made, steering a course to rejoin the Hiryu, which, with its escorts, was running east toward the American carrier position.

The change of course by the enemy caused the first American striking groups to miss their projected rendezvous with the Japanese carriers. All but two groups. While the other carrier squadrons, believing they had come in astern of the Japanese force, flew big circles toward Midway, Lieutenant Commander Jack Waldron with his squadron of fifteen Douglas torpedo planes and his thirty men, and Lieutenant Commander McClusky (not to be confused with "Go Get 'Em," the fighter pilot) and his dive bombers turned to the north.

For an hour they flew great circles, always to the northward. Waldron and his torpedo planes were in the lead. Finally they saw two smudges of smoke on the horizon. They were from the burning Soryu and a cruiser, apparently the only two ships hit by the Midway planes.

Waldron and his men were running short on gasoline, and after reporting contact he asked permission to withdraw to refuel.

"Attack," was the answer.

So he attacked.

With no fighter escort, no help from the dive bombers, who still were some miles astern, Jack led his squadron in. Thirty Zeros dived at them from the clouds ten miles out. Every ship in the force turned its guns on them and opened fire.

Torpedo 8 was flying the Douglas Devastators, good planes but slow and vulnerable, and long since outmoded. They were no match for the Zeros.

Waldron's plane was the first to go down. Ensign George H. (Tex) Gay, Jr., of Houston, saw Jack's plane hit the water, its motor flaming, and saw him struggle vainly to push back the plastic cover over his head.

"Hadn't we better stop to help them?" Tex's radioman and rear gunner asked over the interphone.

"We've got a job to do," Tex answered grimly, continuing his run.

"Our planes were falling all around me in flames," Gay said. "The Zeros were concentrating on the leaders. I was bringing up the rear. Which was lucky for me, as I was the last one they attacked."

Gay doesn't remember much about those crowded seconds while his squadron was being decimated there in front of his eyes. He was closing the range at better than a hundred and fifty knots, aiming for the Akagi.

He was still a mile away when he heard his rear gunner yell, "They've got me." Taking a quick look he saw the boy hanging lifeless in his safety belt. Tex himself had been hit in the arm and leg.

The Akagi was looming up ahead of him, as big as a hotel. He pressed his torpedo release, then pulled the emergency lever.

"I was only about five hundred yards away," he estimated, "and I barely pulled up over her flight deck. As I cleared her I heard a big explosion, which I am sure was my torpedo hitting. I don't believe I could have missed at that range.

"I thought about crashing my plane on the Akagi's deck," Gay

[167

continued, "but I vetoed that quickly as I thought I still had a chance of getting away. After all, my plane still was flying."

The Zeros, disregarding their own antiaircraft fire, had followed Gay on in and were on him, blazing away with their machine guns and 20-millimeter cannon, as he flew across the Akagi. Half a mile away a cannon shell knocked out his controls and he crashed into the sea.

"By the time I got the cover back and got out of the plane, it was sinking tail first," he said. "I could see my radioman slumped in his seat. I dived to try to release him, but couldn't get the cover pulled back. Finally I had to surface to get another lungful of air, and before I could dive again the plane was gone. I'm sure he was dead, though."

Using his light parachute pack as a life preserver and pulling a seat cushion over his head to shield him from the Japanese pilots, who, he was afraid, might strafe him in the water, Gay, the only survivor of Torpedo 8, watched the Japanese force blasted by the American carrier planes.

McClusky and his Enterprise dive bomber group were the first ones in. They picked up the Kagi, the other big Japanese craft converted from a battleship to a carrier after the 1922 Washington disarmament conference, and set her on fire from one end to another.

Following the Enterprise group came the Yorktown squadrons, whose pilots had the advantage of Waldron's contact report and had to waste no time searching for their targets.

The Yorktown squadrons had kept together as they moved toward the enemy force, the fighters covering them clear into the attack.

From the bridge of the heavy cruiser Astoria we could hear them calmly talking over the situation.

The Zeros again concentrated on the low-flying torpedo planes, as they had on Waldron's squadron, but this time they had the Wildcats to deal with.

"Let's go down and give the boys a hand," said one of the pilots calmly, as he saw the enemy planes attacking.

Making a coordinated attack, the Yorktown squadrons literally blasted the Akagi out of the water. Lieutenant Commander Leslie, leading a dive bomber squadron of seventeen planes, lost his bomb on the way, through faulty release mechanism, but made his dive anyway. Fifteen of the sixteen planes that followed him laid their explosive eggs across the big Japanese carrier's flight deck. One pilot reported his bomb went down one of the carrier's elevator shafts, up which the elevator was rising with a plane.

"How am I doing, Joe?" we heard one enthusiastic dive bomber pilot shout.

"That sounds like a pilot who has just put one down a Japanese smokestack," observed one of the listening officers.

"The Japanese had a big red circle painted on their flight deck," Leslie said. "It made a beautiful point of aim for a dive."

The Japanese planes had returned from the Midway attack and were refueling and rearming when the American planes drove in and sank the carriers.

Meanwhile the other carrier squadrons, which had gone in to Midway and refueled, returned to the attack along with survivors of the Midway air force.

When the three carriers of the striking force were hit, the other Japanese ships, except for a few destroyers, hauled out of the area as fast as they could go. The late American arrivals, seeing the three Japanese carriers in a condition to which the Japanese must have become accustomed by that time, took out after the other vessels. Two heavy cruisers were heavily bombed and one destroyer was sunk.

From Ensign Gay's view under his seat cushion, which he said he was wearing like a Merry Widow hat, pulled down on both sides, Torpedo 8's lone survivor watched the pursuit and destruction of the enemy. A Japanese destroyer fired a spread into one of the stricken carriers, he said, after taking off her

[169

survivors; there couldn't have been many. One of our own submarines came up to the Soryu in the late afternoon and pumped a spread of torpedoes into her.

The other carrier, burning fiercely, drifted over the horizon, abandoned by the other enemy ships.

While our land-based Midway planes and the squadrons from the carriers were attacking the Japanese striking force, the enemy support group, spearheaded by the Hiryu, was streaking eastward.

Our own three carriers, the Hornet and the Enterprise in the lead and to the southward of the Yorktown, were still speeding westward, closing the gap between the two forces.

On the bridge of the Astoria, which was one of the two cruiser escorts for the Yorktown, we were anxiously awaiting the return of the Yorktown's planes. Shortly after 1 P.M. they began to come back, first the fighters, then the dive bombers, all seventeen of them.

The first one had no more than landed on the Yorktown's deck than Admiral Fletcher sent a message to all the ships within visual range:

"One enemy carrier sunk."

The message was broadcast over our loud-speaker system. The kids around the guns cheered like mad.

Up on the bridge, however, the tension was increasing.

Lieutenant Commander "Dave" Davidson, the communications officer, hurrying past on an errand, told me we had been sighted by an enemy scout plane. It had been shot down, but not before it had gotten away a contact report.

"It won't be long now," said Dave, grimly.

It wasn't.

The Yorktown waved off the last of her returning planes and began to launch her reserve fighters. The flag hoist which means enemy planes approaching shot up to her yardarm.

"Stand by to repel attack" went the command booming over our loud speaker, and a moment later, "action starboard."

First visual evidence from the Astoria's bridge of the approaching attack group of eighteen dive bombers was several big splashes to starboard as the enemy bombers began to jettison their loads as our fighters hit them. Then, following the bombs, flaming enemy planes began to fall. In a matter of seconds five twisting columns of smoke marked the death of as many enemy dive bombers.

"They were in three V's of six planes each at about fifteen thousand feet," said Scott (Go Get 'Em) McCuskey, who was up with the Yorktown fighters to protect his carrier, "Adams," his wing man, "and I went at them from a beam approach. They scattered like a bunch of pigeons and we drove right through them. I knocked one out of one side of the V, then went on across and got one on the other side. Adams got another."

The trailing enemy formations, diving under or zooming over the first section, which was the target of the American fighters, continued on toward the Yorktown.

From the Astoria's bridge we saw the end of one Japanese plane. He came diving down out of the fleecy white overcast with a Grumman Wildcat on his tail. He pulled out close to the water and started radical evasive maneuvers.

"Don't let him get away," the marines on the antiaircraft battery just under the bridge were pleading. "Shoot him down."

The Wildcat fighter pilot, as if answering the pleas he couldn't hear, swooped twice at the fleeing enemy plane. After the second pass, it plunged into the sea to explode in a mass of flames.

Say this for the Japanese fliers, though. They kept on coming. Eleven were shot out of the air before they reached dropping distance, but the other seven won their way over the carrier and peeled off.

Every gun in the force was yammering away at the enemy planes as they plummeted, black as hate, out of the white clouds. The whole starboard side of the Yorktown seemed to burst into flame as her gunners poured out red-hot shells at the enemy bombers.

Standing in the port wing of the Astoria's bridge, watching the carrier two thousand yards away, Captain Frank Scanland saw her begin an evasive turn and called to Lieutenant Commander Bill Eaton, the navigator, who always takes the deck during action:

"Better give her twenty-five right, Bill."

The casualness of his tone was so striking I stared in amazement.

The enemy planes were coming down now, one a second, out of the twelve-thousand-foot overcast. I don't know how it is with others, but for me it was like watching a slow-motion picture. It seemed to take minutes for the planes to come down from first sighting to bomb-dropping distance.

The first one down, making a beautiful dive at an angle of about seventy-five degrees, put his bomb on one side of the flight deck, not far from the midships island structure. There was a great flash of fire when it landed. The next one missed, his bomb falling alongside the carrier, throwing a great column of spray in the air. He never pulled out of his dive but flew flaming into the sea.

The air was full of black antiaircraft bursts, through which the first two planes dived unscathed. The third man, however, was hit while still some five thousand feet above the carrier's deck. His plane seemed to hang in the air a moment, then turned a complete somersault. As it straightened out again, the bomb, looking almost half as big as the plane, broke loose and started falling. As though running on a wire, it fell straight for the carrier's smokestack. It hit a quarter of the way down the big pipe, penetrating almost to the fireroom before it exploded. Thick black smoke poured out.

Four more made their dives and dropped their bombs, but only one more hit was scored, with an armor-piercing bomb that penetrated the flight deck forward and exploded four decks down.

The Japanese bombers were paying little attention to the

cruisers or destroyers. One, however, after dropping his bomb, turned toward the Astoria and gave us one squirt from his machine gun. It was his last one. As he flew past the cruiser at bridge level, the 20-millimeter guns went to work on him. His gunner already was slumped over as he flew past the ship and as he passed the bridge, only fifty feet above the water, he too was hit and sagged down against the side of his cockpit. His plane never came out of its shallow glide, but plunged into the water astern.

The Japanese dive bombers were identified by our gunnery officer as Baugeki '97s. They had long, tapering wings, and long, slim fuselages. Red circles were painted on the wing tops. There were two red bands around the fuselage about halfway back. They were painted a mottled brown.

After the bomb went down her stack, the Yorktown slowed to five knots. A great column of black smoke was pouring up amidships, and thinner wisps of smoke could be seen around the forepeak, seeping up from the fire deep in her forward compartments.

Soon her signal searchlight began blinking and to the Astoria came the message: "Send small boat for admiral and staff."

The bombing had knocked out the ship's radio, and the admiral had to be where he could communicate with the other ships and shore stations.

Captain Scanland turned the Astoria to send her across the bow of the slowly moving carrier, and one of our motor sailers was launched, with Lieutenant Willie Isham at the helm, to bring Admiral Fletcher to us.

Pulling under the side of the burning Yorktown, the little boat took a line from the carrier down which the admiral and eight of his staff clambered, including Captain Spencer Lewis, his chief of staff, Commanders Gerry Galpin and Harry Guthrie, Lieutenant Commander Sam Latimer and Lieutenant Harry Smith.

They came aboard dressed in smoke-begrimed coveralls, look-

[173

ing like refugees from a chain gang. Admiral Fletcher moved in with Admiral Smith. His staff set up housekeeping in Captain Scanland's outer cabin, which they dubbed "Boy's Town."

Just as our boat was completing the final trip, two of the Yorktown's dive bombers that had been circling the formation ran out of gas. Seeing the Astoria stopped, they came in and landed alongside. Both pilots set their planes down beautifully in the roughening sea and were out of the cockpits and in their rubber boats without even getting their feet wet. Our small boat picked them up. One of them was Lieutenant Commander Leslie, who had led the dive-bombing attack on the Akagi.

As the boat was picking up the pilot and radioman gunner of the second plane, a lookout reported a torpedo approaching the ship from dead ahead.

Looking down from the bridge, fifty feet above the water, Lieutenant Commander Davidson said he saw what he also believed was a torpedo passing parallel to the ship and not more than fifteen feet away. It may have been a fish, he said later, since there were no more torpedoes seen, and the destroyers patrolling around the stricken Yorktown made no contacts. If so, it was the biggest, fastest moving one he ever saw. It was running deep, at an estimated speed of forty-five or fifty knots, and leaving a clearly defined wake.

Anxious to get his boat under way, if there were enemy submarines about, Captain Scanland at that moment saw our small boat going back to take aboard the rubber boats the pilots had used.

"Get that damn boat aboard," he roared. "What in hell do they think they are, a salvage crew?"

Aboard the Yorktown, meanwhile, the fire was being brought under control. The smoke from the fire forward had thinned out to only a few small white wisps. Amidships, the black column of smoke pouring up out of the damaged stack had turned from black to brown. The holes in her deck had been repaired. She was picking up speed.

174]

There was a cheer from our cruiser as a new ensign, bright as the morning, was hoisted to the yardarm to replace the smoke-blackened one that had been flying since dawn.

Knowing that the first attack probably would not be the last, Admiral Fletcher had asked for help to protect the stricken carrier, and two cruisers and two destroyers came boiling over the horizon.

The force was now back in cruising formation, the carrier flanked on either side by two cruisers. Ahead and on either side the destroyers patrolled.

"My speed is fifteen knots," the carrier signaled. Then it was seventeen, then eighteen.

There was a momentary scare as a large formation of planes was reported approaching from the southwest. Then they were identified as friendly. Flying high and fast, they passed overhead on a northerly course. Vengeance for the attack on the York-town was soon to be had. One of the Yorktown's scout planes finally had located the one undamaged Japanese carrier, the Hiryu, and Admiral Spruance had sent a striking force from the Enterprise to attack.

The American striking group hardly was out of sight when the ominous report, "many bogies bearing 350 degrees" came up from the flag plot. ("Bogies" was the voice code for unidentified aircraft.) That could mean but one thing, another attack. It was 5 o'clock. It had been three hours since the first attack.

Up to flank speed went the destroyers and cruisers, driving to place themselves between the carrier and the incoming enemy planes. The Yorktown, too, could be seen picking up speed. White water was curling away from her bow.

"She's launching fighters," someone on our bridge yelled. Off the patched flight deck the little Wildcats were roaring out to the attack. There was no preliminary circling this time. Straight for the enemy they flew, throttles full out.

Far to the north we saw the first evidence of the attack—the flash of exploding planes. At the same time came the report from the attacking fighters that the enemy planes were torpedo bombers, the Kogekiki '97s.

As they came in visual range, flying about five hundred feet off the water and in a fast, downward glide, every gun that could be brought to bear opened fire. One of the cruisers nearest to the approach was using her main batteries, firing into the water to raise the splashes that could be as deadly for an approaching plane as a direct hit.

The northern sky was black with AA shellbursts, forming a deadly curtain of steel in front of the approaching Japanese formation.

One group of five enemy bombers zoomed up and over the shellbursts, and then spread to attack the cruisers and destroyers. One of our 5-inch guns, firing point-blank at the enemy pilot that had picked the Astoria as his victim, got a direct hit. The enemy bomber blew up in a great flash of flame. Another skidded into the sea, leaving a flaming trail of burning gasoline a quarter of a mile in length.

Two of the Japanese pilots were very brave men. Right through the curtain of antiaircraft fire they flew, straight for the Yorktown. Captain Elliott Buckmaster, on the Yorktown's bridge, saw them and started an evasive turn. The "Mighty Y," lacking her usual speed, couldn't quite make it. The two enemy bombers, flying within a hundred yards of each other, made their drops not over five hundred yards out from their target. The big two-thousand-pound torpedoes, slanting down to the water, porpoised once or twice, then ran straight and true for the American carrier.

A great column of water splashed over the Yorktown's deck at the first explosion, and she shuddered as though she had hit a stone wall. The other hit within seconds, apparently entering through the hole torn by the first explosion, and exploding deep in the ship.

"I can't bear to watch it," said a young ensign who himself

was to die two months later in the Solomons, and he turned away, his face set, tears in his eyes.

As the smoke and spray of the two explosions fell away we could see the big carrier heeling ominously to port.

"My God, she's going to capsize," Captain Scanland whispered, incredulously.

She went over fifteen degrees, twenty, twenty-five, thirty. Waves were lapping at the port edge of the thwartship passageways, through which the setting sun was shining.

"What's that signal?" the captain called to a signalman on the deck below as two colored flags could be seen going up to the Yorktown's yardarm. But it was unnecessary to ask again. They could be plainly seen, whipping in the wind. They were HL (hypo love, to use the phonetics of the fleet). They meant, "I'm abandoning ship."

From below decks blue-clad and khaki-clad figures could be seen climbing topside. Soon they were sliding down the lines to the water.

The "Mighty Y" was fighting hard to save herself. As she rocked on the long Pacific swells, she would seem, at times, to regain some of her trim. Then she would lean over again, as though tired of the struggle. The water rushing through the hole in her side apparently had smothered whatever fires the torpedo explosions had set.

All vessels in the area had their small boats over the side, while the destroyers nosed in as close as they could without endangering the swimming men, and started pulling survivors up onto their low decks.

The oil-covered sea was alive with bobbing heads, small rafts and 5-inch shell casings that had slid off the decks, or had been blown off by the force of the torpedo explosions. Unless you looked closely to see they were not leaving a wake, it was difficult to distinguish them from a submarine periscope.

For over an hour the work of rescue went on. Then, convinced there were no more survivors to be picked up, the escort vessels took up their small boats and the force formed up and headed east. One destroyer was left on guard.

As we headed toward the darkening eastern sky the Yorktown was silhouetted against the setting sun. Viewed from broadside her steep list did not show and she looked as battleworthy as she had that morning.

Two days later, just at dusk, one of the Japanese submarines that were in the area found her and drove two torpedoes into her starboard side. Hitting opposite to the hole torn by the aerial torpedoes, the new torpedo hits opened up new compartments that filled with water and corrected the list. Other bulkheads continued to give way during the night and she sank the morning of June 7. Captain Buckmaster and a picked crew had gone back aboard her from the destroyer Hammann that day and were on her when she received her death blow. The Hammann, which was lying alongside the carrier, furnishing her power and light, also was hit by two torpedoes and sank. For some reason, the Hammann's depth charges had not been set on "safe" and when she went down they exploded, killing several of her men who had not been injured by the torpedo hits.

It was announced that the submarine that sank the two ships probably was destroyed, but men of the destroyer guard that attacked them said they believed the submarine, or at least one of the two that made the attack, got away. It was seen on the surface, making good speed, before darkness foiled further pursuit.

Members of the Yorktown's former crew lined the rails of the rescue ships as long as they could see their ship. Many of them were crying as she faded out against the dying afterglow.

Just before dark, the Enterprise and the Hornet came within visual range of the Astoria, and Admiral Spruance sent a message to Admiral Fletcher saying the Yorktown had been avenged.

"Fourth carrier found and our planes successfully attacked," he said.

178]

So ended the first day of the Battle of Midway. Against the American loss of sixteen planes, some three hundred men and the disabling of one aircraft carrier stood enemy losses of four aircraft carriers, one destroyer, one heavy cruiser, and damage to several other vessels. Three and perhaps four ships had been sunk out of the transport train in the attacks the previous day and night by the Flying Fortresses and the Catalinas.

That evening a decision was made that saved the Japanese from an even worse disaster.

The reports were not yet in from all sources. Admiral Spruance knew that the Japanese had been dealt a heavy blow, but just how heavy was not then known. It was days before it was known the Hiryu definitely had been sunk. Thirty survivors, who had been abandoned aboard her, were picked up from a lifeboat. They said she sank the night of June 4–5.

The maneuvering during the day had taken the American carrier force within a hundred miles of the Japanese. It was known they had battleships with their force. Despite erroneous press reports in the States at the time, we had none.

Instead of continuing the pursuit during the darkness, which would have put the American carriers at dawn within striking distance of the disorganized Japanese striking force and the enemy transport train that continued blindly on toward Midway, the two American carriers and their escorts ran eastward during the night.

The American carriers turned westward again at dawn but made no contacts that day. Marine and army planes, however, the latter carrying navy observers to guard against any more attacks on our own vessels (the army had announced the sinking of a light cruiser that turned out, on examination of photographs, to be an American submarine that made a crash dive and escaped unscathed) found some enemy vessels on June 5 and attacked, scoring possible hits on three damaged enemy cruisers.

The Japanese forces were in complete disorder. The air was

[179

filled with frantic messages, the ribald version of one, which Admiral Halsey likes to repeat, being:

"Send help. Send it fast. In saving my face I lost my ass."

Many high navy officers believe that the ranking admiral of the force must have been killed aboard the Kaga or Akagi, perhaps more than one admiral; and the Japanese had no "plan" as to what they would do if they met heavy opposition.

When he saw that he had lost contact with the remnants of the enemy striking force, Admiral Spruance set his course west of south to bring him within striking range of the enemy transports. Much slower than the combatant ships and not so well protected, they should have been duck soup for the dive bombers, which were about all the striking planes the American carriers still had, so many torpedo bombers having been lost June 4.

Someone in Pearl Harbor or Washington, however, probably not knowing his position, ordered the admiral to concentrate on the combatant ships. When the message was received he was almost in position to launch his planes against the transport, but he obeyed orders and changed his course to the northward. Later an order came for the destroyers to close the enemy ships for a torpedo attack. It came at a time when they had only enough fuel for six hours' fast steaming. That order was disregarded.

After turning north, the carriers located two groups of enemy ships and attacked one consisting of Japan's two most deadly 8-inch gun cruisers, the Mogami and the Mikuma, and three destroyers. The Mikuma and one destroyer were sunk by dive-bombing attacks, and the Mogami was heavily hit. She also was thought to have sunk, but the Japanese may have been able to salvage her.

By nightfall of June 6 all contact with the fleeing enemy had been lost. Some of the ships had gone to the north to join up with the diversion forces that had attacked Dutch Harbor and later occupied Kiska and Attu. The transports had headed south at their best speed and now were under the protection of the land-based planes from Wake and the Marshalls.

Midway was the most stunning and one-sided defeat ever suffered by a major fleet. In a period of a month the Japanese had lost six of their eleven major carriers, most of the air groups from them, five heavy cruisers, at least five destroyers, three or four big transports, and perhaps fifteen thousand to twenty thousand men. Many other ships, including three battleships, had been damaged. The naval odds in the Pacific were evening up.

Strategically and tactically, the operation had been up to all expectations. Our airmen had proved themselves far superior to the Japanese, and our ships had shown a much greater ability to beat off opposing attack than had the enemy.

The last big Japanese offensive, one which, had it been successful, would have changed the whole picture in the Pacific, had been stopped cold. The Japanese navy had been punished as never before in its history. From that day the Japanese have not been able to take one forward step. Nor have they attempted one.

GREEN DRAGON IN ITS LAIR

A camouflaged Navy motor torpedo boat, which the little bandy-legged men of Japan learned to fear in the South Pacific, tied up for repairs at a secret river base on New Guinea. They hid in inlets and along the rivers during the daytime and sailed out at night to attack enemy supply lines.

RELIC OF MIDWAY

A Japanese 8-inch gun heavy cruiser of the Mogami class after United States carrier dive bombers had worked her over during the great air-sea battle north of Midway June 4-7, 1942. Copies of this photograph were widely posted throughout the Hawaiian Islands to convince any skeptical Japanese as to who had won.

HONORS FOR THE BRAVE

Rear Admiral Charles E. Rosendahl, America's leading lighter-than-air expert, wearing the Navy Cross awarded him for the courageous fighting of his heavy cruiser in a night battle against the Japanese in the Solomons. Secretary of the Navy Knox pinned on the decoration. Admiral Rosendahl returned from the Pacific to take command of the Navy Air Ship Training Program.

PART IV

THE OFFENSIVE PHASE

CHAPTER I

Battle of the Solomons

THE DECISIVE defeat of the Japanese at Midway, following by only a month the carrier actions in the Coral Sea that had turned back the enemy's attempt to extend his conquests in the Southwest Pacific, at long last made it possible to concentrate our thinly spread naval and marine forces for an offensive of their own.

The balance of sea power still swung heavily in favor of the Japanese, despite the loss of their four carriers at Midway and the two in the Coral Sea, but the odds were narrowing. The upsetting of their timetable also had made it quite probable that they could not be ready for another offensive thrust for some months. Organization of expeditions such as the twin-pronged thrusts toward Port Moresby and New Caledonia in the South in May and against Midway and the Aleutians in the Central and North Pacific in June involves problems in logistics that cannot be solved in a matter of weeks.

Decision was reached to strike in the Solomons, at the air-and-naval bases the Japanese were building on Guadalcanal and on Tulagi, which lie only twenty miles apart across a small inland sea, at the southeastern end of the Solomon Island chain.

A strong Japanese naval-and-air base at that point in the Solomons would be a dagger pointed at our Australian supply line at the stretch where it was weakest. We had to move quickly before the Japanese could complete the field and get installed there the air strength that would make any attempt later much more costly.

The enemy already was established in the Upper Solomons. He had moved in on Tulagi and Guadalcanal early in May. It was the ships of his occupation forces that fliers from the U.S.S.

Yorktown attacked there on May 4, the first action in the Battle of the Coral Sea.

The move against the Solomons was not an improvisation. An attack in that area had long been planned. In the previous January Admiral Nimitz, in discussing with correspondents at Pearl Harbor the gigantic problem facing our forces in the Pacific, had swept his hand across the map over the Solomons and said that we must of necessity attack from that direction.

Considerable work already had been done in preparing for it. We had air bases and naval bases in process of construction, or already in operation, in the Fijis, at Tongatabu in the Tonga islands to the south of Fiji, at Noumea and elsewhere on New Caledonia, and at Efate and Espiritu Santo in the New Hebrides. The latter base was only six hundred miles from Guadalcanal.

The first marine division had been training under Major General Alexander Archer Vandegrift in New Zealand and was ready to go.

The move was improvised only in that it was made before we were entirely ready, a fact that became painfully evident in the early stages of the campaign when we failed for various reasons, but largely because of the unpreparedness and timidity of our high navy command, to keep reinforcements moving in and to give the marines on the island the air-and-naval protection they needed. It was not until November that this handicap was finally overcome and the possibility of losing the positions that had been won so cheaply finally dissolved before a tide of men and planes and supplies.

Our 1942 offensive in the Solomons, in New Guinea, and in the Aleutians will probably be given a rather small place when the final story of our war against Japan is told. And rightly so. All of these operations were on a small scale, compared with the Russian, North African, and Italian campaigns, and those yet to come in the Pacific and on the continents of Europe and Asia.

They were important at the time, however. They forced Japan on the defensive. They gave our sea, air, and land forces the knowledge that the Japanese is only a second-rate fighting man. They provided a pattern of attack we did not have before and which could be learned only the hard way.

The greatest effect of the three campaigns in a military sense was the losses inflicted on the Japanese navy-and-air force. Those losses were out of all proportion to the strategic value of the island bases involved. They were losses the Japanese could ill afford to take, and which it is doubtful they have been able to replace.

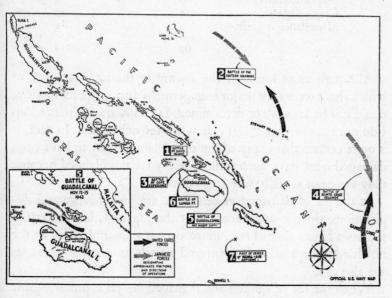

In a period of three days in mid-November, in the waters around Savo Island, off Guadalcanal and up "the slot" of the Solomons toward Bougainville, the Japanese navy lost to United States planes and surface ships one or perhaps two battleships, either six or seven heavy cruisers, two light cruisers, six destroyers and twelve transports, six of them of fifteen thousand to twenty thousand tons.

In the six months of the Guadalcanal campaign, from August 7, 1942, to February 10, 1943, when Major General Alexander

[187

M. Patch, U.S.A., announced that the island was "secure," United States Navy communiqués announced the following Japanese losses:

	Sunk or probably sunk	Damaged
Battleships	2	7
Carriers	1	4
Cruisers (light & heavy)	11	31
Destroyers	22	51
Transports	24	13
Oilers	0	2
Seaplane tenders	0	2
Cargo vessels	5	15
Miscellaneous craft	4	1
	69	113

Although exact losses of the enemy in the night actions, of which there were four major engagements during the six months, could not be accurately determined, from my own observations I do not believe the official claims are far out of line. In fact, it is quite certain that many of the ships claimed only to have been damaged must have been sunk. They were not claimed because they were not actually seen to go down.

In the list of damaged vessels there are probably several duplications, since it was known that the Japanese, lacking repair facilities closer than Truk, more than a thousand miles to the northwest, kept slightly damaged vessels in combat areas, as we also did.

When the list of sunken and damaged vessels is put alongside the estimated Japanese fleet strength at the start of the war, the cost to them of the Solomons campaign becomes truly staggering: more than half of their battleship strength sunk or heavily damaged; more than half of the carriers they had left after the Coral Sea and Midway; three-quarters of their cruisers, and three-quarters of their destroyer strength. This truly was vengeance for Pearl Harbor in overwhelming measure.

In addition to these major ship losses, the Japanese also lost hundreds of barges and landing craft. The beaches of Guadalcanal were littered for miles with the wreckage of them.

Our fleet losses during the same period, from surface engagements, air attacks, and submarines, were:

	Sunk
Battleships	0
Carriers	2
Heavy Cruisers	
(including the Australian Canberra)	6
Light Cruisers	2
Destroyers	15
Destroyer Transports	
(converted four-stackers)	3
Transports	1
	29

Two of our battleships, two of our carriers and several of our cruisers and destroyers were damaged, but all have now been repaired and are back with the fleet. Some of them, damaged in early engagements, were back in time to take part in the final phases of the Guadalcanal campaign.

The Japanese losses in men have never been accurately determined, but the total, both afloat and ashore, must have been fifty thousand or better. Radio Tokyo put the losses on the island alone at 16,743, and it never has been known to overestimate such matters. On the twelve transports destroyed by the Guadalcanal fliers on November 14 and 15 were an estimated thirty thousand to forty thousand troops. Many of those certainly did not escape. Losses from combatant ships sunk also must have been heavy, as none of the Japanese sailors who were pulled from the sea by our rescue boats wore life belts.

Authenticated Japanese plane losses were 797, and many more damaged planes probably never got home. Lacking self-sealing gas tanks, any puncture of their fuel supply, even if it did not set the plane on fire, spelled for the crew a forced landing in hostile territory. Many of our fliers were sheltered and taken safely back to base by friendly natives when forced down off shore or on one of the jungle islands. The Japanese fliers got their throats cut.

Our own plane and personnel losses during the six months have never been made public, but they were only a fraction of the Japanese totals. We lost more men killed and missing in the sea actions than were killed ashore.

Tropical diseases, especially malaria, were a more crippling foe than the Japanese. We lost almost as many planes on the ground or in operational accidents as we did in combat.

Our combat losses, in comparison with the Japanese, were almost unbelievably small. For instance, from October 16 to October 31 our fliers, operating from Guadalcanal, army, navy and marines, accounted for seventy Zero fighters, eighteen two-motored horizontal bombers, nineteen dive bombers, and five float planes, with a loss for our side of only seventeen planes and but four pilots. Surely a shining tribute to American fighting men of the air and the sturdy planes they flew.

The marines under General Vandegrift set a pattern of jungle fighting that has been followed in all subsequent campaigns, on Rendova, New Georgia, Bougainville and New Britain. His men did not move without reconnaissance, a lack of which cost the army much prestige in the Aleutians. They moved only in the daytime, digging in and holding strong points at night, firing at anything that moved, and infantry was never used to do what artillery could do.

Japanese prisoners captured on Guadalcanal said the most terrifying thing they had to undergo was the incessant day-and-night shelling, the shattering impact of the marine artillery, which often threw a barrage only fifty yards ahead of our advancing troops.

The best summary of the Guadalcanal campaign was written by General Vandegrift in his farewell message on relinquishing command to General Patch, December 8, 1942. Although there still was heavy fighting to be done, the issue was no longer in doubt.

Titled a "Letter of Appreciation for Loyal Services," the general's division order said:

"In relinquishing command in the Guadalcanal area I hope that in some small measure I can convey to you my feelings of pride in your magnificent achievement and my thanks for the unbounded loyalty, limitless self-sacrifice, and high courage which have made these accomplishments possible.

"To the soldiers and marines who have faced the enemy in the fierceness of night combat; to the pilots, army, navy, and marine, whose unbelievable achievements have made the name 'Gaudalcanal' a synonym for death and disaster in the language of the enemy; to those who have labored and sweated within the lines at all manner of prodigious and vital tasks; to the men of the torpedo boat command slashing at the enemy in night sorties; to our small band of devoted allies who have contributed so vastly in proportion to their numbers; to the surface forces of the navy associated with us in signal triumphs of their own, I say that at all times you have faced without flinching the worst that the enemy could do to us and have thrown back the best he could send against us.

"It may well be that this modest operation, begun four months ago today, has, through your efforts, been successful in thwarting the larger aims of our enemy in the Pacific. The fight for the Solomons is not yet won but 'tide what may' I know you, as brave men and men of good will, will hold your heads high and prevail in the future as you have in the past."

CHAPTER 2

The Marines Land

THE TULAGI-GUADALCANAL expeditionary force sailed into the Coral Sea on August 5 and headed north along the line of the 160th degree of east longitude toward the Solomon Islands.

It was the largest American force ever assembled in the Pacific

Ocean. There were three carriers, the Saratoga, Enterprise, and Wasp, the new thirty-five-thousand-ton battleship North Carolina, a dozen light and heavy American cruisers, three Australian cruisers, including the Canberra, and many transports, supply ships, and tankers. The total was sixty-nine ships.

The force had been gathering for almost a month. It was under tactical command of Vice Admiral Frank Jack Fletcher, who had been given another star after Midway. The strategic commander was Vice Admiral Robert Lee Ghormley, who had his headquarters in New Zealand. In charge of the landing force was Rear Admiral Kelly Turner, who recently had gone to the Pacific from Admiral King's staff in Washington. General Vandegrift was commanding officer of the marines, which included the first division and the first raider battalion, in charge of Colonel Merritt Edson.

A full-scale rehearsal of the landing had been held a week before. The various units of the force, which had come from New Zealand, from Australia, from Pearl Harbor, and from the Atlantic by way of the Panama Canal, had rendezvoused south of the Fijis. High winds and low tide had interfered with the landing attempt, but at least the men had received the benefit of a day's practice getting in and out of the small boats.

On August 5 the weather was entirely too pleasant for comfort, with a calm sea and a clear sky. Planes from the three carriers kept a tight patrol around the force to shoot down any enemy snoopers who might come around.

The morning of August 6 also was clear, but by noon the weather had begun to close in, and the big force steamed north the rest of the day under the protecting cover of a low overcast and occasional rain squalls.

As the tropic night came down, the American force was within less then two hundred miles of Guadalcanal. Apparently it had not been detected.

It should be explained here that the Japanese, in all their operations through New Guinea and the Solomons, seldom ventured far inland. They seized only the harbors and the narrow coastal plains which they needed for airports. One reason for this was because the Japanese quickly alienated the natives, who had been well treated by the Australians and the British. The blacks soon learned to hate the arrogant little men from the north. The Japanese were terrified of the knife-swinging, bushy-haired Melanesians.

The main Japanese installations were on the small islands of Tulagi, Gavutu and Tanamboga in the Tulagi Harbor area and along the northern coastal plain of the big island of Guadalcanal.

Guadalcanal, which appears as Guadalcanar on many old maps and is so spelled by New Zealand and Australian newspapers, is the second largest island of the Solomons group. Only Bougainville is greater in area.

The islands were given their name "The Isles of Solomon" in the sixteenth century by a Spanish promotion group that had financed a voyage of exploration by Don Alvaro de Mendaña de Neyra. When he returned in 1567 with tales of the tropic paradise he had discovered, the promoters, probably to stimulate colonization, gave out the story that these were the fabled islands whence had come the gold of King Solomon.

(There's gold in them thar hills, all right, but it wasn't found for almost four hundred years, and then by an Australian prospector, not a Spaniard.)

The Solomons are six hundred miles long, lying in a southeasterly-northwesterly direction between longitudes 155 and 162 degrees East, and latitudes 5 degrees and 11 degrees South. From Bougainville they stretch southeastward in roughly parallel columns, separated by an unnamed sound that the marines of Guadalcanal called "the slot." They are of volcanic origin, mountainous and well forested. Cold streams flow down out of the high hills.

The Lower Solomons, which include all of the group except

Bougainville and Buka, had been taken under British protection in 1893. At about the same time the two northern islands were claimed by Germany. After the first world war, Buka and Bougainville were mandated to Australia.

The Japanese occupied the Upper Solomons in March, establishing air bases and anchorages at Carola Harbor on Buka and at Kieta, Tonolei and Buin on Bougainville. There already was an airfield at Kieta. They also moved into the Shortlands and established an air-and-naval base at Faisi.

In April they moved down to Gizo Island, just south of Kolombangara and to Rekata Bay, on the north shore of Santa Isabel. In May they occupied Tulagi and Guadalcanal. They had small groups elsewhere, on Florida, Malaita, Kolombangara, Vella La Vella, New Georgia and Choiseul, but had not yet built airfields on those islands.

On the islands in Tulagi Harbor the Japanese were building a naval-and-seaplane base. It is not a particularly good harbor, being open to the south, from which direction come the prevailing winds. There are shoal areas along the eastern edge of the entrance. It had the advantage, for a naval base, of docks, oil tanks, houses, and a shallow inland passage across Florida island to Indispensable Straits.

On Guadalcanal the Japanese were building an airfield to the east of the Lunga River on a part of what had been Lever Brothers coconut palm plantation. (Lever Brothers is an American company, the makers of Lux soap.) The Japanese had cleared away the palm trees, had built parking spaces and on August 7 were within a few days of completion of the airfield.

Flying Fortresses of the eleventh bombardment group, under the command of the former West Point football star and coach, Col. Laverne (Blondy) Saunders, flying from Espiritu Santo in the New Hebrides, had been bombing the Japanese positions on Guadalcanal and in Tulagi Harbor for several days prior to the assault. At the same time bombers from New Guinea were raiding Rabaul and Buka, although not in any great strength.

The American force moved in on Guadalcanal during the predawn darkness, the transports and the cruisers that were to cover the landing going ahead of the carriers, which cruised to the west and south. The landing hour had been set for 9 A.M.

At 5:30 A.M., an hour before sunrise, the carriers began to launch their planes. That day I was riding the cruiser Minneapolis, flagship of a division, with Rear Admiral Carleton Wright in command. She was one of the carrier guard.

Because of the darkness, the carriers used their deck lights for the takeoff. As the planes took off they also turned on their running lights, to avoid collisions in the darkness. Against the dark sky the blue deck lights, the red and white running lights of the planes, and the blue flames of their exhausts gave a Christmas-tree effect against the eastern sky.

One of those small tragedies that are more poignant than a major disaster occurred as the planes of the Saratoga were taking off. One of the first ones away must have misjudged his altitude, for he turned sharply as he cleared the deck, and plunged into the sea. There was an explosion, then only darkness. The Minneapolis swung to one side so as not to run through the spot where he had fallen, and a destroyer dropped back to look for him. He never was found. Since this was to be the Saratoga's first combat, it also would have been the first one for the missing flier. And now he was gone before he had a chance to strike a blow for his country.

The other planes were away without incident, circling the formation until the squadrons were complete and then heading eastward toward the lightening sky and the enemy, their running lights growing dimmer and dimmer until they were gone.

We had run out of the overcast weather during the night, and the morning was one of those beautiful, cool sunrises when everything seems to be in tune except the men who inhabit the earth. A few scattered white clouds only accentuated the gold of the rising sun, the blue of the sky, and the verdant green of the great mountain peaks of Guadalcanal, which rise abruptly

[195

from the southwest shore of the island to an altitude of more than eight thousand feet.

The news was good, and immediate. The first group of fighters to arrive over Tulagi, a squadron from the Wasp led by Lieutenant Commander Courtney Shands, found eighteen Japanese planes on the water or pulled out on the beach for overhaul. Our fighters destroyed them in the time it took them to make their strafing runs. Other squadrons of fighters and dive bombers from the Wasp and the other carriers were ranging over the islands of Tulagi Harbor and the Japanese barracks and gun positions on Guadalcanal.

For an hour and a half, aided by thunderous barrages from the cruisers and destroyers off shore, they bombarded and strafed every Japanese position in the area.

Lieutenant Commander John Grider, the Minneapolis's communications officer, had provided me with a pair of earphones, and I listened in on the attack.

Each group had its station, on which it stayed until it was relieved. As each relief group came up, the retiring leader would brief the new commander on the position.

The squadron leaders were directing their men to where they would do the most good.

"There are three camouflaged sheds right in the middle of that field," one said. "Drop a few clunks on them. They look like ammunition sheds to me."

"Strafe along the edge of the woods beside the airfield," one of the fighter commanders ordered his men. "I see some people moving there."

"Get that archie," world-war term for antiaircraft, one of the fliers yelled. "Get him. There, at the corner of the field."

He must have been got because he wasn't mentioned again.

Aboard the carriers and the direction station on Admiral Turner's flagship, the transport McCawley, the reports of the fliers were being coordinated. At 7 A.M., half an hour after the attack had been launched, the situation looked so good that the landing hour was set ahead from 9 A.M. to 8 A.M.

The transports had gone to within about three miles of the shore, put over the Higgins boats, tank lighters and amphibious tractors, and the marines were ready to go.

Brigadier General William H. Rupertus, then second in command to General Vandegrift and later head of the first division as a major general, was in charge of the assault on Tulagi and Gavutu, the two selected for the first day's capture. General Vandegrift took charge of the landing on Guadalcanal.

On Guadalcanal and Tulagi the landings went as smoothly as if it only were practice. The Japanese, apparently thinking it was just another air raid, had abandoned their exposed beach positions and taken to the hills, as they had been doing when the Fortresses had come over on previous days. Warm food was found in the kitchens, and some on the tables.

Colonel LeRoy R. Hunt led the first wave to the Guadalcanal beach, landing to the east of the Lunga River. As only feeble opposition was encountered, the other waves followed as quickly as they could get into their boats. By noon they had penetrated to the airfield, the main objective. The last ones ashore went in swimming in the Lunga, which is really only a creek but is cool, and at that time, before it was polluted by dead bodies and construction activities farther inland, provided an inviting swimming hole.

The Tulagi garrison also was taken by surprise, and the marines were ashore and up on the ridge before meeting any serious opposition. Landing on the north and northwest shores of the island, they quickly joined forces and started pushing southeast on the three-mile-long island toward the town, prison, and hospital, which are grouped along the shore at the southeastern tip. Our fliers were bombing and strafing the Japanese in that area.

The stiffest opposition was encountered on Gavutu and Tanambogo, the two small islands to the east of Tulagi. It was on

[197

these islands and near by the seaplanes had been destroyed. Both are small hills sticking out of the water. The first landings were made on Gavutu, which was seaward of Tanambogo. Destroyers covered the landing boats until within a thousand yards of the beach, but then lifted their fire. Immediately the Japanese rushed out of their dugouts and manned their machine guns. It was on Gavutu that the bulk of the first day's casualties of two hundred men were received.

By nightfall the first day, the marines who had landed on Guadalcanal had control of the airfield and over two miles of the beach. Gavutu had been cleared of the enemy garrison, of about five hundred men, some of whom had escaped across the causeway to Tanambogo. The Japanese on Tulagi were penned in the southern end of the island, with the marines above them on commanding heights.

The American carrier bombers, who had maintained a shuttle service all day from the carriers lying fifteen to twenty miles off the island and the Japanese positions, were begging in late afternoon for the marines ashore to give them some targets on which to lay their eggs.

"I've got a bomb I haven't used," one would say. "Tell me where I can put it so it will do some good."

The Japanese sent down a plane strike of dive bombers from Buin in midafternoon. The carrier fighters met them west of Savo and shot down ten or twelve with the loss of only one of our own planes, the pilot of which was saved. The Japanese pilots scored only one hit, on the destroyer Jarvis. (The Jarvis left the next night under her own power but was never heard of again. The supposition is she was torpedoed.)

At the end of the first day the situation seemed to be well in hand. We had complete control of the air and sea; Gavutu was entirely ours; we had numerical superiority on Tulagi; the Guadalcanal beachhead was well established; the partially completed airfield was in the hands of the marines; patrols were ashore on Florida and Malaita.

The American carriers maneuvered west and south of Guadalcanal during the night, while the cruisers and destroyers inside patrolled the two straits on either side of the small island of Savo, which lies between Guadalcanal and Florida. Japanese submarines were reported in the area, but no surface vessels. A night attack on our positions on Tulagi was thrown back in hand-to-hand fighting.

At dawn the next day the carriers' planes were back over the island. The marines by then had set up shore radio stations and were able to direct our planes to specific targets.

The Tanambogo garrison had been reinforced during the night by Japanese swimming over from Florida. A reserve force of marines was thrown against them in Higgins boats, while small tanks that had been landed on Gavutu waddled across the partially demolished causeway. The landings were supported by both destroyer fire and strafing and bombing by carrier planes. By noon the last Japanese had been cleared off the island.

On Tulagi our troops also were advancing against the last spots of resistance. As they approached the hospital, on a ridge near the southern end of the island, the marines thought they saw women at the windows. Orders were given for a reconnaissance. As the marines approached within grenade-throwing distance the women, or men dressed as women, disappeared from the windows and the reconnaissance party was showered with grenades and brought under machine-gun fire.

The marines withdrew, and called for supporting fire from the ships. Steaming slowly along at point-blank range, the destroyer Monnsen opened on the hospital. The first hit set off an explosion that flattened trees for yards on either side. The Japanese had been using the hospital as an ammunition dump. It was the first of many violations by the Japanese of the rules of civilized warfare (if there can be such a distinction in the business of killing).

The Japanese, better organized now, sent down two plane

strikes that day, one a force of an estimated twenty to thirty two-motored Mitsubishi '97s from Rabaul. Some of them carried torpedoes.

Again the fighters engaged the Japanese planes far from the target.

Our ships all were under way by the time the survivors had won through the fighter screen. They threw up an annihilating barrage of antiaircraft fire. One Japanese bomber, disabled by bullets from the ships, crashed on the after deck of the George F. Elliott, setting a fire that got out of control. The old ship, the former Baltimore mail liner Los Angeles, of about ten thousand tons displacement, had to be abandoned.

Neither on this day nor the day before had the Japanese bombers discovered the carrier force, a much more inviting target than the transports and supply ships.

As night fell on August 8 the first offensive by the United States in the Pacific was an unqualified success. Air, sea, and land forces had operated as a team for the first time. Our losses were small. We held Tulagi, Gavutu, Tanambogo and Makambo —the four small islands that enclose Tulagi Harbor. The marines on Guadalcanal had extended their lines and already had started to work completing the airfield the Japanese had begun. Japanese laborers who had been on Guadalcanal, most of them undersized, undernourished little men, obviously army rejects, were being rounded up by marine patrols led by natives. Unarmed, they offered no resistance.

Work of unloading the boats was slow because all the docks had been destroyed and everything had to be manhandled ashore from Higgins boats or small tank lighters, the only type of amphibious equipment we had at that time. Another day would see that completed, then the transport fleet could return to base and start bringing in reinforcements and supplies.

Dinner aboard the Minneapolis that night was turned into a celebration.

CHAPTER 3

The First Battle of Savo

THE EVENING of August 8, 1942, off Savo Island was overcast. Occasional rain squalls swept in from the east. Heat lightning played along the horizon.

The transports of the invasion fleet maneuvered slowly off Kukum Beach, on Guadalcanal, and off Tulagi Harbor. All the troops were ashore, but much material still remained to go into the boats. It was a slow process, with only the bobbing Higgins boats and tank lighters to do the ferrying. The crews of all the ships were exhausted by two days of nerve tension and the hardest kind of work. At least one more day of unloading was ahead for most of the ships.

At the westward entrance to the sea area between Guadalcanal and Florida, a sea which has no name on the hydrographic office maps but is known throughout the islands as Savo Sound, the screening force of cruisers and part of the destroyers that had covered and supported the landings of the marines were steaming a defensive patrol. Destroyers were on guard at the eastern end, where two channels lead into Indispensable Straits, Sealark Channel in the center and Lengo Channel to the south, along the shore of Guadalcanal. Through that area were many small coral heads and uncharted pinnacles.

The screening force, as well as the transports, was under tactical command of Rear Admiral Turner, whose title was Commander Amphibious Forces South Pacific. The second ranking officer was Rear Admiral Crutchley of the Royal Navy. He had his flag on the Australian cruiser Australia.

Admiral Turner had planned to move his headquarters to the United States heavy cruiser Astoria that night, but for some reason he changed his mind and asked the British admiral to come to the McCawley for a conference. That left the screening force without an officer of flag rank. The captain of the United States heavy cruiser Vincennes, being senior, technically was in command.

That afternoon two Japanese task forces had been sighted heading south from Truk. One, consisting of three heavy cruisers, two aircraft ships, which carry eight to ten seaplanes for scouting work and light bombing, and three destroyers, was on a course for Rabaul on New Britain Island, the main Japanese base in the South and Southwest Pacific. The other force, of three heavy cruisers and several destroyers steaming at a speed of twenty knots, was on a course for Guadalcanal. Plotting the position and speed of the latter force on the map, it was evident that if it was heading for Guadalcanal it should reach Savo Island about 2 o'clock the next morning.

To cover adequately the passages on either side of Savo Island, our force was divided. To the south were three Australian cruisers, one American heavy cruiser, and three destroyers. To the north were the American heavy cruisers Astoria, Vincennes, and Quincy, and three destroyers.

The American forces were steaming at ten knots to conserve fuel and also because there was not too much sea room for fast maneuvering in either passage. The passage between Savo and Cape Esperance, on Guadalcanal, is about seven and a half miles wide. The northern passage, between Savo and Florida Island, is about fourteen miles wide.

Like the men of the transports, the crews of the combatant ships were dog-tired. They had had little rest for forty-eight hours, had done a lot of bombarding and had fought off three attacks by enemy planes. The best they could hope for, until the transports were unloaded, was a heel-and-toe watch bill; that is, watch on and watch off. Most of the ships were standing that sort of a condition watch that night.

Late in the day Admiral Turner had made his customary evaluation of the situation, a sort of progress report, which he had broadcast to his command. In it he called attention to the contact report on the enemy force headed for Guadalcanal, but made the guess that they probably would stop for the night at Rekata Bay, on the north shore of Santa Isabel. He had asked Admiral Fletcher, who was south of Guadalcanal with the carriers, to try to locate the enemy ships the next morning and hit them with dive bombers and torpedo planes.

The commanders of the American force knew the enemy was aware where they were, since the Japanese still had positions at Cape Esperance, on Savo Island, and on Florida, but they apparently believed with Admiral Turner that so small a Japanese force would not attack that night. No extra precautions were taken. One captain did not even include the contact report in his night orders, and the young officer who had the deck did not know of the presence of the enemy force within striking distance of his ship until they opened fire. On most navy ships only heads of departments are allowed to read the secret dispatches. If there is anything the captain thinks the junior officers should know, he puts it in his night orders.

Too, everything had gone so well the first two days that everyone was feeling a little cocky—an old American habit—despite fatigue. Conditions were ripe for disaster.

Shortly after midnight two planes flew high over the force. They were not identified as friendly, but they showed running lights and they dropped no bombs. No one opened fire on them. They remained in the vicinity, watching the allied ships maneuver. The enemy fliers must have noted that they were sailing a square, in column, and were making only ten knots.

Just before 2 A.M., steaming at an estimated twenty-five knots, the Japanese force cleared Savo Island to the south and engaged the Australian-American force. The innocent-appearing planes silhouetted the allied ships with flares. Making a coordinated gun-and-torpedo attack, the Japanese cruisers and destroyers quickly put the Canberra out of action, hurting her so vitally that she sank a few hours later. The United States cruiser with that force, the Chicago, took a torpedo in the bow. The destroyers Ralph Talbot and Patterson also were hit.

Sweeping around Savo close to the shore, the Japanese vessels engaged the American vessels. In quick succession they hit the Astoria, Quincy, and Vincennes, some of them with both torpedoes and eight-inch shells. The Quincy blew up and sank almost immediately. The Vincennes and Astoria remained afloat for some hours. Then they, too, went down.

Our force had been caught like a flock of ducks sitting on the water, and offered no effectual resistance. The Astoria, riddled by an estimated one hundred to a hundred and twenty-five hits by 8-inch and 5-inch shells, fired only eleven salvos. Many of her men were killed before they ever reached battle stations in answer to the general quarters alarm. Our gunners discovered that night, too, that some lots of star shells were no good. One cruiser, attempting to illuminate the destroyers making a torpedo attack on her, fired a hundred star shells and got only five flares out of the lot.

Our casualties on the four ships were approximately one thousand men.

The action was over in a matter of minutes as the Japanese force, probably untouched, swept on around Savo and out the northern passage. The enemy ships did not come within fifteen miles of any of our transports, and made no effort to attack them.

It may be that the Japanese were heading for the transports when they came into Savo Sound that night. The navy communiqué said they were, and that they had been "intercepted" and "forced to retreat." In view of the plane reconnaissance the enemy had made, that would seem open to question. To those on the spot it appeared that the Japanese had done exactly what they intended to do, had done it masterfully, and that the United States Navy had suffered an even more humiliating defeat than at Pearl Harbor.

Damage control work aboard the stricken cruisers was not

up to standards achieved later. Fires raged unchecked. Emergency apparatus failed to work. Today, the Astoria probably would be saved.

The news of the disaster threw the fleet into what approached a panic. Admiral Fletcher took his carrier force out of the area at high speed. The partially unloaded transports were ordered to leave as soon as possible. They pulled out through the night and the next morning. Ashore marines grimly dug in and awaited the worst the enemy could send against them. As the enemy bombers came over Guadalcanal August 9, we could hear the radio control station vainly imploring, "Any friendly planes in the area please answer." On the ships, far to the south, navy men were ashamed to look at each other.

CHAPTER 4

Battle of the Eastern Solomons

THE JAPANESE required two weeks to organize a major effort to attempt the recapture of Guadalcanal and Tulagi.

In the meantime they were harassing the marines with daily bomber raids from Rabaul and night shellings by submarines and destroyers. But they were doing little damage. Two efforts to put flanking groups ashore, one with radio equipment to replace that which they had abandoned on August 7, had met with disaster. The radio-equipped party of thirty men was killed and their equipment was seized.

The second attempt was more ambitious, an estimated eight hundred men landing from destroyers one night to the east of the marine beachhead, which now had been extended to a distance of three miles along the shore, and a mile to two miles inland. The marines met this larger force at the Tenaru River and annihilated it, killing all but thirty men, who were taken prisoner. The colonel leading the Japanese force committed suicide.

The marines completed the airfield on August 19, and the next day the first contingent of marine planes flew in to Henderson Field, named for Major Lofton B. Henderson, who had dived his burning bomber into a Jap carrier at Midway. They had been ferried to the South Pacific on an escort carrier, which took them within range of Guadalcanal, then launched them. The force consisted of twelve Douglas Dauntless dive bombers and nineteen Grumman Wildcats. Lieutenant Colonel Richard C. Mangrum, of Seattle, a former star tennis player, was in command of the dive bombers, and Major John Smith, who was to shoot down nineteen enemy planes before he was relieved in mid-October, led the fighter squadron, the famous VF223. Among the fighter pilots was Captain Marion E. Carl, of Hubbard, Ore., who received his baptism of fire at Midway, where he was credited with two Japanese planes. He got fourteen more while flying from Henderson Field.

General Vandegrift, in discussing one day the three major events of the early months of Guadalcanal, said the arrival of the first planes was the biggest. The tired, battered marines who had been forced to take to their dugouts every time the Japanese bombers came over without means to fight back, almost mobbed the pilots when they landed.

The American fliers had arrived just in time. Even as their wheels touched the brown loam of Guadalcanal for the first time, the Japanese were starting down from the Marshalls and the Carolines with a major force.

The Japanese force, spearheaded by three carriers, was spread out in a great arc north of Guadalcanal. One small carrier, the Ryuzo, or Ryujo, was on the eastern point of the arc. Farther to the west, almost due north of the island, were two larger carriers of the Zuikaku (which means "Lucky Stork") class. Cruisers and destroyers were with the Ryuzo. There were battleships as well with the two other carriers.

Ahead of this striking force was a group of several transports, escorted by cruisers and destroyers. Another enemy force of supply ships, transports, and destroyers were gathering at Gizo Island to the west.

American search planes first sighted the small carrier on August 23, and a strike of planes was launched from the Saratoga. The enemy ship apparently had sighted the American snooper, for the Saratoga planes could not find her. They searched until they were so short of gas they had to go on to Guadalcanal for the night instead of returning to their ship.

Admiral Fletcher ran south during the afternoon and early evening, but turned back north during the night to search again at dawn, with his carrier scouts, the area where the Japanese force had been sighted the day before. He had only two carriers with him, the Saratoga and the Enterprise. The Wasp was south, refueling, and the Hornet was too far to the east to join up for the battle.

At 1005 hours the morning of August 24 army Flying Fortresses sighted the Ryuzo, which was headed south with an escort of two cruisers and several destroyers. At almost the same time another search plane sighted a destroyer and two light cruisers several miles west of the Ryuzo; a third reported a force consisting of a battleship, a heavy cruiser, five destroyers, a transport, and a fleet oiler, south of the Shortland Islands on a course for Guadalcanal; and still a fourth reported several transports north of Santa Isabel. Things were building up to a climax, fast.

The American force continued north and west, closing the range with the Ryuzo. At noon we were east of Stewart Island, one hundred and fifty miles northeast of Guadalcanal. Aboard the carriers, on Henderson Field, and on supporting army bases, every available plane was being readied. At 1245 the Enterprise launched her air group to attack the Ryuzo. The whole force was at battle stations, ready for the show to begin.

The season was what passes for midwinter ten degrees south of the equator. It was hot in the sun but pleasant in the shade. A few white clouds sailed gracefully in the deep blue waters of the sky and cast their reflections on the surface of the even bluer sea.

Captain Frank J. Lowry, the Minneapolis's skipper, who was one of the most courteous gentlemen, best skippers and coolest men in a crisis I met in twenty months in the Pacific, called my attention to a ripple in a large white cloud to the west.

"It looks like a wagon track through a snow field, don't you agree?" he asked, pretending to wipe the sweat off his forehead. Captain Lowry had been born and raised in Iowa and always was talking of the farm he'd like to buy back in the Middle West when his navy days were over, of how he would stock it and plant and run it. Most of his service in recent years had been in warm climates, and he bemoaned the lack of change of seasons.

There was little time, however, for talk of snow fields, or the colors of the elms and maples and oaks in the fall. We were still admiring the cloud and talking of Iowa when two fighter pilots discovered an enemy plane several miles to the east of the force.

"He looks like a Jap to me," one of them said.

"We've got plenty of time," his section leader said, "look him over."

It didn't take long.

"He is a Jap," the first voice yelled excitedly.

"Okay, go get him," said the other, calmly.

At about that time one of the lookouts on our cruiser reported an unidentified plane approaching on the starboard beam.

The report had hardly been relayed to the bridge when there was a great flash of flame in that direction, some ten thousand to fifteen thousand yards away, and then the great funeral tower of smoke that marked the end of another Japanese plane.

I had seen many planes fall since that first one off Wake six months before, and when there was fire it was a 100-to-1 bet it would be a Japanese. Our fliers used to mention in their prayers at night the man who had invented self-sealing gas tanks and failed to include the Japanese on the secret in time for them to equip their planes with it. Many an American flier owes his life to those rubber tanks.

As the enemy plane fell flaming to the sea we made out the small, snub-winged American fighter following him down.

"Nice going, Dick," the calm voice said, still unexcited. "Come on, now, join up."

"Who shot down that plane?" the Saratoga fighter director asked. There was an unintelligible answer, which the director must have heard because he said:

"Well done, Ramsey. Well done."

The enemy plane, a four-motored Kawanishi patrol bomber, had approached so close to the force before "Dick" got him that there could be little question he had reported our strength, speed, and course, a course to which the force was committed so long as it had a striking group aloft seeking the enemy. Everyone stood by for the enemy attack that now was inevitable.

The first attack was only a feint by fighter planes. Intercepted by our fighters, they turned away, somewhere out in the blue sky beyond the reach of our binoculars. We heard only the fighters reporting their approach and then cursing them as they turned and fled.

"They were speed boys, all right," we heard one pilot report. At 1415 hours (2:15 P.M.), fifty minutes after the Kawanishi had gone down in flames, another Japanese search plane, this one a two-motored land bomber, was discovered twenty miles astern of the force. He met the same fate as the first snooper. The fighter who got him swooped so low as he made his lethal pass at the low-flying Japanese craft, his wingtip hit a wave.

[209

"Jeff, did your plane hit the water back there?" we heard a fellow pilot ask.

"Yes, it did," Jeff said.

The fighter director asked for the identity of the pilot, but they must not have heard him, for there was no answer. Later we saw a Wildcat landing aboard the Saratoga with a battered starboard wingtip. It was still flying as sturdily as ever.

An hour passed with no further alarms, and Captain Lowry relaxed general quarters and ConditionZed to let the men below get some fresh air. He put on a show of his rope tricks for the bridge force. He could make a rope do as many stunts as could Will Rogers.

Then an army Fortress picked up a single carrier, apparently the Ryuzo, reported that he had dropped four bombs at it and missed with all of them, "damn it to hell."

"There don't seem to be any fighters around," he reported. "This baby should be duck soup for some dive bomber."

He was a prophet not without honor. Within minutes we heard some of our attack group talking. They were dividing the assignment.

"We'll get the carrier, you take that cruiser on the left," we heard someone tell someone else. They plastered the carrier with several bombs and at least two or three torpedoes.

Late that evening a search plane reported the Ryuzo afire and listing, dead in the water, with destroyers removing the survivors of her crew.

Still another hour passed, and just as the American force had about decided the Japanese had expended their energy attacking Guadalcanal—a large force of planes had approached the island shortly after noon and had been chased away by the marine fighters with a loss to the attackers of seven bombers and five Zero fighters—the report was flashed through the fleet that "many bogies" were approaching out of the northwest.

The Saratoga and the Enterprise began launching their reserve fighters, and the force went up to flank speed.

"Here they come, Hank," we heard one fighter pilot tell another.

"Very good, I see them. About twenty-six bombers, don't you think?"

"Yes, let's go."

"Come on, Barney, peel off."

"Here I go."

"Hit 'em hard!"

"Come on, let's go, nobody's hitting them."

"Paul, on your left."

"I see them. I see them. We've got to get them."

"Drop those belly tanks and get going," another voice broke in.

"Okeh, Johnny. Let's go, gang. Give 'em hell! Whoopee."

All this was out over the horizon, but soon we saw thin streaks of flame falling toward the water, and we knew the boys were "on them" and giving them hell.

Then the ships of the force opened up.

The planes had come in on the Enterprise side and were concentrating on her and the North Carolina, which was seeing her first action.

The big, thirty-five-thousand-ton battleship, bristling with so many antiaircraft guns that she looked like a porcupine, seemed aflame from one end to the other as she opened up against the planes diving on her and the carrier. Those two American ships were big game for the enemy planes, if they could get in on them.

The bombs were dropping now. Ten miles away we could feel the shock through the water as a cluster landed astern of the Enterprise, spattering her with fragments and killing several men. I didn't learn it until weeks later, but the first bomb had killed Bill Williamson, a young lieutenant I had met at Art Wyeth's home in Honolulu only a month and a half before. I never had seen anyone so full of the joy of living as Bill that July afternoon at the Wyeths'.

The Japanese attack was not well coordinated, the dive bombers arriving well ahead of the torpedo planes. The sky was still black with the twisting smoke of the antiaircraft bursts, however, when from our bridge we saw a group of low-flying torpedo planes heading for the North Carolina. The big battlewagon's fire control must have seen them too, for suddenly her whole starboard side flared with the flash of her guns. A wall of black shellbursts, so compact and thick it was as though someone had pulled a black curtain across that sector of the sky, blossomed among the torpedo planes. As the wind began to whip it away not a plane was in sight, but from the water rose several wisps of smoke from burning oil and gasoline.

The firing had begun at 1710 (5:10 P.M.). At 1725 it was over. An estimated eighty enemy planes had launched the attack. When the reports of all the fliers and ships were tallied, seventy-one were accounted for. Forty-seven fell before the chattering machine guns of the Wildcat fighters, and the almost unbelievable total of twenty-four were shot down by the antiaircraft guns of the force.

The Enterprise had been hit and set afire, putting her out of action for a few weeks, but she was able to steam under her own power and before nightfall was recovering her planes and heading south with the rest of the force. The Wasp was speeding north to rejoin. The Hornet also was coming up, with more marine planes for Guadalcanal.

The marine and navy fliers on Guadalcanal, in addition to turning back the strong enemy air attack, also had struck at the Japanese transport force north of Santa Isabel, off Bradley Reefs. They had hit a cruiser, a destroyer, and four transports. With the customary marine-navy disinclination to claim any hits they were not absolutely sure had been made, the fliers reported that night serious damage only to a cruiser and a transport. A search plane flew over the area next day and found six burning ships. All had been abandoned. They were so wreathed in flame and smoke that he could not be sure of the class of any of them except the cruiser. The others, he thought, were transports.

The second round of the Battle of the Solomons had been won as had the first. Having no crystal ball, we could not forecast that the next few weeks were to see written one of the saddest chapters in the history of the United States fleet, which ended with the recall of both Admiral Fletcher and Admiral Ghormley, the two ranking navy commanders in the South Pacific.

The marines' desperate fight to hold what initially had been won so cheaply had just begun.

CHAPTER 5

On the Defensive

DARKNESS HAD fallen before the last plane was recovered on August 24. The Saratoga and other ships of the force had to turn on their running lights to guide the stragglers home. Finally the last one was aboard, the lights went out, and the force turned southward, escorting the crippled Enterprise out of the danger zone.

The Japanese carriers, their air strength chopped down to almost zero Zeros, also had turned tail and were running north for Truk, to get under cover of land-based planes and to secure air replacements for those shot down in the day's fighting.

To many of us who didn't have to make the decision, it looked as though we were missing a golden opportunity to deal the Japanese a much heavier blow than had been struck. The Saratoga had lost few planes, and those had been more than replaced by homeless birds from the Enterprise, who had been forced to seek another flight deck when the big E's rudder jammed because of the pounding she had taken and she went out of control just as she was getting up speed to recover planes. The Wasp was coming up at full speed with full fuel tanks.

Why not go after the retiring Japanese ships? The Ryuzo undoubtedly had gone down. She was burning and dead in the water. One of the big carriers had been hit by the Flying Fortresses. The Japanese fleet would have to gear its speed to that of the damaged flattop. By morning it might be possible to catch them. With little plane protection they should be fresh meat for our striking forces.

The memory of August 8–9 apparently still lingered on. The American force withdrew as fast as the Enterprise could go. By morning we were beyond any possibility of catching the retiring Japanese fleet.

Withdrawal of the Japanese striking force and the destruction of the transport train near Bradley Reefs did not mean that the enemy had given up on Guadalcanal. It was several weeks before the Japanese carriers came back, but transports, supply ships, destroyers, and cruisers began to pour down from the Japanese fourth-fleet base at Truk. Every day the search planes hopefully would report ten to twenty ships in the Shortlands, in Gizo Island anchorage, or en route down "the slot" to Guadalcanal.

The reports of enemy vessels headed for Guadalcanal with supplies and reinforcements became monotonous and routine. One pilot, one day, instead of sending the usual message that such-and-such a number of enemy ships was proceeding on course 120 at twenty knots (the course for Guadalcanal) merely reported the enemy position, then added "usual course, usual speed."

The Japanese were using the Upper Solomons as staging bases for their ships bound for Guadalcanal. They would make those harbors one day and lie there over night. The next afternoon they would start for Guadalcanal. They timed their runs so that even if they were sighted they had little to fear. Our planes from Guadalcanal could not reach them before dark.

By morning they would have unloaded their men and supplies and would be back under their own air cover. Night dive-bombing attacks on these ships were made by the marines, but with no great success.

"Why in the name of all that's holy don't we run up the south side of the Solomons at night, and work over those babies some bright dawn?" was the question the navy men were asking each other all through the force. "We're just submarine bait out here, running up and down between the New Hebrides and Guadalcanal."

There were lengthy wardroom discussions on just how such missions could be accomplished with little risk. It would have been feasible, if the admiral didn't want to risk the carriers for such a strike, to send in light surface forces for night bombardments. Our planes could illuminate the harbor, as the Japanese planes had illuminated our screening force off Savo, and the ships could give them a shelling that should be more effective than a dozen bombardments by horizontal bombers. The limited number of Fortresses were working industriously, but if the enemy ships were under way they had little chance of hitting them. There were few worthwhile targets ashore.

A contributing factor to the shackling of the navy was the division of authority in Oceania. Demarkation line between the Southwest Pacific and the South Pacific commands was longitude 160 degrees East, up which we had walked the chalk en route to attack Guadalcanal. Theoretically, all forces to the west of longitude 160 degrees East were under General MacArthur. Those to the east were under Admiral Ghormley. The fleet had orders to stay east of 160.

It was a situation that cried for correction, but the change was not made until the spring of 1943, when General MacArthur was given strategic command of all the South and Southwest Pacific areas. Navy wardrooms and army messes seethed with mutual recriminations.

Fate caught up with us in just twenty-two days. It was exactly what everyone had expected. The stock question at breakfast was, "Did anyone get torpedoed last night?"

When the Japanese fleet had started south on August 22, as usual they sent a screening force of submarines ahead. When the enemy fleet retired after the Battle of the Eastern Solomons, the submarines stayed. The navigator's chart was dotted every day with red crosses marking enemy submarine contacts. The American carriers and their escorts steamed daily through the area where they were thickest. As many as twenty would be plotted at one time.

The carriers' planes and the destroyers, ranging all round the task forces, took a toll of the undersea boats, making three probable kills in three days, but that in itself was a measure of the danger. One of the carrier planes got a sub on August 25, and so did a destroyer. On August 27 a carrier plane got another, sending the laconic report after the attack, "Sank one submarine; returning to ship."

The intensive plane search probably kept the enemy submarines down during the daytime, but the long, dark nights gave them a sufficiency of operating time to recharge their batteries and sweep their stations. It is quite probable the force had been sighted by some of them. If they watched very long they could even tell the course. We were wearing a groove in the ocean. One day we ran through a big oil slick where a submarine had been attacked on the force's track the day before.

On September 15 the Wasp force ran into a whole pack of submarines. It was the first time the Japanese undersea boats had been known to run in a pack, raising the question as to whether the little men might be getting from the Germans some expert advice, and perhaps even some submarine commanders. Three torpedoes hit the 14,700-ton carrier just forward of her island. Her gasoline stores became ignited, and after two hours of vain fighting, her skipper, Captain Forrest P. Sherman (not to be confused with the former Lexington captain, Frederick C. Sherman, now a rear admiral) had to abandon her.

Among the casualties was young Jack Singer, International News Service correspondent.

The destroyer O'Brien also was hit. Although she made port safely for emergency repairs, she had been hurt so badly that she broke in two while under way back to Pearl Harbor for dry-docking.

Since August 24 the carriers had not made a single offensive gesture. It would have been much better had they retired to a rear base behind torpedo nets and sat out that month.

The morale of the fleet was going down like an express elevator. The men wanted to fight. They wanted to give the marines on Guadalcanal some support, get along with the war. Instead they were kept on a chain, sweltering in tropic heat, in waters fairly crawling with hostile submarines.

The old adage that no general or admiral ever wins a battle, the other fellow loses it, took on a topical aura of truth.

Where, a month before, the military situation seemed well in hand, it now was rapidly getting out of control. We had only one undamaged carrier left in the Pacific, the Hornet. The Japanese were pouring men and supplies in to their forces on Guadalcanal every night. Our old four-stack destroyers, the valiant expendables, and some small supply vessels were taking some material in to the marines, but it was only a dribble where a flood was needed.

The Japanese navy, probably puzzled by the American fleet's failure to attack, was becoming bolder. They were sending battleships to bombard Henderson Field. More of our planes were being destroyed on the ground than in combat. The United States had surrendered both sea and air control. The thin line of marines holding the beachheads on Guadalcanal, which was only about two miles deep and five miles long, was under increasingly heavy pressure.

CHAPTER 6

The First Reinforcements
Go In

WHEN THE marines first landed on Guadalcanal the "scuttle-butt" both ashore and afloat was that they were to seize the position, then turn over to the army the job of holding the island while they moved on up for another assault.

Somewhere that plan, if it was a definite plan and not just an idea, went glimmering. The Americal division that had occupied New Caledonia the previous April went on building roads and unloading ships. The first reinforcements to go to Guadalcanal were more marines.

We picked up the seven transports at the base and turned back toward Guadalcanal. The Minneapolis, which I had boarded July 4 in Honolulu, still was the luxury liner on which I was touring the South Seas. Now she had a new skipper, Captain Charles E. Rosendahl, America's leading lighter-than-air authority. What he was doing risking his precious knowledge down there on a heavy cruiser I never understood, except that navy regulations say a captain must have a command at sea to hold his rank.

On September 14 we pulled out of port and headed for Guadalcanal. The Wasp and Hornet were up to the north of us providing air protection.

The situation was considerably befogged as we weighed anchor and stood out through the mine field. An army search plane, chug-chugging along on patrol near the Santa Cruz islands, had sighted what he first reported as seven enemy carriers. Shades of Neptune, the man was reporting all the remaining Japanese flattops in one place. The report was so unbelievable that it wasn't believed. On a second look he guessed that it was two battleships, four heavy cruisers and one destroyer. That still sounded screwy, but there must be something doing for he reported there were carrier fighters buzzing around. We set sail for Guadalcanal with some trepidation.

The force which was under the command of Admiral Turner aboard the McCawley, with Admiral Wright on the Minneapolis in command of the screening force, continued on north through the night and the next afternoon. Then came the report of the torpedoing of the Wasp and the O'Brien. We countermarched and started south as fast as the old tubs of transports could go, which wasn't very fast. Not as fast as the transport I served on in the last war that had hauled some twenty thousand soldiers to France—which is a tragic commentary on the progress the American merchant marine had made in twenty-five years.

All the 16th we continued south, having one submarine contact at noon.

Then came a desperate plea from the marines for support. The heavily reinforced Japanese troops were attacking the perimeter defense lines, within rifleshot of Henderson Field. The marines had to have help, and fast. Our transports carried several artillery units, the most pressing need. We turned around at dusk and headed north.

To everyone in the force it appeared we were in for a very rough time. Captain Rosendahl sent our four cruiser scout planes back to base. This was done to reduce the fire hazard in case of a night attack. The Astoria might have been saved on August 7 had it not been for the monster bonfire her planes and aviation gasoline and lubricating oil had made.

At dusk we were off San Cristobal, southernmost of the Solomons. At 3 A.M., September 18, we were straightened out for the run through Lengo Channel. On our port hand Guadalcanal loomed up black and still.

It was a moonless morning but the heavens were full of stars, in whose dim radiance we could see the waves breaking along

[219

the Japanese-held beach. The air was cool and damp. A little wind was blowing off the island, bringing with it from the marshy lowlands a fragrant odor I never was able to identify. Someone said it was mimosa, but I never confirmed that. With the pleasant odor was mixed the sour smell of marshes and rotting vegetation.

Captain Rosendahl, who was born in Illinois and raised in Texas, said it smelled to him like alfalfa.

Our friendly argument about the odor, in which several officers joined, was carried on in low tones. If the Japanese couldn't already see us they certainly couldn't hear us. But the night, the feeling of danger, and the realization that on shore, not a mile away, were little men peering at our ships who would have cut our throats as cheerfully as we would have cut theirs, put an effective damper on loud talking.

Ahead of us we could see the white wake of our destroyers, while astern was the larger bulk of the light cruiser Boise and the Australian 6-inch-gun cruiser, Leander. With the Minneapolis and the destroyers they constituted the screening force for the transports. And this was in an area where enemy battleships were operating.

There was a momentary flurry as one of the destroyer captains opened up on the voice-radio circuit to announce that a torpedo wake had just crossed his stern. A moment later he corrected his report.

"I believe it was a beach wave," he said, apologetically.

It was still pitch black as the force cleared Lengo Channel, but a prearranged signal from the marines on the beach indicated it was safe to proceed. The transports swung in toward the beach. The screening force swung out to cover them.

As the light quickened we could see the Higgins boats and tank lighters already in the water around the transports starting the daylong task of ferrying the men and guns and stores ashore.

Up through the coconut trees came thin spirals of white smoke from the marines' cooking fires. The summits of the green mountains were wreathed in white clouds. High above them a patrol of Grumman fighters could be seen circling, black dots against the blue sky. Peaceful was the morning.

From where we were patrolling out in the sound we could see the small boats plying back and forth from ship to shore and shore to ship. They left feathery white wakes and looked for all the world like the water bugs you see scooting across sunny pools on warm summer days.

Eight o'clock came, at last, and then 9, and 10, and 11. Now it was "Tojo time." The bombers from Rabaul had been running on such a clocklike schedule that the hours between 11 and 2 o'clock had been given the name of Japan's premier and current war lord. The lookouts were told to double their vigilance.

Although it had been cool as we steamed in during the early morning hours, cool enough for a leather jacket, the day hadn't stayed in that condition long, once the sun was up. Heat waves were dancing on the steel decks as though a fire burned under them.

At 2 o'clock I gave up my watch on the bridge and went below for my customary after-luncheon shower and nap.

This propensity of mine to take an afternoon nap in the face of anything except a major battle had long been a subject of comment on the bridge. When I came back topside at 4 o'clock, considerably refreshed, I found a rhyme on the top of my notebook, which read something like this, if my memory serves:

> Neither snow nor rain, nor cold nor heat
> Can keep Foster Hailey on his feet.
> Blow high, blow low, blow soft, blow hard,
> When the sun crosses over the foretop yard
> He drops his pencil, jams on his hat
> And hies away to his caulking * mat.
> Life goes on, sadly or gaily,
> But in the pilot's seat, no Hailey.

* In the days of sailing ships, the men who filled the seams with tarred ropes (caulked them), used large mats on which to lie when working on the lower strakes. Sluggards were wont to crawl under the boats and take a nap on these mats. Ever since that time when a sailor takes a nap in the daytime he is said to be "caulking off" or, as it has been adulterated, "corking off."

The doggerel was not signed, but Dan Godsoe, the Chief Quartermaster, looked most guilty. The chief was what the boys call "a character," and a grand guy to have around when the going was tough, as they all found out on the Minneapolis in those same waters two-and-a-half months later.

While I had been sleeping, two of the destroyers had been detailed to go up the beach off the Japanese-held positions and do a little shelling. Captain Rosendahl was about to spit because he hadn't been asked to take the Minny up and lay in a few 8-inch salvos.

"Why do they want to fool around with those pop guns," (5.38-inch rifles), he said bitterly. "If they'll let us up there we'll blast the damn camp clear over into the Coral Sea."

Rosy's reaction was typical of the men all through the fleet. The monotony of days and weeks at sea with no enemy to fight gave them the same ineffectual feeling that a heavyweight has when shadowboxing. This near the enemy, it seemed a shame not to let them throw a few shells at least.

"Why don't you ask the admiral for permission?" I suggested.

" 'Tain't being done this year," said Rosy, and he resumed his pacing, interposing an occasional "damn" as he watched the two destroyers throwing shells into the Kokumbona Village area, where the Japanese had set up headquarters after being chased out of Kukum Village on August 7. The shells must have hit some Japanese storage dumps, because a good fire was soon burning.

During the afternoon two destroyers came boiling in through Lengo Channel with gasoline for the marine planes. A small supply ship also had come in during the morning. The beach was piling up with stores.

Shortly after sunset the force was unloaded and ready to move out. The last hour of work had been speeded by a contact report from a plane search saying a force of enemy cruisers was headed down "the slot."

At 7:30 P.M. the last small boat was back aboard the transports and we headed out Lengo Channel at our best speed, the transports ahead this time and the cruisers bringing up the rear, just in case the Japanese skippers poured on the coal and got there ahead of their usual hour, which was between 11 P.M. and midnight.

There had been some Japanese reconnaissance planes around during the day, but they had not come within visual range. For the first time in two weeks the daylight hours had passed without an air raid. There had been no submarine contacts. The only planes we had seen had been our own, one of which, unfortunately, was mistaken for an enemy and shot down by the transport's gunners with the death of one man and injury to the other.

For the men of the combatant ships the day had been a terrific letdown. For the marines the quiet day was a welcome relief, and the arrival of the first large reinforcements and supplies a matter of major importance.

September 18, said General Vandegrift, was the second best big day on Guadalcanal. The first had been the arrival of the first planes.

As we cleared the eastern end of the channel and headed southeast between Guadalcanal and San Cristobal we saw reflected against the clouds over Savo Island, thirty miles astern, a burst of star shells. The Japanese force had arrived, but too late.

CHAPTER 7

Rear Base

"Now HERE IT IS," bellowed the boatswain's mate of the watch through the loud-speaker system. "There will be a fruit-picking party to shove off at 1000; ten men from each division. At 1500 there will be a swimming party. Division officers please turn in lists as soon as possible. That is all."

It was mid-September. The Minneapolis had returned from escorting the first big convoy of reinforcements to Guadalcanal and was anchored in Segund Channel off Espiritu Santo. Her crew was going ashore for the second time in two-and-a-half months.

The island of Espiritu Santo is in the northern New Hebrides. It was the closest base to Guadalcanal. It was from there the Flying Fortresses took off to soften up the Japanese for the August attack. It was to Espiritu Santo and the navy hospital headed by Captain Joel J. White (MC) USN, that the Guadalcanal wounded and sick were brought by the faithful, daring pilots of the navy and the marine transport planes, the DC3's, and the army C-47's.

The New Hebrides chain is composed of eighty islands, stretching over some five hundred miles in a southeast-and-northwest direction on the eastern edge of the Coral Sea, six hundred miles southeast of the Solomons. They are jointly administered by French and British resident commissioners. The two countries moved in originally to protect the native Melanesians from slave traders.

The administration is known officially as a condominium, but more widely as "a pandemonium."

The preponderant white population is French, but there were only seven hundred and fifty of them according to the 1937 census. Most of them are planters. The less than two hundred British subjects were mostly plantation managers or employes of trading companies. The French imported some eleven hundred Tonkinese for work on the plantations. The native population, kinky-haired, coal-black Melanesians, is estimated at about forty thousand.

There is a lot of Espiritu Santo, but it isn't much. There was a small Burns, Philp Ltd. store, and another small store run by a Frenchman. There were a few tin houses along the beach, a Catholic church and hospital, staffed by Sisters of Mary and with a resident French doctor, and coconut plantations. This, with

Noumea on New Caledonia, was the "recreation area" for the fleet.

After weeks at sea, or a trip into Guadalcanal, any base was a welcome change. From the original bomber strip, and other airfields that were built, planes flew wide searches over all the surrounding sea. There were two or three light bombing raids the first nine months of the occupation, and twice a submarine shelled the beach. But these did little harm.

Like the fruit-picking and swimming parties arranged for the Minneapolis's crew the first day back, each ship made its own fun. Later there were baseball diamonds and cold beer, but that was months in coming. The fruit was free. When the Japanese threatened the New Hebrides by occupying the Lower Solomons, most of the white planters sent their families to New Zealand or Australia. When the United States army and navy moved in and started building up the island as a major base, they also gave up their plantations. They were well paid, however, for use of their land and were awarded $50 damages for each palm tree cut down.

Cool streams run down through the hills. Near the original fighter base one of the streams widens out to form a pool some forty by fifty feet in area. It was like something out of a South Seas movie and was called "Lamour Pool." On the hottest days of summer, which runs from January through March, the water in the streams, protected as they are by overhanging trees through most of their length, seldom gets above seventy degrees. For those who preferred salt-water bathing there was the ocean all around. Fish could be caught by surf casting.

All of which reads well, but Espiritu Santo was something less than Paradise. The sun beat down there with a burning fury as it did on Guadalcanal. If you were in the shade and sitting still it wasn't so bad, but any exercise brought the perspiration pouring off you in streams. A sour, damp smell hung in the air, rising from the rotting vegetation that lies twenty feet deep in the jungles that cover most of the hills and all the ravines.

Then there are the flies. They look no different than flies else-where, but they are the most persistent winged insects a soldier or sailor ever swatted. They could not be scared away by a wave of the hand. They had, literally, to be brushed off. With darkness the malarial mosquitoes rose out of the swamps.

In the early days there never was enough transportation on the island, and a trip on foot along the coral sand roads, over which the dust hung in choking clouds most of the day, mixed with your perspiration to make a gooey mess that required two full baths to remove.

After a couple of trips ashore most of the sailors stayed aboard ship even when they could have had liberty, or went only on the swimming parties. During the daytime, except for the de-stroyers, which are too small to afford shade for many, it was much more pleasant to be on a ship lying out in the stream, than ashore.

At night there were movies on shipboard and ashore. They were shown in the hangar on the bigger ships and on the fantail of the destroyers. There were never enough good movies to go around, however. I sat through more "B" pictures in two weeks than I had in all my previous limited movie-going experience.

It was pleasant though, out on the open deck, the starlit sky above, lights gleaming through the trees from the tents ashore (blackouts are reserved for places like Honolulu and San Fran-cisco and New York City) and Betty Grable showing her legs and singing "The Song of the Islands." The sailors preferred such light fare. War movies left them cold. They were too near reality to accept the overdone flag-waving of Hollywood.

I generally stayed ashore when in Espiritu Santo. For a time I lived with Lieutenant Commander E. L. (Red) Monagin, who was Captain of the Yard. Red, who was deaf as a post from in-juries suffered as an amateur boxer and who had been out of the navy for several years, somehow had talked his way into a com-bat zone. Someone finally caught up with his medical record back in Washington and he was ordered to go home. Then I accepted the kind invitation of Captain White to share his tent, and that was my home when I was ashore there.

Nearly every evening at Captain White's, up on a hill behind the hospital, a few kindred spirits would gather for a brief libation before dinner. If you sat on his porch long enough you met everyone of consequence on the island.

Brigadier General Rose, the island commander, was a frequent visitor. Admiral Fitch occasionally dropped by, and Admiral Sherman, the former skipper of the Lexington, now commander of a task force. Colonel Evans Carlson, of the second raider battalion, came up occasionally, sometimes bringing along Major Jimmy Roosevelt, then his second in command. Jimmy later brought down his own raider outfit.

Major General Twining, head of the Thirteenth Air Force, came over soon after he had been rescued from the sea after being lost in a Flying Fortress. Major General Roy Geiger and Brigadier General Louis Wood, the first marine air wing bosses, made the captain's tent a frequent port of call.

One of the attractions was the genius of Commander Joseph A. Bowen, (MC) USNR, the hospital's executive officer. Being an old Kentucky Colonel, suh, from Louisville, the good doctor wasn't content on the island until he had tracked down some wild mint and started domesticating it in a bed outside his tent. Thomas Harris, the Burns, Philp representative on the island, furnished what goes best with mint. The mess steward furnished the ice. The result was straight from heaven, frosted, inviting, appetite-stimulating.

Dr. Jean Pouliquen, the little French doctor at the hospital, sometimes had a few friends in for dinner. His Tonkinese boy could conjure up a chicken dinner with which Oscar of the Waldorf could have found no fault.

For men who long had been under the strain of battle the cool evenings on the hill, followed by a movie in the hospital area, where the screen was set up in a gully so it could be watched from both sides and seen from some of the quonset wards, were a relief beyond calculation.

There was little distinction between the lot of officers and men, so far as living quarters and food went for the first few months. Later the officers pooled their resources and opened a club in which, with considerable optimism, they installed a powder room. Beer tents were opened for the men on Aore Island, where several baseball diamonds were laid out.

The transformation of the base was something to watch. The advance party had landed there only in May, 1942. When Captain Rosendahl and I toured the island with Red Monagin in a jeep in September, 1942, which was the roughest ride I ever took, roads of a sort had been cut through the jungle; a bomber strip was operating, and had been for over two months; bridges had been built across the deep jungle streams; coastal-defense guns covered the beaches, and antiaircraft bristled from camouflaged nets at many places.

Every trip back saw improvements. Screened quonset huts took the place of tents in the hospital; military highways of packed coral sand replaced the rutted, loam roads; new air strips were hacked out of the jungle. Quarters for both officers and men were improved. Finally, even a dock was built, which greatly speeded unloading of heavy cargo. The first few months everything had to be taken ashore in boats or big lighters and manhandled ashore through the surf. Ships lay for weeks waiting to be unloaded. A liberty ship that had been built in a record thirty days lay idle for ninety days off Espiritu Santo.

All of this delay was not due to lack of unloading facilities. It was partly due to the navy policy of using the ships as floating warehouses. Material was kept in much better condition aboard ship than ashore, and was ready to be moved on up the line on short notice. Although it tied up valuable bottoms, it made for mobility.

At these advance rear bases there was little friction among the services, or rather between the army and the navy, since the marines seemed to get along well with everyone. When the President Coolidge sank off Espiritu Santo in October after running through our own mine field, the several thousand soldiers aboard her were largely re-outfitted from navy stores. Many of the officers were taken in by navy officers and ate in the navy mess. Later, when cigarettes ran low, the army wasn't allowed to purchase the more popular brands, such as Chesterfields and Camels, in the navy canteen; but that was the only case of non-cooperation. It was a distinction I could not understand. Then the army had no officers' club and could not be accommodated at the navy club. The army, however, had the rationing of what liquor supplies were received by Burns, Philp Ltd., and that was pretty much a closed corporation.

One thing that became more and more evident the more a person traveled through the rear areas, was how much depended on the individual. Where the officers in command realized that regulations applying farther back could not work in forward areas, things went very well. Where some paper pusher had to look for authority "in the book" before he would issue a pair of pants or a keg of nails, matters became maddeningly snarled.

There probably were many others, but the three navy men with whom I came in contact who impressed me most were Red Monagin, Lieutenant Russell Burke and Lieutenant (jg) Dobbins. The latter two were connected with the navy air transport service. They all seemed to have the idea that the main object was to keep the material and the men moving on up to where they were needed. If regulations interfered with efficiency, to hell with regulations.

Lieutenant Dobbins was a classic example of what ingenuity, lots of brass, and a contempt for red tape could do to speed the war. A former American Airlines traffic employe, he had been sent to the base to handle mail and freight and passengers for the shuttle service run by the converted PBY's and PBM's among the South Sea bases.

When he arrived there he found nothing to work with. He had to beg a boat from someone whenever one of his ships came in. Finally he secured a small whaleboat. Then a fifty-foot motor sailer. He saw some jeeps being unloaded one day, and brazenly appropriated one. He parlayed that into a carryall.

"He's a ball of fire," one of the PBM pilots told me admiringly. "Formerly when we arrived at the base, we'd lie out in the stream for hours waiting for someone to come out and refuel us and take off the stores we had brought. Then we'd have to run down ourselves any cargo or mail waiting for us. Frequently we couldn't get anything to eat.

"How things changed when that big lug arrived! He would be alongside in his motor sailer before our engines had stopped turning over. He'd have all the cargo and mail ready. If we were late and didn't have time to go aboard some ship or ashore for lunch, he'd have figured that out and would have sandwiches and hot coffee with him."

On the base itself, Lieutenant Dobbins didn't wait for anyone to bring cargo or mail to him. When he knew he had a plane coming in he'd call the various stations and ask them what they had going out. If they couldn't bring it to him, he'd get in his carryall and go after it.

"After Dobbins arrived we always left with a full load," the pilot said.

Here are two examples on the other side of the ledger: A destroyer I had been riding for several weeks came in to be repaired. She had been operating out of Tulagi for weeks; she had been dive bombed by a Japanese carrier group, losing three men killed, sixteen wounded and collecting fifty-eight holes in her side and superstructure from bomb fragments. She hadn't had any fresh vegetables for weeks. When the supply officer tried to get some he was told none were available. Yet one of the officers, going aboard a tender for lunch, was served fresh orange juice and fresh sliced tomatoes.

Another time, many of the officers and chiefs on the same destroyer were in need of khaki pants and shirts. There wasn't an unpatched uniform on the ship. They made up a list and sent a junior officer to a supply vessel to get them. He was told an inventory was being taken and to come back in two or three days. He explained that his ship was leaving that night for Tulagi. That made no difference. He didn't get the uniforms, although there were stacks of them behind the counter near where he was standing.

Supply vessels would come south full of the spirit of service. But after a few weeks at a rear base too many of their officers became infected with the I'll-look-out-for-myself-you-do-the-same attitude, and the men who were doing the actual fighting up in the Solomons went on short rations and wore patched, stained uniforms.

The bigger combatant ships, the cruisers especially, knew what a tough time the destroyers were having, and few pleas to them ever went unanswered. Their officers had enough rank to make it unwise for a supply ship to refuse them what they asked for, so they loaded up beyond their needs and passed it on to the tin cans. Whenever one of them, for any reason, was going back to Pearl Harbor or the States, they would strip themselves to the essentials of food and gear and charts needed to make the voyage, pile everything else out on the quarterdeck and tell the destroyers to come and get it.

When the Minneapolis was ordered back to Pearl Harbor in October of 1942, Lieutenant Commander John DeWitt and his supply department worked for almost thirty-six hours without rest handing out everything from frozen beef to setscrews to the destroyers and other vessels that were staying down south.

Marines, army and navy men ashore always were welcome to come aboard the cruisers for a bath and a meal, and they availed themselves of the opportunity. One heavy cruiser became so famed for her hospitality she was dubbed "The U.S.S. USO."

Captain Joy said they served over three hundred extra meals one day, and sold fifty gallons of ice cream to visitors at the ship's store.

Those were heartwarming things. That was democracy at work, even in the navy.

CHAPTER 8

Derailing the
Tokyo Express

THE SINKING of the Wasp on September 15, 1942, left the Pacific fleet with only one operating carrier, the Hornet. Of the carriers with which we had started the war, the Wasp, Lexington, and Yorktown were gone. The Enterprise was damaged and back at base being repaired. The Ranger still was in the Atlantic. Several escort carriers were in the Pacific, but they were being used only as plane ferries and escorts. None had been given combat missions.

The fleet also had lost in other categories. Of the two new battleships in the South Pacific, the South Dakota was out of action. She had hit an uncharted pinnacle, damaging her keel and bottom plates.

The loss of three American cruisers and the Australian Canberra, and the damaging of the Chicago in the First Battle of Savo had whittled down the cruiser divisions. The destroyers Jarvis, Blue and O'Brien had been sunk, as had three converted destroyer-transports, the Little, Gregory, and Colhoun.

In addition to the ships actually lost, many of those still operating were in need of dry docking and repairs to put them in full combat condition. Many still were inadequately fitted with anti-aircraft weapons.

The South Pacific fleet was as weak as it had been, or was to be. It chose this time to drop its defensive policy, which had cost it so heavily, and go on the offensive.

Who was responsible for this change of tactics I do not know. Admiral Nimitz made a visit to the South Pacific about this time. It may have been, since Admiral Ghormley had observed British operations for two years in London and was a believer in decentralized control, that he turned loose his task-force commanders and they conceived the daring, offensive actions.

There were only two striking forces available at that time. Every other ship still afloat was on escort duty, moving supplies into Guadalcanal and the various supporting bases. On October 2 the Minneapolis and Chester had escorted three transports and a supply ship, loaded with marines and seabees, to Funafuti in the Ellice Islands, where they set about building an airstrip.

One striking force, built around the Hornet, was commanded by Rear Admiral George D. Murray, former captain of the Enterprise. The other was a surface force, composed of the heavy cruisers San Francisco and Salt Lake City, the light cruisers Boise and Helena and several destroyers. It was under the command of Rear Admiral Norman Scott.

The Hornet was the first to strike.

The Japanese were pouring men and supplies into Guadalcanal and their other operating and prospective bases. The harbors of Buin, Kieta, and Kahili on Bougainville, Faisi in the Shortlands, Gizo, and Rekata Bay on Santa Isabel, were filled every day with ships, either waiting to run down to Guadalcanal or putting men and material ashore to build up the bases at those points. The enemy also had started work on the Vila field on Kolombangara and at Munda on New Georgia Island, across the Kula Gulf from Vila plantation.

The Hornet started up the Solomons the afternoon of October 4, just as we often had talked about such an operation two months before, when we had four carriers instead of one in the South Pacific. She picked a squally evening, when Japanese search planes would be hampered by the weather. Surprise was essential if the show was to come off, as she could not risk a fight unless it was forced on her.

Although the prevailing storms come in from the southeast in the southern latitudes, local conditions often developed around the islands about which our forces received only scanty information. One of these storms developed in the Bougainville-Shortland Islands area the morning of October 5. Regardless of the weather, Admiral Murray decided to launch his planes.

Despite this disadvantage, which made the flight over the Bougainville mountains to Kieta a trial of skill instead of fighting ability, the Hornet planes found their targets and carried out their attack.

A dive bomber found a heavy cruiser and hit it. Torpedo bombers swooped in on the Buin anchorage and got hits on at least one tanker, one transport and a seaplane tender. In Faisi anchorage two cargo ships were hit by light bombs and a cruiser and a destroyer were strafed by Hornet fighter planes. Four Kawanishi patrol bombers were found on the water at Faisi and destroyed. Six others were damaged. Fighters shot down two seaplanes and two Mitsubishi '97 bombers. The airfield at Kieta was strewn with bombs, although no planes were caught on the ground there.

The bad weather held on as the Hornet turned south, and she sent in a strike at Rekata Bay on the way back. Two small transports and twelve planes were found there. All were bombed and strafed and set on fire. By nightfall the Hornet was out of the danger area without having been attacked. The only Japanese plane to get near the force, a search plane, was shot down by the Hornet's fighters.

Now it was Scott's turn. With only the air protection that could be given him from Henderson Field he could not go as far up the Solomons as had the Hornet force. His plan was to inter-

234]

cept the Express at night just before it reached Guadalcanal. As described before, the Express ran on a fairly regular schedule, arriving off Savo Island about midnight. That allowed the Japanese two hours to unload and four more hours of darkness to run back northwest to the shelter of their own air cover.

Knowing it would be a night action, Admiral Scott had been drilling his force assiduously in after-dark tactics and firing. For two weeks they had been operating out of a base in such practice, going out to fire at night, returning to the anchorage in the daytime.

The afternoon of October 11 the Scott-led force of two heavy cruisers, two light cruisers and four destroyers was south of the Solomons when word came that a force of Japanese ships identified as three heavy cruisers, three or four transports, and six destroyers was sighted heading down "the slot."

The night was moonless as Scott, in the San Francisco, led his force in from the south past West Cape and on up toward Cape Esperance. They crossed the south passage and went on past Savo, a black blob against the only-slightly-lighter sky, without sighting any enemy ships. The plan was to hold on north past the north passage and then sweep to the west. Just as the flagship cleared the north tip of Savo, enemy ships were contacted to the northwest. They were in two columns, each led by a cruiser. Scott turned his force to engage them.

One of the enemy heavies has been identified as of the Nati or Atago class, each of which mounts ten 8-inch rifles in five turrets. There were six destroyers, one of which may have been a light cruiser, mounting 6-inch guns.

Against this enemy combatant force Admiral Scott sent his two heavies, the thirteen-year-old Salt Lake City with ten 8-inch rifles and the newer San Francisco with nine, the two lights each with fifteen rapid-fire 6-inch rifles, and four destroyers, each carrying four 5.38's, and torpedoes. He was outgunned in caliber, but at short range, where all guns could be used, the advantage on the enemy's side was not as great as the figures would seem to indicate.

Having gauged the enemy's speed and course in a few minutes' run toward them closing the range, Admiral Scott turned 90 degrees left so all his guns would bear, and gave the order to open fire.

The enemy force, meanwhile, had continued steadily on its course, apparently not having picked up the United States ships.

Two salvos were in the air from the American ships before there was any answering fire from the Japanese vessels. One enemy cruiser was hit on the first salvo and burned merrily.

In making the turn, however, our cruisers had pulled away from the destroyers, which were making a valiant effort to overtake them and resume station ahead and on the flanks. Apparently blinded by the flash of the guns, someone on the admiral's staff mistook some enemy vessels at which the force was firing for our own and the order was passed to check fire. All of our vessels except the Salt Lake City, which was sure of her target, knocked off.

During this pause the enemy vessels recovered some control and opened a heavy fire on the Boise, hitting her in three places and setting her afire.

By this time our destroyers had come up and started a run for the enemy vessels to launch a torpedo attack. They got at least one sure hit on one of the enemy cruisers.

The flagship, meanwhile, now had become oriented and all the American vessels were ordered to resume fire. The crippled Japanese cruiser quickly was polished off, and two other enemy vessels were set afire.

The Boise, however, was having heavy going. Her fires gave the Japanese a point of aim and they were concentrating on her. One enemy heavy was not more than five thousand yards away, which is not a great distance at sea.

Captain Ernest G. Small of the Salt Lake City saw the Boise's plight and put his ship between the crippled American light cruiser and the enemy heavy. The Salt Lake City's first salvo hit just forward of the Japanese vessel's bridge, putting both forward turrets out of action.

"How was that?" fire control asked the Salt Lake City bridge.

"Very nice," was the answer. "Now put the next one a little farther aft."

"Can do," was the response. Again the Salt Lake City's turrets belched bright flame against the black night.

"Every damn shell of that salvo went into the Jap, right where it was ordered," said Lieutenant Commander Dave Hawkins, the Salt Lake City's navigator, "and she turned over and sank."

The Japanese by this time were in complete rout and attempting to escape. Admiral Scott turned his force 90 degrees right, to put them on a course of 320 degrees, to the northwest past the Russell Islands. As they steamed through the enemy force they polished off several destroyers and other vessels that had been hit previously.

When the Boise was hit and started to burn she had dropped out of line. As Admiral Scott ordered the pursuit discontinued and turned his force back, he thought that she had been sunk. Out of the dark night as the force retraced its course, loomed an unidentified ship. Guns were trained out. Then a recognition signal was flashed. It was the Boise. She was down by the bow and leaking fuel oil, but all her fires were under control and she was making twenty knots. The American force turned triumphantly south and started for a rear base. One of the destroyers, the Duncan, had been badly hurt and was left behind. The Salt Lake City had been hit three times, but she was still seaworthy and had lost only five men. Less than two hundred had been killed on the Boise.

Another of the destroyers had been detached to stand by the Duncan. At daylight it became evident that the latter was doomed, so her men were taken off. She had lost sixty killed and several more wounded, of a complement of two hundred and fifty men.

Although the official communiqué claimed only one heavy cruiser sunk that night, the men who fought the battle insisted they saw three enemy heavies, one transport, and five destroyers go down. The next day the fliers from Henderson Field found two enemy cruisers in the general area (whether they had been in the night action was not known), hit one with a torpedo, and scored several near misses on another. Another group later attacked a Japanese cruiser also in the same vicinity, and scored at least one direct hit on her. It is possible not a ship of the Japanese force escaped.

The Tokyo Express finally had been derailed. In November it was to be stopped for good in the three great night actions off Savo and Tassafarango Beach. The navy was on the march.

CHAPTER 9

Bull, Son of Battle

THE RAID by the Hornet on the Japanese bases on the Northern Solomons on October 5 and the interception by Admiral Scott's force of the enemy's vessels off the Russell Islands the night of October 11–12 only halted, it did not stop, the Tokyo Express.

The next night the Japanese sent down the biggest task force they had used for the night shellings and plastered Henderson Field with 14-inch, 8-inch and 5-inch shells for an hour and ten minutes, from 1:40 to 2:50 A.M. Two battleships were believed to have been in the attacking force. Observers on Tulagi said at least three hundred and fifty rounds were fired.

The same night the Japanese made a large-scale landing only three miles east of the marines' positions, putting ashore the equivalent of two-and-a-half regiments. That day the first army reinforcements arrived. They consisted of one regiment, the 164th infantry.

Two enemy air raids were made during the daylight hours of October 14. That night the Japanese again shelled the marine positions, killing few people but knocking out several of the all too few planes that were left. At the same time search planes reported a large Japanese force moving down from the north. It consisted of two or three carriers, two or three battleships, heavy and light cruisers, and destroyers.

General Vandegrift, whose dispatches generally were a model of understatement, sent out an urgent plea for assistance. He estimated he would need a division of fresh troops to hold his positions on the island, and he pleaded for naval-and-air support. The Grumman Wildcats were more than holding their own against the Japanese Zero and the enemy bombers, but the export version of the P-39's, the Airacobras, that had been sent him, were of little use against air attack. Designed as a low-altitude fighter, they could not get up to interfere with the Japanese attacks. The enemy bombers would come sailing over at twenty-four thousand feet with the Airacobras at their best altitude vainly circling five thousand to ten thousand feet below. They were being used only for strafing.

Enough Wildcats were not available to supply all requests for them, so it was suggested that perhaps General MacArthur could lend the marines some of his P-38's, the two-motored Lightnings.

The only immediate answer to General Vandegrift's plea was to send a few more P-39's, two destroyers, and four motor torpedo boats, two of which were lost the first night they operated.

In the meantime the Japanese had heavily shelled Henderson Field again, knocking out all but four of the marines' planes. On October 15 they unloaded seven transports in daylight in full view of the marines, who could do little about it. The situation was so desperate that Major Jack Cramm hung a torpedo on General Geiger's staff plane, a PBY, and twice attacked the transports through a swarm of Zeros, an act that was "above and beyond the call of duty" if any action ever was.

The problem on Guadalcanal was not how soon the island could be cleared of Japanese, but whether it could be held. Newspapermen who asked General Vandegrift whether they should stay were advised to leave. Some stayed to take their chances with the marines.

"The old man was sitting in his tent when I took the message in to him," one of General Vandegrift's staff recalled. "He read it, read it again, and then exploded straight up in the air and let out a warwhoop. It's the only time I ever saw him excited."

The message announced the appointment of "Bull" Halsey as COMSOUPAC, succeeding Admiral Ghormley.

Perhaps what was later done to win Guadalcanal would have been done anyway. No one knows. I do believe that Admiral Halsey's appointment at that time did more to raise the morale of the fleet than anything else that could have been done.

Ever since the previous May, when Halsey had been forced to return to the States to consult a specialist about the skin malady that was making life almost unbearable for him, I had been asked innumerable times by officers I met if I had heard anything about Halsey, or when and if he was coming back.

"I'd take Halsey sick in bed as a commander over anyone else in full health," one high ranking officer had said.

As leader of the first three raids on Japanese-held bases, the Marshall-Gilbert raids on February 1, the Wake-Marcus raids in February-March and the Doolittle attack on Tokyo in April, Halsey had established himself with the fleet as a daring, keen, hard-hitting leader. The navy didn't have enough admirals with reputations like that. They needed him back.

Admiral Halsey allegedly had no idea that he was to be tapped for the South Pacific job when he left Honolulu in October in a PB2Y, the four-motored Consolidated patrol bomber that was being used as a navy transport, to go south. He must, however, have known something was in the wind. Vice Admiral John H.

Towers had been appointed Commander Air Force, Pacific. It was hardly likely that a senior three-star admiral, such as he was then, would go back to command of a task force.

His orders were given him when his plane landed at Noumea.

"They've certainly handed me a hot potato," he is said to have exclaimed. They certainly had. But he soon showed he was the man who could handle it, if anyone could.

Admiral Halsey is not the paragon of all virtues that he has been pictured. He is brusque, impatient, bull-headed and intolerant of criticism. He is not happy behind a desk. His arrival did little to unsnarl the red tape or ease the supply problems that bedeviled operations in the South Pacific. He is inclined to back subordinates long after it is obvious they are unfitted for their jobs, merely because they are his men and, by God, no one else can criticize them. He is primarily a tactician, not a strategist. He probably would have been much happier in command of a carrier force attacking Japanese positions instead of giving orders to other men.

But he certainly was what the doctor ordered for the South Pacific in October, 1942.

"Take off the neckties," was his first general order.

"Strike-repeat-strike" was his second.

In his first interview he said his only idea was to "kill Japs, kill Japs, keep on killing Japs." He carries a personal hatred for the little men of the Rising Sun beyond that of any other person I ever met.

His first two weeks as COMSOUPAC of necessity had to be spent in Noumea organizing his staff, moving his headquarters ashore from the small vessel on which Admiral Ghormley had lived, conferring with New Zealand commanders and our own army officers, who theretofore had been treated as outsiders. General Patch was accustomed to buttonhole newspapermen who had been "up the line" in order to find out what was going on. Halsey changed all that.

Then he started out to visit bases under his command. Accom-

[241

panied only by his flag lieutenant and Colonel Julian Brown, of the marines, his intelligence officer, he arrived on Guadalcanal by plane on November 8. That afternoon he went with General Vandegrift to the front line, then out west of the Matanikau River. Half an hour after their jeep had passed along a stretch of road near Point Cruz a Japanese sniper was killed there.

That night in the General's tent, lighted only by a dim blue bulb, he talked with reporters. The gruffness and nervousness he showed back in the rear bases was missing, as he shook hands with us and settled down in a rattan armchair the Japanese had left behind and General Vandegrift had appropriated. He was relaxed and affable. Obviously this was what he liked, being up where there was fighting going on.

He reiterated his policy for winning the war, of "killing Japs." "We must exterminate them," he said. "And we can't do that by holding back and defending this place or that place or any other place. We've got to go out and hit them. We've got to get control of the seas. The man who controls the sea is the one who will win the war in the Pacific."

The naval situation was fine "from our viewpoint," he continued; and he said he hoped soon to make it impossible for the Japanese to continue reinforcing their troops on Guadalcanal.

"We'll lose ships doing it," he prophesied, adding, "but hell, you can't make an omelet without breaking eggs and you can't fight a war safely or without losing ships."

General Vandegrift, who had been begging for naval support, was grinning like a Cheshire cat. That was the kind of talk he liked to hear.

The discussion went on from there to the role of the battleship—which Halsey warmly defended and which was to prove itself in a week within ten miles of where he was sitting—and to what it would take to completely lick the Japanese.

Asked if he thought a landing on the Japanese home islands would be necessary, he said he hoped so.

"I want to be there," he added grimly. Then he went on to

describe exactly what he wanted to do to Admiral Yamamoto. It isn't printable, nor is much more of the admiral's talk. Profanity seems a natural way of talking with him and is never offensive, as it is from some people. Exact quotations, however, do not read well.

After a quiet night, interrupted only briefly by naval gunfire when two Japanese destroyers sneaking around Savo, apparently to bombard Henderson Field, were intercepted by a PT boat, the admiral decorated several men the next morning and then started back for his headquarters.

Although there was no announcement to the marines of his visit, the word got around quickly and was a big lift for their spirits. No longer did they feel alone and forsaken. Not when Mr. Big himself had flown in to tell them help was coming.

With a man at the helm whose only thought was to fight, reinforcements and supplies began to pour into Guadalcanal. Then came the three big night naval battles off Savo Island and Tassaforango Beach. Guadalcanal was ours.

Perhaps it was not Admiral Halsey's fault, but things began to bog down after that. It was not until February that the Russell Islands were occupied and the following June before an amphibious force, composed largely of army troops, moved on up to take Rendova Island, then Munda and Vila and Vella La Vella and set the stage for Bougainville and the drive against Rabaul, which was the immediate big objective of the Solomons and New Guinea campaign.

It was during such periods of readjustment and preparation for new advances, such as followed the victory at Guadalcanal, that Admiral Halsey's talents showed to least advantage. When there was no fighting to do, only a mass of detail work to wade through, he became irascible and bogged down in red tape. The patience and infinite capacity for taking pains that is the outstanding characteristic of Admiral Nimitz is lacking in Admiral Halsey.

It was no surprise when General MacArthur, instead of Ad-

[243

miral Halsey, was given supreme strategic command of the Southwest and South Pacific, a consolidation of command that was long overdue.

The admiral was born to the navy at Elizabeth, N. J., October 30, 1882. His father, who retired as a captain, was a lieutenant of the line at that time. The admiral's younger years were spent following his father to various stations.

He always wanted to go into the navy, and after a year of pre-medicine at the University of Virginia he entered Annapolis, July 7, 1900, under presidential appointment.

Most of his years at sea were spent in destroyers, with only short tours ashore as naval attache at Berlin, in navy intelligence, as discipline officer at the academy, and as commandant of the naval air station at Pensacola, Florida.

Despite his identification now as an air admiral, Halsey still impresses as being at heart a tin-can skipper, of which he was one of the best. Most of the stories about him, and the legends, were born during his days with the cans. Like them he is built for offensive action. Defensive maneuvers bore him.

Long before the Japanese gained a reputation as night fighters, Halsey was proving with his squadrons that light vessels could tangle with the big boys and get away with it. He convinced the scoffers of this when he took a squadron against the battle line one night. The attack was delivered at such close range it caused damage to two of the battleships, although the torpedoes he fired carried only dummy heads. At the investigation, which always is made when a navy vessel is damaged, he was asked the reason for the ferocity with which the maneuver was carried through.

"I was under orders to attack," he said. "I attacked."

Another carryover from his tin-can days are the breezy, slangy messages he sends. With the destroyers, all relations are more informal. Most naval communications are couched in stilted, correct terms. Not Halsey's. When a vessel was out of position, instead of hoisting the position flag and the vessel's call letters, he would send a visual signal, something like this:

244]

"Would you mind getting the hell over where you belong?"

This breeziness did not indicate any sloppiness in ship handling or a deviation from good practice. Although he did not live "from the book" and actually disliked a lot of the formality of navy life, as witness his first order as COMSOUPAC to "take off the neckties," he always ran a taut ship and a taut squadron.

"When Halsey took a squadron out of a harbor," a previous commander under him said, "it went out in correct order and kept formation once it was outside."

Halsey always has had a rugged constitution. He played fullback for two years at Annapolis, where he acquired his nickname of "Bull," and he is a rabid golf bug. He never let a late party the night before interfere with his golf game.

"I've seen him come aboard with a full load at 4 A.M.," one of his golfing pals said admiringly, "and be up at 6 o'clock for eighteen holes of golf, apparently as chipper as if he had had all night in."

In the navy, even more than in civil life, a man must be able to handle his liquor if he is to have the respect of his fellow officers. Halsey could.

As many other high ranking officers did during the '20's, among them Admiral King, the Commander in Chief, Halsey took his flight training at Pensacola as a captain. He and the others did not expect to become combat fliers, but they wanted to learn about aviation. Many of them have since dropped any pretensions as pilots. Halsey, however, still keeps his hand in at the controls, although of course not in the fighters or big bombers. He takes his air time in training planes.

His flight training gave him a first-hand knowledge of planes, their capabilities and their limitations. When he returned to sea he went as a carrier captain. In March, 1938, he was nominated to be a rear admiral and was given a carrier division. He was promoted to three stars in June, 1940, and became Commander Aircraft Battle Force, Pacific, with his flag on the Enterprise. He was at sea on December 7, 1941, having taken some marine planes to

[245

Wake, when the Japanese struck. He was to have been in Pearl Harbor that morning, but an engine casualty on one of the escorting cruisers and high seas had delayed his return.

The Enterprise planes were en route in to Pearl that morning when the Japanese struck. Some of them were shot down by the Japanese fighters and by our own antiaircraft. With his few planes Halsey made a search for the Japanese carriers. He didn't find them, which probably was just as well. Otherwise he and the Big E, as the Enterprise was called, might not have lived to do the things they did.

If Admiral Halsey retains his health and is not killed on one of the frequent visits he still makes to the front whenever he can get away from his desk, much more will be heard of him before this war is over. It would be altogether fitting if he and the Big E could lead the battle procession into Tokyo Bay when that great day comes.

CHAPTER 10

The Battle of Santa Cruz

AFTER THE desperate days of late September and early October, prospects began to brighten for our side in the South Pacific. Halsey was in command. The defensive phase was over. His orders were to strike, strike, strike. And he was getting something with which to hit the enemy.

The bomb damage sustained by the Enterprise in the Battle of the Eastern Solomons had been repaired, and the Big E rejoined the South Pacific fleet. The damage sustained by the South Dakota when she ran on a reef also had been repaired and she was running interference for the Enterprise, along with cruisers and destroyers. Two more AA cruisers of the Atlanta class,

246]

FIGHTING MARINE

Major John Smith, skipper of VF-223, the first Marine fighter squadron to reach Guadalcanal. In two months of desperate air battles John Smith (what an apt name for an American air hero!) shot nineteen Japanese planes over and around the Lower Solomons to become the leading American air ace to that time, mid-October, 1942.

THE DAWN CAME UP LIKE THUNDER

Japanese positions on Tulagi Island, the Solomons, are blazing from attacks by American carrier planes and surface vessels August 7, 1942. United States Marines have landed at the upper end of the island and are advancing down the island toward the main Japanese forces. The action was completed two days later.

THE CONQUERORS OF GUADALCANAL

Admiral William F. Halsey, Jr., and Major General Alexander Archer Vandegrift (now Lieutenant General and Commandant of the Marine Corps) who made "the bandy-legged little monkeys," as Admiral Halsey always describes them, yell uncle in the campaign for Guadalcanal. They were the two top fighting men of the first two years of the war in the Pacific. This photograph was taken in Admiral Halsey's headquarters as the Guadalcanal campaign was nearing its successful conclusion.

bristling with AA guns, had joined up, as had several of the fast 6-inch-gun cruisers of the Brooklyn class.

The Hornet, after her bold raid on Bougainville, had dropped back south and east. Alone, the only serviceable carrier in the Pacific, she could not risk more than one such foray. When most of the marines' planes were knocked out by the night battleship bombardment of October 13 she went up and lay off the island to give the marines air cover. When air reinforcements went in, she retired. On October 18 she and the Enterprise joined forces.

Enemy naval forces that had been milling around between Truk and the Solomons, occasionally under observation by some of the search planes from Funafuti or Tulagi, finally got organized about this time, and started south. Halsey ordered the Hornet and the Enterprise to intercept them. A reconnaissance report on October 25 indicated they were within striking distance, and the Enterprise air group went after them but failed to find the enemy vessels.

When morning general quarters sounded through the vessels of the American force on October 26 they were east and north of the Santa Cruz islands, in almost the same position the Big E and the Saratoga had been two months and two days before. An early morning search was launched. At 8:20 A.M. one of the scout planes reported part of the Japanese fleet two hundred miles away, almost due north. The attack was launched.

The Japanese force had its scouts out early too, that morning, or perhaps a submarine had sighted the American force. As the first wave of American planes was sixty miles away on its trip to attack the Japanese ships, it met the Japanese planes en route to attack the American force. The enemy had the jump on the Americans. The Japanese force of planes was larger than the American group, indicating they had more carriers. It looked like a rough day.

The weather was none too good over the American force. There were broken clouds, some as low as fifteen hundred feet.

[247

They provided a good cover for the enemy planes, hiding them both from the defending American fighter pilots and from the antiaircraft gunners on the ship.

As the two striking air groups passed each other there was brief, desultory fighting between the fighter planes, but the main body of each pressed on. Their job was to attack the others' ships. Their own ships would have to look out for themselves.

The collision of the two air groups, however, had one bad effect. It forced the American fighter pilots who engaged the enemy to drop their emergency tanks, thus decreasing their range. It left them little reserve for the fighting ahead, which has to be done at full throttle. Some of them did not get back to the carrier, probably because of exhaustion of their gasoline supply.

The Japanese forces were spread out over a wide area in their usual tactic of dispersion. The warning from their air group that the American planes were on the way had given them time to get their fighters into the air. Too, they had numerical superiority of planes, enabling them to hold back more fighters for defense than could the American forces. Although only two enemy carriers had been reported, it developed there were three or perhaps even four. The attack group from the Hornet was met by Zeros seventy-five miles from their target.

Despite the opposition, the American dive bombers and torpedo bombers pressed on, maintaining the tradition that no American carrier group ever had turned back from an attack once it had the enemy in range.

As they sighted the enemy carriers they were met by a terrific antiaircraft barrage. Combined with the Zero attack, it became too hot for the torpedo bombers, and they turned away from the carriers to attack a heavy cruiser, on which they secured several hits, probably sinking her.

The dive bombers, whose pilots and rear gunners had successfully fought off the Zero attackers, pressed on against the bigger carrier, identified as of the Zuikaku class. Eleven of them dived and laid their eggs all along her flight deck. If she survived, the

248]

Japanese have better damage-control methods than has the American navy.

Other American planes from the Enterprise were attacking other vessels of the enemy force. Two scout bombers, loaded only with 500-pounders, made an unsupported attack on another carrier of the Zuikaku class. Both got hits.

In addition to the bomb hits on the two carriers and the torpedo hits on a heavy cruiser, American attack planes also scored against a battleship of the Kongo class, on two light cruisers, and two other heavy cruisers. One of the latter was identified as of the Mogami class, reputedly the best of the enemy heavies. Two of that class were sunk at Midway.

Two hundred miles to the south, the American ships were battling for their lives against the Japanese planes. Warned of the approach of the enemy, every available fighter was in the air when the Japanese pilots bored in, but the clouds made interception difficult.

The American fighters picked them up well out from the carriers, and attacked. Burning Japanese planes began to fall through the overcast. There were so many of them—an estimated seventy-two in one group alone—that the limited number of American fighters could not get them all, although they followed the enemy planes right into the antiaircraft barrage from their own ships.

Aboard the American ships all was ready. All hands were at battle stations. Watertight compartments were closed off. Hose lines were strung. Damage-control parties were distributed through the ship at the most vital spots. Every gun was manned. Then they waited.

That is the most trying time of any battle, the waiting for the attack to begin. Once the firing starts, the mind seems to be closed off to everything except the task in hand. The few minutes, or seconds, before are like what it must be to drown. Thoughts race through the mind, of past mistakes and future hopes. And every man wonders, secretly, whether he can control his nerves sufficiently to face enemy fire without flinching. The more highly civilized and imaginative the person, the worse the strain.

Shortly after 10 A.M. the attack opened, a coordinated dive-bombing and torpedo attack out of the fleecy white clouds. The Hornet was on the approach side and took the brunt. Planes were falling like tenpins before her AA fire and that of the escorting cruisers and destroyers, but the Japanese pressed on.

One Japanese pilot, his plane out of control, crashed into the Hornet's signal bridge just forward of the stack, his two one-hundred-pound bombs and one five-hundred-pounder unexpended. The two smaller bombs exploded. The larger stuck in a lower deck, but was shored up and its fuse pulled to make it harmless. Another Japanese plane crashed on the flight deck, part of it falling down one of the plane elevators and setting a fire on the hangar deck. She also had been hit by one or two other bombs of undetermined poundage.

The worst damage, however, was done by two torpedoes that tore into the Hornet's side, stopping her engines and opening up watertight compartments that quickly filled and caused her to list to starboard. She was dead in the water. One of the bombs severed her main water line, and her crew had to fight the fires with emergency equipment, small pumps run by gasoline, foam-ite buckets, hand fire extinguishers and good old-fashioned bucket parties.

Shortly after the attack on the Hornet began other Japanese poured out of the clouds against the Enterprise and her big escort, the South Dakota.

Aircraft-defense tactics of American task forces are exactly the opposite of the Japanese. When an attack is coming in, all escort vessels close with the carriers to put up an umbrella of steel. They follow her maneuvers. It was so this day.

The big thirty-five-thousand-ton battleship, with almost as much speed as the carrier, twisted and turned with the Enterprise, her great battery of antiaircraft guns blazing at the attacking planes.

The Japanese carrier pilots, who are obviously the picked groups of the enemy fliers and much more tenacious and skilled than the army fliers any of our people have encountered, were not to be denied.

Diving out of the low clouds, they laid two bombs on the Enterprise flight deck. One exploded, doing considerable damage but not enough to interfere with continued operation. The other, apparently an armor-piercing projectile, struck the flight deck forward and at an angle. It tore through two decks and out through the side of the ship, not exploding until it hit the water.

The South Dakota also was hit. A Japanese dive bomber laid a five-hundred-pound egg squarely on her No. 2 turret. The hardened armor plate, several inches thick at that place, protected the turret from damage, but fragments spattered the bridge. One man was killed and Captain Gatch, who later was to tell his ship's story in two articles in the *Saturday Evening Post*, received a fragment in his neck. Only the quick work of a doctor, who held the severed artery with his fingers, saved his life. In falling to the deck, Captain Gatch also hurt his left arm.

That day the big battleship proved herself able to more than handle her own against an aircraft attack. Although claims of planes shot down frequently are difficult to evaluate, where many ships are firing at the same group at the same time, the South Dakota claims to have destroyed more than thirty of her attackers. Her armor had proved to be impervious to a hit by a contact bomb.

The initial attack on the two forces had lasted not more than five minutes. The Enterprise still was steaming at full speed and able to handle planes. Of the escort ships, the destroyer Porter had been sunk by a torpedo, and the South Dakota had been hit.

On the Hornet, fire-fighting crews gradually brought her flames under control. Her list had been held to less than ten degrees, and prospects of saving her seemed bright. Destroyers went alongside to help fight her fires, and the heavy cruiser Northampton was detailed to take the helpless flattop in tow.

After the torpedo hits, when the ship started to list, Captain Charles Perry Mason ordered preparations made to abandon ship, but quickly canceled them.

Then the Japanese came back. When unidentified planes were reported approaching shortly after 4 P.M., six hours after the first attack, the Northampton dropped her tow and the big carrier lay helpless in the water. Disregarding the other ships, the Japanese concentrated on her. Despite her helplessness to maneuver only one torpedo hit was scored. The list increased, but still her guns blazed and her men stayed aboard.

Half an hour after the torpedo attack, a flight of dive bombers appeared. They did even more poorly than the torpedo planes, scoring only near misses on their sitting target. A lone plane, whose pilot apparently had become separated from the others, came in five minutes after the others. He hit her with his bomb, the sixth that had found its mark.

The third torpedo hit and the near misses of the bombs had so shaken the already-damaged ship that she began to list further, and Captain Mason ordered her abandoned. The destroyers closed in to take off the men just as the lone dive bomber appeared.

More than an hour later, as the last party was swimming away from the carrier toward the rescue ship, a fifth attack was made, this one also by dive bombers. At least one more bomb of heavy caliber hit the stricken vessel. Still she refused to go down, and our own destroyers had to be sent in to sink her with torpedoes and shellfire. Just before sundown, she wearily turned over and disappeared. She had been in commission just a year and six days.

When the Japanese fliers sank the Hornet, they made good in part one of Tokyo's boasts. The big carrier had been identified by the Japanese as the Shangri-La from which Jimmy Doolittle and his fliers had taken off for the raid on Tokyo, and the propaganda agents on the wavebands directed toward the Hawaiian Islands had been boasting for months that the Hornet would be hunted down and sunk. She had been sunk, but not hunted down. It was she and the Enterprise that had done the hunting.

The Japanese fleet limped back north after the day's battle, never to return again in that great force or again to threaten seriously the supply lines to Guadalcanal.

The American ships turned south, the Hornet's surviving planes aboard the Enterprise, to repair the damages and gird themselves for the other battles ahead.

The box score was in favor of the American force. Against the loss of the Hornet and Porter and the damage to the Enterprise and South Dakota, the American fliers tallied two enemy carriers damaged, one probably sunk, heavy damage to an enemy battleship and three heavy cruisers, lesser damage to two other ships, and more than one hundred and fifty enemy planes destroyed. Seven of them had fallen before the guns of Lieutenant Stanley (Swede) Vejtasa, of Fighter Ten, who thereby took his place with the outstanding navy fighter pilots of the Pacific fleet.

Again it had been proven that plane for plane, ship for ship, man for man, the Japanese was no match for the American.

"When we first started out," Admiral Halsey was quoted as saying, "I held that one of our men was the equal of three Japs. I have now increased this to twenty. They are just monkeys, and I say monkeys because I cannot call them what I would like to call them."

CHAPTER II

Jungle Warfare

THERE NEVER will be another Guadalcanal. It was the first American amphibious operation in the Pacific. If for no other reason it will have its place in history as that. But there are many other reasons.

On the mountain slopes of that rugged, eighty-mile-long island, along its sandy beaches, through its matted jungle ravines, the marines and army troops wrote with blood and sweat one of the most inspiring military chapters of United States history.

They proved in that steam-heated paradise, in the skies over it and the seas around it, that the American foot soldier, the American sailor, the American flier and the American engineer was almost as good as his country hoped he was and that he was infinitely better than the bandy-legged little men of Japan who in their previous conquests had accumulated an unwarranted reputation as supermen.

With Guadalcanal behind them, our fighting men now know what to expect when they storm other beaches, move through the jungle, maneuver in black nights at sea against the enemy. At Guadalcanal they faced the unknown.

The marines who charged ashore in the Solomons on August 7 were typical American youngsters, led by officers who were civilized men, men whose business was killing but who wanted to do no more of it than was necessary. The first prisoners captured were so delighted to discover they were not to be tortured and shot, they grinned happily for the camera. Their wounds were treated by navy doctors with the same care as those of the wounded marines. When a Japanese was seen approaching with his hands in the air, the troops held their fire.

The marines soon were stripped of any illusions that the

enemy they were fighting had any compassion for a wounded or helpless man. They soon found that a white flag was not a sign of surrender but a trick to get the marines to drop their guard. Wounded Japanese shot hospital corpsmen who answered their cries for help. Colonel Frank B. Goettge and a squad of twenty-six men who went to Matanikau Village to scout conditions there were ambushed and all but three brutally killed. The Japanese slashed and bayoneted the wounded. The bodies were mutilated. This was the law of tooth and claw, kill or be killed, the creed of the jungle. After the first few days, few prisoners were taken. Any live Japanese found was shot before he had an opportunity to kill an American.

Guadalcanal was a testing ground for nerves and stamina and fighting skill. In no other theater of war were men under such continuous physical and mental strain for so long as were the marines in the Solomons. It was forty-one days before reinforcements arrived. Twice they were shelled by cruisers and battleships in what veterans of the first world war described as a far worse bombardment than any artillery barrages they were subjected to in France. They were attacked almost daily and nightly by enemy bombers and strafers. Fanatical Japanese snipers constantly penetrated their lines, sometimes lying hidden for two days before opening fire. There was no rear area. The narrow beachhead for weeks was all front line.

The division of men that was put ashore on August 7–8 outnumbered the Japanese defenders. But after the first few days the enemy steadily reinforced his troops until the odds were heavily the other way, as the marines' ranks were depleted by death, wounds, and illness. The first two groups of enemy troops to arrive were wiped out, over eight hundred of them at the Battle of the Tenaru River August 21; but by mid-September the Japanese were on the offensive. In the Battle of Bloody Ridge, September 13–14, they almost breached the perimeter defense line around the airfield. Again, in late October, several regiments that had been landed east of the marines' positions stormed the defense lines at Coffin Corner and almost broke through the Seventh Marines before the third battalion of the 164th regiment reinforced them. At the Battle of Point Cruz the Japanese used newly landed tanks to run over marine positions.

The major actions on Guadalcanal, however, were few. Largely the fighting was a battle of patrols, of small groups of men advancing from tree to tree, ravine to ravine. There were no fixed defense lines, with barbed wire and trenches in depth. There were not enough marine defenders to man such a barrier. Each man dug his foxhole or machine-gun pit and stayed in it at night, firing on anything that moved.

The Japanese did most of their fighting during the hours of darkness. They would start chattering and singing, and then go charging at the thin marine defenses. It took courage of the highest order to stand firm under such an attack, especially during the first few weeks, before the American men (most of them only boys) learned how foolhardy were the Japanese tactics and how effective the cross fire of machine guns. Always, though, a few got through, and then there was hand-to-hand fighting in the foxholes with trench knives, fists and teeth. The feared jujutsu proved far less effective than a right to the jaw.

The Japanese were masters of just one art. That was camouflage. With their grass coats, sprig-decorated helmets, and brown faces they blended into the jungle scenery like animals. After a time the marines came to think of them as just that, animals. It made the killing of them easier.

In all that has been written about the fanaticism of the Japanese soldiers on Guadalcanal, it seldom is mentioned that no American on Guadalcanal, so far as anyone knows, ever surrendered to the Japanese. If the Japanese are fanatics, then so are the marines and the army troops who fought so valiantly against them.

What made the American so much more effective a fighting man than the Japanese was that his brand of bravery was not the suicidal kind that would send him charging unarmed against an enemy machine-gun nest. When he advanced he went with a beltful of grenades. Too, he did not have to be led by an officer waving an ancestral sword.

Some men sacrificed themselves, but they did it under no hysterical stimulus of wine or opium, and it always was done to save a larger group. Such was the action of Corporal Reuben Heer and PFC John Weigel of the 164th infantry one sweltering day out west of the Matanikau at the start of the final drive to rid the island of the Japanese. Their company had charged over a ridge following an artillery barrage, only to find itself pinned down by machine-gun fire from Japanese emplacements which the artillery could not reach. The only hope was to retire down the ravine to the beach.

"Go ahead," the two young soldiers told their fellows, "we'll cover you."

"Armed with Tommy guns, they kept up a constant fire on enemy positions while the rest of our men were withdrawing," said Staff Sergeant Gilbert Shirley. "They'd fire until their magazines were empty, then drop down, reload, fire again, drop down to reload, and so on.

"The Japanese were so busy firing at them, the rest of us were able to withdraw with few casualties."

Heer was killed. Weigel escaped, to die a week later with a sniper's bullet in his head.

Then there was the calm, considered bravery of eighteen-year-old marine private Joseph Champayne, of Lewiston, Me. He was dug in with his platoon along the beach at Point Cruz, near the Matanikau River, when the Japanese threw some newly landed light tanks against them. One of the first tanks penetrated the marine lines and was overrunning machine-gun posts, crushing the American defenders under its heavy treads. Some of the men attempted to retire, and were shot down by machine-gun fire from the tank.

Young Champayne held his ground directly in the path of the charging Japanese tank, gambling that it would straddle his

[257

foxhole. It did. As the enemy machine rumbled over him he calmly armed a grenade and stuck it in the tank treads. Five seconds later it exploded. The tank, out of control, spun to the left and ran into the sea before its crew could stop it. All of them were drowned. Private Champayne was awarded the Navy Cross. Admiral Halsey pinned it on the youngster's stained blouse on his first visit to Guadalcanal.

And these are not isolated cases. There were many more. The decorations do not half cover the deeds of heroism.

There can be no question, though, as to who was the outstanding hero of Guadalcanal and of the first two years of war in the Pacific. It was General Vandegrift, later commandant of the corps.

By the very scheme of things the awarding of medals is little more than a lottery. For every man who is decorated there are two who performed individual feats just as heroic but which went unnoticed or unrewarded. Out of regard for those unhonored heroes, I wrote few hero stories out of the Pacific. When I did write one I always took pains to make it clear that those of whom I wrote were only a few among many.

Too, medals often are awarded to men who do one heroic act and then do not live up to their reputation. The medal, however, cannot be taken back.

General Vandegrift won his Congressional Medal of Honor the difficult way, by no single act of outstanding bravery but by four months of calmness under fire, by showing great patience in the face of great difficulties, by leadership in the finest sense of the word. Ernest Hemingway's definition of courage as "grace under pressure" fits the commandant of the Marine Corps as a bayonet fits its scabbard.

The first American commander of Guadalcanal was the weld that held together the steel parts of the marine machine. He did not expose himself unnecessarily, but when it was necessary he did it calmly and matter-of-factly. He seldom lost his poise, and so disposed his forces and conducted his campaign that American losses were only in a ratio of 1 to 10, one of the greatest military records of all time.

On Guadalcanal he set the pattern for all such island warfare. He never used men where artillery could do the job that had to be done. He felt, as do most American commanders I have met, that his men were the one weapon he had that should not be expended unnecessarily.

"We could do this a lot faster if we wanted to lose the men," he explained one day, as he sat outside his tent in the sweltering heat of a Guadalcanal morning, "but I don't intend to do it. Whenever it is possible we will not attack without artillery preparation, no matter what element of surprise we lose, and we will storm no enemy strongpoint that possibly can be leveled or softened up by shells."

The discussion had been inspired by an example of his methods that Ira Wolfert and I had witnessed the day before on the western front beyond the Matanikau River. Several of us had been at a forward observation post watching an advance over a ridge a mile or so ahead. We saw the marine skirmish line pinned down by Japanese machine-gun and mortar fire from a wooded ravine. A few moments later, after we had returned to Colonel John Arthur's command post, we sat in on the artillery attack on the Japanese positions.

By telephone from the front line, Lieutenant Colonel Van Ness, the regimental chief of staff, was able to locate exactly on his map the location of his skirmish line and of the Japanese positions. This information was relayed to a battery of 105's several thousand yards to our rear.

"On the way," sang out the telephone talker. Then over our heads screamed the shells, the sound of their passing preceding the distant boom of the guns' discharge. We heard the shells land in the Japanese positions and explode. Eight times the guns roared in the rear, the shells passed overhead, and exploded in the ravine.

[259

"How is that?" Colonel Van Ness asked the officer in charge of the company up front.

"Very good," was the answer. "I think that has done it. We're advancing again."

"Those shells were landing only fifty yards in front of our men," Colonel Arthur explained. "I wish you would give credit in your stories to the marvelous job Colonel del Valle's artillery has done in this campaign. It never has failed us, and it has been so accurate we do not hesitate to ask for a concentration as close to our lines as the one just fired."

Like most of the other officers who commanded troops on Guadalcanal, Colonel Arthur had little regard for the Japanese tactics, or for the ability of the enemy as a fighting man.

"They [the Japanese] are good fighters but poor soldiers," he summarized. "They are brave enough, but we think their tactics are poor and they waste men every day. These snipers that come in every night, for instance. They never get out again, and about the best they can hope for is to get one of our men before we get them."

Colonel Arthur's command post, which was fairly typical, was in a coral cave in the side of a ravine, a mile behind the fighting line. It was one previously used by the Japanese. In the outer part of the cave, some ten feet square, was set up a small table, on which were maps, message pads, and pencils. Behind this the cave closed down to not more than three feet in height. Colonel Arthur and Colonel Van Ness had their ponchos in there, spread over two stretchers. That was where they slept.

When "on the line" the men carried emergency canned rations with them, but generally hot food was taken to them. In the rear areas only two meals a day were served. Breakfast was at 8 A.M., dinner at 4 P.M. Only those doing the fighting rated three meals a day. Whenever it was humanly possible they got them. They ate out of their cups, and with a spoon. Those utensils, a poncho, and a roll of toilet paper were all the personal equipment they carried.

Reinforcements always arrived with full blanket rolls and packs. They would start up to the front line with them. After the first day they were down to the equipment listed above. A mile behind the front line there always were great piles of abandoned packs and blankets. One reason for this was that in the steaming heat of the jungle paths anything that was not essential to life was just too much of a burden to carry. One captain told me that his men one day threw away their extra packs of cigarettes.

"Those few ounces were just too much extra weight to carry," he explained, "and then they needed their pockets to stow extra clips of ammunition."

One advantage the marines held over the Japanese on Guadalcanal was the friendliness and cooperation of the natives. British administration of the islands always had been humane. The natives quickly reacted to the arrogance and brutality of the Japanese—who stole their pigs, their gardens, and their women—and drove them into the bush to starve.

The marines organized the former plantation workers into labor battalions, which were used in building airstrips, roads and gun emplacements. The marines paid only the pre-war British wage of a shilling a day, which in the South Pacific was equivalent to 17½ cents; but they fed the natives on marine rations, which was much better food, poor as it was, than they ever had been able to provide for themselves. Sanitary measures that were instituted raised the health level.

In August the marines organized the former native constabulary into the Guadalcanal Defense Force, who proved themselves valiant fighters.

There is the story of a big Melanesian named Voulla or Vouza (it is difficult to spell phonetically the native names; most of the men took descriptive English names, such as one of the plantation drivers, who was called Charley Motorcar). Voulla was captured by the Japanese and tortured for information by a Japanese intelligence officer whom he recognized as a former

[261

tailor on Tulagi. They bayoneted him several times and left him for dead. He chewed his bindings with his teeth and returned to the marine lines. Later he toured the South Pacific islands as an instructor in jungle warfare for other native forces.

The most interesting part of Voulla's story to me was the fact that a Japanese army officer had done menial work as a servant for several years at a British post. It shows how far ahead the Japanese had planned. It also showed to what lengths their officers would go. It is difficult to imagine an American army officer sacrificing several years of his life in such a situation, no matter how important the information he might secure.

The value of these natives in aiding patrols was strikingly shown in the exploit of a group of twenty men under the command of Lieutenant Frederick T. Flo, USA, of Los Angeles. Aided by native guides and native bearers, the patrol operated through the Cape Esperance area for eighteen days, made a complete reconnaissance of enemy billets where more than twenty-five hundred men were stationed, killed eleven of the enemy they caught in the bush, and escaped themselves without a casualty.

"After we had learned to rely on the natives we had no hesitation about going anywhere," Lieutenant Flo said. "They were marvelous in the jungle, reading sign. When they were on guard or scouting ahead of us we knew we were safe. We even bivouacked one night within a hundred and fifty yards of a Jap camp and slept without any worries."

What was true of the natives on Guadalcanal was also true of those of the other islands of the Solomons chain. The record of recovery of our aviators, who had to bail out of damaged planes over territory ostensibly held by the enemy, is proof of the native cooperation. One youngster, Edward Hartman, tail gunner in a Flying Fortress shot down off Choiseul, was taken two hundred and fifty miles to Tulagi by natives in a dugout canoe. The natives asked no reward.

Exceptions to this loyalty and cooperation of the natives were found only on Malaita, where the British administrators and the missionaries never had been able to gain much of a foothold, and on Bougainville and New Britain, which had been administered by the Australians. Many natives of those islands cooperated with the Japanese.

Many stories could be told of Japanese brutality in the Solomons. The one which shows them at their worst is that of a little Chinese girl five or six years old, who was left for dead after being struck behind the ear with a rifle butt and slashed in the arm with a saber, or knife.

Her father and mother had taken to the hills with her when the Japanese came. The enemy finally penetrated to the village where they had taken refuge. The father and mother were killed. Friendly natives found the unconscious little girl and carried her to the marines. She was turned over to Father Frederick P. Gehring, a Catholic chaplain with the navy, who had spent many years in China. It was thought he might be able to talk with her, but she did not appear to understand him. He named her Patsy Lee, and took her by plane to the mission hospital at Espiritu Santo. There the wounds in her small body quickly healed. The terrible ones of the spirit proved more difficult. For weeks the little girl did nothing but cry or sit staring at her hands, folded in her lap. Finally, under the gentle ministrations of the sisters, she began to take an interest in her surroundings and, the last I heard, was resuming a normal child's life at an orphanage at Vila, in the New Hebrides.

In times of peace the most peaceable of people, as the police records of the Hawaiian Islands indicate, in the Solomons the Japanese soldier showed himself a brutal animal.

"Kill the bastards," was the marines' battle cry.

The Ides of November

AFTER THE BATTLE of Santa Cruz on October 26, the Japanese navy retired to lick its wounds.

The Japanese high command at the same time must have decided that a major expeditionary force would be needed to retake Guadalcanal from the marines. It eased off its piecemeal reinforcement of its garrison and started gathering ships and troops in the Upper Solomons for a mass movement in mid-November.

The situation for the American forces, both afloat and ashore, was improving. With Admiral Halsey at the helm, reinforcements began to move in volume. The loss of the President Coolidge, loaded with artillery in one of our own mine fields while en route to a base, was the only serious blow we received during this period.

The second raider battalion, led by Colonel Evans Carlson, had come south from its Makin raid. It spearheaded a force that landed November 3 at Aola Bay, twenty miles east of Henderson Field, to flank the Japanese eastern beachhead between Kola and Taivo points. The Japanese had been reinforcing their troops there. At the same time a mixed force of marine and army troops under the command of Brigadier General E. B. Seebree, of the America Division, started a drive against the Japanese from the west. In a week the estimated three thousand to four thousand enemy troops were cut up into small groups, which were methodically hunted down and destroyed.

Early in November, too, General Vandegrift launched a drive to the west across the Matanikau, calling over some of his forces from Tulagi and Florida to join with army troops for the attack. One of the objectives was to push the Japanese back out of artillery range of Henderson Field.

Ever since late in August, when the Japanese began to get artillery ashore, one or two long-range Japanese guns, called by the marines "Pistol Pete" or "Millimeter Mike," had intermittently shelled the western end of the field and the marine position in that area. The shelling never had done a great deal of damage nor interfered greatly with operation of the field, but it was a nuisance.

The evening of November 11, several marines and a couple of correspondents were sitting after chow on Fantasy Hill, a ridge near the Press Club (a bomb-shredded squad tent with eight cots and a table), digesting their food and smoking a last cigarette before blackout. The sun had dropped behind the hills to the west, and it was pleasantly cool there. Everyone had just gotten comfortably settled when "whe-e-e-e-e" came the whine of a shell overhead.

"It's that Pistol Pete again," grumbled one of the marines as he shouldered his way into the nearest dugout.

It became obvious after the first two shells, one of them a dud, that the Japanese were ranging on the airfield half a mile away, so we all returned to the brow of the hill where we could see what damage, if any, the shelling was doing.

The third shell also was a dud. We heard the "whe-e-e-e-e" overhead and then a dull "plop" as it hit in the mud to the west of the runway. Number four was the same, another dud, and so was number five. By that time the hill was crowded. In the division headquarters area below us, too, everyone was outside his tent. As the Japanese gunners continued firing and the shells continued to be duds, some of the men began to laugh. The laughter was joined in by everyone within earshot.

For fifteen minutes, while the Japanese fired ten shells, the whole area knocked off work to watch the show. There would be the whine of the shell overhead, the dull plop in the mud, but no explosion. Then the raucous belly laughter from the whole area.

It really was funny. We could imagine the little Japanese sweating over their 150-pound shells (Pistol Pete fired a fixed-charge shell that must have required two men to carry it) hopefully sending them on their way, and then listening vainly for the explosion.

There was little laughter around headquarters that night, though. Several large enemy task forces had been sighted steaming around the Northern Solomons, and the harbors were filled with big transports. General Vandegrift decided he had better shorten his lines to the west, so he pulled Colonel Arthur and his marine and army forces back across the Matanikau.

It was obvious that something was in the wind. After six days without a daylight raid, nineteen Zeros had made a reconnaissance over Guadalcanal on November 10, apparently attempting to provoke our fighters into a scrap to deplete the defense force. The Grummans refused to attack, being content to knock down one chap, who made the lethal mistake of straggling behind the tight-knit enemy formation.

November 11, the Japanese came back with a two-pronged air offensive. At 9:30 A.M. twelve dive bombers and twelve Zeros attacked a convoy that was unloading off Kukum Beach, but failed to get more than near misses. At 11:30 twenty-five Mitsubishi '97's came over in two big V's at twenty-five thousand feet and dropped their bombs near the airfield. They killed some men, but did no damage to the field or the planes. The Grummans knocked down four of the Zeros and one of the dive bombers, with two other probables, and six of the two-motored bombers and one Zero from the second wave of attackers. The new Airacobras that recently had arrived got one of the two-motored bombers. Our total losses were one Grumman, from which the pilot parachuted to safety.

The morning of November 12 saw another convoy off the

beach, unloading additional men and supplies. At 3:30 the Japanese sent in an attack of twenty-five Mitsubishi '97's, this time carrying torpedoes. The flight was led by two float planes, whose pilots apparently were doing the navigating. They had an escort of ten or twelve Zeros.

Captain Joe Foss, who was to become America's ace of aces, with twenty-six planes to his credit, was waiting for them with his VF-121 squadron of Grummans. The torpedo bombers were down low, the Zeros at twenty thousand feet. Joe and his gang were nine thousand feet higher, hiding in the clouds.

"We went past the Zeros so fast they never knew we were there," Joe said. "We knocked off the two float fighters and barreled on in on the torpedo bombers. It was like shooting ducks."

Of the twenty-five enemy planes that were in the nicely spaced formations when the Grummans fell on them out of the clouds, only nine remained as the American ships came into view. The rest had been shot into the water.

The convoy, under the shepherdage of Rear Admiral Dan Callaghan and Real Admiral Norman Scott's cruisers—the San Francisco, Portland, Helena, Atlanta, and Juneau, the latter two light AA ships—and eight destroyers, put out from the beach and was steaming at full speed.

As the nine surviving Japanese planes flew in at them they laid down such a hail of antiaircraft fire that not a single bomber was able to drive home his torpedo. One of the Japanese planes disintegrated in midair over the stern of the San Francisco and part of it fell to the deck, killing thirty men, but otherwise the force escaped unscratched. The integrity of the American cruiser had not been weakened.

One of the antiaircraft guns the Japanese had abandoned on August 7 and which the marines had been using since, brought down one of the Japanese bombers. The enemy pilot had turned away from the ships, apparently in trouble and headed for the beach for a crash landing. The marines manning the Japanese

40-millimeter triplet mount opened on him as he came into range and shot him down a thousand yards off the beach.

After the attack the convoy resumed unloading, and with darkness headed back for another load. The cruiser force left with them.

The situation still looked critical. Search planes had reported Japanese forces closing on the islands. They included battleships. Guadalcanal braced its collective spine for another night shelling such as those of mid-September and mid-October. The date was right. It seemed to require two or three weeks for the Japanese to steam back to their main bases, load ammunition and provisions, and get organized for another strike at the marines.

Shortly after midnight the old ship's bell that was used as an air alarm in the division command area began to clang. All hands climbed out of bed, pulled on trousers and headed for the dugouts. Soon we heard the putt-putt-putt of "Maytag Charlie's" old two-lunger over the area, and then a few flares burst into brilliance high over the field and floated down.

That always was the signal for the firing to begin from the Japanese ships off shore. Sure enough, there came the boom of guns. But they were not followed by the whine of the shells. It was a naval battle. Making good on his promise to the marines that the night shellings would be stopped, Admiral Halsey had ordered Callaghan and Scott to take their small force back in and intercept the Japanese.

From the shore we could see only the flash of the guns, momentarily outlining the ships, and the occasional searchlight beams as the Japanese vessels illuminated ours long enough to get the range. Star shells and flares occasionally cast a ghostly light over the scene. We could not, however, tell friend from foe. As three ships blew up in a matter of seconds, we did not know whether to cheer or cry.

The next morning, as the Higgins boats began to bring in survivors, the story began to unfold. It was days before the pieces all were fitted together. This is the story:

The American force was in column, four destroyers in the lead, then the light cruiser Atlanta, the heavy cruisers San Francisco and Portland, the light cruisers Helena and Juneau, and four more destroyers.

"We picked up the Japanese ships at 0150, just south of Savo," said Captain Samuel Power Jenkins of the Atlanta. "One of the Japanese vessels, I believe it was a light cruiser, turned a searchlight on us just as we fired our first salvo.

"Almost immediately another Japanese vessel, a heavy cruiser, opened fire on us. He hit the bridge with his first salvo of 8-inch shells, and in a very short time we had lost control of the ship from there."

Captain Jenkins saw two destroyers crossing his bow, apparently screening the heavy cruiser, and shortly thereafter his bridge was hit by another salvo from 8-inch guns on the starboard side. He did not know whether it was the same cruiser or a second enemy ship that fired at him from the starboard.

Fires followed the explosion of the shells, and two Japanese destroyers swept in on the Atlanta, pasting her with their 5-inch guns. She was hit with two torpedoes amidships, lost way and fell out of line. She had been in action just ninety seconds. Captain Jenkins believed her guns had damaged the light cruiser that had illuminated her.

The second salvo that hit the bridge killed Admiral Scott and his first lieutenant, Lieutenant John Christian Isham, who had been a shipmate on the Astoria at the Battle of Midway. Of the twenty persons on the bridge only three, in addition to Captain Jenkins, were alive. Those four all were wounded.

As the American force engaged the enemy ships coming through the south passage, between Savo and Cape Esperance, a second column of enemy ships, including two 14-inch-gunned battleships of the Kongo class, cleared the north passage, between Savo and Florida, and opened fire.

The four American destroyers that were leading the column had swept on past the southern force before the firing started, and they drove in against the new force steaming toward them.

"We were so damn close, I should judge not more than three hundred or four hundred yards, when we ran into the battleships that our torpedoes did not arm in the short run and failed to explode," said one of the survivors of the destroyer Laffey, the first of our ships to be sunk. "Then what a pasting we took."

As the Japanese forces closed in from north and south on the outgunned, outnumbered column of American ships, all the vessels became engaged.

The destroyer Cushing, which also was in the leading four, was hit and stopped. She fired her torpedoes at a battleship as she lay dead in the water. Her crew said they saw the torpedoes explode.

When the northern group of enemy ships was sighted, Admiral Callaghan swung out around the burning Atlanta and led his cruisers toward the newly engaged Japanese force. Following the San Francisco were the Portland, Helena, and the Juneau.

The three American cruisers had continued firing on the enemy cruisers that were pounding the helpless Atlanta as they passed. As they came within range of the northern force, they engaged them too. Driving through the Japanese, still in column, they often were firing at vessels to port and starboard at the same time.

The Japanese battleships concentrated their fire on the San Francisco and the Portland. One of the enemy turrets hit the San Francisco's bridge. One 14-inch shell penetrated the flag bridge, another the navigation bridge, and a third the fire-control platform. The holes, one above the other, were spaced as evenly as if they had been measured with a yardstick.

Admiral Callaghan and his staff were killed, as were Captain Cassin Young on the navigation bridge and the gun boss on the fire-control platform. Commander Rae Arison, the navigator, was severely wounded. The senior unwounded man on the bridge was Lieutenant Commander Bruce McCandless, the communications officer. He had been in the conning tower, the

270]

steel turret where Captain Young would have been for a day engagement. He was knocked unconscious by the explosions but soon regained his feet and took command.

The senior officer of the ship was Commander Herbert Schonland, but he was busy below decks with damage-control parties, and told Mr. McCandless to take charge.

Without notifying the other ships of the catastrophe that had struck the San Francisco, he continued to lead them through the Japanese force and then turned east to run to safety.

Aboard one of the trailing four destroyers, the Monssen, Lieutenant Commander Charles E. McCombs, who had taken command only a few days before when Commander Roland Smoot became ill, had a ringside seat for the early phases of the battle and then a tragic part in it.

"We were next to last of the destroyers to go into action," said the tin-can skipper. "We were astern of the Barton, which was one of the first ships you saw blow up out there. She apparently was hit by a torpedo.

"We saw our ships up at the head of the column open fire on the enemy ships to port. Then we heard the Japs were crossing over. I ordered all torpedo tubes trained to starboard and ordered them to fire, without further command, at any worthwhile target, preferably a capital ship.

"The first ship we saw was what the torpedo officer thought was a battleship. He said she appeared to be stopped. We were coming up astern of her, and when we had her almost on our beam we fired a spread of five torpedoes. She was about three thousand to four thousand yards away.

"Both the torpedo officer and the chief torpedoman believed they saw two of them hit her just about midships. I didn't see them myself. I was too busy watching out ahead, to be sure I didn't run into someone. Some of the other men thought they saw three explosions.

"Just before the first spread of torpedoes hit, the men at the forward tubes saw another large ship, which they believed to have been a heavy cruiser or an other battleship, just forward of the other ship. They fired a spread of five at her.

"The chief torpedoman was killed, but he had told one of his strikers who survived that he thought a hit also was scored with that spread.

"Since the first ship appeared to be already damaged and dead in the water when we fired at her, she may have been the one on which another can had scored three torpedo hits. I don't see how she could stay afloat with that many hits in her, but it may be she was the damaged battleship the fliers found the next morning."

The Monssen had not yet been brought under fire as she steamed steadily in. Shortly after she had fired her torpedoes at the two large enemy ships, she opened fire on an enemy ship that was firing at the Atlanta.

"About that time," Mr. McCombs continued, "star shells started bursting to starboard of us, and I turned hard right and went up to flank speed in an attempt to avoid being silhouetted. As we turned, a Japanese destroyer, a two-stacker with a low superstructure and with two white bands painted around her funnels, crossed our bow not more than a thousand yards ahead. All our 20-millimeter guns opened on it, sweeping its decks, and our number 4 gun, under local control, pumped several shells at it.

"We still hadn't been hit, and I had hopes of driving on through the Jap force and getting clear, to the north of Florida Island. Shortly thereafter, however, more star shells started bursting to starboard of us—the bulk of the Japanese force now was to port—and by their glare I saw two torpedoes coming at us. I swung hard right and missed them, one by not more than five yards. Some of the crew claimed they saw three more pass under the ship.

"I thought the star shells might be ours, they burned like the kind we have, and I blinked a recognition signal at the ship that had fired them. Immediately two searchlights hit us, from two different ships. We opened fire on the nearest one and the lights went out. But just then all hell broke loose. We started getting hit with heavy caliber shells on both sides. We estimated we got about ten amidships, and ten around the bridge. One hit number 1 gun, killing all the men there, another penetrated the engine room, another the chief's quarters, setting a fire in the handling room next to it, and another went into my cabin. The action had started at 1:50. It now was 2:40. We had expended all our torpedoes, every 5-inch gun was out of action, we were dead in the water and afire badly amidships, so I ordered the ship abandoned."

The fight was about over. There was more intermittent firing as ships of the two forces passed each other attempting to rejoin their own columns, but each group of vessels now was trying to disengage. In the confusion of the melee, as the American ships steamed through the Japanese forces, some of the Japanese vessels were seen firing at each other.

Three of our destroyers, the Laffey, the Cushing, and the Barton, were gone; the Monssen was afire, but did not sink until daylight. South of Savo the crippled Atlanta was helplessly drifting. Near her was the cruiser Portland, which had been hit near the stern, disabling her steering gear so that she was able to go only in circles.

The San Francisco, the Helena, and the Juneau were headed out of the area at their best speed, accompanied by the four surviving destroyers, including the Fletcher, the O'Bannon, the Aaron Ward and the Sterrett. The San Francisco had been hit, but had lost little of her watertight integrity. The Juneau had taken a torpedo amidships, but still was able to make fifteen knots. The destroyer Aaron Ward had been badly hit, and had to be taken in tow. The other vessels had not been touched.

Exact losses of the Japanese fleet will not be known until the war is over and the enemy admiralty records become available. Daylight revealed a Kongo type battleship badly damaged and attempting to escape, with an escort of five destroyers.

[273

Another enemy ship was dead in the water and burning. She was in the vicinity of the Atlanta and the Portland. The latter asked the former to identify the ship, which Captain Jenkins thought was either a light cruiser or a destroyer leader. The Portland opened fire and sank her.

The surviving American vessels, with both admirals dead, were to suffer still another loss before they cleared the area. As the force steamed south of San Cristobal at noon, an enemy submarine hit the crippled Juneau with a torpedo on the side opposite where she had received a torpedo a few hours before. She broke in two and sank in thirty seconds. There were only a handful of survivors from her crew of seven hundred men.

Three of the Juneau survivors, Lieutenant (jg) Chuck Wang, of Philadelphia, Signalman 2/cl Joseph Hartney, of New Britain, Conn., and Seaman 1/cl Jim Fitzgerald, of Manchester, Conn., made the island, which was only forty miles away, after five days in a small rubber boat dropped to them by a Flying Fortress. A PBY found five more on a raft a few days later.

Chuck, whom I saw six months later in a hospital at Mare Island, his leg still in a cast, suffered a compound fracture of the right leg. He owes his life to the fact that when they landed on San Cristobal the natives who found them took them to the home of Henry Kuper, a German plantation owner on nearby Santa Ana Island. There one of Mr. Kuper's half-caste sons, a graduate of the medical school in Suva jointly supported by the South Pacific British colonies and protectorates and the Rockefeller Foundation, treated him for shock and had the good sense not to bother the wound, which was full of maggots. The maggots kept it clean of infection. When Chuck was taken by plane to a rear base, the navy doctors there were able to save both his leg and his life.

Dr. S. M. Lambert, of the Rockefeller Foundation, to whom the major credit should go for establishment of the hospital and who tells of the work of its graduates so eloquently in his book,

A Yankee Doctor in Paradise, has Chuck's everlasting gratitude. Other native graduates of the school, called NMP's, Native Medical Practitioners, have saved the lives of many fliers. The golden bread cast on the waters of the South Pacific by the Rockefeller Foundation has returned manyfold in the lives of American fighting men.

Dive bombers and torpedo planes from Henderson Field were in the air at dawn to work on the damaged battleship and other enemy ships in the area. They were joined in midmorning by dive bombers and torpedo planes from the Enterprise, which had steamed up to join the fight. Both the Enterprise groups did some yeoman work on their way in. The dive bombers attacked an enemy force of six cruisers and several destroyers, and sank two cruisers and damaged three more.

The Big E's torpedo planes, led by Lieutenant Al P. (Scoffer) Coffin, of Indianapolis, discovered the damaged Japanese battleship and threw three torpedoes into her.

"We knew things were going on around here, but no one had told us about that big baby out there," said Scoffer as he landed at Henderson Field. "I had plenty of gas, so instead of coming straight in I decided to take a sweep west of Savo, before landing. Then we saw her."

While their fighter escort of Grumman Wildcats dived at the destroyers and the battleship, Scoffer and his nine planes attacked. The battleship still was under way then, but she soon stopped.

All day long the Enterprise planes and the marine and navy fliers from Henderson Field worked on her. Lieutenant Harold H. (Swede) Larsen, who had succeeded Jack Waldron as skipper of Torpedo 8, took his squadron out against her. So did Captain George Dooley, of the marines. Major Joe Sailer and Major Frank Richards, both of the marines, led their dive bombers in attacks.

As Lieutenant Coffin came back from his second torpedo run on the battleship he settled down wearily on a log and observed that "the damn thing apparently is going to float until the war is over.

"Better not let this news get back to Washington or the admirals will start building battleships again," he added, wryly.

Before darkness fell the fliers had put nine torpedoes and at least five thousand-pound bombs in the battleship. She was afire from stem to stern, her sides glowing cherry red, when last seen that night. The enemy destroyers had steamed away and left her to her fate. She was not around the next morning.

"Scratch her off the list," said Brigadier General Louis Wood, the marine commander of the field.

The United States sailors and fliers had won the first round, although the losses had been heavy. The Atlanta was scuttled only a few thousand yards off the beach during the afternoon. When she sank it made the United States losses two light cruisers and four destroyers. The Portland had to be taken in tow but finally made port safely and was back with the fleet in a few months. The other ships soon were repaired.

But still the Japanese came on. That night the ship's bell near General Vandegrift's tent again aroused the area at 2 A.M. as "Maytag Charlie" came overhead. His arrival was followed in a few minutes by the boom of enemy guns near Savo Island. For half an hour they banged away at Henderson Field, until the PT's could get out from Tulagi. When the torpedo boats attacked, getting a hit on a light cruiser, the Japanese force retired. Although the guns had sounded to me no larger than 5-inch, some of the craters on the field indicated there may have been a heavy cruiser or battleship in the force.

Before dawn the fliers were up and after the Japanese. All the Enterprise planes except a few fighters had come in the previous day, and stayed overnight. One of the Big E's elevators had jammed, and she had headed for base.

The first strike that went out found two light cruisers and two destroyers, perhaps the bombardment force of the night before, and attacked with both bombs and torpedoes. They put two heavy bombs on the deck of one of the cruisers, and three torpedoes in the other.

As the morning wore on, however, the job ahead began to look bigger and bigger. A large enemy force composed of one enemy carrier, two battleships, one heavy cruiser and eleven destroyers was discovered 150 miles to the northwest. Another force of two battleships, a heavy cruiser and ten or twelve destroyers was off New Georgia, headed down "the slot." The map in the operations tent was bristling with red pins, showing Japanese ship contacts.

At noon came the big news. A Flying Fortress droning up the Solomons sighted the Japanese transport train near Vella La Vella, headed toward Guadalcanal. This was what all the preliminary shelling and maneuvering had been for. The "softening up" period was ended. This was the payoff.

Lieutenant Colonel Albert D. Cooley, bombers operations officer, went quietly around among the crews sounding his familiar battle cry: "Come on, boys, let's go."

Henderson Field soon was a cloud of dust as engines began turning on every plane that could fly. Seventeen had been damaged by the night's bombardment, but the ground crews had repaired all but two or three of them. They also taxied up to the line.

When it was first sighted, the transport train was more than two hundred miles from Henderson Field. That was about the limit for the fighters, if they were going to have any fighting time over the target, but they took off with the dive bombers and torpedo planes anyway.

"There were twelve ships when I got there," Scoffer Coffin reported to operations. "Six of them were big babies. About the size of the big Matson liners, probably twenty thousand tons. They were loaded with troops."

Although estimates as to the enemy strength vary, it was believed not less than two-and-a-half or three divisions were on the Japanese transports.

A Japanese task force of battleships and destroyers was operating near the train when it first was sighted, but as the American air attack went in they shoved off, leaving the transports only with a destroyer guard and what fighter opposition could be mustered from nearby fields (Munda and Vila were not then in operation).

From midafternoon until after sunset the American fliers attacked—dive bombers, torpedo planes, and fighters. All of them strafed the troop-laden decks. As fast as they unloaded their bombs or torpedoes and exhausted their ammunition, they streaked for home at full speed to reload and take another crack at the enemy.

Before darkness put an end to the slaughter, four of the big transports had been sunk; four more were dead in the water and on fire. The sea was filled with men and debris, and covered with oil.

All during the attack the Japanese ships had continued to steam on toward Guadalcanal. Four of the smaller ones, only lightly damaged, were still making good speed. The tired fliers crawled into their beds with the realization that another full day's work lay ahead.

The American losses had been relatively light in men and planes, but the marine fighter squadrons had lost their best leader. Lieutenant Colonel Joe Bauer, the fighter operations officer who, General Wood said, was "worth a squadron of planes," was shot down between the Russells and New Georgia. His rubber boat failed to release. The nearest land was Buraku Island. The colonel had fallen ten miles away.

Joe Foss, who had been with Colonel Bauer when two Zeros jumped him and set his plane afire, said he had seen Joe in the water, with his Mae West inflated, swimming strongly, so he believed he was unhurt. The rescue plane, a little amphibian scout called a "duck" by the fliers, took off with a fighter escort, to look for Joe. It already was after sundown. Led back by Foss to the place where Joe had gone down, they quartered the area

Official U.S. Navy Photograph

NIGHT ACTION OFF MUNDA

An American war vessel of a South Pacific task force had just fired a full broadside at the Japanese airfield at Munda, New Georgia Island, the Solomons, as this photograph of night action was snapped. Silhouetted in the flare of the leading ship's gun is an American light cruiser. This was one of several softening up raids made against Munda preceding its capture by an amphibious task force in July-August, 1943.

"STAND BY FOR AIR ATTACK"

Already hit but still fighting, the aircraft carrier Hornet—the "Shangri La" from which the Doolittle fliers took off for the raid on Tokyo—battles three attacking Japanese planes. An enemy Aichi dive bomber is plunging toward the bridge of the American vessel trailing smoke while two Kogekiki torpedo bombers that already have launched their tin fish scuttle for safety.

until complete darkness made a further search impossible. They saw no trace of the missing flier. He never was found.

During the afternoon, when contact reports on enemy vessels were coming in thick and fast, one search plane reported a force of two battleships and four destroyers south of the Solomons. A quick check was made with navy headquarters. They were ours. Washington and Lee were on the way.

Rear Admiral Willis A. Lee, Jr., had his flag on the U.S.S. Washington, the sister ship of the thirty-five-thousand-ton North Carolina. With him was the South Dakota, with her injured skipper, Captain Gatch, still aboard. The five-hundred-pound bomb which "Battleship X" had taken on her turret at Santa Cruz had hardly more than scratched the paint. With the two big battleships as an antisubmarine screen were the four destroyers. If the Japanese kept on coming tonight they were going to have 16-inch guns to argue with.

Admiral Lee approached from the south and west, sweeping the mouth of "the slot," then turned through the north passage past Savo to see if by chance some of the Japanese vessels already were in Savo Sound.

He continued on southwest until he was almost opposite Lunga Point, then turned back west again. As the American force turned, three ships were seen coming through the north passage. The range was about twenty thousand yards.

"Commence firing," the admiral ordered.

The six massive turrets on the two ships, from each of which the blue snouts of three 16-inch rifles protruded, rumbled slowly on their turntables. Then the black night was split by the flash of eighteen 16-inch guns belching flame and smoke almost in unison.

High above the battle an American search plane was maneuvering.

"It was the damnedest thing I ever saw," the pilot reported. "One minute there was a ship there, I believe a heavy cruiser. I saw the flash of the guns and then the red-hot shells hit. When my eyes had recovered from the flash of the explosion, there wasn't any ship. It had just disappeared."

While still steaming westward, the four destroyers on the outside of the formation and nearest Savo, the battleships shifted targets and hit the other two enemy vessels.

As the American force drew abreast of Savo the Japanese, who again had split their force, sending part of it through the northern passage and part through the southern passage, came in from the north and the west. An enemy cruiser or destroyer threw its searchlights on the South Dakota.

The enemy destroyers here made a fatal mistake. Instead of trying to get through the thin American destroyer screen and launch their torpedoes at the American battleships, they threw everything they had at the American cans. The sea was full of torpedoes. In quick succession the Walke, the Preston, and the Benham were hit and fell out of line.

The American battleships steamed on through the southern passage, engaging both prongs of the attempted Japanese pincer. Two Japanese battleships, that were with the enemy force coming in from the west, opened fire on the South Dakota.

For twenty minutes the most intensive big-ship battle since Jutland raged. All guns were working on the American battleships, the secondary battery pounding the nearer, smaller ships, the 16-inch rifles reaching over them to hit at the enemy cruisers and battleships.

From Fantasy Hill the roar of the big guns was like thunder, echoing back again and again from the mountainsides. It was difficult to tell whether the flashes against the clouds were ships blowing up or merely the flash of a full broadside from the battleship turrets.

The Japanese force that was moving toward the southern passage turned west when it was engaged, and headed back up "the slot." Admiral Lee paralleled its course, hoping to run among the surviving Japanese transports to complete the destruction the fliers had started so well the previous afternoon. He did not abandon the pursuit until almost 5 o'clock, when, the remaining Japanese ships having pulled out of range, he turned south and steamed away from the area. One of the damaged destroyers rejoined, but was so badly damaged it sank later that day.

Although again no one on the American side could definitely assess the hurt done the Japanese force, a closer estimate could be made than for the one two nights before. This battle had been fought at a longer range and with fewer ships on the American side. It had not been the free-for-all of the other action. Admiral Lee reported his force definitely had sunk one enemy battleship and severely damaged another; that his ships, guns, and torpedoes had disposed of three heavy cruisers and one destroyer, and that another cruiser and another destroyer had been damaged.

Daylight revealed that despite the battering they had taken, the Japanese had sent their four remaining transports into the island. The ships must have been damaged in the previous day's attack, for they were beached instead of being anchored off shore. The fliers started to work on them.

Several Flying Fortresses and two-motored B-26 Marauders had come up from Espiritu Santo and they joined the navy and marine dive bombers and torpedo planes in attacking the four Japanese ships. In two hours the enemy vessels were afire from one end to the other. The destroyer Meade cruised slowly past Tassaforanga and threw scores of rounds of 5-inch shells into the blazing hulks.

Army Airacobras, their 20-millimeter cannon and machine guns blazing, swept the beaches to destroy any material put ashore and kill the men attempting to handle it. It was estimated that not more than twenty-five hundred men had gotten ashore of the original force of thirty-five thousand to forty-five thousand that had left Rabaul and Buin so confidently a few days before.

At noon the Airacobras and scout planes reported that large quantities of enemy material still were stacked along the beach. The Japanese were attempting to move it inland. At about the same time a cache of incendiary bombs was found near Henderson Field. They had been brought ashore several days before, but somehow had been overlooked.

"How about taking a load over, Scoffer?" General Wood asked Lieutenant Coffin. The latter readily agreed. Part of his squadron was out on another mission, but he rounded up two other planes and their crews, and they took off.

Wanting a closer view of the Japanese positions than I had been able to get, I went along with the Scoffer, riding in the belly of the plane, from where I had a view to either side and down.

"This is going to be a wild one," B. W. Dahl AOM 3/cl, warned me as we crawled into the plane and he took his place in the top gun position. "We're going in at treetop level."

Taking off from Henderson Field in a cloud of coral dust, the three Grumman Avengers climbed to two thousand feet and then headed back up into the hills to the headwaters of the Poha River.

After a few miles we were down to treetop level, as Dahl had warned, flying so low that the leafy branches were almost brushing the bottom of the plane. The hillsides were deeply gullied, and we flew down in the ravines and then up over the ridges. It was like riding the Thunderbolt at Coney Island.

Back in the foothills there was little evidence of Japanese emplacements, but as we headed down the Poha River at two hundred knots we began to see machine gun emplacements and foxholes here and there on the far sides of the ridges. They all seemed to be deserted, as there was no movement around them as we swept past.

In the palm trees on either side of the river near its mouth were the stores the planes had been ordered to destroy. As we swept over the area, three abreast, the incendiaries tumbled out of the bomb bays and spewed fire and destruction along the beach.

As the formation swept out over the sea, Scoffer's plane passed between two of the burning transports. It was like looking down into the crater of a volcano. The decks had been burned away, leaving only the hulls, which were a bright red on the outside. Inside the hulls there was nothing but flames in which there appeared to be many small explosions, probably of small-arms ammunition.

At sunset that night the whole Japanese-held beach was covered with smoke from burning stores. The four beached transports still glowed red against the dark background of the palm trees and the shadowed hills.

The Battle of Guadalcanal had been won. The next morning search planes failed to find a single enemy vessel within two hundred miles of the island.

In three days of as bitter sea-and-air war as ever was waged the Japanese had been completely routed. They had lost two and perhaps three battleships, eight heavy cruisers, six light cruisers, as many as a dozen destroyers, and twelve transports, six of them of the largest size. Forty-seven of their planes had been shot out of the air. The personnel casualties may have been as high as thirty thousand or forty thousand men.

The Japanese made only one more major effort to reinforce their Guadalcanal garrison. On November 30 they sent down a force of transports, cruisers and destroyers, that was intercepted off Tassaforanga Beach by a task force of United States cruisers and destroyers before it could get its men and material ashore. In a short but bloody engagement six, or perhaps nine, of the enemy ships were destroyed.

Rear Admiral Wright, on my old ship, the Minneapolis, led the American forces in that engagement. It was hastily organized, with part of the destroyer screen not even having the communications plan, and suffered heavy losses when the enemy destroyers made a torpedo attack while the American ships were firing on the transports. The Northampton was torpedoed and sunk, and three other American cruisers, the Minneapolis, the New Orleans, and the Pensacola, were damaged. But by the heroic work of their crews, all of the damaged cruisers were saved and taken safely back to the States. All were back with the fleet within a year.

Army reinforcements continued to be poured into Guadalcanal, and on December 7, four months to the day since the marines first had landed, General Vandegrift turned over the command to General Patch and took his sick, tired, battle-weary marines out for a rest.

Six days later I was at Lennon's Hotel in Brisbane at dinner with Commander Fred Bell and Lieutenant Commander Frank Peters, whose ships had convoyed the marine transports through the Coral Sea. At a table on the far side of the room was a party of twelve. All but two of them were in their shirt-sleeves. All of the uniforms were clean, but some of them were unpressed. The tall man with the two stars on his collar wore a khaki jacket he must have borrowed from someone; it didn't fit very well.

Our waitress, accustomed only to the most correct dress in the dining room, looked somewhat askance at them.

"Who are those men?" she asked in that kind of a voice.

"Just some marines from Guadalcanal," I answered.

It was, of course, General Vandegrift and his staff. They were having their first meal "outside" in almost five months. Others in addition to the waitress stared at them.

As miles go, it often is not far from the front-line islands to a rear base. But it is a road that should be traveled slowly, coming out. A man forgets, in a foxhole, that the war is not as personal to the people back home as it is to him; that clothes sometimes count more than the man.

Night Raid on Vila

AFTER THE great night surface battles of November, the heavier units of the Japanese fleet were withdrawn from the Solomons, those that were still floating, and the Japanese threw in air strength to take their place.

The American fleet had received several new additions in the meantime, light cruisers of the Brooklyn and Cleveland classes. Striking forces were organized to give the enemy a taste of the night shelling that had proved so discouraging to the marines on Guadalcanal.

On January 5 the first raid was made on the Munda airdrome, which the Japanese had recently put into operation. They had been very cute about the building of it, constructing the strip around the palm trees so it was not visible from the air. Then one day they pushed over the palm trees—and there it was. The Guadalcanal fliers had been pasting it since that time, but a ship bombardment is much more efficacious than air bombing against such wilderness establishments.

Rear Admiral W. L. Ainsworth took his force of light cruisers and destroyers safely in past Rendova Island without a scratch. On the way home a striking force of Japanese dive bombers reached the American force ahead of their air cover from Guadalcanal, and scored a hit. Fortunately no great structural damage was done.

I missed the raid by twenty-four hours when I was delayed in getting air transportation. Anxious to see some action, I joined a destroyer squadron which had been operating with Admiral Ainsworth's force and was being sent to Tulagi to do any odd chores that might be found, such as sidetracking the Tokyo

Express if it should attempt resumption of the old schedule down "the slot."

The squadron was composed of new twenty-one-hundred-ton destroyers that had come to the South Pacific only a few months before, just in time to participate in the night battles off Savo. It was under command of Captain R. L. Briscoe, who had on his staff a familiar profile, Lieutenant Robert Montgomery. Bob had practically stowed away on a light cruiser, boarding her with only verbal orders, to reach the South Pacific. Being something of an expert on PT boats, Bob joined the destroyer squadron as a liaison officer for the PT squadrons with which we would be working around Tulagi and Guadalcanal.

Ever since the Germans had chased Bob and the rest of the ambulance drivers of the American Field Service out of France in June of 1940 and he had joined the navy, he had been attempting to dodge the hand-shaking, bond-selling jobs they wanted to saddle on him. After several months in London on the staff of Admiral Ghormley he had returned to the States to PT school. They were trying to put him in a radio show, when he talked his commander into saying he could go south if he could get anyone to take him. That was all the authority he needed. He reported to Captain Heard on the cruiser and had been acting as her personnel officer. Now he wanted to see some action. He did.

The squadron ran up to Tulagi at good speed. It was good to be going places in a hurry again. That is one of the lures of the tin cans; they travel fast. They're hard-hitting, tough-living, hell-for-leather ships, the cowboys of the fleet. In addition to the Nicholas the other ships of the force were the O'Bannon, which I was riding, the Radford, and the DeHaven.

After a quiet day on the hook in Tulagi Harbor, without a day or night air raid to stir up the hot air or increase the bodily temperature, the squadron spent most of the next day in a coconut shoot against the Japanese positions around Kokumbona Village. The sides of the ravines there were very steep, and the marine and army artillery could not get a high enough trajectory to reach the slope nearest them. The Japanese would lie in their foxholes on that side in comparative safety, ready to mow down any American foot soldiers coming over the brow of the ridge. The job of the destroyers was to chase them out.

With marine and navy observers aboard to call the shots, and a spotter ashore in communication with us by short-wave radio, the squadron made four firing runs, plastering the eastern side of the ravines with several hundred 5-inch shells. At times we were firing only fifty yards ahead of the troops, who were moving in behind the sea-and-shore barrage before the Japanese could reform their shattered defenses.

"Excellent and effective," was the final report from the shore. "Thanks."

The boatswain, helping clear away empty shell cases that were rattling around the deck, grinned up at the bridge and yelled:

"We certainly did our share for the scrap campaign today."

The shore bombardments by the "cans" were the most enjoyable events of a trip to Guadalcanal. There seldom was any return fire from the shore, so the cans went in so close you often could see the Japanese running around like mad looking for good deep foxholes in which to hide. General Patch rode the Nicholas, and reportedly was amazed at the accuracy of the destroyers' fire and their ability to change targets almost from second to second and hit the new one on the first salvo.

Late the next afternoon Captain Briscoe signaled the squadron to form up outside Tulagi, and we headed back to refuel, replace the ammunition we had fired at the Japanese, and prepare to take the cruisers up for a strike at Vila, on Kolombangara Island, to the west of New Georgia across the Kula Gulf.

The Japanese were building an airfield there. They also were using it as a staging base for Munda, running supplies in to Vila and trans-shipping them to barges, which ran the shallow Hawthorn Sound to Munda airfield.

[287

We left with the cruisers the next afternoon. Admiral Ainsworth had his flag on a light cruiser. The other cruisers, all the 6-inch lights, included the Helena.

We boiled along through the night and the next day.

That night there was a high overcast, through which the moon sent a soft diffused light, blurring the silhouette of the ships and the hills of New Georgia, which we had on the port hand, as we headed for Visuvisu Point on the northwestern coast of the island. The force was in column, with the O'Bannon in the lead.

At midnight, two hours away from the target, three planes came into view. They flew up our column of ships, at about two thousand feet altitude, and then crossed over, half a mile in front of us.

When we saw them fly past the other ships without a challenge, we assumed they were our own planes, although Bill Simmons, the O'B's gun boss, followed them with his director and his guns.

As they drew abreast and then crossed in front of us, so close we could almost have hit them with a potato, we got a good look at them.

"They're Japs," yelled Doc MacDonald, the O'B's skipper and he jumped to the radio microphone to notify the flagship and request permission to open fire.

"Wait," came the answer.

As the planes turned down the starboard side of the formation to take another look at us, we saw signal lights blinking from the pilot's cockpits. They were sending two dots and a dash, the letter "U" in International code. It apparently was the enemy recognition signal for the night. None of the American ships answered.

Bill was tracking the planes in earnest now, our guns turning in unison to follow them down the line of the ships. Any moment we expected either to see them start a bombing run at the cruisers, or to see our ships open fire at them. Nothing happened.

The Japanese pilots flew on down the line of American ships, crossed astern and came back up the other side. All three were still flashing "U," "U," "U," over and over again.

Finally Doc could stand it no longer. He again reported to the flagship.

"Those are enemy planes," he said. "Request permission to open fire."

Again came the answer, "Wait."

Fuming and puzzled, we stood on the wing of the bridge and watched the three planes circle the force. Each time they crossed our bow at a low altitude and so close that the roar of their motors drowned out conversation. There could be no question about their identity. They were Mitsubishi '01s, the new model of the standard two-motored enemy bomber.

"What the hell is going on, has an armistice been declared?" we asked each other as the planes, with a final blinking "U," turned away from the force and headed southeast toward Guadalcanal. Somebody was crazy. Did the Japanese think we were a force of their ships? The light wasn't that bad, surely. The Japanese had no ships even remotely resembling our light cruisers. The destroyers might be difficult to identify from the air, but not the cruisers.

We had other worries ahead, though, and we soon forgot the enemy planes, especially as no more appeared and there was no reaction from the enemy-held beach which we were paralleling, only a few thousand yards out.

Shortly after 1:30 we raised Visuvisu Point and turned to head down the Kula Gulf toward the Japanese base.

The cruisers and destroyers went up to flank speed as they started down the gulf, hugging the New Georgia shore.

The night was as silent as a tomb, the water smooth and oily-looking. Our wake made a neat, geometric pattern across its face. We could see the hills of Kolombangara plainly. In the center was the cone of an extinct volcano. Mist was drifting down the narow valleys from the hilltops toward the sea.

Promptly at 2 o'clock the American cruisers opened the bombardment. There was a great flash of light, then the red-hot shells arched across the sky toward the Japanese positions. After a ranging shot or two, on which the PBY's circling high above the enemy positions spotted for the cruisers, all the bombarding ships began rapid fire. The shells were pouring across the sky like fireballs from a battery of roman candles.

The story was going through the fleet that after the Munda bombardment on January 5 a message was intercepted from the Japanese base commander, reporting: "Honorable enemy has new secret weapon, 6-inch machine gun."

There was little evidence during the first five minutes of the effect of the shells on the Japanese positions, but finally we could see small fires begin to glow against the clouds, and then a great pillar of flame rose from the beach.

Staff Crowley, my former shipmate on the Salt Lake City, who had been promoted to lieutenant commander and attached to Admiral Ainsworth's staff as air officer, said several small fires appeared to merge to form the big one, which was in fuel stores along the beach. Staff was watching the show from one of the PBY's. He said they dropped a few bombs in the biggest blaze just to help it along and spread it.

"It was a beautiful shoot," Staff told me the next day as we met on the flagship, back in Tulagi Harbor. "We rocked the salvos back and forth across the Japanese bivouac and storage area. If there were four thousand men in there when we started shooting I'll bet three-fourths of them went to their ancestors."

For fifteen minutes the light cruisers and destroyers hosed 6-inch shells into the enemy positions.

Halfway through the bombardment the planes spotted two small destroyers or corvettes and a small supply vessel sneaking out from behind the shelter of the small island that lay between the American ships and the enemy base. Admiral Ainsworth ordered the Helena and the DeHaven to bring them under fire. The fliers saw at least one hit on the supply ship. One of the destroyers made a feint as though to launch a torpedo attack on the American vessels, but when it was brought under fire it quickly turned tail and ran.

As suddenly as it had begun, the firing stopped and the misty night again was silent as the American ships, turning up their maximum speed, headed out of the gulf. In fifteen minutes they had thrown 405,000 pounds of shells into the enemy base, a weight of metal it would have required fifty Flying Fortresses, each carrying four tons, to equal.

The cruisers and their escorts raced away at flank speed. We took up our previous post at the head of the procession. The bombardment job was done, now to get back under the protection of the Guadalcanal fighters before daylight. We had almost two hundred miles to go to Tulagi Harbor.

The force, again in column, destroyers ahead and astern, had hardly cleared Visuvisu Point when we got our first evidence that we were not going to get out as easily as we had gone in. A float light came down from a plane several miles ahead of the formation, and then another and another. They burned for several minutes on the water, marking the path of the American force.

The snooper planes made no attempt to attack us, and the force steamed on through the pale night. Soon we were being shadowed by two planes, one on either side. As Admiral Ainsworth changed course to turn us toward a big squall that was sweeping southeast along the shore of Santa Isabel to the north, they dropped red and green flares to port and starboard, respectively.

We were almost in the edge of the squall before the attack planes arrived. Six of them came in from astern, at about five thousand feet altitude. They immediately were brought under fire by the trailing destroyers and the Helena. They turned away without completing their bombing runs, separated, and lined up on either side of the force, apparently preparing for individual attacks from six directions at once.

The O'Bannon was in the squall by then, and rain was drumming on the decks. The squall was not large, however, and soon we ran out of it. As the light increased one of the Japanese planes, of the same type as had circled us at midnight, came roaring out of the mist and passed us not more than two thousand or three thousand yards away. Before our guns could train on him he had disappeared in another storm cloud a mile or so ahead of the force.

Intermittently for the next three hours the Japanese planes stayed with us. After two or three runs at the force, during one of which the Helena gun boss thought he knocked down two of the big bombers, they stayed discreetly outside the range of the force's antiaircraft weapons, seemingly content merely to escort us home.

The eastern sky was lightening as we picked up the Russell Islands to the southeast of us, and soon we saw four Grumman Wildcats headed in our direction. The Japanese planes must have seen them too, for they shoved off in a hurry.

We had cleared the squall area as we neared Savo Island, and the whole eastern sky was golden from the rays of the rising sun. Up to the yardarm of the flagship whipped bright-colored signal flags, spelling out the message: "To all hands, well done."

Just as Lieutenant George Philip, Jr., the capable young executive officer and navigator of the O'Bannon, was passing the word about the admiral's message over the loud speaker to the crew, out of the east, flying high and fast, came a strike of more than fifty American planes, torpedo and dive bombers. Above them was their escort of Wildcats. They were headed for Vila, to add to the damage the surface force had done five hours before.

"Look to the sky," George ordered, dramatically. "There goes the might of the United States. The enemy is on the run."

Tired youngsters, manning the rail, raised a cheer.

We heard later that the fliers found Vila a scene of desolation, with several fires still burning, accompanied by small explosions as the flames reached new piles of ammunition or gasoline. They dropped fifty tons of fragmentation and incendiary bombs.

For the crews of the American ships the dawn had brought an end to the fears of the night and a deep satisfaction at a job done skillfully and without loss. For the Japanese the new day brought only new disaster. The antiaircraft fire against the American planes was desultory and weak.

There was a conference aboard the flagship while the force was refueling, and then the cruisers steamed out of Tulagi on a southerly course. DesRon* Umpty-Ump took them out to Sealark Channel, then turned back to sweep toward Savo for a large and a small submarine that had been sighted by a scout plane a few minutes before. There was little rest or liberty at rear bases for the men of the tin-can navy.

But they liked the life they led. It was action against the enemy. No one had to worry about their morale.

CHAPTER 14

Savo Nights

AFTER THE night strike at Kolombangara DesRon Umpty-Ump again took up its vigil at Tulagi.

Another destroyer had joined up, and Captain Briscoe shifted his flag to her. The O'Bannon had to go back for an engine overhaul, and again I packed my bag, closed my typewriter, and moved back to the Nicholas. I was just in time to tell Commander Bill Brown, the Nicholas's skipper, goodbye. He was going to Rear Admiral Tip Merrill's staff as operations officer. Lieutenant Commander Andy Hill, the former executive officer,

* The navy's abbreviation of "destroyer squadron."

who had spent a year at the University of Missouri, my own alma mater, before going to the Academy, took her over.

We spent the day in the harbor "on the hook," but shoved off soon after sunset for a night patrol west of Savo looking for two Japanese submarines that had been sighted in that area during the day. We didn't find them. At dawn we returned to Tulagi and spent another sizzling day at anchor. With the inflammable linoleum removed from all decks, the inside of the destroyers fairly crawled with the heat. Every patch of shade was thick with sprawling sailors, who found even a steel deck topside preferable to a bunk in the steaming quarters below. Up there at least you could breathe.

Shortly after noon we received a warning "to all ships" that a Japanese raid was coming in.

"The condition is red, the condition is red," the loud speaker on the bridge bawled.

General quarters was sounded, and we made preparations for getting under way. You never know, when a strike is coming, whether it will be high-flying horizontal bombers, dive bombers or torpedo planes. At anchor is no place for a ship to be, in any case.

There was the usual cloud of dust over Henderson Field, twenty miles across the sound. We could see the fighters climbing to intercept the Japanese attackers. As they gained the higher altitudes they left behind them long vapor trails, like skywriting. It must have been an unusual atmospheric condition that day, as ordinarily this does not occur in the tropics, although it is a common phenomenon in cooler latitudes.

As we stood out of the harbor we saw the Japanese attack coming in, over Savo Island, high-flying Japanese bombers in the irregular V of V's they always use. Then the Grumman Wildcats and the P-38's hit them. At first it was difficult to distinguish our fighters. The first evidence that they were attacking was a flaming Japanese plane falling. Then the whole Japanese formation disintegrated, like a flock of ducks scattering

294]

before the plummeting charge of a hawk. Down below them we saw our fighters pulling out of their dives and climbing back to renew their attack.

The Japanese bombers' escort of Zero fighters must have been caught napping, because we saw at least a dozen of our fighters dive through the bomber formation, spraying death on the vulnerable Mitsubishis, before the Zeros dropped down to do battle.

Now the vapor trails began to take crazy patterns, whorls, and crisscrossing streamers that hid from view the hurtling little fighters that were making them. To the west of Savo we could see several columns of smoke rising from the sea where burning Japanese bombers had crashed. The Japanese formation, now broken into many small groups of two or three planes each, was streaking westward as the Zeros and Wildcats and Lightnings battled behind and above them. Apparently not a single enemy bomber had won through to the airfield, the target toward which they were heading.

It was not long until our own fighters began returning. As they headed down toward the field to reload and rearm, a new patrol took over. One group of Lightnings, their bluish-white bellies flashing silver against the sun, swept over our line of destroyers, and following them came a group of little stub-winged Grummans. Soon headquarters came back on the air to announce: "The condition is green, the condition is green." That meant the Japanese were gone.

The night passed without alarm, so we remained at anchor in Tulagi. It was almost impossible to sleep below decks, however, and everyone who could find a place had taken his mattress topside and stretched out there under the stars. Strange as it may seem, you get accustomed to even a bed of rivet heads, which poke through the thin mattress malignantly. The darkness, stirred occasionally by a sea breeze, was refreshing after the steamy heat of the buttoned-up spaces below.

Men at sea in the tropics in wartime suffer much more from the heat than those ashore. The ship must be closed up tight at sundown. With no time for a cooling-off period, the heat that has collected during the day from the sun beating on the thin steel decks and side plates is closeted with the crew and makes of the below-deck sleeping places a Turkish bath. The breeze from the electric fans serves only to stir up the steaming air and brings little relief. Men lose as much as four or five pounds just sleeping under such conditions, and rise from their sodden bunks to greet the blood-red sun of a new, hot day almost as tired as when they turned in the night before. Always it was a relief to spend a night cruising away from the land. There at least you were stirring up a breeze of your own, even if none was blowing, and every mile between the ship and the shore seemed to bring a decrease in the temperature.

The daylight hours of January 26 also passed quietly. The crew saw a movie during the afternoon, the men sitting in the steaming mess room in their skivvies (navy slang for underwear) or in dungaree trousers.

At dinner that night the skipper suggested to Lieutenant Commander Lou Snider, the Exec, that perhaps we could have a movie shown in the wardroom. This was accomplished by setting up the projector in the narrow passageway just aft of the wardroom and projecting it through the port, or doorway, against a sheet hung on the forward bulkhead. Because the crew's messroom was so small, the chief petty officers generally skipped that one and came up to the wardroom, which was on the main deck just under the bridge, for their recreation.

There was some discussion at dinner as to what one of five movies we had aboard should be shown. It was finally settled that we should see "Thunder Afloat" with Wallace Beery and Chester Morris in the leading parts. It was an old film, as most of them were that found their way to the combat zones. The good ones apparently were being held back in rear areas, where morale was more of a problem than it was in the front lines, afloat and ashore. "Thunder Afloat" was a portrayal of antisubmarine patrols off the East Coast in the first world war. We were going sailing on our day off.

The picture was just approaching an exciting part, with Beery barging off in his Eagle boat, the 1918 version of the PC's, in search of a German submarine when the "beep, beep" of the general quarters alarm rang through the wardroom. Japanese night raiders had been detected coming in to attack. In nothing flat the wardroom was deserted.

By the time we had reached the bridge the anchor was already being heaved in and, with the rest of the squadron, we soon were on our way out. It was to be one of our most rugged nights.

"Damn them, why couldn't they stay home at least one night?" Lieutenant (jg) Johnny Everett, the torpedo officer, muttered as he checked his men to be sure everyone was at his post.

The moon was not yet up as we cleared the two small islands at the mouth of the harbor and turned toward Savo. There was only a light, broken overcast, however, and the stars, once the eyes became accustomed to the darkness, give a surprising amount of light.

Lying closest to the open sea, the Nicholas was the first of the squadron outside, and we made a big circle as the three others cleared the harbor and fell into formation. We were steaming in column, following the leader.

"This may be quite a night," the skipper said, as we stood in the darkened wheelhouse, where the only illumination was a dim light in the binnacle stand, and peered out of the forward ports at the foaming wake of the destroyer ahead of us.

The sea was glassy calm. Off to our left, as we approached Savo, was the black, ominous bulk of Guadalcanal. It lay like an island of the dead, not a light showing either around Henderson Field or farther west where the Japanese still had a tenuous beachhold. The enemy bombers had not yet arrived.

As we cleared Savo on a course toward Santa Isabel several planes were seen bearing toward us, and almost immediately the

[297

leading destroyer opened up on them. It was followed by the DeHaven, which was next in column, and soon we were all blazing away, the red-hot tracers from the 5-inch guns and automatic weapons arching out across the star-studded sky in a beautiful if terrible pattern, reminiscent of some of the fireworks displays at the New York World's Fair.

One of the Japanese planes was hit and fell blazing toward the sea. Whether the accuracy of our fire was the reason, or the enemy pilots had been given other fish to fry, the formation turned away from us and continued on toward Tulagi and Henderson Field. Darkness and silence again fell over the line of destroyers, broken only by the muffled roar of the big blowers forcing air down to the pounding engines.

Captain Briscoe now headed south for the Russell Island group, which the Japanese then were using as a staging base for reinforcing Guadalcanal. They would put men and supplies ashore there one night and then, the next, run them across the twenty-two-mile-wide strait to Guadalcanal in landing barges.

By this time the Japanese bombers were over Tulagi and Henderson Field twenty miles to the east, and the searchlight beams were probing for them against the sky. We saw one caught full in the concentrated glare of several lights, the ack-ack bursting all around him. He was diving and twisting to escape. Finally they lost him. We were too far away to hear the sound of the antiaircraft, or the bursting of the bombs the Japanese were dropping; but soon there was a dull red glow from the direction of Tulagi that waxed and waned for half an hour.

We learned later that the bombers that approached Tulagi flew over once without dropping a bomb. As they returned for another run, one of the 20-millimeter batteries, that had no chance of reaching the bombers at the height they were flying, opened up. It was followed by other AA defenses. Their target ringed for them by the flash of our guns, the Japanese, this time, laid their eggs. One hit a fuel-and-ammunition supply dump. That was the blaze we saw. Several ships in the harbor, including an old engineless fuel barge, were straddled and got some bomb fragments aboard but were not damaged.

The Japanese had sent down a strong air force and some of our own planes, the big amphibious Catalinas, or PBY's, that made almost nightly nuisance bombing raids against Munda and Vila airfields, on New Georgia and Kolombangara islands, respectively, also were in the air. It was difficult to tell friend from foe.

Finally Captain Briscoe did something about it.

"Any Black Cats" (as the night-raiding Catalinas were called), he said over the warning net, "do you know where we are?"

"Yes, generally," came the answer.

"Then get the hell away from here," he bellowed.

Before we were sure, though, that all friendly planes had left the vicinity two of the Japanese pilots, guided by our foaming white wakes, made a run on us and dropped at the Nicholas. We were the last ship in the column.

They came in so suddenly, plummeting down from a high altitude, that our guns did not open fire until they had made their drops and were on their way.

We never saw either one from the wing of the bridge, but we heard clearly the roar of their motors and then the sound of the bombs bursting. Two fell some fifty yards astern, and two were so close ahead that spray from the small geysers of water they threw in the air fell on the forecastle. There was no damage, though, to the ship or injury to the men.

We had been caught off guard because of the presence of our planes. But we were not going to let it happen again.

"Fire on any plane that comes within range," Captain Hill grimly ordered Fire Control.

By midnight we were down off the Russells, sweeping between Lamon Rock and Cape Esperance.

Japanese planes remained in the area most of the rest of the night, and twice more we opened fire on them, bagging at least one more enemy scout, which fell in the water and exploded less than a mile from the formation. No more bombs were dropped at us, however, and as the sun came up over Cape Esperance, heralding the beginning of another blistering day, we headed back past Savo for Tulagi.

There was little rest for the weary crews. We refueled and remained at anchor through the hot morning, but soon after lunch orders were received to make an antisubmarine sweep to the north. One of our planes had sighted and attacked an enemy submarine that morning, and when there was one there generally were others that escaped detection. We finally caught up with one of them that night.

After the afternoon sweep the squadron patrolled along, just taking it easy. There was an early sunset behind a bank of black clouds in the west as we headed up "the slot." A striking force of our dive bombers and torpedo planes, which had attacked a Japanese convoy off Kolombangara, sinking one destroyer and damaging one cargo vessel and a tanker, came out of the sun, racing the storm clouds back to base, and swept low over our formation.

The squalls started coming an hour after the tropic night had dropped down, cooling the ships but reducing visibility; and we took up a patrol between Cape Esperance and the Russell Islands. The enemy barges always picked a black night to make their runs to and from Guadalcanal, and it was our hope to intercept and sink some of them if they tried it.

It was just before midnight, as we were cruising along, that men on the Nicholas and the Radford sighted what they thought was either a large barge or a submarine running on the surface. The Radford must have sighted it first, because just as our officer of the deck was reporting it to the commodore, the other destroyer put on speed, crossed our bow, and attacked.

The submarine, for that was what it was, apparently saw or heard us at about the same time, as it attempted to dive without attacking. The Radford was over him before he had reached a safe depth, and dropped two depth charges, or "ash cans" as the sailors call them. The rest of the squadron then turned for a run over the target, but no one else got a contact and the Radford, which had made her run at high speed and had used up several hundred yards of seaway turning for a new attack, also lost the sub. In the faint night light we could see a large oil slick bubbling up, and it appeared certain the enemy craft had been hurt.

The rest of the night passed without further alarms, but with continuing squalls that apparently grounded both our planes and the enemy pilots.

Ominous reports meanwhile had been coming in from our search planes of the presence of large enemy naval forces, including battleships and carriers, between Truk and the Solomons. Other groups of destroyers and cruisers were seen in the Shortland Islands area, off Bougainville, and enemy air activity was increasing.

Our oil tanks being full, we didn't go back to Tulagi that day but stayed out west of Savo. Other and strong United States task forces were speeding up from the south, hoping for a decisive naval engagement if the Japanese should keep on coming, but Squadron Umpty-Ump was the only United States naval group actually around Guadalcanal. If battle were to be joined, it appeared we would be the ones who would start it.

The enemy position on Guadalcanal at this time was desperate. We had complete control of the air over the area they still held along Tassaforanga Beach, west of Kokumbona Village, and they were strafed by day and bombed by day and by night. Our forces, now greatly superior in numbers as well as in fire power, and also in physical condition, were pressing on each day behind heavy artillery barrages.

The presence of the enemy ships it was thought indicated a Japanese decision to rush in more troops and hold the remaining beachhead. As was proved later, it was a desperate and costly effort to remove as many of the survivors as possible, especially the higher officers.

Anyway, there our squadron was, out west of Savo, holding

on to its collective hat in anticipation of a knock-down, drag-out fight with enemy ships and planes.

Many planes were sighted early in the evening, but they left us alone as we swept back and forth between the Russells and Cape Esperance. There were some of our own planes up, as well as the enemy's, and late in the evening one of the Black Cats reported what he thought was a Japanese submarine, some fifteen miles west of our position at the time. We swung over that way and cruised through the area twice without making a contact.

Meantime, the report had come in that a force of our cruisers and destroyers had been attacked by Japanese torpedo bombers soon after dark near Rennell Island, some seventy miles to the south of Guadalcanal, and that the heavy cruiser Chicago had been hit. The planes we had sighted earlier in the evening apparently were the ones that had made the attack.

Shortly after midnight the moon came up, burnishing our wakes with silver and making a long track from the ship to the horizon. The sea's face was like a millpond on which the flying fish, disturbed by our passing, left long wakes as they skimmed the surface, beating the phosphorescent water to a froth with their tail fins.

At daybreak the squadron slid in past Savo to take up an anti-submarine patrol in the passages on either side of the island. A large convoy of our ships bringing fresh troops and supplies had come in during the early morning and was now lying off Koli Point and Lunga Point, discharging. Our task was to see that no submarine got in on them from the west.

There was an air alarm at 3:30 P.M., but the Japanese raiders were turned back before they got even as far as Savo. We saw our fighters going to intercept. Again they were leaving long vapor trails as they passed over Savo.

As we learned later, the intended attack on the island apparently was only a feint to distract attention while Japanese torpedo bombers made a daylight strike at our cruiser-destroyer task force that had been hit the night before. Coming in this time in broad daylight, thirteen torpedo bombers attacked the crippled Chicago, which was under tow. Although twelve of the thirteen attackers were shot down, they all apparently got within launching range first, as six torpedoes hit the cruiser. The Chicago, with eight torpedoes in her guts, turned over and sank. The destroyer Lavallette was hit but made port safely.

The Chicago was the seventh and last cruiser we were to lose in the Guadalcanal campaign, now drawing rapidly to a successful conclusion.

January 30 passed quietly for the squadron. There were no contact reports, or air alarms, so we remained at anchor in Tulagi harbor overnight. Because of the heat it wasn't much of a rest cure for the crew. Too, they had a lot of ship's work to catch up with. The many days and nights of cruising around Savo had given little time for paint chipping or repair work.

Shortly after midnight the watch had a radio side seat at the ramming and disabling of a Japanese submarine by one of the four New Zealand corvettes that had been operating with us out of Tulagi on antisubmarine patrol. When an enemy task force was around, the New Zealanders had to play doggo in some harbor behind shore-defense batteries, having no armament with which to tangle with the enemy surface vessels, nor enough anti-aircraft to combat a plane attack. Fortunately for them there were generally more worthwhile targets around for the Japanese planes, and they went through many raids unscathed. Against submarines, however, at least those the Japanese were using in the Solomons, they were more than a match, having more deck armament than the subs and the same listening devices and depth charges as the bigger American destroyers.

The Kiwi was cruising along off Cape Esperance that night when her lookout sighted a Japanese submarine on the surface. Opening first with her deck guns, to which the Japanese replied with automatic weapons, the Kiwi then rammed the enemy undersea boat at full speed, slid off, wheeled and rammed him again.

The Kiwi had one dead man and several injured aboard. She

had rammed the submarine so vigorously she had put a permanent wave in her own bow. She was still seaworthy though, and ready and willing to accept congratulations. It had been a long, nerveracking patrol out of Tulagi for the little corvettes, and this was their first chance to crow. No one begrudged them it. There was no question about that victory.

The night of January 31 was unlike the day. It was "Condition Red" at 9 P.M., so away the squadron went, chasing the flying fish past Savo.

It was as black as the inside of a curly-haired man's hat, as Kim Hubbard once phrased it, and we saw and did nothing except cruise back and forth between Cape Esperance and the Russell Islands all night long.

At dawn, however, a plane spotted what it thought was some undamaged enemy landing barges just west of Cape Esperance, and the squadron leader and the DeHaven went in to work over them. The Nicholas and the Radford were left outside to birddog for submarines while the other two destroyers were raking the beach. They were firing fuse-set shells so they would burst just above the water and thus get a larger destructive spread with each shell.

"Keep our fire right on the beach," the commodore warned over the TBS, the radio voice circuit. "We have some patrols back there in the hills somewhere, and we don't want to mess them up."

After the squadron leader and the DeHaven had worked over the barges to the commodore's satisfaction, the squadron headed back in for Tulagi. As we paralleled the beach we could see our artillery firing at the Japanese positions just west of the Poha River. One of our planes was circling the area to spot for the guns. He occasionally dropped a smoke bomb to mark some Japanese position. Then the artillery would go to work on that area.

We could gauge the progress of our troops ashore each day by the position of the artillery fire. In a week they had moved some two miles west up the beach and now were at Kokumbona Village, one-time headquarters of the Japanese on the island. Our crews were aching for a chance to go in and help out with some more shore bombardments, but our services apparently weren't needed.

At 4 P.M. we saw an air strike of fourteen dive bombers and eight torpedo planes, with an escort of Lightnings up above them, shoving off northeast. They were back shortly after sunset to report they had found a destroyer and a corvette escorting a large cargo vessel through Vella Gulf, apparently headed for Vila or Munda, and had attacked them and left them all badly damaged and dead in the water.

The squadron anchored in Tulagi harbor for a conference among the captains and the commodore on the next day's operations. General Patch was sending a landing expedition around Cape Esperance to set up a "second front" and put a pincers on the Japanese. The squadron was given the job of sweeping the south passage past Savo during the night to be sure there were no enemy surface or undersea craft nosing about and then was to escort the landing craft to the beaches and cover their landing with shellfire, if there should be opposition.

We were underway at sunset for what proved to be the most exciting and tragic thirty-six hours of our duty. We didn't know it then, but before another sunset we were to lose the DeHaven and two-thirds of her crew, and the Nicholas was to barely escape a like fate.

Dive-Bombing Attack

By FEBRUARY 1 the ground forces on Guadalcanal had driven the enemy out of his former headquarters at Kokumbona Village, ten miles west of Henderson Field, and across the Poha River, the last natural defense line for several miles. The decision was made to land a force to the south of Cape Esperance and start a drive from both directions.

To Captain Briscoe's destroyer squadron was given the task of safely escorting the LCT's and the small destroyer-transport around the cape to a landing near Nugu Point. We had gone out west the night before to sweep the area for hostile submarines or surface vessels, as the operation was scheduled to begin at 2 A.M. There was a delay, and it was after dawn before we picked up the small transport train and started past Savo.

It was a hot morning, with high, broken clouds, and we cursed the slowness of the LCT's as they waddled along deep in the water, their sunken decks chock-a-block with trucks and supplies and men. As we cleared the passage with the destroyers patrolling on either side of the line of LCT's, one of the LCT captains must have decided he knew more about the course than the leader, because he took off in a direction that eventually would have landed him on the Russell Islands. The squadron leader had to steam ahead and shoo him back.

The lateness of the start forfeited any element of surprise for the expedition, as we were clearly visible from the enemy-held beach of Guadalcanal. They were undoubtedly in touch by radio with their air bases on up the Solomons and the fleet units that had been reported maneuvering south of Truk.

"We'll probably get the hell bombed out of us," one of the telephone talkers said as we stood on the shaded wing of the bridge watching the slow progress of the train. There were several of our own planes around, however, and we thought we would have plenty of protection.

The first troops were just going ashore at 11:30, several hours behind schedule but apparently without opposition, when headquarters announced an air raid coming in.

"Oh, oh. What did I tell you," the talker said as he dug out his tin hat from its storage place in the flag locker.

For some reason, the planes did not attempt to interfere with the landing operations but centered their attack on Henderson Field. From twenty miles away we could see the black antiaircraft bursts against the white clouds over the island.

The first few LCT's and the destroyer-transport were in nuzzling the beach by then, and the Nicholas and the Radford turned back to sweep astern of the stragglers. Some three miles astern of us were the squadron leader and the DeHaven.

We were steaming along on a northerly course when two miles ahead and at about five thousand feet altitude a large two-motored bomber burst out of a cloud bank.

There was a moment's hesitation, as one of the officers yelled he thought it was one of our own PBY's. Finally, the skipper identified it to his own satisfaction and ordered fire control to open up on him.

"Wham, wham," "wham, wham," the two forward guns began to bark.

Before the shells had reached the plane's position, Lieutenant Johnny Everett, who originally had identified it as a PBY, again was shouting that it was one of our own planes at which the guns were shooting. The captain ordered fire control to check fire.

The Radford meanwhile also had opened fire and was pouring out her 5-inch projectiles at a fast rate.

We waited anxiously for the shellbursts. Directly ahead of the plane one blossomed, then a second. Both had exploded within what looked to be ten yards of the plane. If it was one of our own planes it was just too bad.

"My God, we've shot down one of our own planes," Johnny moaned as the big airship, looming black against the white clouds, nosed over and plummeted straight for the water.

As it fell directly on our course, we got a good look and dissolved any doubts as to its identity. It was a Mitsubishi '01. Just before it hit the water we saw a door open and someone plunge out, then a spurt of flame, but there was no explosion.

As the plane fell, other shellbursts from the Radford blossomed in the area where our own two had exploded, and over the short-wave radio circuit someone on the Radford yelled, "We got him. We got him."

Immediately there was an indignant howl from our bridge, and Skipper Hill strode purposefully to the microphone.

"We got that plane," he said. "We were the first to open fire, and we claim him as ours."

"We opened first," the Radford retorted.

"Knock off the chatter," ordered the commodore.

The Nicholas by that time was passing the spot where the plane had fallen. There was little wreckage. Only a gasoline tank, its aluminum bright and shining, a few scraps of wing and what looked like two or three bodies in life jackets.

We did not stop to investigate, as we knew there must be other enemy planes in the area. Sure enough, in a moment, another Mitsubishi '01 popped out of a cloud. Again the Nicholas and the Radford both opened up. Black bursts were all around the Japanese pilot, and he was smoking and wabbling as he ducked into another cloud, but still flying. It seemed doubtful, however, that he ever would get home.

A whole flock of Zero fighters also passed astern of the force soon after, but they were flying high and fast, made no passes at us, and no one opened on them.

As soon as the raid was over, we turned back to the scene of the crash of the first plane. As we had countermarched, the Radford was now ahead of us instead of trailing, and Captain Briscoe ordered her to investigate the wreckage.

We took the commodore's command as tacit acceptance of the Radford's claim that her guns had shot down the Japanese bomber. The whole Nicholas crew was in a fret. As a wholly unbiased observer, I offered to make an affidavit to the effect that the good St. Nicholas had first opened fire on the enemy and it was her guns that had shot him down.

"You know what I think?" said a young lookout, grinning down from the fire-control platform just above the bridge. "I think we ought to anchor alongside the Radford tonight and go over and talk this over with them, say about three hundred of us."

For two-and-a-half more hours anger bubbled among the Nicholas's crew. Then there came more important things to think about.

The first LCT's to land had completed their unloading at 1 P.M. and headed back for Tulagi. The Nicholas and the De-Haven were assigned to escort them. The squadron leader and the Radford were to bring the others.

We headed north toward Cape Esperance and then turned east through the passage between the cape and Savo Island. The skies were beginning to clear, and there were only a few fleecy white clouds. There was much plane activity. Two Airacobras swept past on a reconnaissance of the enemy-held beaches. High over Henderson Field we could see four or five planes circling, apparently on routine high patrol.

The LCT's, rid of their load, were chugging along at a better pace than they had taken going out; but it still was slow, uninteresting work. The two destroyers were maneuvering on either side.

Shortly after 1430 (2:30 P.M.), headquarters again warned of an approaching air attack, but canceled it five minutes later. The destroyers, which had rung for flank speed when the alarm was given, dropped to a slower pace.

At 1443 headquarters again came back on. His voice sounded more urgent this time as he announced that "the condition is red," and Captain Hill ordered enough turns put on to take the

Nicholas up to a faster speed. As all hands scanned the skies for the enemy planes, we noticed that the DeHaven still was meandering along at slow speed. Apparently Captain Toland thought this too was a false alarm.

There was no sign of unusual activity over Henderson Field. We could see the planes still circling over it, some twenty thousand feet up. There was another large group of planes somewhat to the north of the island, headed our way, but they were too far away to be identified. The planes circling the field seemed to be paying them no attention, so we thought they must be friendly.

We were almost through the south passage, with Savo on the port quarter, when out of a small cloud just ahead of the force and at about six thousand feet altitude we saw a plane diving at the DeHaven. Lieutenant Commander Lou Snider, spending his last day in fire control before turning over the job to Lieutenant Mitchell, ordered our guns to open fire.

The enemy plane must have been sighted at about the same time from the DeHaven because we saw a bubble of white froth at her stern, as her propellers began to thrash a faster beat. Then her automatic weapons opened fire on the diving bomber.

Straight and true the enemy flier dove, at a steep angle, to within less than one thousand feet of the little can, then dropped his bomb and straightened out. There was the flash of an explosion between the DeHaven's stacks, followed by a billowing cloud of black-and-brown smoke.

Other enemy planes were diving and all our guns were yammering.

Then there was a shout from one of our signalmen:

"Plane diving on us, starboard quarter."

Out of the corner of my eye I saw another explosion on the stern of the DeHaven, and then my whole attention was centered on the plane diving at the Nicholas.

The Nicholas was turning flank speed, the wake boiling high

above her fantail as she squatted like a running horse and tore along through the glassy water.

The enemy bomber came over the edge of the cloud and started down. His front view silhouette was as distinct as in a drawing. There was the round cowling of the motor, the two wings like pencil marks protruding on either side and, sticking out below, the two wheels with their wind pants.

"An Aichi," I said to Ensign LaSalle, who was standing beside me.

"Looks like it," he agreed.

Captain Hill had swung the ship hard right when the first report of the bomber diving was received, and the destroyer was heeled far over as she made the turn. Every gun on the ship was firing, the red tracers of the 20-millimeters arching up to a converging cone at the nose of the enemy bomber. LaSalle grabbed up a Tommy gun from the bridge wing and started firing that.

The Japanese pilot was aiming straight for the bridge where we were standing. There was a flicker of fire from his wings as he came within range and opened up with his machine guns and then, out of the belly of his plane, from behind the wheels, we saw his bomb release and start to fall.

I had a feeling of detachment, which is not uncommon, others have told me, as I watched it come down. I was sure it was going to hit. I was standing near the pilot-house door under what protection the apron of the fire-control platform gave, and the flag box cut off my view aft so that I lost the bomb just before it hit. By that time, however, I saw it was going to miss, but by a very narrow margin.

The first bomber had not yet released his bomb when the report came that another was coming in on the port quarter. In not more than three or four minutes eight of them dove at our destroyer, which was twisting and turning at flank speed six thousand feet below them. Big John Stone, the lieutenant in charge of the 1.1 battery just aft of number two stack, said none of the eight bombs missed the ship by more than twenty or thirty feet.

[311

"It was almost miraculous to see our stern swinging just far enough to get out of the way," John said.

Suddenly the guns stopped yammering and the usual sounds of the ship, that had been obscured by the cacophony of war, were heard again, the blowers sucking the air to the boilers, voices on the bridge. Somewhere a man was crying like a heart-broken child.

From the bridge we could see one man lying on the small platform just under the 1.1 battery. It really was only a piece of a man. One arm and half the trunk seemed to be gone. A gunner's mate was standing by one of the 20-millimeters nearby looking in puzzlement at his right hand, from which blood was streaming to the deck. Two men were helping a third into the after dressing station, where young Dr. W. J. Doyle was taking care of the wounded. Several men were lying on the deck.

The ship was steaming steadily at high speed, apparently little damaged. The engine room had reported water coming in through a hole in the side, but they soon had it plugged. Steering control had been lost for a few seconds on the bridge, but it had been quickly restored. The shock of one of the near misses had broken a connection.

Before going aft to check on the dead and wounded, and the damage, I swept the immediate vicinity with my glasses to check on the DeHaven and the LCT's. The little fellows were all right, circling near where a great cloud of black smoke rose up from the sea to a height of hundreds of feet. I could see no ship at the base of the smoke.

"Gone," said Captain Hill, who saw me looking. "I saw a bomb hit her just forward of the bridge. It must have penetrated to the magazine, for there was a terrific explosion and she broke right in two. I doubt if anyone came off the bridge. The explosion just blew it to pieces."

The attack obviously being over, Captain Hill had turned back toward the smoke that was the DeHaven's funeral pyre. As it began to thin we saw the sea covered with debris, and a great

312]

circle of oil that glinted like a rainbow in the afternoon sunlight.

In evading the attack at high speed we had traveled several miles away from where the other destroyer had gone down, and the LCT's, their forward ramps in the water, already were nosing through the wreckage pulling oil-covered survivors aboard when the Nicholas arrived and put over her whaleboat.

In half an hour it was certain all the living had been found, and some of the dead, floating in their life jackets, so Captain Hill ordered the LCT's to come alongside and transfer the wounded to us.

There were surprisingly few. It was live or die on the De-Haven that day. Many of the one hundred and ten survivors did not have a mark on them. Almost two hundred men had died.

One of the most stoical of the survivors was Chief Machinist's Mate R. C. Andrews. He was a big man in his late forties, with a thick black moustache. As he clambered aboard the Nicholas he used only one hand. The other was badly torn. One finger was hanging only by a piece of skin. He examined his injured hand critically—Doctor Doyle was caring for the worst cases first— then reached in his pocket for his knife.

"Here, son, cut this off," he said to a young seaman standing by him.

"Aw, I can't, Pop," said the youngster. "Let it alone. Maybe the doc can save it."

"Nope, she's too far gone," the Chief said; and as casually as if he were cutting off a chew of tobacco he severed the piece of skin and tossed the finger over the side.

One of our own men, Gunner's Mate 3/cl. Lewis Samuels, was almost as casual about his shattered hand. He reported to Doctor Doyle, who cleaned and bandaged his hand, gave him a tetanus shot, and told him to lie down.

"I can't Doc, I got to get back to my gun," Samuels answered.

"You sit down there; never mind your gun. You've lost a lot of blood."

"I had to take care of another patient then," Doctor Doyle

said later. "The next time I looked around Samuels was gone."

Samuels helped get the DeHaven wounded aboard and was busy, with his one good hand, tidying up around his 20-millimeter mount when the doctor found him an hour later and ordered him into one of the Higgins boats that had come to take the wounded to the navy hospital.

Just as we were getting the last of the wounded aboard, the squadron leader and the Radford came boiling up. The squadron leader took aboard the uninjured survivors, and then the three destroyers headed for Lunga Point at high speed to put them ashore. A Japanese task force, first reported as consisting of two heavy cruisers, two lights, and sixteen destroyers had been sighted coming down "the slot." There was no time to mourn the dead or comfort the living. The squadron and half a dozen PT boats were the only force available to stop them. We had to be about it.

"Are you all right?" the commodore asked Captain Hill.

"Two dead, one dying, sixteen injured, and one gun out," was the answer. "Otherwise, O.K."

"Disembark survivors and wounded men and join," the commodore signaled.

As we hurriedly put the DeHaven survivors into the Higgins boats and turned away to follow the squadron leader back out past Savo, the DeHaven's men gave a cheer for the Nicholas. Leading it was Samuels, his bandaged hand now in a sling.

"Keep her floating, you guys," he yelled at his shipmates lining the rail.

We saw him waving with his good hand as long as we were in sight.

At dinner that night, a subdued meal in contrast to the usual uproar, we put all the stories together and decided that six planes had dived on the DeHaven. Three of them hit her. Eight had dived on us. Although some observers reported seeing as high as seven enemy planes go into the water, it was finally decided that not more than four or five had been shot down. We thought the group probably was from a carrier. They had an escort of Zeros. Two-thirds of the DeHaven's crew had been lost, including Captain Toland, who a few days before, when I was preparing to shift from the O'Bannon, had asked me to come aboard his ship. Only three of her eighteen officers had survived.

Lieutenant Mitchell resolved the question of the man I had heard crying. It was Hector Constantino, Chief Radio Electrician.

Hector was a chunky little man who still spoke with an accent. He had come to the United States from Greece just before the last world war. Two days after he arrived he was robbed of his savings by two fellow countrymen. Hector enlisted in the army. After serving through the war he left the service for a few months, but then enlisted in the navy. He had been in the navy since that time. He was one of the most deeply patriotic men I ever knew. To him the United States meant everything he cherished.

"It's no pose with Hector," Mitch explained. "He cries whenever he hears of one of our ships being lost. He did the other night when the message came through about the Chicago. He just happens to be built that way."

It was an emotionally and physically exhausted crew that took the Nicholas out west of Savo that night. Few of them had had any sleep for forty-eight hours, since we had been out on patrol all the previous night. They had seen their shipmates killed and wounded and a sister ship destroyed in exactly six minutes. The deck was still slippery with blood in places. There had been no time to clean up. Now they were going out to intercept the Tokyo Express. Three ships against twenty. All other American ships in the area—freighters, tenders, corvettes, and the escorts —had been ordered to leave.

Months later, in my notebook, I found this: "The mighty Davids go out to tackle Goliath. What a story if it comes off!"

The sun set early behind a bank of clouds, and the dark came down. Heat lightning was playing along the horizon. Far to the left, as we cleared Savo, were visible the hilltops of the Russell Islands. Thirty miles to the northwest loomed the bulk of Santa Isabel. Between the two lay "the slot," empty, quiet, ominous. Back up its 250-mile length, somewhere on the way down, was the enemy force.

Captain Briscoe, the commodore, led us out the north passage and then southwest toward the Russells. We were in column, the squadron leader, in advance, then the Nicholas, and behind us the Radford.

If there were 8-inch-gun and 6-inch-gun cruisers in the enemy force, as was the first report, the only chance for the three out-gunned, outnumbered American cans was to surprise the enemy and be within torpedo-launching range, inside ten thousand yards, before we were discovered. It would be suicide to go in against the fire of the heavy guns.

Before leaving the vicinity of Tulagi, Captain Briscoe and the PT squadron commander had agreed on search areas. The destroyers were to cover the approach from the south, and the PT's the approach from the north. Search planes were up "the slot" to watch for the Japanese.

As the early hours passed with no further report on the enemy, it appeared possible they had turned back. They were almost past Savo at midnight before we saw them. At almost the same time the PT boats, sweeping the north channel, ran smack into them.

"My God, it's the whole Japanese navy," we heard one of the young PT skippers exclaim.

The Japanese ships opened fire as the PT's attacked, sinking two of them and so damaging a third that it had to be beached. But not before they had scored a hit on one destroyer, which caught fire and burned for some time before it sank. Dive bombers from Guadalcanal also joined the fight, and the clouds above Savo were lighted for half an hour with the flash of guns and bombs and the flares dropped by the planes.

316]

When Captain Briscoe made contact with the enemy force, now identified as twenty destroyers, he turned the squadron north and headed for the Japanese ships. They were about twenty thousand yards away at this time.

Planes had been around all the evening, but none had attacked, and we did not know whether they were enemy or friendly. As the squadron turned toward the Japanese ships, however, the planes turned toward the three destroyers and started dropping flares to mark our course. The commodore turned away.

For two hours the Japanese force stayed inside Savo, losing two more ships either to our planes or to mines, which had been sown off Tassaforanga Beach in anticipation of just such a visit, and then they pulled out at high speed.

When the commodore saw them coming out he again attempted to close, but again the enemy planes probably warned their ships of our approach, and again we turned away.

Circling, we followed them up "the slot" for several miles, but we never got close enough for a torpedo attack. Planes from Guadalcanal still were harassing them as they retired. At daylight other planes took up the chase. They found sixteen destroyers, and scored a hit on one and a near hit on another.

At the time it was thought the enemy force was bringing reinforcements in to the dwindling Japanese garrison on Guadalcanal. Instead they were evacuating the officers. The men were left to die.

As we steamed past Savo the next morning en route to Tulagi we saw many abandoned Japanese small boats in the water and debris from damaged or sunken Japanese ships.

That afternoon the commodore, whose original squadron of five destroyers now had dwindled to three, and one of those damaged, recommended that the squadron be withdrawn. The commodore's logical evaluation of the situation was that his ships were too valuable to use on suicide missions and the force wasn't big enough to really slug it out with anything the Japanese would send down. Admiral Halsey must have agreed with him, for orders came for the Nicholas to return for repairs and for the others to join up with a force of cruisers maneuvering south of the Solomons. Late that afternoon we said goodbye to Tulagi with no regrets.

CHAPTER 16

On Up the Solomons

THE GUADALCANAL campaign drew rapidly to a close in February. The Japanese made one more major rescue attempt after February 1, sending down another force of twenty destroyers that was heavily punished by marine and navy dive bombers and torpedo planes both going and coming. Then they left the rest of their people on Guadalcanal to die, again pulled all their heavy ships out of the Solomons, and poured in air reinforcements to their air bases at Munda, Vila, Buin, Faisi, Rekata Bay, Kahili, Kieta and Buka.

At the same time the American task forces that had been operating south of the islands withdrew to our rear bases. The late-January, early-February maneuvering was the first time during the Solomons campaign that both fleets had been at sea in force without a meeting. Apparently neither cared to risk another carrier battle. We had only the Enterprise and Saratoga operating in the area along with several smaller converted carriers that had yet to prove their mettle.

As a whole our fleet was stronger. Our heavy cruiser divisions had been riddled, but the battleships and the light cruisers that had been sent down had more than made up for the losses. Destroyer losses had been replaced, and some of the jobs they previously had been doing, such as off-harbor antisubmarine patrol, were being taken over by the PC boats. The PT squadrons were being augmented and assigned to offensive patrol against Japanese barge concentrations.

When the marines landed on Guadalcanal the only amphibious equipment in the South Pacific was the Higgins boats, small tank lighters, and a few amphibious tractors. Men of the force had been reading in the magazines about the wonderful new equipment that was being built, the LST's, LCI's, and the others; but they hadn't seen any. In the early months of 1943 these also began to move south. Most of the captains of these smaller vessels were inland tug captains or harbor sailors who knew nothing about navigation. For the long ocean voyage from the West Coast to Australia or the Solomons, they sailed in squadrons using follow-the-leader tactics. Men who could navigate were put on one ship. The rest tagged along.

Before moving against Munda and Vila, which were almost two hundred air miles from Henderson Field, our Solomons forces needed a closer fighter base, so the Russell Islands were occupied in mid-February and an airfield was built there.

The Japanese had used the Russells as a staging base during the Guadalcanal campaign, but they withdrew after the evacuation of the Guadalcanal officers, and the American move was made without opposition. It was several days before the Japanese even sent an air strike against the American ships that filled the narrow, dangerous waters of the anchorage off Pavuvu Island. Completion of the airstrip on the Russells put American fighter planes sixty miles nearer to Munda.

Both air and surface units were used in the softening up of the Japanese positions on New Georgia and Kolombangara. Dive bombers, torpedo planes, Flying Fortresses and Liberators subjected the Vila and Munda camps to almost daily bombardments, the PBY's kept them awake at night with nuisance raids, and task forces of light cruisers and destroyers made several runs up "the slot" to bombard them.

During this period the Japanese were striking back by air, but

[319

not as hard as the Americans were pounding them. They had taken such heavy punishment from the American fighter planes in the daylight attacks that they had almost abandoned such sorties and started paying only nocturnal visits. Although they lost few planes they also did little damage. Night bombing by small units against combat positions has little value except to keep the garrisons awake.

I was still riding the Nicholas during the early phases of the softening-up process. She had returned to base to have the holes in her side patched and her No. 5 gun, which had been temporarily disabled the afternoon of February 1 by a bomb fragment, put back in first-class shape. Then she had rejoined the squadron. The O'Bannon previously had rejoined, after getting her engine repaired. Once more there were four destroyers in the squadron.

While there, word had come of the final investment of Guadalcanal. The force we had set ashore to the south of Cape Esperance on February 1 met the main body driving west on February 10. All organized resistance had ended a day or two before. In a few days the last remaining Japanese on the island were either captured or killed.

When we rejoined the squadron we found it attached to another task force under command of Rear Admiral Ike Giffen. He had his flag on one of the 8-inch-gun cruisers. Under Admiral Giffen was a division of lights. Their division commander was Rear Admiral A. S. (Tip) Merrill, who had only recently been promoted to flag rank. Our old friend Commander Bill Brown, the former skipper of the Nicholas, was Admiral Merrill's operations officer.

While waiting for the force to start north to cover the Russell Islands occupation, the Nicholas did two days' patrol off the harbor entrance. The second night we had what seemed to be a good submarine contact and made two attacks. There was no wreckage around the next morning, so if it was a submarine he must have escaped with only a jolting.

The visit to the base was a complete washout. We arrived the

320]

day after its officers' club, set up in a former plantation owner's home, ran out of fluid stock. No one had had a drink for so long, abstinence was getting to be a habit. At the last minute of our call at another base I had finagled a case of gin, but we had pulled out so suddenly we hadn't had an opportunity to attack it.

On February 20 we ran up to Tulagi with the light cruisers to cover the Russell Islands occupation, but when it became obvious that the Japanese surface forces were not going to interfere we went back south to join Admiral Giffen's heavies.

For several days the force did squads left and right, and right about, wearing out the book on maneuvers for practically any contingency of day or night fighting that could be imagined.

The Nicholas was glad to escape for two days to escort a light cruiser back to port. When she left the cruiser outside the harbor and headed back to rejoin the force everyone on the ship felt as though on vacation. She had been operating under a commodore or admiral for so long, Captain Andy Hill could hardly believe he finally was on his own, if only for a day.

Even the weather was propitious, sunny and cool, as the Nicholas turned north. We spent the morning firing at a target the First Lieutenant had made and that afternoon had an unofficial fireworks show, shooting off some pyrotechnics that had been condemned. One of the flares misfired when it was being shot and landed in the whaleboat just under the bridge. While the rest of us were ducking for cover Lou Snyder skinned down the ladder, jumped into the boat and threw the bomb over the side. It exploded as it hit the water, only a fraction of a second after it had left his hand. Lou will get no medal for his act, but it took plenty of courage.

When we rejoined the force we found plans had been made for a double-barreled night raid on Munda and Vila, which lie only twenty miles apart. The plan was for the light cruisers and destroyers to go in from the north, through the Kula Gulf, and hit Vila while Captain Briscoe took his four cans off Munda Bar to plaster the Munda airstrip.

The destroyers refueled from the cruisers on March 3 (one cruiser sent the Nicholas some walnut ice cream while the oil was being pumped) and we shoved off and headed north. After the loss of the Chicago the heavy cruisers never again went in range of the Japanese air arm around the Solomons.

While in port the Nicholas's doctor, Doctor Doyle, was transferred to the hospital. He had contracted what he had diagnosed as a slight case of cat fever but which developed into pneumonia. For several days he was running a fever of 104 degrees in a climate that was almost as hot. When the Nicholas left for the strike at Munda, she had no physician aboard. Although any one of the young doctors at the navy hospital would have jumped at the chance to see some action, none of them could be spared. Few wounded patients were being received from up the line, but the hospital was filled with sick marines and sailors. Pneumonia cases especially were increasing among the men of the ships, debilitated by the long watches they had to stand and the terrific heat.

The afternoon of March 4 the force headed north. This was getting to be a milk run for the Briscoe squadron. The ships passed through Sealark Channel without slackening speed, having to change course for a fleet of LCT's headed for Tulagi who never got out of anyone's way, and headed out past Savo at dusk.

The sunset was one of the most gorgeous the tropics ever had put on display. There was not a cloud in the sky. That night, for one of the few times of the many I had watched, I saw the green streamers shoot up across the sky just as the sun went down. Seen through binoculars, it rivals the aurora borealis for splendor.

Soon after sunset the force separated. Admiral Merrill led his group up "the slot." Captain Briscoe turned the destroyer squadron southwest through the passage between the Russells and New Georgia, to head up past Tetipari and Rendova for the attack on Munda.

The night was moonless and cloudless, and the heavens were

crowded with stars. There was the usual play of heat lightning along the horizon.

The squadron was in column. The squadron leader set the course and the speed. The others followed, running in her wake. On nights when it was difficult to see the bulk of the ship ahead the white phosphorescent wake always was visible.

The American ships, mere shadows in the night, slipped past Tetipari and then Rendova, which is shaped like Humpty Dumpty, a fat body with one leg sticking out toward Tetipari.

As we drew abreast of Baniata Point two planes came into view. The commodore turned out to sea, to give the squadron more room to maneuver, but they must have been friendly, for they turned away, apparently on sighting us. We knew there were to be PBY's over the enemy airfields to watch the bombardment and spot for the cruisers.

When no attack developed, the commodore turned back on the course, starting in past Rendova toward the firing course paralleling Munda Bar, a sand-topped coral reef that lay some two miles off the beach.

The squadron was half an hour from the firing course when we heard Admiral Merrill order his ships to commence fire and we saw, across the low-lying southwestern tip of Munda, our cruisers engaged in Kula Gulf. The enemy cruisers had chosen to defend Vila.

The flash from the 6-inch guns of our own cruisers was unmistakable. It was obvious they had gotten in the first licks. They must have had two or three salvos in the air before there was any return fire from the two enemy ships, and then it was in small volume compared to the hurricane of shells pouring from the turrets of the American cruisers.

The action had not been under way five minutes when there was a great explosion, then another smaller one from the area where the enemy ships had been seen firing. The smaller explosion was followed by a fire that waxed and waned. The American ships ceased firing.

[323

Captain Briscoe continued to lead the squadron in to do the job assigned, and promptly at 1:30 the squadron leader turned on the firing course and opened fire. An instant previously we saw the cruisers open up again and their shells arching across the sky toward the Vila target. Counting the flashes, we could see the force was still intact.

Following the squadron leader the other three destroyers turned on the firing course and opened on the Munda airstrip. There was no immediate answering fire from the beach, although the engagement between the two enemy vessels and the American cruisers in Kula Gulf had destroyed any element of surprise. The whole area must have been alerted.

Lieutenant Mitchell, the new gun boss, was firing the Nicholas guns in full salvo, and soon the destroyer was rocking back and forth from the recoil of the five 5.38's going off in unison. The South Pacific fleet did not then have flashless powder, and the blinding flash of the four destroyers' guns blinded those of us who were watching from the bridge. The only way to see at all, we found, was to count the seconds between salvos and close our eyes just as Mitch pushed the firing button. That way it worked out very well.

Methodically and at a sedate speed the squadron moved along on its firing course, rocking its salvos back and forth across the enemy airstrip from one end to the other. (An air strike that followed up at daybreak said Munda airstrip had been so torn with shells it was unusable; and no planes were attempting to operate from there when the American bombers arrived over the field.)

There still was no answering fire from the shore as the four American destroyers completed their run and turned southwest for the haul back home. The Radford was slow to turn out after the other three ships, and the commodore ordered sharply:

"Join up. Let's get the hell out of here."

After the flaming ten minutes of the bombardment the night seemed twice as black as all hands strained their eyes watching for the enemy torpedo boats supposedly operating in protection of the Munda Beach. The sea was glassy calm, without a ripple showing, and we could have seen the wake of a PT for five miles. If there were any around they never got close.

Carl Pfeiffer, the O'Bannon's chief engineer, had been having trouble with his repaired engines; and before we had gone in that night Doc MacDonald had reported to the commodore that he would not be able to make top speed. Remembering that, the commodore held the squadron leader to the speed of the O'Bannon as we started the retirement.

The squadron had put about six miles between it and the beach when the Japanese finally climbed out of their dugouts and fired a pattern of star shells in our direction. They were two thousand or three thousand yards short, but they acted like a shot in the arm for the O'Bannon. She was just astern of us in column when we saw her start to move up. We were running in the squadron leader's wake at her speed, and the O'Bannon was almost up on our fantail before she discovered she had closed the interval. She turned out just in time to avoid ramming, and shot past the Nicholas as though the latter had been tied.

The commodore saw her moving several knots faster than Carl had said she could make, so he stepped up the squadron leader's speed and soon the whole squadron was hightailing it at maximum speed.

As we were retiring we saw the cruisers open up again on the enemy ship they had hit when going in for their run. They had left her burning behind them, made their run and then worked her over again on the way out. We saw the American shells pouring in on the enemy vessel. Then the fire disappeared. We heard the next morning, when we were refueling back in Tulagi, that the American force had met the two enemy ships coming out of Kula Gulf after apparently having made a sweep of the lower end in search for the American ships. Admiral Merrill opened fire and hit both of them before they had fired a gun. One blew up and sank almost immediately. They left the other burning and dead in the water, went on in for their firing run, and then sank her on the way out.

The bombardment had been so effective that not an enemy plane got off either field, and the force returned to base without an attack. One of our own planes came over Rendova as we cleared Baniata Point, but he quickly got out of our way when the Radford fired a few shells at him. After the Nicholas's experience west of Savo the night of January 26 and the loss of the DeHaven, the squadron was under orders to fire at night on any plane that came in range without identifying itself.

Several weeks later I saw Dick Tregaskis of International News Service at a rear base, and learned that Dick was in the PBY the Radford fired on. He had flown up from Guadalcanal to watch the bombardment. The shells burst all around the plane and gave them quite a shaking up, Dick said, but did not injure or kill anyone and did little damage to the plane. It was entirely too accurate shooting for their comfort, though.

When we returned to base I said goodbye to the Nicholas and to the squadron, which now had a new commodore, and started what developed as a long and laborious trip to the Aleutians.

The Battle of the Solomons was not over, but it was the beginning of the end. In seven months Guadalcanal had been seized and built into a major air base and a staging island for further moves up the chain. The Japanese had withdrawn their badly battered fleet, and although they continued to feed in planes to Rabaul and Munda, Vila and Bougainville air bases, the United Nations held control of the sea and the air.

On June 30 an invasion force of the army landed on Rendova Island, from where Munda airstrip could be brought under artillery fire, and after two months of heavy fighting cleared it and all of New Georgia of the enemy. Shortly thereafter the Japanese, outflanked by another American landing on Vella La Vella, began withdrawing their forces from Kolombangara, abandoning their now useless base at Vila.

General Vandegrift, promoted to a Lieutenant Generalcy and placed in charge of the first amphibious corps of marines, sent them ashore November 1 at Empress Augusta Bay on Bougainville.

On the second anniversary of Pearl Harbor, the only question remaining was how long it would take to complete the conquest of all the Solomons, an outcome that was as certain as the course of the sun and the moon and the stars.

The Japanese navy made only three ineffectual efforts to interfere by sea with the American advance from Guadalcanal. On July 6 and 12, while the battle for Munda still raged, forces of American cruisers and destroyers defeated light Japanese flotillas in the Kula Gulf, with loss of the light cruiser Helena and the destroyer Gwin; and in November an American surface force turned back an attempted surface strike from Rabaul at the Empress Augusta Bay bridgehead.

The pincers were closing on Rabaul, the principal target of the American drives through New Guinea and up the Solomons.

General Vandegrift's prophecy in his farewell to his command on Guadalcanal in December—" 'tide what may' I know that you, as brave men and men of good will, will hold your heads high and prevail in the future as you have in the past"— was being gloriously fulfilled.

PART V

THE ALEUTIAN CAMPAIGN

CHAPTER I

Diversion for Midway

As THE GREAT Japanese invasion fleet with which the little men of the Rising Sun hoped to seize Midway and to bomb Pearl Harbor into uselessness moved northward and eastward from the Marianas, the Marshalls, and the Bonins, in early June, 1942, a part of it split off and turned even farther to the north.

In the early morning of June 3, as the fog that had hung over the Aleutians for three days began to lift, planes from the two small carriers that were the heart of the Japanese force struck at Dutch Harbor.

Their arrival was not unexpected. Like Pearl Harbor, our other island bases, and the West Coast, Dutch Harbor and Alaska had been on the alert for several days.

There was little, however, that our forces in the Aleutians could do to prepare for an attack, except take a deep breath and pull in their belts. There wasn't time. Six months after the start of the war, Dutch Harbor still was little more than a seaplane anchorage and naval fueling station. It had no airfield. One hundred and twenty miles to the southwest, the army was building an air station at Umnak and already had a strip built and a squadron of P-40 fighter planes based there. But Umnak was the last military installation out the thousand-mile chain. On Kiska there were only ten weather observers, and no fortifications. The rest of the islands were inhabited, and guarded only by a score of white fishermen and trappers, a few hundred Aleuts and thousands of ravens, gulls, ducks, and eagles.

The first attack on Dutch Harbor was by fifteen Japanese fighters, who strafed a PBY in the harbor, the only plane there, and ships and shore installations. They were followed by a few horizontal dive bombers. Twenty-five men were killed at

Fort Mears, the army camp at Dutch Harbor, the major casualties of the two days of intermittent attacks.

On the way back to their carriers, which were lying southwest of the American base, the Japanese planes inadvertently flew over Umnak, of which they apparently had no prior knowledge. The P-40's knocked down several of them and also some of the bombers that had followed the fighters over Dutch Harbor.

The aim of the Japanese in attacking the Aleutians probably was twofold. First, and primarily, their purpose was to pull our fleet, that was then maneuvering north of Pearl Harbor, away from Midway to clear the way for their large invasion forces approaching that westernmost United States outpost. If the Japanese ruse had been successful it is doubtful if the forces based on Midway could have repulsed the Japanese, since most of the marine and navy fighters, dive bombers, and torpedo planes from Midway were shot down in the first few hours of combat. The big army bombers alone could not have stopped the Japanese.

Secondly, the Japanese wanted to test our Aleutian defenses. If they found them weak enough they might have attempted a landing much farther up the chain than Attu or Kiska. They did not have a large force of landing troops with them, however. Some of the estimated ten thousand to twelve thousand men who made the unopposed Attu and Kiska landings were with the Midway attack group originally, and were diverted to the Aleutians when the Midway attack failed.

Whatever the Japanese plans, the unexpected opposition from land-based army fighters undoubtedly dissuaded them from attacking Dutch Harbor. The Japanese carriers—whose commanders by that time had received the news of the disaster that had struck their Midway forces—retired to the westward. On June 7 the weather station on Kiska reported: "Unidentified ships are entering the harbor." After that, silence. A smaller force occupied Attu at the same time. They were to stay on

Attu for almost a year and on Kiska for thirteen months before they were chased out.

Much has been written to indicate that the Japanese occupation of Attu and Kiska was a direct threat to the continental United States. One writer made the absurd claim that the Japanese force that attacked Dutch Harbor had intended to go on and assault Seattle. If they had so intended, what stopped

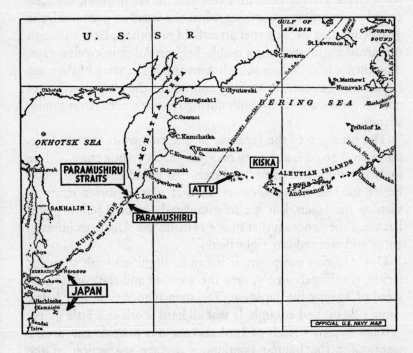

them? Certainly not a few army fighters and a handful of navy PBY's, and army B-17's and B-26's making a few contacts and ineffectual attacks on them in fog and rain those first two days. The Japanese have made many fanatical and foolish moves, but it strains credulity to imagine that they had any hopes of reaching and attacking the Canadian and United States mainland with a force consisting of only two small carriers, three or four cruisers, and a dozen destroyers.

[333

It is doubtful if the Japanese would even have attempted a landing on Attu and Kiska had they met any opposition from the shore at those two places or if we had had any surface forces available to oppose them in the Aleutians.

No evidence was found at either Attu or Kiska, after we had captured the former and occupied the latter, to indicate they had plans for building up either place as a possible invasion base for a strike farther east. In a full year of occupation, opposed only by intermittent bombing when the weather permitted, the Japanese failed to construct an airfield on either place, although our army engineers built a usable field on Adak in twelve days. The enemy installations at both Attu and Kiska were of the most rudimentary nature, in striking contrast to the plush-lined bases and monster airfields we built during the same period, on similar islands.

The presence of the Japanese on the two westernmost Aleutian island groups, although no great threat to our coast, did tie up many ships and planes and men that could have been much better used in active theaters. In that way it was a strategic victory for Japan. But it also stimulated our base building and hastened the program that now has made the Aleutians impregnable and secured our right flank.

Our Aleutian campaign, if it can be dignified with so major a title, was largely one against the weather and the country instead of against the Japanese. The men who waged that battle cannot be praised enough. It was all hard work and little glory.

That barren stretch of land and sea did provide the dreary setting for the longest continuous surface sea action of the Pacific War and of modern naval history. The Battle of the Komandorskis, of March 27, 1943, waged by an American task force of one heavy cruiser, one old light cruiser, and four destroyers against a Japanese force of two heavy cruisers, two lights, and six destroyers, lasted for three and a half hours. It turned back the last major effort of the Japanese to reinforce their Aleutian garrisons.

334]

The Aleutian campaign, because it was to be largely naval and amphibious, had the navy in command, but all three services —the navy (which included the Coast Guard), army, and marines—participated in preparations for and operation of the Attu and Kiska shows. Marine participation was largely training, under the command of Major General Holland McT. Smith, later to command the Tarawa-Makin operation. He also had trained the troops that set up the beachheads in North Africa. Marine officers participated as intelligence officers in the Attu and Kiska landings.

Vice Admiral Thomas C. Kinkaid, who had been at Midway, was in over-all command. At sea, in tactical command of the task forces that supported the Attu and Kiska landings, was Rear Admiral Francis W. Rockwell, who had been commander of the Philippine naval district at the start of the war. Each naval task force also included one or two admirals. Major General Albert E. Brown was in charge of the army troops who made the landing on Attu. He was relieved, after six days, by Major General Eugene M. Landrum, "Landrum of the Andreanofs," who had been in command at Adak. Major General Charles H. Corlett was in charge of the army troops that made the Kiska landing.

The other two high-ranking army and navy officers in the Aleutian-Alaskan sector were Lieutenant General Simon Bolivar Buckner, Jr., and Rear Admiral John W. Reeves, Jr., who were in command of the army and navy shore establishments, respectively.

The air officers were Major General W. O. Butler, in command of both army and navy air forces based on shore, and Commodore L. E. Gehres, in command of the navy air wing.

The multiplicity of commands was not nearly as confusing as it appears on paper, and the cooperation and good feeling among the various services was outstanding.

Toward the end of the campaign this was beginning to change for the worse, with army men barred from the navy canteen when supplies ran low, and army officers persona non grata at the navy officers' club on Adak except as guests of navy officers or newspaper correspondents. Plans had been made for an army officers' club, but when the prohibitionists began to warm up in Congress, liquor was banned on army posts or in army officers' clubs. Since that is the main attraction of any such establishment, the plans of the army officers were dropped. The navy had its club, the army had none—and didn't like it. That the fault was not the navy's was easily forgotten.

These may seem like small matters, but they are important to men who are stuck in isolated posts with no means of entertainment except what they concoct themselves.

The army was slow to react to the Japanese occupation, but it was hampered, as elsewhere in the Pacific, by lack of ships and men and materials with which to operate. The first major move west was made in August 1942, when General Buckner gathered an expedition and occupied Adak. He used everything from a modern freighter to two old four-masted schooners to get his men and their gear out to Adak from Cold Bay, a base east of Dutch Harbor. The new base put the army within easy bomber range of Kiska, two hundred and fifty miles to the west, and of Attu, one hundred and fifty miles beyond Kiska.

On January 12, 1943, with the base at Adak rapidly becoming our major military establishment in the Aleutians, the army moved on out to Amchitka and started building a base and an airstrip there. On Amchitka the army was only sixty miles from Kiska and only twenty-two hundred miles from Tokyo, the closest any American foot soldier had come to the Japanese capital.

Then, on May 11, 1943, came the attack on Attu. The operation was completed June 2, with extermination of the Japanese garrison of twenty-three hundred men. On August 15 came the occupation of Kiska, which had been abandoned by the Japanese. They had successfully evacuated their force of six thousand to ten thousand men—perhaps by submarine.

Even before Kiska was taken, offensive operations against Japan were underway. The first bombing of Paramushiru, Japan's Kurile Island base, was planned for early July. On July 10 a few B-25's, the Billy Mitchells that have proved themselves our best two-motored bombers, did fly over Paramushiru and drop a few bombs through the fog, with undetermined results. The larger part of the force marshaled for the first bombing effort, however, was diverted to attack a group of small Japanese supply vessels that had started up from Paramushiru either to reinforce the Kiska garrison or to aid in their evacuation. Hit by the big bombers in a skip-bombing attack, a technique of bombing that had been initiated by the British and perfected by our own air force, the four ships turned back. Three of them were sunk; the fourth was badly damaged.

On July 18 the first real attack on Paramushiru was made. Its object was to get photographs. The bombing was only secondary. The strike was made by six four-motored bombers led by Major Robert E. (Pappy) Speer, of Eugene, Ore., who had logged thirty-three months in Alaska and the Aleutians. Taking off from Attu, the six planes made the two-thousand-mile run to Paramushiru and back to Adak without incident. A few float-type fighters took off to pursue them, but none caught up. They brought back more than two hundred excellent photographs, giving our people the first good look at Paramushiru they had had since 1920, when the Japanese allowed the last visitors there.

The fliers reported both Paramushiru and Shimushu, the smaller adjoining island, as well fortified and having large operating naval bases in Kashawabaro and Kataoka bays. The antiaircraft fire, once the Japanese woke up and got their guns manned, was heavy but inaccurate. When the photographs were developed they showed a considerable Japanese force of cruisers and destroyers lying in Kataoka Bay. A light cloud layer had obscured them from the view of the American fliers eighteen thousand feet above them. Seven-and-a-half tons of bombs were dropped, hitting the Japanese main camp on Shimushu and straddling several large transports in Kashawabaro Bay.

A second raid, on a slightly larger scale, was made on August 11. Nine Liberator bombers, the four-motored B-24's, made this attack. Two failed to come back, but one of these made a safe landing on Kamchatka Peninsula, at a Russian base.

The object of this raid was to do damage, and the big bombers carried considerably greater bomb loads than those that made the strike of July 18. More than eighteen tons of bombs were dropped on the naval base at Kataoka Bay and on the army staging areas on the shores of Kashawabaro Bay.

Since the previous raid, the Japanese had brought land fighters up from Honshu and our bombers had to fight a forty-five-minute running battle with the Zeros on the way home. In addition to the two planes lost, others sustained minor battle damage. One flew all the way home on three engines. Five of the attackers were shot down for sure, and there were some probables.

There have been other raids since that time, and there probably will be more. The weather is so uncertain, however, both over the Aleutians, from which the bombers must fly, and over the Kuriles, which also are fog-bound most of the year, that bombing is made both hazardous and uncertain. Any damage to our planes means they can't get back home. A man will live less than thirty minutes in the icy waters of the North Pacific, and probably not more than a day or two on a rubber raft.

With the occupation of Kiska in August, the reconquest of the Aleutians was complete. Except for Wake and Guam, no enemy forces remained on American soil.

Many persons, noting only the geographical location of the Aleutians, call them a "bridge to victory," the shortest invasion route to Japan, and other nice-sounding names. Military men, who must weigh all the factors, think the Aleutians of doubtful tactical value.

They might be used as a base from which to carry on bomber shuttle service over Tokyo with the new long-range bombers that are said to be in production. They were too far removed from Japan, with the closest point twenty-two hundred miles distant, for any bombing by the bombers of 1943. Any frontal assault on Paramushiru would require a good many more ships and a lot more aircraft carriers than we can afford for a venture of such doubtful value.

The value of the Aleutians is somewhere in the dim future when, if Russia should have come into the war on our side, they will lie along the main supply route to our ally and Paramushiru will have fallen anyway. The war in the Pacific will be nearing its end then, not the beginning of the end, as it was at the close of the first two years of the war.

CHAPTER 2

Base Building

"This war up here is largely men and machines against weather," said Major Henry W. Hall, a former investment broker of Portland, Ore., who was a member of the original landing party on Adak, and the army port commander.

He made the remark as he and Morley Cassidy, of the *Philadelphia Bulletin* and the North American Newspaper Alliance, and I were drinking coffee in his quarters, one foggy, windy afternoon in early August just before the Kiska attack, and discussing that first landing on Adak almost a year before.

The major's quarters, the day we were there, were a well heated quonset hut. Coffee bubbled on the diesel oil stove in the middle of the area set aside as living space for himself and the two officers who shared that end of the quonset with him. The other end was his office. A small cubicle, boarded off to afford a small degree of privacy, was his sleeping nook.

[339

The quonset sat on the side of a ravine in the midst of the area where the island command of Major General Landrum was situated. Graveled paths connected the various huts. Little wooden bridges crossed the stream that ran down the ravine. There was a grill of boards outside the quonset entrance on which to scrape the mud from your shoe pacs or mukluks, the Alaskan snowboot. All of the quonsets were heated. Some of them had their own shower baths and flush toilets.

The major's quarters marked the change that had come over Adak in its year of occupancy by the American army and navy.

When the vanguard of the odd armada that had taken the army westward a year before arrived at Adak, they had found no humans and only one house, a one-room shack built by Walter Kansack, an Aleutian guide. There were no docks, no roads, no anything except the spongy tundra, the fog-wreathed, snow-capped mountains.

Now, in addition to Major Hall's quonset, there were several hundred more of the same, five movie theaters, thirty miles or more of all-weather roads, a modern airfield as large as La-Guardia field, hangars, warehouses, mess halls, two deep-water docks, a naval officers' club with a fireplace, a turkish bath where you could get a bath and massage for 10 cents, a limited amount of Scotch and rye whiskey, and fifty thousand soldiers, sailors and marines.

The stupendousness of the undertaking—building a city for fifty thousand men—can be appreciated only by realizing that everything except the sand and gravel for the roads had to be brought in by ship. Every bite of food everyone ate had to come by the same means.

Adak, although the biggest, was only one of many bases in the Aleutians, built up in the same way in the year after the Japanese occupation of Kiska and Attu.

The whole contour of some of the islands was changed. Lakes were drained and their beds filled for airfields on both Adak and Amchitka. It was easier to do the job that way than to attempt to dig through the spongy tundra to solid ground elsewhere. Roads were cut through the hills and some smaller hills were leveled in securing fill for low spots where some military installation was needed.

And all this work was done in a cheerless, wind-swept, treeless chain of islands where the sun shines less often, winter or summer, than on any other place in the world; where there are no good beaches, where the weather all year is as unpredictable as a Marx Brothers movie.

Surprisingly enough, the Aleutians are the healthiest place where our army is quartered. The incidence of sickness there is less than 1½ per cent. Much of that is caused by exposure or overwork, revealing organic weaknesses that might not have shown up under other circumstances. The year-round chill, which varies from a few degrees above zero in winter to an average of between 45 and 50 degrees in the summertime, apparently is as deadly on germs as it is hard on men's spirits.

It is the lack of sun that is the most depressing aspect of the Aleutians. There are only two months in the year when there is anything like clear weather. Those are April and October. The rest of the year the fog varies from thick to thicker, with only an occasional clear day. In four months in the Aleutians I saw the sun perhaps a dozen times, but I never saw it rise or set. During July the army bombed Kiska every day it was possible either to take off in comparative safety from one of the air bases then operating—Adak, Amchitka, and Attu—or the fog was low enough over Kiska to enable the fliers to get a bearing on Kiska volcano to make a run over the main camp around the harbor or over Gertrude Cove. That was just twelve days out of thirty-one. There were not half a dozen days that month when the air was clear enough over Kiska for any worthwhile pictures to be taken of the Japanese positions.

The work of base building in this treeless wilderness of volcanic peaks, sticking up from an ice-cold sea, was the toughest any men ever undertook. Down in the South Seas, men could cool off with a swim in a cold jungle stream after the day's work. There was tropical fruit to pick and eat. It was exciting. They were near the fighting, even if they weren't in it. Up in the Aleutians no one ever got completely dry or warm. Men worked in spongy tundra, that strained the leg muscles; in fog, and sleet and rain and cold that penetrated to the very marrow of the bones. It was the only place in the world, as several persons have been credited with first saying, where you could be in mud up to your waist and have dust blowing in your face at the same time.

Worst of all was the fact that men in the rear bases—and most of the bases became that in short order, once an airfield was built and our planes could give it protection—never saw a Japanese, never got an opportunity to fire a gun at an enemy. They were doing the hardest work, living in the most disagreeable circumstances they could have dreamed of, and getting the least pay for it. They wanted to fight a war, not to work their way through one. They didn't like it.

Just reading the temperature charts of the Aleutians, it doesn't sound like such a bad place. The islands sweep southwestward in a long arc from Alaska, almost to the same latitude as Vancouver, British Columbia. The Japanese Current to the south moderates the temperature in the winter and the cold Bering Sea to the north keeps them cool in summer.

As at all bases carved out of a wilderness, it is the lack of conveniences, the unpaved roads; no sidewalks, no street lights, detached toilets, and mess halls blocks away from working and sleeping quarters, that make living such a nightmare.

"If I was back home in Seattle, I wouldn't mind weather like this," a young officer said one day as we stood in the rain outside the navy officers' mess waiting for the line to move past the cashier's window. The temperature was about 50 degrees. "It's a normal winter day for there. It's this damn mud and eternal fog that drives me nuts, and no privacy. Sometimes I'm like Garbo, I want to be alone."

342]

AS TOUGH AS HE LOOKS

Major Joe Foss as he looked on Guadalcanal when, as a member of a Marine fighter squadron at Henderson Field, he shot down twenty-six Japanese planes to tie Captain Eddie Rickenbacker's record in the first World War. Most of Joe's bag were Japanese Zero fighters. In the background are the fliers' tents along Henderson Field. Joe himself titled this photograph, "Me and My Working Garb, Some Days."

JUNGLE LUMBERJACKS

Four men of a Navy Construction Battalion, better known as "Seabees," who did most of the construction work in the Solomons. Composed largely of older crafts-men, they furnished a lot of the sweat and some of the blood needed to drive the Japanese off Guadalcanal.

BATTLE OF THE KOMANDORSKIS

The American heavy cruiser, Salt Lake City, outfighting and outmaneuvering a Japanese task force that was trying to take supplies and reinforcements in to Attu and Kiska on March 26, 1943. The American cruiser is fighting from behind a smoke screen laid by American destroyers.

Adak in the late summer of 1943 was a fairly civilized place, where you could have coffee in the middle of the afternoon in a cozy quonset like that of Major Hall. A bus line connected the main establishments dispersed over the island.

"The convoy that took this place was the damnedest sight you ever saw," Major Hall said. "We had bought or leased every old scow along the Alaska coast. Some of our equipment we brought out in barges, towed by tugs.

"We had bad weather on the way out and one of the tugs, the Klihyam, Grant Evans, skipper, had to seek shelter for the night in a bay. He put out to sea again the next morning, failed to find the rest of the fleet, and came on ahead to Adak all alone. Somehow he passed us and arrived here first. He was lucky the Japanese weren't on the island.

"Our men went ashore with only combat packs and lived in the open, with only canned rations for six days. It was the most miserable time I ever spent anywhere.

"We had to manhandle everything ashore from barges, wading in icy water up to our waists."

Everything was subordinated to the work of building the airfield. Twelve days after the machinery to build it was ashore, the field was ready to receive planes.

Because the Seabees have a catchy name and had a good press agent in Alaska and the Aleutians, John Kenny, they have received credit for doing much more of the construction work than the army engineers. It was the army engineers who built Umnak, who built Adak, who built Amchitka and did the bulk of the heavy work at other Aleutian bases. The Seabees finished Dutch Harbor, after the civilian contractors had been removed. It was they who built the various comfortable navy towns along the chain and also some navy airfields, where the two services maintain separate establishments, but the army engineers did the major share.

A large dock first was built at Adak, being completed after thirty days. In January a deep-sea dock which had been prefabricated in Alaska and taken to Adak knocked down, was erected. The Seabees built a companion piece.

The Japanese, either because of the weather or because of their limited search planes, did not discover the army's presence on Adak for thirty days. Late in September a float observation plane dropped down through a high fog and buzzed the harbor. At the first burst of antiaircraft fire he scurried back into cloud cover, but the next day he returned with a friend and dropped light bombs that did no damage. Another attack was made the following day, but with the completion of the airfield the Japanese made no further attempts to interfere with the base.

The story of Amchitka is even more one of men and machines against the weather. The landing there was made January 12, 1943, with the weather much worse than it was at Adak in the late summer. On the second day of the landing a gale made up, driving one supply ship ashore and wrecking most of the barges. The lake that was drained there had to be filled.

Amchitka also received more attention from the Japanese than did Adak. A reconnaissance plane flying from Kiska, seventy-five miles away, discovered the Americans on the island on January 23. After that, they bombed it intermittently, whenever the weather permitted, until the fighter strip was completed on February 16 and the first eight P-40's went in. The enemy had only float-type planes at Kiska, carrying only small bomb loads, and in all their attacks they killed only one man and did little damage, either to the island installations or to the ships in Constantine Harbor, that were the prime target.

The Japanese learned about completion of the airfield on Amchitka the hard way. On February 18 they sent over the usual bombing mission of two float planes. The P-40's caught them before they reached the island and shot them both down. This must have had a very depressing effect on the Japanese garrison at Kiska. It was the last bombing attack on Amchitka.

On March 1 the Amchitka-based planes began to pay back the Japanese. That day the P-40's, which were used largely as fighter-bombers and ground strafers because there was no enemy air opposition, paid their first visit to Kiska. They made many more.

When the time came for the Kiska "invasion" in August, Amchitka had been transformed from a barren, tundra-covered island to a major base. More than a hundred fighters were based there to provide the air cover for the Kiska show. There were several squadrons of bombers, and transport planes to carry paratroops, if they were needed. Docks had been erected and a sea-wall built to protect Constantine Harbor from the storms that sweep down out of Bering Sea in winter at an eighty-knot pace. The island garrison was sheltered in quonset huts. The men had been visited, if not entertained, by a USO show.

Two men, who never were mentioned in communiqués, were given much of the credit by the army and navy men with whom they worked, for the speedy construction of the Aleutian bases. They both were Alaskans who were called into the service at the start of the war, Lieutenant Colonel DeLong by the army and Commander Anderson by the navy. I never found anyone who knew the first name of either. Colonel DeLong merely was called "DeLong" and Commander Anderson was called "Squeaky."

Neither of them had much knowledge of army or navy regulations. Both cared less. But when there was a tough job to be done, they were the Johnnies who could do it. For both of them it was a step down in a money way to take the commissions they had. Colonel DeLong, before the war, was Alaskan superintendent for the Morris and Knudsen Construction Company, Boise, Idaho. Although the Amchitka expedition was in command of Brigadier General Lloyd Jones, army men I talked with said Colonel DeLong was the fellow who made the thing tick.

Squeaky Anderson—he wouldn't tell his first name when he was asked merely say, "Call me Squeaky, everybody knows Squeaky"—was a chunky, straw-haired man who had gone to Alaska as a boy, where he trapped, ran his own trading schooner, fished for salmon, and finally became a salmon packer. Squeaky was one of the most deeply patriotic men in the Aleutians. His age, in the forties, would have protected him from the draft. His business was essential. Squeaky figured if the Japanese weren't licked there wouldn't be any business. The United States had been good to him, he said. He wanted to pay his debt in a more personal way than buying bonds and voting regularly, and obeying the law.

Squeaky and Colonel DeLong always were with the forward echelon. When that was Dutch Harbor, they were there. When it was Adak, they were at Adak. When it was Attu they were at Attu. They were among the first ashore on Kiska. Colonel De-Long drove the first jeep across Kiska from the landing beach on the west side to Gertrude Cove. When he made the trip it wasn't a certainty that the Japanese already had gone. But the Colonel was no more afraid of a Japanese than he was of any other man.

The Pacific war during the first two years was largely one of base building in an attempt to overcome the twenty-year head start we had given the Japanese.

It was men like Squeaky Anderson and Colonel DeLong who won that battle. Unsung and little honored, they deserve the gratitude of their country in only slightly less measure than those who actually came to grips with the Japanese. Theirs not the honor and glory, only the satisfaction of a necessary job well done.

Battle of the
Komandorskis

WITH THE battle for the Solomons going full blast five thousand miles to the south of the Aleutians, the Pacific fleet could spare few combatant ships for duty in the North Pacific and the Bering Sea during the fall and winter of 1942.

In the spring, however, the Japanese pulled out of the Solomons their heavy vessels or what few were left of the fleet based on Truk, and Admiral Nimitz was in a position to strengthen his northern force.

Among the ships sent to the North Pacific was the heavy cruiser Salt Lake City. Already the old "Swayback Maru" had seen more action than any other American heavy cruiser. She had been with the Marshall-Gilbert, Wake-Marcus, and Tokyo raids. After a tour of duty with the Australian squadron, she had joined up for the Guadalcanal occupation and on October 11, off Savo Island, had fought heroically in the first interception of the Tokyo Express. It was the action of her captain, Ernest Small, now a Rear Admiral, in driving in between the flaming Boise and the Japanese heavy cruisers that had saved the American light cruiser.

Under a new captain, Bert J. Rodgers, the Salt Lake City arrived at Adak in early March and was assigned to a task force led by Rear Admiral C. H. McMorris. They soon headed west to patrol between the Kuriles and Attu and Kiska to intercept any reinforcements for these two Japanese-held Aleutian islands.

In addition to the Salt Lake City, an 8-inch-gun cruiser, there was an old 6-inch-gun light cruiser, the Richmond, aboard which Admiral McMorris had his flag, and four destroyers.

As will be made plain later, it was fortunate, so long as there was only one heavy American cruiser, that it was the Salt Lake City. She is one of only a few that have two turrets aft. More modern types have only one turret of three guns firing over the stern.

Anyway, there they were, in the birthplace of storms, looking for a fight. The sea was calm that morning, March 27, and the wind, for a change, was blowing out of the southeast and at only eight knots.

The force had been out several days, but until that morning all the officers of the deck and the lookouts had seen was the gray, restless sea; they had felt the bite only of the bitter wind that blows off the Arctic ice pack a few hundred miles to the north. It was to be just another precautionary muster on station, the crew thought as, hearing general quarters sounded, they stumbled in their heavy Arctic clothing across icy decks and up steep ladders to their battle posts.

The force was in scouting formation, in the van the flagship. They had been south and west during the night and were headed back toward Attu on a northeasterly course. With the sea calm and the temperature just above freezing, it was, relatively, a pleasant morning.

Shortly after 7:30, an hour before sunrise, one of the destroyers relayed the order from the flag, "Concentrate on me," and shortly thereafter the further signal, "Set boiler condition one," which meant everything on the line. Something was up, but from the fighting top of the heavy cruiser the horizon still was an empty waste of sea and cloud.

At 7:45 the flagship, still some distance in the van, signaled that it had "Three to five targets bearing ooo degrees (north)" then "Expedite concentration."

Excitement ran through the ship like a flame. This is what they had been looking for, a chance to catch the Japanese at sea in the daytime. "Prepare for action," ordered Captain Rodgers.

348]

The American force, in fighting formation, turned north at flank speed toward the enemy convoy.

From the foretop of the Salt Lake City the lookouts could see the enemy ahead on the horizon. They reported to the bridge it appeared to consist of two or three AK's or AP's (navy designation for, respectively, supply ships or transports) and one DD (destroyer). Soon came the further word that the escort appeared to be two DD's and one CL (light cruiser).

It looked like a field day for the American force. A light cruiser and two destroyers could not stand long against the fire power of a heavy cruiser, and, with a full day ahead for the job, the AP's probably could be overtaken before dark and sent to the bottom with their loads of men and supplies.

The first optimistic evaluation was short-lived. At 8:37 came the report from the lookouts that another enemy ship had been sighted, fourteen miles away, and that it "may be a CA (heavy cruiser)." It was on a collision course with the American ships.

The two forces—American and Japanese—were closing at high speed, and it was only a matter of minutes until the full score was on the board.

Against the American force of one heavy cruiser, one light cruiser, and four destroyers, the Japanese were deploying a battle line of two heavy cruisers, later identified by lookouts as of the Atago and Nachi classes, two light cruisers of the Natori and Kuma classes, and six destroyers.

The two enemy AK's, or AP's, escorted by another light cruiser and two more destroyers, had turned northwest at their best speed when the American vessels began closing, and stayed on that course as the Japanese battle force, which had been ahead of them, countermarched and drove in against the American ships.

At 8:40 the leading enemy heavy cruiser opened fire on the American flagship from about twenty-five thousand yards, or fourteen land miles, getting a straddle but no hits with her second salvo. The light cruiser answered, but the range was too great for her 6-inch guns.

The Salt Lake City, meanwhile, her engines pounding away at full throttle, had been closing the Richmond to interpose her heavier armor and armament between the flagship and the enemy, and at 8:42 she let loose with her two forward turrets in a salvo at the enemy ship that was firing on the flag.

Since the first enemy ships had been picked up an hour before, the whole picture had changed. Instead of a stern chase of an inferior Japanese force, the Americans now were faced with a fight for their lives. It was they who must run. Admiral Mc-Morris turned his flagship hard left to head southwest, and the heavy Salt Lake City followed him around minutes later. The pursuer had become the pursued.

With the Richmond now drawing away, the enemy turned their guns on the Salt Lake City.

The range had closed to less than sixteen thousand yards, and the enemy formation was clearly outlined against the gray eastern sky. The two enemy light cruisers and four destroyers were in column, with one of the cruisers leading and one trailing. On their port beam were the two Japanese heavies.

"It seemed like the whole eastern horizon was full of enemy ships," said Captain Rodgers.

The first few salvos directed toward the Salt Lake City fell wide, but the Japanese gunners were not long getting the range (their gunnery was excellent throughout), and soon the leading enemy CA straddled the American cruiser.

A "straddle" in navy parlance occurs when shells from one broadside fall on both sides of the target. If you're the target, it's time to duck, for it means the enemy has the range and deflection right and if he can keep on you he's bound to get a hit. Captain Rodgers swung his ship sharply.

From topside, where the fall of shot could be clearly seen (you can actually see the shells coming), it was known no hits had been made. They were so close, however, that below decks where the sweating engineers were coaxing every possible revolution out of the big engines, they thought the enemy had scored.

"The concussion was so great," said one of the assistant engineers, "it felt like someone had hit me on the back with a heavy club and I had to grab a stanchion to keep my feet."

The Salt Lake City meanwhile was blazing away with her two after turrets at the enemy heavies, getting frequent straddles; and at 8:46, just four minutes after opening fire, she scored the first hits on the leading CA. From the spotting post at the top of the foremast a great ball of fire was seen to mushroom up from the vicinity of the enemy cruiser's bridge, and then a column of heavy black smoke. The Japanese cruiser ceased firing and began to drop back.

"I believe the commander of the Japanese force was on the bridge and was either killed or badly wounded," Captain Rodgers said. "Certainly there was little evidence of intelligent direction of the Japanese force after that. With their superior speed and fire power they could have murdered us. I wish the odds had been the other way. They wouldn't have gotten away from us."

As the Nachi dropped back the other enemy heavy, the Atago, came on and continued fire; but the battle had been going on for a good twenty minutes before the Japs scored the first of five 8-inch-gun hits on the Salt Lake City.

When the leading CA was blasted, the Salt Lake City concentrated all her fire on the Atago and got several straddles. Whether hits were scored was not definitely determined, but she also slowed and began dropping back, keeping station on the Nachi.

Admiral McMorris, meanwhile, had been making small course changes to put his ships on the same northwesterly course as the retiring transports, and at 9:51 Captain Rodgers suggested a further change to the right "so all my guns will bear."

Up to that point the Salt Lake City, except for the opening

salvos from her forward turrets, had been able to use only her five after guns, while the Japanese, showing more speed, were able to close the range and then swing right or left to let go at the American cruiser with full broadsides. Against the five-gun salvos the Salt Lake City was firing, the Japanese were answering with twenty guns.

The fight had not gone badly, despite the odds. The Salt Lake City had been hit, but not in a vital spot, while she had seriously damaged one of the enemy heavy cruisers (the American destroyers reported later that the Nachi was apparently able to fire from only one forward turret), and probably had scored some hits on the other. One of the enemy destroyers also had been hit when it crossed the line of fire and had disappeared astern, with another enemy destroyer standing by.

An enemy spotting plane, launched by one of the Japanese cruisers at the start of the battle, also had twice been fired on by the Salt Lake City and the destroyer's batteries and had disappeared into a cloud, smoking, after several bursts in its vicinity.

The enemy light cruisers, still in column formation with four destroyers, had crossed astern of the Salt Lake City and were paralleling her course, outside of range but in position to spot fire for the enemy heavies. The heavies still were on the port quarter, but dropping back.

Reporting to Admiral McMorris that the heavies were dropping astern, Captain Rodgers asked for another change of course to the right at 9:53 "so we can take this light cruiser" (the nearest enemy ship).

"Go ahead," came the answer.

The Salt Lake City then swung right twenty degrees, putting her on a course east of north, and opened up on the leading enemy light cruiser, plastering her with eight salvos, most of which straddled. The enemy ship turned sharply away, finally making a complete turn, in which she was followed by the destroyers and the other cruiser, and the Salt Lake City turned back again to fall in astern of the Richmond.

The respite was short. While the Salt Lake City was changing course to engage the light cruiser, the heavies, their damage apparently under control, again had come up within firing range and again opened on the Salt Lake City, jarring her with several salvos, and getting another hit.

Then occurred one of the minor accidents that plagued the American heavy cruiser all day and which except for the speedy and calm repair work of her officers and men, might have proved fatal. Due to the shattering concussion of her own 8-inch guns, an electric connection was broken in the steering engine and control of the ship from the bridge was lost. It was quickly repaired, then broken again.

Now the situation was really bad. The enemy heavies again were blasting away with all the guns they had left, and Captain Rodgers, unwilling to use more than a few degrees of rudder for fear it would jam and leave him circling helplessly, was forced to forgo the radical maneuvering with which he had been avoiding the enemy salvos.

"Having steering trouble," he signaled the flagship.

Admiral McMorris immediately ordered two of the four American destroyers "Report to Bert" (that was Captain Rodgers's nickname). "Screen him with smoke."

Back from their place on the flanks came the two little tin cans, black smoke rolling from their stacks as they increased the oil flow and shut off the air, to swing back and forth across the stern of the limping heavy cruiser.

"It was like something you see in the movies," said Lieutenant L. B. Ramsey, who had the spotting post in the foretop. "They'd go tearing across our stern, belching smoke and throwing bow waves twenty feet high, then turn, still at full speed, and come back again. Every time they crossed they were in the line of fire of the enemy cruisers. It must have been interesting to hear those shells whistling overhead."

Blinded by the smoke, the enemy cruisers checked fire momentarily but kept closing, resuming fire whenever there was a rift in the screen. It was through one of these holes that the Japanese gunners scored their last two hits on the American cruiser, and the most damaging. One penetrated the hull below the water line, sending oil and water cascading into the engine room. The other landed topside, on the starboard catapult, and caused the only casualties on the Salt Lake City—two dead and thirteen wounded.

As the Salt Lake City began to list from the water she was taking in through her ruptured skin, the remaining two American destroyers left the Richmond and joined the two making smoke. They were ordered to make a torpedo attack, but before they could get under way they were recalled as the Salt Lake City, which had lost speed because of her flooding, got all her engines operating again.

And still the Japanese feared to close. The Salt Lake City, despite her damage, was still blazing away at the enemy cruisers whenever she could get a range on them, and the gallant little American destroyers, doing half a dozen things at once, kept the enemy light cruisers and destroyers at bay with their 5-inch-gun fire.

"We were up above the smoke," said Lieutenant Ramsey, "and had a real bird's-eye view of all this. We could see where the smoke was thinning and the Japs on a course that would open us up to them. They never disappointed. They'd come past that hole and then 'bloom, bloom, bloom,' would come the shells. When they'd open up with all five turrets, it looked like they were on fire from stem to stern."

Admiral McMorris meanwhile had been gradually edging away from his northwesterly course, and at 11 o'clock he turned left to head almost due south, followed by the Salt Lake City and the four destroyers, the flagship some twenty-five hundred to three thousand yards ahead. The Salt Lake City still was listing badly, but her engineers, working in one engine room in water almost up to their necks, were gradually bringing order out of chaos and had her churning along at a good speed.

At about this time the Japanese admiral, or whoever was now in charge of the enemy force, suddenly must have awakened to the fact that he had been outmaneuvered as well as outfought, and at last he split his forces and attempted the same enveloping tactics that had worked so well for the British light cruisers in their epic battle with the Graf Spee off the Uruguayan coast in the early days of the war.

He kept one light cruiser and two destroyers to starboard of the American forces but sent the other two to port. He apparently also ordered a torpedo attack, which he had not attempted up to now despite the fact all Japanese cruisers, as well as destroyers, are believed to carry tin fish. The flanking enemy cruisers began to close. The Richmond here got in her effective licks in the battle, opening on the starboard cruiser so accurately that it turned away. The destroyers opened up on the other, and that Japanese captain also must have decided discretion was the better part of valor, because he also slowed and turned his ship.

The battle now had been going on for three hours, and the after turrets had been pumping out shells so furiously that their magazines were running low. Details were assigned from the AA batteries, and they started carrying shells and powder from the forward magazines over the open decks to the after turrets.

This was during a slight lull in the battle when the Japanese force, seeing the American destroyers forming for the torpedo attack that was delayed, turned ninety degrees right and momentarily dropped back out of range, crossing astern of the American ships.

They turned back when the American destroyers were recalled, and again opened fire, but it was only for a few minutes. At 11:52, for reasons that only they knew, they again turned right ninety degrees and headed west, at the same time opening up with all their AA batteries into the low-hanging overcast, in the apparent belief that the American bombers, which had been ordered out from our Aleutian bases, had arrived. Those skippers must have been at Midway or in the Solomons campaign and wanted no part of an American air attack.

It is possible, too, that they were running short of ammunition, as they had fired many more shells than the American ships, or it may have been that the Nachi-class cruiser was in more serious trouble than was apparent from the Salt Lake City. Whatever the reason, they turned away, voluntarily abandoning a battle that could have been disastrous for the outnumbered American force.

The Japanese maneuver was not immediately observed on the American cruiser, which still had her worst moments ahead. The hits aft and the many near misses had so strained the bulkheads and fuel lines feeding the engines that salt water had leaked into the fuel tanks and at 11:55, three minutes after the Japanese had turned away for the last time, the Salt Lake City's fires went out and she began coasting to a stop. As she two-blocked the three flags of the signal "mike speed zero" an 8-inch shell from one of the retiring Japanese ships passed through the "zero" flag, tearing it to shreds.

"I don't suppose there was anyone on the ship who didn't believe that was the end," said Lieutenant Commander John N. Boland, the antiaircraft officer, "but there was no outward evidence of any panic. I remember one of the men below asked, over the battle telephone circuit, what was going on."

" 'Oh, we're just hiding in the smoke to let the Japs catch up with us,' another man on the circuit told him. 'Then we're going to jump out and sink them.' "

Captain Rodgers, however, knew the score, and he asked the admiral to order now the torpedo attack by the destroyers. It looked as though that was the only thing that could save the Salt Lake City from certain destruction. Dead in the water, she would have been an easy target for the Japanese ships, if they had been ready to take advantage of her plight. The attack was ordered and Captain Ralph S. Riggs, commodore of the destroyers, ordered them into formation.

"Protect the Salt Lake City," he signaled to one destroyer; and to the other two: "Form on me. Speed 32." Then a few seconds later: "Target is the big boys. Course 270."

"Roger," said one destroyer.

"Roger," echoed the other.

Turning from their cruisers and toward the enemy, the three destroyers bored in for the attack.

It was one of the most chilling and most magnificent sights they ever had seen, those aboard the Salt Lake City who witnessed it were agreed.

When the destroyers started in, all the enemy ships knocked off firing at the American cruiser and turned their guns on the three little cans.

"I didn't see how they could live through it," one observer said. "The shells from the enemy ships were falling around them like hailstones."

For seven minutes, from 11:55 until 12:02, the destroyers could only take it as they charged ahead toward the retiring enemy forces. Then Captain Riggs told his force:

"My course 300. This is the firing course. Get ready."

Reporting later, he said he launched his attack at ten thousand yards and got at least one hit and perhaps two with his torpedoes on the Nachi-class cruiser. The American destroyers also were firing at the enemy with their five-inch guns as they attacked, and it is believed some hits were scored with those.

Back aboard the Salt Lake City the fires under the boilers had been relighted and at 12:02, just as the destroyers were making their gallant attack, the big ship began to push her way through the water again, following the Richmond back east toward the protection of the American bases and the army planes that were on their way out to attack the retiring Japanese ships.

The Salt Lake City fired a parting salvo at the retiring enemy at 12:05. It was the last shot of the battle.

The tension was not ended for the American force, because they did not know but what other enemy ships might be in the

[357

vicinity, looking for them, and there was still the possibility the enemy vessels, now retiring, might return. One destroyer now was having heavy going, having been hit by an 8-inch shell during the torpedo attack, and was limping along far astern.

"Do you want me to join you?" another DD asked.

"Keep on as you are," Captain Riggs ordered. "I will come along as fast as I can."

As the afternoon wore on the tension eased. An enemy plane shadowed the force for a time, but later there were friendly navy planes in the vicinity—late in the day the PBY's found and bombed the enemy supply ships—and every hour brought the Americans closer to their Aleutian bases.

Evaluating the conduct of his men during the three-and-a-half-hour naval battle—the longest continuous surface engagement of modern naval warfare—Captain Rodgers and his executive officer, Commander W. S. Bitler, noted so many instances of conduct beyond the call of duty that they found it difficult to select the really outstanding examples.

From the freshest-caught boot, there was not a single man who faltered at his post during the long engagement. After the battle was over there were a few cases of hysteria, but they were quieted quickly by the doctor.

Even the newer men, which included more than 50 per cent of the crew, men who had been at sea only a few weeks and never under fire before, stood up heroically to the long strain, several distinguishing themselves by their coolness and bravery. For instance, Rex Leist, a 21-year-old second class seaman from Exilia, Ohio, who had been in the navy less than six months and at sea for only two weeks. He volunteered as one of a small party that went aft under the very mouths of the after guns to chop ice and open valves of the smoke generators on the fantail.

"Considering his inexperience," said his citation, "and relative lack of instruction regarding the smoke generators, his actions in securing makeshift tools from scattered toolboxes to open frozen valves on an oily, slippery, rolling deck, were all the more commendatory. Regularly occurring blasts from mounts over his head did not cause him any apparent concern, nor deter him from his task."

"That battle changed the whole complexion of things up here," said Lieutenant General Buckner, "and was one of the bravest and most brilliant ever fought. If the Japanese had been able to get those reinforcements and supplies ashore we would have had a far more difficult job taking Attu."

There is only one memento of the battle, aside from her scars, on the Salt Lake City. It is a small piece of copper, for which a priority number had to be secured before it could be retained. It was formerly a part of the rotating band of a Japanese shell that hit the cruiser during the battle. It now adorns the top of a silver cigarette box in the Captain's sparsely furnished cabin.

It was presented to Captain Rodgers by his officers, who liked a skipper who liked to fight, who, when the going was toughest, took time out from gulping hot coffee brought to him by a shivering but loyal mess boy, to watch an enemy salvo fall fifty yards short and bellow down the wind "Yah! Yah! Yah! Missed us again."

The cigarette box was inscribed:

TO THE GALLANT LEADER
OF A GALLANT SHIP.
CAPTAIN B. J. "KOMANDORSKI" RODGERS, U.S. NAVY.
IN THE U.S.S. SALT LAKE CITY
FROM THE OFFICERS HE LED
IN THE
BATTLE OF THE KOMANDORSKIS.

No gift ever brought more pleasure to both receiver and donors.

CHAPTER 4

Attu Is Taken

THE BIGGEST invasion fleet since Guadalcanal was massed early in May, 1943, in Cold Bay, on the Alaskan Peninsula near where the Aleutians begin.

With Adak a big and growing base and Amchitka firmly established as an army fighter-and-bomber station, the time had come to begin chasing the Japanese out of the islands.

The little men with the big teeth were right where they had stopped almost a year before, on Kiska of the Rat Group and Attu of the Near Islands. It was thought they might also be on Agattu, to the south of Attu, but the fliers could see little evidence of construction there. Later, reconnaissance showed they had been on Agattu, but not in force. They even had abandoned Attu in the fall of 1942, but when our forces failed to move in they went back.

Kiska was the most strongly held of the two main islands. Aerial reconnaissance indicated a garrison of ten thousand to twelve thousand men. Attu was less strongly held. The pre-invasion estimate of twenty-five hundred men was within less than two hundred of being correct. The decision was made to attack Attu first.

One reason for the decision to make the first assault on Attu was that it was an amphibious operation, and the army had used on the North African invasion all the men it had trained in that most difficult science of war. The troops selected for the Attu show had some training on how to climb down a cargo net into a Higgins boat and how to get themselves and their gear ashore, but not much. They had been training in Southern California for the mobile warfare of North Africa, where infantry and artillery move at forty-five miles an hour, not foot by foot as is often the case in landing on an enemy beach. Attu was to be their education. No one wanted to make the first lesson too costly, as an assault on Kiska might have been.

Another reason for making the original attack on Attu was that it was a hundred and fifty miles nearer to Paramushiru. The generals were desirous of having a look at that northernmost Japanese base, and a bomber strip on Attu would give them a safer margin, with the limited range of their planes, for the trip. Also, with Attu in American hands a shuttle bomber service could be run across Kiska to soften it for the assault that would follow.

In the invasion force in Cold Bay on May Day were battleships, heavy and light cruisers, and destroyers. The men of the former had a personal score to settle with the Japanese. The ships they were riding were among those the Japanese fliers had damaged or sunk in Pearl Harbor in the sneak attack that touched off the war. Now, raised and repaired, they were ready for action. There also was a small carrier, one of the converted C-3 freighters, with squadrons of Grumman Wildcat fighters to do the ground strafing for the invasion and fight off any Japanese air reactions. Transports carried an invasion force of 12,000 men. Rear Admiral Rockwell was in charge of the force as long as it was at sea. After that his job would be to furnish supporting fire. Major General Brown was in charge of the army attack team.

The force had planned to get under way May 2 but a bad storm blew up, the first of many unforeseeable events that helped make Attu so costly a venture, and departure was delayed twenty-four hours.

"D" Day had been set for May 7, but as the big force neared Attu, the transports together, the heavier ships out ahead and on the flanks to guard against surface interception, a pea-soup fog settled down and refused to lift. The force turned away and milled around in the Bering Sea for three days. Finally when the weather report indicated better weather was coming, the force turned back and started in. It arrived off Attu the morning of May 11.

Attu is the westernmost island of the Aleutian chain, only two hundred miles from the Russian-owned Komandorski (Commander) Islands and less than four hundred from the nearest point of Kamchatka Peninsula, off the southern tip of which lie the Japanese Kuriles. Like the other Aleutian islands it is of volcanic origin. It is approximately sixty miles long by twenty miles wide. Its mountains range from two thousand feet to four thousand, and are snow-capped the year round.

The Japanese had pitched their main camp on the northeastern end of the island, around Holtz Bay, one of three fair anchorages. Smaller installations were at Massacre Bay, directly south across the island, and in Chichagof (pronounced Chi-cha'-gof) Harbor and adjoining Sarana Bay at the eastern tip.

The plan of attack was for one battalion, with supporting artillery, to land on a small beach to the north and west of the main Japanese camp on Holtz Bay. The main force would land on the south shore, on Massacre Bay and fight its way through the mountains to a junction with the Holtz Bay beachhead party. That would hem the Japanese in at the eastern end of the island, where they could be reached by bombardment from the sea, and would allow air bombing of a concentrated target. It was estimated it would take a day and a half for the main force to fight its way from Massacre Bay to Holtz Bay. It actually required just five times that long.

(Massacre Bay got its name two hundred years ago from the slaughter there by Cossacks of several hundred Aleuts who had resisted the intrusion of Russian fur trappers and traders.)

"H" Hour was set for 9:40 A.M. but at that time the fog was so thick that ships a few hundred yards apart could not see each other. It was no kind of weather for small boats to make a landing on a hostile beach, so the hour of attack was postponed.

Finally, at 3:30 P.M. they started in. The late hour was not so important, as sunset does not come in those latitudes in May until after 2200 hours, 10 P.M.

No opposition was encountered on the beaches, either at Massacre Bay or Holtz Bay, and the first day there was only preliminary skirmishing. The enemy had apparently been caught by surprise by the Holtz Bay landing, made on a small beach that would accommodate only two landing boats at a time. The enemy had only patrols in Massacre Bay. The bulk of their men were on the ridges on either side of the valley and in the high passes leading to Sarana Bay and Chichagof Harbor.

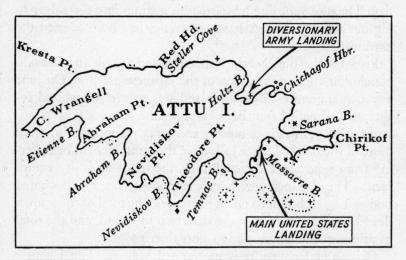

The Holtz Bay forces under command of Colonel Frank L. Culin and Major Albert L. Hartl, made steady progress toward the Japanese main camp. They met only light, sporadic resistance as the enemy began his withdrawal to Chichagof Harbor. On March 17 the Americans occupied all the Holtz Bay area.

On the other side of the Attu range things were not going so well. General Brown attempted to advance up Massacre Valley to the planned junction with the Holtz Bay forces. The Japanese dug in on the ridges on either side and poured down a lethal

[363

fire. Colonel Edward P. Earle, the second in command, was killed by a sniper the first day.

The Japanese had planned their defense well. They had dug holes back into the ridges concealing the openings with the long, brown tundra grass. Often they would hold their fire until advancing American troops had passed their position, then fire at them from the rear. Whenever our men, untrained for this sort of Indian-style fighting, congregated, artillery would be directed on them.

General Landrum, still limping from a recently fractured leg, was sent in to take command. He arrived the night of the fifth day. The next morning he started his men up into the ridges to dig out the Japanese. A lesson in tactics had been learned the hard way.

From then on the American attack moved steadily to its bloody conclusion, the extermination of the Japanese garrison. On June 2 it was announced that the island was secure. Organized resistance had ended four days before. American losses were announced as 342 dead, 58 missing and 1,135 wounded. Hundreds more of the original force of twelve thousand were ill or suffering from exposure and trench foot, the result of faulty equipment. The Japanese dead were announced as 1791 counted bodies. Eleven had been taken prisoners. The total of the known dead later was raised to more than two thousand, and the total of prisoners taken increased to more than a score.

Organized Japanese resistance ended May 29. The Japanese had been under steady pressure and concentrated artillery and ship fire, and aerial bombing and strafing. Many of them were wounded. They had no rest day or night.

The night of May 28, Colonel Yasuyo Yamasaki, the island commander, issued his last order. They were to attack. Every man who could walk had to participate. They were to attack through the pass into Sarana Bay and attempt to fight their way into Massacre Bay. Those of the wounded who could not be moved were to be killed, or were to be given grenades to kill

364]

themselves. The remaining rations were distributed equally. So were the guns and ammunition. Men who had no rifles tied bayonets or knives to sticks.

What ceremonies preceded this final assault were not learned. American soldiers on the ridges looking down on the Japanese positions thought they heard organ music or singing.

Shortly after midnight, when the subarctic night was at its darkest, they attacked. Screaming their falsetto battle cries, they charged through the pass, bayoneting and slashing American soldiers in their sleeping bags. Those who could speak English screamed obscenities.

"We drink American blood like wine," some of them yelled.

It was not warfare on any known pattern. There apparently was no effort to keep the men in platoons or companies. It was a wild, disorganized mob, drunk on blood, a mob whose only thought was to kill. In the darkness they must have slashed and shot and bayoneted many of their own fellows.

They surged through the pass and into Sarana Valley. They overran a first-aid station and bayoneted wounded men on their litters. A chaplain was killed in his tent.

Lieutenant Colonel James Fish, in charge of the advance command post, near which was grouped a battery of the 37-mm. dual-purpose guns that had proved so efficacious against enemy machine guns and mortar concentrations, left his tent in the darkness to find out what was going on. He was found next day, shot in the head, his pistol in his hand. His Chinese mess boy, Chong, lay beside him, his face and body mutilated by bayonet and knife thrusts and sabre strokes.

By daylight the Japanese charge was spent. Its last eddies broke against a ridge at the head of Massacre Valley, where the army engineers were encamped. General Landrum, apparently with a premonition of impending disaster, although he explained it as merely taking all precautions, the day before had ordered the engineers to be on the alert and had issued extra rifles and grenades. They turned back the surviving Japanese.

[365

When order was finally restored in Sarana-Chichagof Pass, the full picture unrolled. The Japanese, exhausted by their eighteen days of fighting, their mad frenzy spent, had charged as far as they could. Then some had committed suicide. They had armed their grenades and held them over their hearts. Many of these were found with the chest scooped out, one hand missing.

With the modern refinements of artillery, land-based and afloat, and air support, the Attu campaign was Indian warfare on a pattern as old as man. It was never large-scale action. It was man-to-man fighting, small group against small group, attack and counterattack, flank and outflank, gully to gully and rock to rock. The army on Attu proved, as had the marines on Guadalcanal, that the Japanese soldier is no match for the American. He's a second-rate little man fighting a good big one.

The Japanese made no effort to reinforce or evacuate their men on Attu and sent up only feeble air attacks from Paramushiru during the Attu campaign. The first air attack was on May 21, by twelve two-motored Mitsubishi '01's carrying torpedoes. With Massacre Bay filled with ships, the Japanese fliers came in on the other side and attacked a gunboat and a destroyer in Holtz Bay. They dropped five torpedoes, none of which hit. One of the raiders was shot down.

On May 23 they tried it again, with sixteen '01's this time. Forewarned by a scouting PBY, the army air force sent up five P-38's, the twin-motored Lightning interceptors, from Amchitka. They met the Japanese west of the island and shot down five, with a loss of two fighter planes, the pilot of one of which was rescued, swimming. The Japanese jettisoned their bombs and fled.

It was just as well for the Japanese that they did not attempt a surface reinforcement or supply of their Attu garrison. In the hope that they would react as they had on Guadalcanal, our admiralty gathered the largest task force assembled since Pearl Harbor to meet any Japanese sea thrust. Perhaps some of the

Japanese submarines that even then must have been evacuating the Japanese garrison on Kiska sighted this big force through a hole in the fog, for the Japanese fleet never arrived.

General Butler's Eleventh Army Air Force, operating from bases two hundred miles to six hundred miles away, did its part in the cleanup of Attu. Whenever the weather was clear enough for them to distinguish the enemy troops from their own—a mistake was made one day and a small party of Americans was strafed and bombed, but without casualties—the P-38's and the B-25's and B-24's were over the island, bombing, strafing, and spotting for the guns. Their only opposition was antiaircraft. After the first few days there was little of that. The Japanese saved their ammunition to use against our ground troops.

Even before the fighting was over the army engineers and the navy SeaBees were ashore, building roads, setting up quonsets, erecting docks, building an airfield. The strip in Holtz Bay, on which the Japanese had done some work, was poorly situated and was not made use of, even as a starting point. On June 9 the airstrip was usable, and the first transport plane landed there. Early in July it was large enough for the B-24's to use, although they had to wait a few days, after landing, while an additional three hundred feet were added to make the takeoff safe for the Paramushiru raid, on which a maximum load of gasoline and bombs was carried.

In two months' time our engineers and construction men had done ten-fold as much work as the Japanese had been able to do in almost a year. If engineering could have won the war, it would have been over in short time.

The Attu campaign, which would have been miserable enough for the men engaged even under the best of conditions, was made worse by inadequate clothing and a failure to properly evaluate the difficulties of movement over the tundra.

The Attu force, composed of men who had not been acclimated to that sort of weather—it would have seemed to be much the better part of wisdom to have used the army forces already based in the Aleutians and Alaska for the expedition—was equipped with so-called mountain jackets, which furnished no protection for the neck and did not have an attached hood to shed the water, and with leather mountain boots. Anyone who had been in the Aleutians should have been able to foresee the inadequacy of that outfit. Apparently the command would not listen. Each quartermaster has his own idea, and it is a common American trait to learn only by experience.

After a few hours ashore the leather boots were soaked through, and they never dried out. In forty-eight hours the rear areas were covered with men nursing blue, swollen feet, as incapacitated for war as if they had been hit by an enemy bullet. Companies that had not lost a man through enemy action were down to half strength in four days because of trench foot.

The tundra defied even the hardy jeep, which had not met its nemesis in any other sort of going. Tractors and half-tracks bogged down within fifty yards of the sandy beach. Practically every round of ammunition, every pound of rations, had to be carried man-back from the beaches to the men on the fighting lines.

Attu was a bitter lesson, but it apparently was well learned. The men who went to Kiska were well clothed and wore rubber shoe pacs that protected their feet from wet. There was not a single case of trench foot in the first few days on Kiska, where the same weather and terrain conditions were present as were on Attu.

Americans learn, it seems; but learn the hard way.

CHAPTER 5

Kiska Patrol

ALEUTIAN WATERS are a sailor's nightmare. Violent storms sweep the area in the winter. Fog shrouds it in the summer. The islands themselves are poorly charted, often missing by a mile or more the position marked by the Hydrographic Office. The harbors and coastal waters are full of uncharted pinnacles.

Even in peacetime the Aleutians are no picnic for a navigator. Few large ships ever even approached their shores. In wartime, with the ships often operating at high speed, it was enough to give a bald-headed pilot gray hairs.

Especially was it rugged work in the Aleutians for the destroyers, the navy's tin cans. There never are enough of them for the jobs they have to do. They are the antisubmarine screen when the fleet goes to sea. They escort the tankers and the supply ships and the transports. When a shore bombardment is made the little cans go in the closest, in range of the enemy's defense batteries, to throw their bullets.

Toughest of the jobs they had to do in the Aleutians was the Kiska patrol. For many months they operated off that fog-shrouded, bleak island day and night, in fair weather and foul. If there had been enough of them the Japanese might never have been able to evacuate the Kiska garrison by submarine. As it was, the Kiska patrol, in a period of a month, sank or heavily damaged three submarines. The PC487, a one hundred and seventy-foot, four hundred-ton patrol ship, got another.

Typical of the vessels of the Kiska Patrol was a destroyer of the Farragut class, one thousand, three hundred and seventy-five tons displacement, two hundred and twenty-five men. She was named, as are all destroyers, for a naval hero. Typical of the patrol were the two trips I made with her during the month of July, 1943.

I boarded her one rainy, chilly evening in Kulik Bay, Adak, from the mailboat. At the top of the amidships steel ladder that serves as a gangway for the cans, I was greeted by Lieutenant Commander Ray Malpass, Annapolis '30, her skipper. He apologized for not having a bigger reception party. The rest of the officers were down in the crew's tiny mess hall seeing a movie.

"You're a popular man on this ship," Ray said as he led me up to his room and rang for a cup of coffee. "The father of one of my officers sent us your story from the *Sunday Times Magazine* on destroyers. It was the first time we'd even seen the destroyers mentioned in this war. We were glad to know someone appreciated us. We've had it up on the bulletin board for a week, but one of the boys thought it would look a little too much like a plant if we left it there, so when we heard you were coming aboard, we took it down."

We drank our coffee and batted the breeze, talked for a few minutes, until we heard the movie party breaking up. Then I went down to the wardroom to meet the other officers. It didn't take long. There were only fifteen. The other Annapolis men were Lieutenant Stan M. Zimmy, class of '37 and Lieutenant E. D. Lamiman, class of '40, the gun boss. The rest were reserves, most of them having come into the navy only since the start of the war. There were Lieutenant B. H. Brittin, the first lieutenant; Lieutenant (jg) C. W. Schwartz, communications officer; Lieutenant (jg) E. S. Jackson, as assistant gunnery officer; Ensign E. R. Rendahl, the chief engineer; and Ensigns H. G. Towes, Jr., S. B. Rolfe, E. T. Fulham, C. P. Ketzel, J. J. Waters, W. O. Apthorp, J. N. Wessels, T. W. Hoffrichter, the supply officer, and Doctor Dasler.

"They're swell kids," said the captain. "Some of them don't know much, but they're learning."

I had been told at COMNORPAC, Admiral Kinkaid's headquarters, that the cans did a week's patrol, then were in port for three or four days, then out on patrol again.

"Who's kidding who?" said the skipper. "We got in last night at midnight, and we're out again the first thing in the morning. And this is the longest stay we've had in for a month."

I had known none of the men on the destroyer before, but being back on a can was like getting back home to a small cottage after a week in town at a big hotel. The skipper put me in what would have been the division commander's cabin. We shared a head (the bathroom).

We were underway in midmorning, leading a big freighter out through the mine field.

"A little convoy job on the way out to our station," the captain said. "We'll drop her off at Amchitka during the night.

"We claim a piece of that place," he said. "While they were building the airfield there we patrolled off shore to give them an antiaircraft cover. Once in a while the Japanese would concentrate on us instead of the field. They were flying from Kiska in float Zeros and float Aichis." The Aichi is the carrier dive bomber.

As the ship cleared the harbor and turned for the run between Adak and Great Sitkin, the fog, that had been light and broken inside, settled down over us, almost blotting out the loaded freighter wallowing along astern.

"It's always like this," Captain Malpass remarked. "It can be clear as hell inside, but once you turn the corner out here you're in thick fog."

All afternoon and through the night we plowed along through the fog, patrolling in front of the slow freighter to be sure no submarine slipped by us to ram its tin fish home. During the night the destroyer took the freighter into Constantine Harbor and then boiled along at twenty knots on up to Kiska to relieve the division leader.

The fog was so thick at 8 o'clock that the two ships had to maneuver within a few hundred yards of each other to exchange signals. Then the division leader turned for home, and the responsibility of trying to keep the submarines out of Kiska Harbor was ours.

Looking at the map of the Aleutians, with Kiska only a dot near the end of the chain, it would appear like a fairly simple job to set up a blockade that even the submarines couldn't run. If there had been enough destroyers to put one every ten miles around the island it might have been possible. With only two on station at a time, one to the north and one to the south of the island, with more than sixty miles of coastline to patrol, it couldn't be done. The range of the submarine-detection devices is limited. The destroyers had to keep on the move. It would have been, and apparently was, a simple matter for the submarines to lie off the island and run into the harbor through the unprotected areas that could not be covered.

The destroyer did the best she could. Except when other ships were in the area, as on July 6, when a task force of three heavy cruisers, one light cruiser, and several destroyers went in to bombard, she sailed varying patterns off the southeastern shoreline of the island. When the fog was heavy she often went in within a few hundred yards of the shore, feeling her way along the rugged coastline. When the fog lifted and our bombing planes were over the island, she stayed hull down over the horizon. At night she again would sweep the coastline.

As we cruised in and out and around about Kiska we often speculated on what the Japanese there must be thinking, or feeling. When we headed in for the island at night we wondered if alarms were not sounded. They would have been on any American base, we knew. We hoped we were disturbing their sleep, if nothing else.

"I'd certainly admire to throw a few shells in there," said "Guns" Lamiman, the tall youthful gun boss from Detroit, as we watched the cloud shadows pass across the green-brown face of the Japanese-held island. Because it was clear (a rarity), we were some miles to the south, and through the strongest binoculars nothing could be seen of the Japanese installations around Gertrude Cove. Little Kiska Island and South Head were between us and the main camp around the harbor.

It was monotonous work, enlivened only by an occasional echo on the detection gear from the big floating islands of brown kelp. They sent back a "ping" that sounded convincingly like a submarine. Then indicators would buzz in the engine room, calling for more speed, and we would heel over in a sharp turn and rush off in the fog to investigate.

The principal amusement was in watching the fat brown ducks with red bills and feet, and white topknots, as they scurried to get out of the path of the ship. As the sharp prow of the destroyer neared their resting place on the water they would scurry out of the way, wings and feet beating the water to a white froth. The sailors called them Aleutian pigeons.

No one on the ship had ever seen them get off the water. They would skim its surface, up the side of a wave and down through the trough, to subside finally a half mile or so from the ship's track. We occasionally saw a pair of them flying along, speeding brown silhouettes against the gray sky. We decided they must have floated in to the beach and taken off from there.

July 4 was a big day. The cook baked a birthday cake, and we had cake and soft drinks for dessert. It wasn't a bad combination.

Gray day succeeded gray day, with no action. When word came that the cruisers were going to bombard on July 6, all hands had hopefully waited orders for us to join up, but they had sailed majestically on past with only an affirmative to the skipper's message to the admiral asking permission to proceed on duty assigned, a routine at sea when naval forces or ships meet. The junior must ask the senior for permission to carry out his previous orders.

The fog prevented us even from seeing the bombardment. The thunder of the guns came only faintly, muffled by fog and distance.

When the orders came from COMNORPAC on July 8 for us

to start the series of night bombardments that continued until the army invasion of August 15, the news ran through the ship like a flame.

Even the weather was auspicious that day. There was only a high overcast in the morning. At noon it cleared away to reveal a sapphire-blue sky, flecked here and there with fleecy white clouds. The sea, which had looked cold and gray and angry under the fog, reflected the blue of the sky. If it had not been for the wind we could have believed ourselves back in the South Pacific.

The target assigned was Gertrude Cove, the secondary camp of the enemy garrison on Kiska. Singled out for particular attention were some antiaircraft batteries that had been plotted by the fliers. The skipper, the gun boss, and the navigator spent the rest of the morning and part of the afternoon plotting the firing run. Since the bombardment was limited by the orders to twenty-five salvos from our four guns, or one hundred shells, it was decided to spread them out over two runs, firing fifteen the first time and then going back an hour or so later to fire the remaining ten.

Dinner that night was the most pleasant since the start of the patrol. Over coffee, as Samuel Pepys, himself an old navy man, would have said, we fell to discussing various things—John L. Lewis, the labor leader; British Colonies in the Pacific; national cooperation after the war. Doubts were expressed as to an immediate solution of any of them. The radio brought the news at 7 P.M. that Kiska had been bombed the previous day "according to a communiqué from the Navy Department." It was news to us. We hadn't seen any planes or heard any bombing. But then, in the fog, we never were quite sure of anything.

The wardroom and the crew's combined messing and living space was deserted early. All hands not on watch turned in to get a little sleep before the bombardment, which was scheduled for some time after midnight. The skipper had decided to let the Japanese garrison get all tucked in before waking them up.

NORTH PACIFIC BATTLE LINE

Big guns of the North Pacific fleet belching death and destruction at Kiska in the Aleutians. This was one of the many sea and air raids that finally drove the Japanese invaders off their finger-tip hold on the main island of the aptly named Rat Group. An American task force attacked Kiska, August 15, 1943, only to find the surviving Japanese garrison had fled by submarine.

IN MASSACRE VALLEY

A scene during the early phases of the Attu invasion when American troops attempted to advance up the valleys against Japanese rifle, machine gun and mortar fire from the fog-shrouded ridges. Later the Army tactics were changed and American troops fought their way along the ridges to extermination of the Japanese garrison of 2,300 men. Even in mid-May snow still lies on the ridges and in the valleys of the bleak Aleutian islands.

Only the red battle lights and one faint white light were burning in the wardroom at midnight, when those of us who had been sleeping turned out for a sandwich and a cup of coffee before going topside. To shield our eyes from even that faint illumination all of us who were going to be outside wore red goggles. When going from a brightly lighted room to the darkness of the upper decks, it requires from ten minutes to half an hour for a person's eyes to adjust themselves. The red goggles cut the adjustment period to a matter of seconds, an important factor in efficient operation of a ship.

At 12:30 A.M. the "beep, beep, beep" of the general quarters alarm sounded through the ship, and all hands started for their stations.

The moon shone faintly through a high overcast that had covered the blue bowl of the sky at sunset. We were edging in toward Kiska at slow speed.

"It's not too good a night for it," the skipper said, as we stood on the wing of the bridge, protected by the aluminum dodger from the cold wind blowing off the island, "but I'm going in anyway. Just when you would welcome a little fog over the damn place, visibility is unlimited. Their lookouts on Vega Point probably have sighted us already."

The phosphorescent wake of the ship trailed behind us, visible for a mile or more. It silhouetted the men on the after guns like a blue floodlight. Incongruously, I was reminded of the hidden lights at the New York World's Fair that were placed to shine up through the trees.

The ubiquitous Aleutian pigeons left small glimmering wakes on the water as they scurried out of the way. Once the ship ran through a school of fish. They thrashed the water to a phosphorescent froth that seemed to run to the horizon, broad as a moon track.

In the darkness of the bridge you could not distinguish officers from enlisted men. All wore the blue woolen windbreaker jacket and trousers, gathered at the ankles, that were called zoot suits,

[375

topped with a blue knitted watch cap or a blue cloth helmet that buttoned under the chin. The helmet has an apron that can be tucked down inside the collar to protect the back of the neck.

Although the ship was approaching an enemy position that was known to be fortified—the Japanese antiaircraft guns were of 3-inch caliber and on dual-purpose mounts, so they could be used either against airplanes or surface craft—there was no evidence of strain on the bridge.

Inside the charthouse Stan Zimmy, the navigator, was plotting the course, occasionally making slight changes that were transmitted through the loud speaker to the bridge.

Stan's cheerful voice, booming out of the grill over the chart table, was in contrast to the low tones in which the rest of us were talking. The Japanese could not have heard us had we been shouting through a carrier's bull horn, but there is something about being in sight of an enemy position at night that automatically mutes the larynx. I had noticed it before on night runs into Guadalcanal past the Japanese-held shore.

"Five hundred yards to go, Captain," Stan finally announced.

"Tell the gunnery officer we are approaching the firing course," the captain told the talker who stood next to him with a telephone line to the fire-control platform above.

In the stillness we could hear "Guns" passing the word to his crews and then up and down the ship, from the four gun mounts, cracked the command, "load." The steel-jacketed bullets banged into the rifle chambers.

The ship was paralleling the coast now, on a northeasterly course that had carried us opposite the mouth of Gertrude Cove. Then over the speaker came the last change of course to put us on the firing run, and the captain quietly told the fire-control talker, "Tell the gunnery officer he can commence firing."

The first salvo always is the hardest on the nerves. No matter how you brace yourself for it, the crack of the first explosion comes like a blow in the belly. The muzzle flash is a streak of flame that hurts the eyeballs.

376]

As the first salvo of four shells whined off through the night toward the enemy shore, there were three blinks of light from the beach and, seconds later, three sharp explosions near us. A few feet astern and fifty feet in the air blossomed three black rosebuds of smoke. The Japanese had fired fused-set, antiaircraft shells at us. It wasn't a bad idea. At ten thousand yards, or five miles at sea, the chance of getting a hit at a shadow moving along at fast speed was problematical. A shell bursting overhead, however, showers its fragments over a wide area. When the battle ensign was taken down the next day there was a ragged hole in it, singed on the edges, through which a piece of hot metal obviously had passed. If any fragments lighted on the deck, however, they went overboard. A thorough search by the crew, looking for souvenirs, failed to bring a single reward.

Our shells meanwhile were pouring in on the enemy positions, range and deflection being changed after each salvo to correct for the changing position of the ship. As the ship moved past Buktari Point, that separates Gertrude Cove from the two small coves called Mutt and Jeff, the Japanese there opened up on us with their automatic weapons. We could see the small-caliber shells falling a thousand yards or so to port.

In a matter of a minute and a half, that had seemed much longer than that, our fifteen salvos had been fired, and we turned sharply away and increased our speed. The Japanese still were firing from the beach, so the captain ordered the engineer to make smoke. Eddies from the sooty clouds pouring out of Number One stack filled the partly enclosed bridge.

The captain ordered the telephone talkers to enquire if there had been any casualties, which on a ship means either to personnel or to guns or machinery. The answer was negative.

"Tell all hands to stand easy for an hour or so," he then ordered.

"Now," he said, "how about a hot cup of coffee?"

After the chill of the open bridge the warmth of the wardroom was welcome. We unzipped our jackets and drank several cups of the steaming coffee passed out from the pantry by the mess boys.

"So far, so good," said the skipper. "This next time I'm going in from the southeast. That will put Buktari Point between us and the Gertrude Cove batteries. They were getting too close for comfort."

At 1:38 A.M. we again turned toward the island. The breeze from the northwest had freshened. It brought with it the sour, fishy odor of a mud flat at low tide.

"This place smells worse all the time," said one of the quartermasters. "If they don't get the Japs off there pretty soon, it won't be fit for a white man."

With only ten salvos to fire on the second run, we were soon over with that and headed out to the patrol area. As the captain had predicted, the Gertrude Cove batteries had been blanketed by the ridge of Buktari Point. They had fired over it at us but none of the bursts was close.

Our parting salvo was a pattern of star shells that, it was hoped, might fall on some Japanese buildings, or just Japanese, and burn someone. As we withdrew we could see them floating down through the fog that clothed the top of the Kiska ridges. The diffused light made a halo over the Japanese camp.

Admiral Kinkaid apparently wanted a detailed report quickly on what we had done and seen, for at daylight we were relieved by the division leader. We headed for Adak at high speed. By midnight we were in Kuluk Bay, had refueled and anchored. It was too late to go ashore, but it was quiet in anchorage. With the ship at rest and the engines silent, all hands turned in for the first solid sleep in days. No matter how you brace yourself in your bunk, in the destroyer sprawl—face downward with elbows hooked over either side of the mattress and your toes over the bottom—there is always enough roll during a turn, even in a quiet sea, to waken you. Even if you do not gain full consciousness, it doesn't make for a refreshing sleep.

The nights in port were especially precious to the captain. At

378]

sea he spent the nights on the bridge, turning in on a narrow bunk with his clothes on. It was a luxury beyond any experienced in civilian life to take a shower, don pajamas, and crawl into a well mattressed bunk.

The vessel had all the next day in port while the captain went ashore to report to headquarters, but we were under way again that evening, this time headed for the northern patrol area.

On that job there wasn't even the satisfaction of a night bombardment to relieve the tedium of several days more in the fog. The destroyer was under orders now not to fire if the visibility was good.

Ray took her in one night through a pea-soup fog to bombard the main camp area around the harbor, but it was clear inside and he turned away when the Japanese began blinking a red light from North Head, apparently in the belief that we were a friendly submarine coming in on the surface. Before they realized their mistake we were headed out at high speed, rapidly putting a lot of water between us and the six-inch guns the Japanese had installed on Little Kiska Island and in the North Head area. With a long base line with which to compute their range and deflection, they should have been able to hit the American can with the first salvo, if they had fired.

For half a month more the little cans nosed around off Kiska in the fog, bombarding when conditions were favorable. Then they covered the landings of the army on August 15 and 16, took the transports safely back home, and called it a day.

It was not their fault the Japanese escaped off Kiska. No vessels ever worked harder at so disagreeable a job.

CHAPTER 6

The Aleutians Are
Decontaminated

WITH ATTU safely in American hands, plans for assaulting Kiska were speeded.

Each day saw an addition to the weapons with which to do the job. The naval task force that had covered the Attu attack was augmented. A squadron of army dive bombers was brought in for use against the Japanese fixed gun positions that horizontal bombing seemed unable to knock out. The fighter squadrons and medium and heavy bomber forces were increased.

Every day that the weather was favorable, which was only twelve days during July, Kiska was bombed from both high and low altitude. Until the arrival of the dive bombers, which the army designates A-26 and which are the navy Douglas scout bomber under a new name, the P-40's did that job. Air losses from enemy action during this period were one B-25, the crew of which was saved, and one P-40 and the pilot.

The navy bombarded Kiska from the sea eight times during July, once with a task force of cruisers, once with both battle-ships and cruisers. The six other bombardments were night actions by destroyers. On July 26 the Navy PBY's began night nuisance bombings, dropping a few clunks at hour intervals. The first bombing found the Japanese with many lights burning. After that they blacked out.

On Adak, which was used as the staging island for the attack, the assault force of more than twenty thousand troops, including a reinforced brigade of five thousand Canadians, was in intensive training. In the American force was the 17th regiment, that had fought so gallantly on Attu, and a special service force of American and Canadian commandos that was probably the most completely trained unit in the United States or Canadian armies. The commandos were to be used to seize high ground above the American beachheads to avoid a recurrence of the Attu fiasco in Massacre Valley.

On August 12 the task force began to move. That morning in Adak Harbor, one hundred and sixty-nine vessels were counted. The seagoing equipment included every advanced type of am-

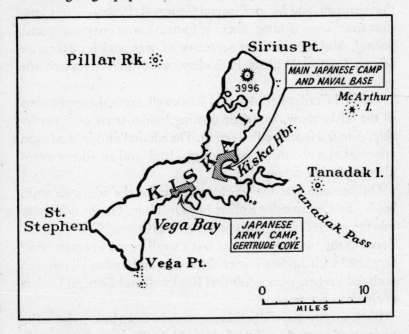

phibious assault craft from the big LST's and LCI's that could carry two hundred or more men, to Higgins boats, tank lighters and amphibious jeeps. Ten army transport planes were waiting on Amchitka to carry paratroopers over the island to seize vital high points.

The expeditionary force was the most completely equipped the United Nations ever gathered and sent on an assault mission.

Every man was briefed on the operation, that is, had it ex-

[381

plained to him in detail. He had been told not only what he and his organization had to do but also what was the task of every supporting group.

In Adak, sitting as the board of strategy for the operation, were, in addition to Admiral Kinkaid, General Buckner and General Butler, of the air force, Lieutenant General John L. De-Witt, commanding officer of the Western Defense Command at San Francisco, under whose jurisdiction were both Alaska and the Aleutians; and Major General George R. Perkes of the Canadian army, commanding officer of Canada's west coast command. John J. McCloy, assistant secretary of war, and his executive officer, Colonel William P. Scobey, were there to watch the operation.

General Corlett and Admiral Rockwell, tactical commanders of the Kiska show, had their floating headquarters on a battleship, Admiral Rockwell's flagship. The admiral's bridge had been arranged as a command post for sea, land, and air forces, complete to the last detail.

On one side was the working space for the admiral's staff, headed by Commander Robert Lee Dennison. On the other side was the general's staff, chief of which was Colonel Carl T. Jones. Between the two larger spaces was a small center compartment, furnished with modernistic chairs, stools, and a setee, all covered with red leather, where Admiral Rockwell and General Corlett could sit to discuss plans.

Big maps covered the bulkheads to show from hour to hour the position of every ship of the force, and the progress of the troops ashore. The chief of intelligence for Admiral Rockwell had a large-scale topographical map of Kiska on which he and his two assistants plotted plane and ship bombardments, and the progress of the landings and advances ashore.

Colonel William O. Eareckson, of the army air force, who was in charge of all tactical air groups for the Kiska operation, had a room of his own from where he was in communication by short-wave radio with the Aleutian air bases and with all planes in the air.

Major General Holland McT. Smith of the marines, was aboard as an adviser. Members of his staff, including his chief of staff, Colonel G. B. Erskine, and Colonel R. E. Knapp, a supply expert, were with the army troops that made the landing. They made frequent reports to Admiral Rockwell and General Corlett.

Short-wave radio connected the floating command post with ships in the vicinity and with the shore parties. During the first two days General Corlett several times talked directly from the ship to his various sector commanders ashore.

Months of preparation preceded the sailing of the big armada from Adak, including a full-scale dress rehearsal on Great Sitkin Island a week before the departure. An amphibious operation poses the most difficult tactical problems of war.

General Corlett had formed his staff in May and had begun preparation of the operations order, a bulky volume of several hundred mimeographed pages. Before writing the order he and his staff had to study the terrain of Kiska, select the best landing beaches, plot artillery positions to guarantee the ultimate support of the infantry, attempt to foresee, on the basis of experience elsewhere, what the enemy would do, and map the basic plans to circumvent any one of several possibilities.

To illustrate: Few of the hills and only two or three of the coves of Kiska had ever been named. The Aleuts may have had names for all of them, but they did not show on available maps. These all had to be marked. Some of them were given quite imaginative names.

Except for the weather, the operation went off as planned. The first landing was made on the west coast, near the southern end of the island. At 6:30 the transports maneuvered off shore and sent in the first wave. At 7 A.M. a battleship, cruisers, and destroyers started bombarding Kiska Harbor and Gertrude Cove from the south.

On the flagship the force commanders and their staffs anxiously awaited word from the advance troops and from the beaches.

"No opposition," was the refrain. "No opposition." "No opposition."

At 9 A.M. the beachhead party reported they were on all the commanding heights above the Cove and had yet to see the enemy. It was too good to be true. It was expected that the Japanese would be taken by surprise, with a landing at the most unlikely spot along the rugged, rockbound coast, but not that much of a surprise.

"Damn it, I want to hear of some guns popping," fumed General Smith. "When you meet resistance, that is when you first get definite information."

Reports came in of abandoned Japanese trenches and gun positions on the hills that rise abruptly from the west coast of the island and then fall gradually away to the east and south toward Kiska Harbor and Gertrude Cove. One discounted report said hot coffee had been found in one of the abandoned trenches. An ammunition dump with some ten tons of small-arms ammunition was found. A crude booby trap was discovered and disposed of.

General Corlett and his staff puzzled over the situation, trying to estimate where the Japanese commander might reasonably be expected to make his stand. It was surmised that he might have withdrawn to the high ground east of Kiska Harbor. If so, the next day's landing in the northern sector would be bitterly contested.

Fog hung heavy over Kiska, as it had over Attu on May 11. Aerial reconnaissance was impossible. Amchitka was socked in and the fighters based there could not get off. Colonel Eareckson, the air boss, was a man with a job but no tools.

The late sunset found American troops on all the high ground, but still no Japanese.

The landing in the southern sector was repeated in the northern sector the next day.

By evening of the second day it was obvious there were no

Japanese on the island. Canadian patrols had penetrated to the main camp area and found it deserted.

An irreverent somebody began humming Gracie Fields' favorite song, "It's the Biggest Aspidistra in the World."

The flight of the Japanese was no great surprise to the fliers. They had been receiving increasingly light antiaircraft fire since the first of August. At about the same time, the Japanese radio went off the air. The night before the Kiska force shoved off from Adak several bomber pilots who had been over the enemy-held island in previous days were betting two to one no Japanese would be found. Our B-25's with the 75-millimeter cannon had gone in at low level to try out their new weapons, and had seen no sign of life anywhere in the main camp area.

Map readers began to notice signs of Japanese abandonment of the main camp in July. Lumber from bomb-wrecked buildings disappeared overnight. One day there were several partially wrecked barges along the beaches in Kiska Harbor. The next time the photographers flew over and took some pictures, the barges were gone.

Just what went on in the conference among the American high command the last few days before the Kiska expedition no one was saying. Why a shore reconnaissance was not ordered was not divulged. It was said to have been urged by some of the conferees, but overruled by others, who insisted that surprise would be a more important factor than exact information as to enemy dispositions.

"We're still a bunch of damned amateurs," said one high-ranking officer disgustedly.

The most widely held theory to explain abandonment of the main camp areas and the disappearance of the lumber and barges was that the Japanese had withdrawn into the hills, where they had used the lumber and the metal from the barges to build camouflaged gun positions.

How long the Japanese evacuation had been under way no one on the American side could determine, even after the whole island

[385

was invested. Some of the Japanese quarters gave evidence that some enemy troops may have been on the island as late as three or four days before the American occupation. Meat was found in garbage cans that could not have been there longer than a week. It showed few signs of spoilage, despite a temperature that never was freezing or below. The musty, unwashed human smell that is typical of Japanese encampments still hung heavy on the air.

Certainly there were many of the enemy still there on July 22 when the navy fired its heaviest bombardment, probably the heaviest ever concentrated on so small a target. Antiaircraft fire was heavy that day, both from the enemy three-inch batteries and from automatic weapons. It was that day the B-25 was shot down. It made a crash landing in the sea to the south of the island. Its crew was picked up by a destroyer.

The Japanese made only a feeble attempt to interfere with the occupation. A submarine fired torpedoes at a destroyer just outside Kiska Harbor, but missed it.

The evacuation of the Kiska garrison by the Japanese navy was a major feat. It apparently was done entirely by submarine. The Japanese took little of their equipment with them. The breech-blocks had been removed from the antiaircraft and coastal defense guns, and some machine guns had been taken from their mounts. Many guns, however, had been left intact, as well as several tons of small-arms ammunition. Apparently the ammunition for the antiaircraft batteries had largely been expended. Only the crudest of booby traps had been set. No mines were found in Kiska Harbor.

Considering the concentrated bombing the enemy camp areas had received, there was a surprising number of installations found intact, or which obviously had been untouched by the bombing but destroyed by the Japanese themselves. The three small two-man submarines in the crude pen at the west end of the harbor had been wrecked by internal explosions. There were bomb craters all around the position but no evidence of hits on the submarines, nor even in the sunken runway where they rested on small cars that had been used to haul them up out of the sea. Yet the sub pen was one of the primary targets of each bombing attack.

The hangar, where the float planes that were used to make the bombing attacks on Adak and Amchitka had been stored, still was usable, only one end of it having been hit. Only a few feet away was an officers' camouflaged hut that had only one small hole in the roof. A building near the beach which apparently had housed the Japanese communications office also was untouched. The Japanese had destroyed the food supplies, splitting the rice bags and puncturing big tins of bread and fish. Oil drums had been similarly rendered unusable.

Naval bombardment appeared to have been more effective than the bombing. The shells, especially the 14-inchers, had blasted great trenchlike holes on North Head around the Japanese gun positions and in the main camp and in Gertrude Cove, covering a greater area than the bomb craters.

The spongy tundra contributed to the relative ineffectiveness of the bombing. It absorbs explosions like a sponge. A direct hit is necessary in such terrain to knock out a gun or do any great damage to a hangar or barracks.

The Japanese camp was in great contrast to the plush-lined American bases along the Aleutian chains. Most of the Japanese had lived like animals in holes in the ground and with the most rudimentary sanitary facilities. The toilet facilities in the officers' quarters near the seaplane hangar consisted of a small cubicle off the entrance with two holes cut in the floor. It adjoined their eating room. An American soldier or marine wouldn't have washed a dog in some of the huts where the Japanese troops had lived for over a year.

The hospital at the main camp was a damp rabbit warren dug back into the hillside. The ceiling had been boarded, but the walls had not. The patients had lain on mats on the earthen floor. In the hospital was found the inevitable supply of male contraceptives, the uses for which were problematical since there were no women on Kiska unless the Japanese brought some along with them.

Before departing, the Japanese had written crude jibes on the walls of their undamaged quarters. There were some recognizable caricatures of President Roosevelt and Prime Minister Churchill. Most of the insults were written in English.

"We will be back and kill out separately Yanki-joker," said one.

"You are dancing by foolische (im Deutsche) order of Rousebelt," said another.

The Japanese had used camouflage extensively. Several gun positions were found to be armed only with logs cut to simulate gun barrels. Their crews were straw-filled dummies. What was thought to have been a military road through the hills was found to be no road at all. The Japanese had merely scraped away tundra and lined the scar with rocks.

Little heavy machinery was found on the island. As on Attu, nearly all the work of construction had been done by hand, including the airfield, which was only half done. Army and navy construction men, working with good American equipment, made Kiska a better military base in a matter of days than had the Japanese in fourteen months of occupancy.

The almost bloodless occupation of Kiska was of course a terrific anticlimax to the Aleutian campaign.

For one thing the departure of the Japanese robbed the Quebec Conference, then in session, of President Roosevelt, Prime Minister Churchill and Prime Minister Mackenzie King of Canada of any important announcement. There was a suspicion in the Aleutians, that would seem to have some basis in fact, that announcement of the appointment of Lord Louis Mountbatten as supreme commander in the Burma theater may not have been intended to be made at Quebec. It was dragged out of the hopper when the expected announcement of a successful assault on Kiska failed.

The holding of a conference in Quebec and at that time would seem to have a close political relationship to the attack on Kiska. The Canadian brigade that was used in the Kiska force was composed of Canadians who had been conscripted for home defense only. In Canada as in Australia, there is no conscription for overseas service. Had the Kiska landing of the Canadians been accompanied by considerable loss of life, Mr. King might have had a difficult political situation on his hands. The airplanes had altered the concept of where a frontier begins (President Roosevelt was quoted several years before our entry into the war as saying the United States frontier was on the German Rhine); but would the Canadian voters have accepted the interpretation that their western defense line lay in the Aleutians if it had been accompanied by a heavy casualty list—especially the French Canadians, who were represented in the brigade by a full battalion?

One big mark on the credit side of the ledger for the Kiska show was the training of the troops engaged. No dress rehearsal ever can take the place of a first night. The men who clambered down the cargo nets and scrambled ashore on Kiska through icy waters thought they were charging an enemy-held island. The first time always is the hardest on the nerves. The next time those men attack they should go in with much more confidence than most of them probably felt as their landing boats approached the fog-shrouded Kiska beaches.

From a mechanical standpoint the Kiska performance was first rate. The arrows on the big charts in the flagship's headquarters room moved right on schedule. If a certain element was scheduled to be on a certain hill at a certain time, it generally was there.

So ended the Aleutian campaign. It had taken fourteen months to decontaminate the islands, but at last they were free of Japanese. The right flank of the seven-thousand-mile-long Pacific battle line at last was secure.

CHAPTER 7

Aleutian Postscript

A SAILOR GOES where he is sent and does what he is told. He isn't required, however, necessarily to like what he does.

Of all the boresome, disagreeable jobs of the Pacific war, the naval operations off the Aleutians probably caused more griping per sea mile than the time spent in any other area.

What most of the sailors probably thought about the Aleutian campaign was expressed in a little rhyme printed in a paper put out once a week by the chaplain of a heavy cruiser which spent several months in that area. The doggerel was signed only "Captain of the Head." It was titled "The Strategic Aleutians," and ran:

> From Nunivak to Attu, we sail the Bering Sea,
> First up and down, then round and round
>   and round again sail we.
> We sail to the eastward, then to the west,
>   with never a friendly lee.
> And what do we see in Bering Sea?
>   We see the Bering Sea.
> The Bering Sea is strategical,
>   The geographers shout with glee.
> As they sketch new maps to sell to saps,
>   like you and you and me;
> It's the future crossroads of the air,
>   the road to prosperity;
> Well if that be true, I say to you
>   God help humanity.
> For of all the fouled-up oceans that ever I did see,
> The worst by far, without a par, is the
>   fouled-up Bering Sea.
> So fie on Luce and Life and Time,
>   Clare Boothe and Homer Lea,
> The sooner we get the hell out of here
>   the sooner it's jake with me.

If we hate the Japs, the so-and-so saps,
    and I think we all agree,
We could do worse than bequeath them the curse
    of this bloody fog-bound sea.
So, Ho for the Sunny Southland,
    far from the bitter tea
Of wind and rain and sinus pain,
    that's brewed in the Bering Sea.

PART VI

THE HARD ROAD AHEAD

The Hard Road Ahead

THE FIRST two years of the war in the Pacific proved two things. First, that the Japanese is a second rate fighting man. Second, that it would nevertheless take a lot of men and ships and planes and time to lick him.

On December 7, 1943, the second anniversary of his sneak attack on Pearl Harbor, he still held all but a few of the islands and all but a few of the square miles of empire he had seized during the first six months of his war against the United States, the British Empire, China, and the Netherlands.

Only in merchant tonnage and combatant ships had the Japanese suffered any crippling losses. His great industrial cities, like those of the United States, were free of any immediate danger of air attack. Only once had hostile planes flown over Tokyo. Then it was a small raid by only sixteen medium bombers launched from a carrier and carrying small loads.

All the wealth of the East Indies—oil, rubber, metals, hemp, quinine—was in his hands. How well he had been able to exploit those riches was not known. He had shown great organizing ability in other ways.

To defend his island and continental empire he had all the advantages of distance, undeveloped terrain, heavily fortified bases, and opponents whose main effort was directed against another and more powerful enemy. He had an army of perhaps a million and a half men, and a fleet that probably still was capable of meeting on even terms any task forces the Allies could send against him in any one area.

On only one flank was he vulnerable—to the north; and he faced no immediate danger of attack there. Russia's resources were too heavily engaged in the west to permit opening a second front, even were she so inclined.

To the east and south were thousands of fortified islands, garrisoned with well trained troops who were billeted in dugouts impervious to all but a direct hit from the heaviest-caliber shell or bomb. The only way to attack them was from the sea, an amphibious undertaking, the most difficult of all military operations. In two years he had been driven from only a few of these bases in the area farthest from his capital.

On the continent the Japanese had to deal immediately only with a China bled white by six years of war, without a seacoast, cut off except by air from the planes and guns she would need to deal effectively with him. The United States had been able to send in and maintain in China only a token air force.

All the advantages of weather and terrain were in his favor on the continent. The torrential rains in Burma made military operations almost impossible six months of the year. Swamps, jungle, and the greatest mountain range in the world were other natural allies.

Behind these natural and man-made barriers, the Japanese leaders probably were content to fight a strictly defensive war. The Japanese had his empire. Let the enemy come to him and try to take it away.

In the strategic planning, the Allied leaders had four possibilities to consider:

First, and most improbable, was a frontal assault on the Japanese home islands. For that the greatest amphibious force in history would have to be organized. Every ship and plane and man that the Allied nations could spare would be needed to mount such an assault. All other areas would have to be weakened to provide the men and materials for such an expedition.

It would sail from the Pacific Coast, the Aleutians and the Hawaiian Islands through the North Pacific. For the last thousand miles it would have to move without air support from land-based planes. On the way the Japanese home fleet would have to be met and defeated.

A second route of conquest would be from Australia, New Guinea, and the Solomons, with the Philippines as the first objective. This operation would be vulnerable to attack from strong enemy bases on either flank. The Caroline Island base of Truk lies to the northeast of such a route. Japanese bases in the Netherlands East Indies lie to the southwest.

An attack on the Philippines probably would be welcomed and aided by the Filipinos. Once ashore the expeditionary force would be at least partially self-sufficient, so far as food is concerned. All other weapons of war, however, would be needed in a continuing flow. They would have to be supplied by sea and air along a route against which the Japanese should be able to throw superior sea-and-air forces.

Such an expedition probably also would involve a full-scale battle with the main Japanese fleet.

Establishment of strong naval-and-air bases in the Philippines would effectively sever the Japanese lifeline to the south, making desperate the position of Japanese troops in all the islands, in Burma, and in southern China; but it still would leave the United Nations more than fifteen hundred miles from Japan proper. That is beyond the range of any bomber planes we had in operation during the first two years of the war, although reportedly within reach of the new super bombers that were in production.

The third possibility was a campaign through Burma, and a construction job, to reopen a supply route to China. Once this was completed, the manpower for a great offensive was waiting. It needed only to be armed.

Lord Louis Mountbatten, one of Britain's top military men, was placed in charge of the operation in the late summer of 1943, which might be an indication of the importance the high command placed on that theater.

Much preliminary construction work, of airfields and roads,

had been done by United States army engineers in preparation for such a campaign.

The weather and the terrain appeared to be more of an obstacle than the Japanese to an advance through Burma.

The fourth route of attack was west and south from the Hawaiian Islands through the mandated island groups of the Marshalls, Carolines, and Marianas to the China Coast and to within bombing range of the Japanese home islands.

That too was an amphibious venture, with a constantly lengthening supply line, but as the power of the fleet expanded it became a feasibility instead of just a dream.

Japan will not be finally defeated until her home fleet is smoked out and brought to battle, and the island route appeared to be the quickest means to that end. In the Solomons, in New Guinea and the Bismarck Archipelago, in the Marshalls and Gilberts, and even in the Philippines, Japan's best hope of extending the war to a point of weariness was to pull back her fleet when she lost air control and depend on her air arm and last-man island defense to hold back the Allied tide. That was her strategy in the Solomons campaign. When our forces finally threaten to seize bases within bombing range of Tokyo, however, then the fleet must come out and fight.

The overwhelming industrial might of the United States and the expansion of the Pacific fleet during the first two years of the war made it possible for the United States to lose battles and still win the war. Japan cannot take such risks. When the Japanese home fleet steams out to battle, the war will be in its last stage, and will remain there despite the outcome of that one great engagement, which will be the greatest sea fight of all time.

There were many cheering indications at the close of the first two years of war that the United Nations were on the march. Despite its position as a secondary front, the Pacific theater was securing merely as an overflow great quantities of war materials from America's industrial machine. Whereas in the first two years no more than one offensive could be launched at a time, allowing the enemy to concentrate against that one, late in 1943 the Pacific forces showed themselves capable of hitting at many different places at the same time. Attacks on Bougainville, the Gilberts, and New Britain were made within a few days of each other.

Although the successful conclusion of the war against Japan probably must await a victory in Europe, it appeared possible that such heavy pressure could be applied in the meantime that when Hitler finally was forced to capitulate, Tojo would not be far behind.

It was a long hard road that stretched ahead, along which much blood and sweat would have to be shed. But the outcome was certain. It was only a question of how long.

The Pacific War

December 7, 1941–December 7, 1943

1941

Dec. 7–8. The Japanese strike without warning at Pearl Harbor, Wake, Guam, the Philippines, Hong Kong.

8. United States, Great Britain, and the Netherlands declare war on Japan.

9. The Japanese attack Malaya. Nauru and Ocean islands bombed.

10. Battleship Prince of Wales and battle cruiser Repulse sunk by Japanese planes off Malaya. Tarawa, Gilbert Islands, raided.

16. Japanese land in British North Borneo.

17. Australian and Dutch forces occupy Portuguese Timor. Portugal protests.

24. Wake falls.

25. Hong Kong capitulates.

26. Manila declared an "open" city. Japanese continue to bomb it.

1942

Jan. 1. Air Marshal Sir Robert Brooke-Popham removed as Malayan commander; succeeded by General Sir Henry Pownall.

4. Marshal Sir Archibald Wavell named commander of all Allied forces in the Southwest Pacific.

5. MacArthur withdraws to the Bataan Peninsula.

11. Japanese land in Celebes, N.E.I.

14. Four U.S. destroyers attack in Macassar Straits; sink nine ships.

18. Japanese raid Sumatra.

21. Lae and Salamaua, New Guinea, abandoned after Japanese air raid.

22. Japanese occupy Rabaul, New Britain, New Ireland, Buka, and Bougainville. Tulagi bombed.

31. British in Malaya retire to Singapore. Japanese seize Amboina, N.E.I.

Feb. 1. Vice Admiral Halsey's force of U.S. carriers and cruisers and destroyers raids the Gilbert and Marshall Islands, sink seventeen ships, destroy forty to fifty planes and bombard two bases.

3. Sourabaya and Port Moresby heavily raided by Japanese.
6. Japanese occupy Samarinda oilfields, Burma.
8. Japanese heavily bomb Rangoon.
15. Singapore surrenders.
19. Combined U.S.-Dutch naval force raids Japanese convoy in Badang Straits, sinking several vessels.
20. Japanese land on Bali, N.E.I.
24. Japanese submarine shells Santa Barbara, Calif.
    Admiral Halsey raids Wake Island.
27. Battle of the Java Sea. Dutch cruisers DeRuyter and Java sunk; also British destroyers Jupiter and Electra. Japanese lose one cruiser, others damaged. U.S.S. Langley sunk by planes.
28. U.S.S. Houston, H.M.S. Perth, H.M.S. Exeter, H.M.S. Encounter, U.S.S. Pope disappear en route from Java to Australia; believed sunk. Japanese losses in engagements unknown. U.S.S. Pecos, carrying Langley survivors, sunk by Japanese planes.

March 1. Japanese land in Java at three points.
4. Admiral Halsey raids Marcus Island, nine hundred and ninety miles from Tokyo.
7. Japanese occupy Rangoon.
8. Japanese occupy Lae and Salamaua.
10. Planes from the United States carriers Yorktown and Lexington attack Japanese shipping at Lae and Salamaua; more than twenty enemy ships sunk or damaged.
17. Washington announces the arrival of United States troops in Australia.
19. General MacArthur named supreme Allied commander in Southwest Pacific.
26. Japanese occupy the Andaman Islands, Bay of Bengal.

April 5. Japanese carrier planes raid Colombo, Ceylon.
8. Japanese occupy Faisi, the Solomon Islands.
9. Bataan surrenders.
11. British aircraft carrier Hermes and two heavy cruisers sunk in Indian Ocean by Japanese planes.
18. Sixteen two-motored Mitchell bombers take off from carrier Hornet and raid Tokyo and adjacent cities.
26. Washington announces that an American Expeditionary Force has landed at New Caledonia.
30. Japanese capture Lashio, Burma.

May 1-2. Japanese occupy Tulagi and Guadalcanal, the Solomons.
4. Planes from carrier Yorktown destroy Japanese occupation force ships at Tulagi and Guadalcanal.

6. Corregidor surrenders.

7–8. U.S.-Japanese carrier battle in Coral Sea. Two Japanese carriers sunk, another damaged, several cruisers, destroyers, and a battleship hit; carrier Lexington, destroyer Sims, and tanker Neosho sunk or heavily damaged by Japanese planes.

13. British announce evacuation of Burma.

June   3. Japanese carrier planes attack Dutch Harbor, the Aleutians; U.S. army and navy planes attack Japanese transports west of Midway and probably sink three.

4–7. Battle of Midway. Japanese lose four carriers, two cruisers, three or four destroyers, three or four transports; other vessels heavily damaged. U.S. carrier Yorktown and U.S. destroyer Hammann sunk by submarine after former damaged by enemy planes.

7. Japanese submarines shell Newcastle and Sydney, Australia. Japanese occupy Kiska and Attu, the Aleutians.

July   22. Japanese land at Buna and Gona, New Guinea, and start drive through Owen Stanley range on Port Moresby.

Aug.   7. United States Marines attack and seize Tulagi, establish beachhead on Guadalcanal, the Solomons.

21. Japanese lose nine hundred dead at Battle of Tenaru River.

24. Japanese effort to retake Guadalcanal turned back by carriers and Guadalcanal-based aircraft in Battle of Eastern Solomons.

30. Army occupies Adak of the Andreanof Islands, 250 miles east of Japanese-occupied Kiska.

Sept. 13–14. Marines repulse Japanese at Bloody Ridge; Japanese use battleships for first time in night shellings of Guadalcanal.

15. U.S. carrier Wasp sinks after submarine attack near Solomons.

18. First reinforcements arrive at Guadalcanal.

Oct.   2. Funafuti of Ellice Islands occupied by U.S. Marines.

5. Planes from U.S. carrier Hornet raid Bougainville bases.

11. Rear Admiral Norman Scott's force of U.S. cruisers and destroyers intercepts "Tokyo Express" west of Savo and sinks three cruisers, five destroyers, and one transport. Our only loss U.S. destroyer Duncan.

26. In carrier battle of Santa Cruz U.S. fliers damage three enemy carriers, one battleship, five cruisers; U.S. carrier Hornet and destroyer Porter sunk.

Nov. 13–15. In air and surface battles in Solomons two enemy battleships, six to eight cruisers, and four or five destroyers, and eight transports sunk; other enemy ships badly damaged. Our losses were two light cruisers, Atlanta and Juneau, and destroyers Laffey, Cushing, Barton, Monssen, Walke, Preston, and Benham; other ships damaged.

30. Six and perhaps nine Japanese cruisers, destroyers, and supply ships sunk in night battle off Tassaforanga Beach on Guadalcanal. U.S. cruiser Northampton sunk, others damaged.

Dec. 7. Major General A. A. Vandegrift of the marines turns over command of Guadalcanal to Major General Alexander M. Patch.

14. MacArthur's forces take Buna Village, New Guinea.

1943

Jan. 5. Task force of South Pacific fleet makes night raid on Munda.

12. Army occupies Amchitka, seventy miles from Kiska in the Aleutians.

18. Australians capture Sanananda as they move westward on New Guinea.

24. Task force of South Pacific fleet makes night raid on Vila.

30. U.S. cruiser Chicago sunk by Japanese torpedo planes near Solomons.

Feb. 1. U.S. destroyer DeHaven sunk by Japanese dive bombers off Savo.

10. Organized Japanese resistance ends on Guadalcanal.

21. Russell Islands in Solomons occupied by army.

Mar. 3–4. American Army fliers, using skip-bombing technique, sink entire Japanese convoy in Bismarck Sea—three cruisers, seven destroyers, twelve transports. Fighters shoot down fifty-nine enemy planes. Estimated Japanese personnel losses, 15,000 men.

6. South Pacific task force raids Munda and Vila; two enemy cruisers sunk attempting interception in Kula Gulf.

April 8. Thirty-nine of ninety-eight attacking enemy planes shot down off Guadalcanal by marine, army and navy fighters.

May 11. Army attack force lands on Attu.

June 2. Attu secure; all but few of Japanese garrison of two thousand three hundred killed.

16. Marine, army, navy fighters shoot down seventy-seven of one hundred and twenty Japanese planes attacking Guadalcanal; antiaircraft guns get seventeen more.

30. Navy transport McCawley sunk by enemy planes, submarine off Rendova.
Army seizes Rendova Island.

July 1. In three days of attacks on Rendova beachhead one hundred and one enemy planes destroyed.
3. South Pacific task force turns back Japanese task force attempting attack on Munda, damaging a cruiser, three destroyers.
6. Japanese defeated in naval battle in Kula Gulf; U.S. cruiser Helena sunk.
7. Army lands on Munda and begins battle for airfield.
12. Japanese defeated in second Kula Gulf battle. U.S.S. Gwin sunk.

Aug. 8. In second battle in Kula Gulf one enemy light cruiser and two destroyers are sunk.
15. Army occupies Kiska; the Aleutians are cleared of Japanese.
28. Organized Japanese resistance at Munda ends.

Sept. 7. Parachute troops land behind Japanese lines at Lae, New Guinea.
16. Lae taken.

Oct. 2. Combined United States-Australian force takes Finschafen.
12. One hundred and twenty-three Japanese ships, one hundred and seventy-seven Japanese planes destroyed in all-out air attack on Rabaul.
15–16. Attempted Japanese retaliation for Rabaul raid costs them one hundred and four planes in attack on New Guinea.

Nov. 1. Marines establish beachhead at Empress Augusta Bay on Bougainville.
2. U.S. cruiser force defeats Japanese force attacking Bougainville beachhead.
20. Marines and army invade Tarawa, Makin and Abemana in Gilbert Islands; four thousand Japanese killed or captured on Tarawa at cost of one thousand three hundred marine dead, three thousand wounded.